The End o

The End of Finance

Massimo Amato and
Luca Fantacci

polity

First published in Italian as *Fine della finanza* © Donzelli Editore, 2009

Polity Press
65 Bridge Street
Cambridge CB2 1UR, UK

Polity Press
350 Main Street
Malden, MA 02148, USA

ISBN-13: 978-0-7456-5110-1 (hardback)
ISBN-13: 978-0-7456-5111-8 (paperback)

A catalogue record for this book is available from the British Library.

Typeset in 10.5 on 12 pt Plantin
by Servis Filmsetting Ltd, Stockport, Cheshire
Printed and bound in Great Britain by the MPG Books Group

Contents

Introduction

Far more than a temporary setback in an economic system with no practicable alternatives, the financial crisis that broke out in 2007 is also the crisis of a way of understanding and engaging in finance. The innovations that appeared in previous decades to promise indefinite economic growth by increasing the financial leverage and liquidity of the markets have suddenly become factors of fragility, recession and contagion.

If we take the trouble to examine it, history shows that this reversal is not only a recurrent event, but also a *permanent possibility* of the financial markets as they have built up throughout the modern era. It can, however, also show us something more. The crisis can be seen as heralding the end, not of finance, but of *one* form of it, finance based on financial *markets*, and hence the end of the idea of money *as commodity*.

On this view, the crisis is not only an event to be described or a problem to be solved, but also – and far more deeply – an *opportunity* for raising the question of reforming the system of finance and credit forcefully and for reopening discussion of the principles and ends to be taken as our starting points and goals if a truly healthy relationship between economy and finance is to prove thinkable and practicable.

The crisis affecting all of the world's financial markets during the last year, with results that are still largely unpredictable today, is accompanied by an equally disturbing loss of bearings at the theoretical level. Paraphrasing Marx, we could say that the 'practical panic' gripping the system's public and private actors for some time now has been accompanied by 'theoretical bewilderment' of a no less serious and widespread nature. Perhaps the most alarming aspect of the crisis is in fact the general and disconcerting incapacity to explain it, or indeed even to understand what form its explanation could take. This incapacity is shared by economists, bankers, politicians and journalists, the most honest of whom have acknowledged it explicitly. As the economist Axel Leijonhufvud writes: 'There are two aspects of the wreckage from the current crisis that have not attracted much attention so far. One is the wreck of what was until a year ago the widely accepted central banking doctrine. The other is the damage to the macroeconomic theory that underpinned that doctrine.'[1]

For the most part, however, we are still left with vague assertions, which are very sketchy in their *pars destruens* and, above all, completely devoid of a *pars construens*.

In any case, the crisis has been accentuated by the difficulty, which is practical no less than theoretical, of understanding its nature. There are at least two reasons for this, the first being an almost total lack of clarity as regards the relationship that must be possible between creditors and debtors. The most recent financial innovations, for instance the securitized subprime mortgages, initially fostered *indiscriminate confidence* in debtors – who should by definition have been denied access to credit within the framework of traditional fiduciary relations – from creditors who were disposed to grant it because they were freed from the attendant risk precisely by the possibility of shifting it immediately onto a liquid market. A simple reversal of expectations was thus capable of generating, in creditors, a *general lack of confidence* towards debtors. When it is not clear where confidence is to be placed, there is rudderless oscillation between two extremes. During some periods, those with money to invest are willing to lend it to anyone at all, regardless of risk, as happened over the last ten years on a global scale. During others, they will lend only to governments regarded as reliable, or at very high interest rates, or indeed not at all, preferring to hold the cash. The 'crisis of confidence' is a crisis of the deep structures of confidence and tends to be accompanied by an indiscriminate contraction of credit, which in turn depresses investments and the economic system's prospects of growth, with obvious repercussions on expectations and confidence. In the *cyclone* of this vicious circle, a financial crisis therefore becomes real due to a structural lack of clarity about the relationship that should obtain between creditors and debtors; to be more precise and concrete, between those who must lend money and those who must spend the money lent, that is, in the final analysis, between finance and what is commonly known as 'the real economy.'

The second reason why the lack of understanding worsens the crisis is the fact that, as a result of the policymakers' incapacity to grasp its nature, the measures taken to find a way out of this crisis may instead simply pave the way for the next. By relying almost exclusively on unprecedented injections of liquidity, the central banks and governments have revealed their failure to understand that *liquidity is not simply an amount of money*, regardless of whether it is generated by the market, as happened during the boom, or made available by monetary authorities, as in the present crunch. What robs every intervention of its power and clarity is the failure to take into account a concept so simple that it is overlooked – first of all in economic theory. This concept can be expressed as follows: *money is not money if its circulation cannot be ensured.*

If this is how things stand, the basic problem is not the lack of money, but the possibility that all the money potentially available today is neither spent nor lent, but simply kept out of circulation, and in this sense accumulated. This is why we claim that the last resort measures adopted are to be seen, first and foremost, as paving the way for a probable crisis – a new and bigger one – rather than judged in terms of their immediate effectiveness. The monetary expansion with which the Fed, under Alan Greenspan, engineered a way out of the crisis of the new economy has in any case been recognized, albeit only retrospectively, as a fundamental contribution to the indiscriminate optimism from which the present crisis was to stem. This precedent is hardly encouraging.

If the present theoretical bewilderment is on such a scale, it might be thought that history could provide some clues, or even lessons. Our incapacity to decipher the crisis on the basis of current practical and theoretical knowledge has indeed prompted many to turn to the past. Since the beginning of the crisis, the need has been felt to find a precedent every time the economic indicators have registered a drop. This crisis thus started to be described as the worst in recent years, following the bubble of the new economy or the Wall Street crash of 1987. As the situation plummeted still further, the spectre of 1929 and the ensuing decade of depression was inevitably raised. We may in fact have something to learn from the comparison of this crisis with its most probable precedents, *but only if we ask the right questions*. The customary exercises of collective memory tend instead to assign history the task of comforting us, which is too easy and too demanding at the same time. The established retrospective readings suggest that, if we have already experienced crises, then we have also survived them. And we therefore feel authorized to conclude that all crises come to an end sooner or later. *But no one bothers to ask how and at what cost.*

If we are instead determined to respond adequately to this task of comparing, we must ask about the nature of finance. What does finance mean? What is the proper function of the financial system? What forms of the relationship between debtors and creditors are consistent with this function? How are the instruments developed by financial innovation, and the very principle of a self-styled 'democratization of finance', to be judged with respect to this function? What does it mean to say that finance must be 'at the service' of the real economy? What relationship must obtain between finance and trade? What is the role of international capital movements?

These simple questions run up against a widespread and more or less conscious tendency to avoid them. This is why we decided to make all the necessary preparations in order to pose them with all the necessary rigour.

The first part of the book is therefore devoted to a *phenomenology of finance*, through which we endeavour to show in what sense the structural characteristic of finance, in accordance with the latter's original meaning, is connected with a loan agreed upon *with a view to payment*, with a relationship between creditor and debtor constituted *with a view to a set term of maturity*, with the opening of an account *with a view to its closure* – in short, with a beginning *with a view to an end.*

Despite its apparent ambiguity, the title of this book is designed to make a precise point: the end *as purpose* [*il fine*] and the end as conclusion [*la fine*] coincide in the case of finance. It is not a question of imposing 'sound' ends on finance, but rather of recognizing that the purpose of finance as a set of economic operations regarding loans coincides with the end of such operations, which must be able to conclude with the agreed payment. In this sense, finance is designed to foster economic relations, or what Jacques Rueff aptly called 'the meeting of all debtors and all creditors'.[2]

This meeting is precisely what the financial system as we know it tends to make increasingly impossible and, above all, to prevent from taking place in accordance with due and agreed forms. The meeting does not take place in periods of crisis due to the manifest impossibility to pay debts – that is, due to the insolvency of debtors, whose bankruptcy makes their creditors insolvent too, with the risk of spreading the contagion. But it does not take place in periods of growth either, because the moment of payment can then be constantly delayed. Growth itself and the optimistic expectations it arouses have the effect of generating an expansion of credit, and hence of loans, with no regard to the effective possibility of payment, in a constant raising of the stakes.

'Delaying payments or reimbursements and causing such delays to overlap perpetually with one another: this was in short the great secret of the modern capitalist system, which could perhaps be most precisely defined as a system that would perish if all the accounts were settled at the same time.' This definition formulated by Marc Bloch, to which we will return in due course,[3] casts a piercing light on the modern history of the global financial system up to the current denouement, by suggesting that, at the root of the dangerous oscillation between euphoria and crisis, there lies a radical incapacity to perform the *exquisitely financial* function of settling accounts.

It is possible and useful to examine history on the basis of this insight. The second part of the book puts forward a thesis that makes Bloch's definition still more radical: the modern financial system not only prevents the closing of accounts, but also takes the shape of a system dispensing with any need for closure from the very outset, one in which it is possible for accounts not to be settled and for debts never to be paid. Striking evidence of this, to which we shall return at various points in the book, is the fact that our financial system rests on an *unredeemable debt* consisting of the banknotes of the central banks and, at the international level, of the dollars stockpiled in the currency reserves of the Middle and Far East.

This observation suggests another possible reading of the title, namely that the present crisis marks the end of a conception and practice of finance grounded in the systematic suppression of the end, understood as maturity and closure: here comes to its end a financial system that wants nothing to do with any end. We must therefore try to understand how it was possible for such a system to begin.

The objective pursued by the book in working its way back through the history of the western monetary and financial system is not to find comforting precedents, but to identify the key watersheds that have led up to the present situation step by step; to show that they were watersheds not through the pressure of the necessities of an evolutionary process with no alternatives, but precisely by virtue of decisions taken *and not taken* at the institutional level; and, finally, to show that the watersheds of this history are mostly connected with the overruling requirements of *war finance*.

On the one hand, therefore, the historical path winds back through the changes in the international monetary regime: from Nixon's cancellation, in 1971, of the convertibility between the dollar and gold – which in fact replaced the international currency, gold, with an unredeemable debt, the dollar – to the initial identification of gold as the international currency – which took place at the exchange fairs of Bisenzone in order to make possible, on this basis, the emission of an unredeemable debt by the dominant military power of the time: the Spain of Philip II.

On the other hand, and in parallel with this process, our examination traces the course of financial innovation, in other words of a *securitization* that ends with ABS (Asset-Backed Securities) and CDOs (Collateralized Debt Obligations), but begins with the first forms of unredeemable paper securities: the notes issued by the Bank of England, the British government's consols, and the Spanish *asientos*.

On both sides, the history is not one of natural and progressive evolution; it is rather one of decisions taken with greater or lesser awareness, but never by chance.

Clear knowledge of the decisions behind us may help to improve our understanding of those before us and, above all, of what is at stake in this crisis and can no longer be ignored. The more strictly *political* third part of the book therefore asks how we can think of finding a way out of the crisis.

As readers will see, the focus of our considerations is on the thinkability of reform, and therefore on *reformability*, even before the individual provisions that can and must be adopted.

We will distinguish between expedient and reform in the light of the fundamental political question raised by the crisis – namely how to find a way out of the present financial system, which is based on disowning both its purpose and its conclusion, and into a financial system that may be in harmony with its truest functions. The question about reformability asks how we can inaugurate a form of finance turned upon the end/conclusion – the settlement of accounts – as its only properly economic end/purpose.

If it is to be established, such a form of finance must be thought out. Thinking finance today entails distinguishing things that are too often confused: money and credit, money and merchandise, the market economy and capitalism. And it is with respect to these distinctions that we shall put forward not only, and not so much, specific reforms but also, and rather, indications as regards what is to be reformed as well as the criteria and principles that any truly new system must be able to meet and take as its cornerstones.

Even though the need to get to grips with the financial system and its structural deficits is now commonly acknowledged, both the repeated slogans and the suggested remedies tend to remain on the surface of things. Calling for a 'new Bretton Woods' without saying what Bretton Woods represented in monetary and financial history, or proclaiming the need for 'new rules' without asking what a rule for finance can and must be – more than anything else, these seem to be ways of concealing a basic difficulty, which concerns the apparently self-evident meaning of the term 'finance'. Everyone knows what finance is. Or at least so it seems. Nonetheless, perhaps for this very reason, nobody states clearly what it is, or what exactly in the system really needs reforming, or what exactly the rules should apply to.

This is why we set off from the simple question of what finance really is. The book's approach is therefore not evaluative. The point is not to pass judgement on the soundness or unsoundness of finance, but to ask what it is that makes a financial act economically important.

While Keynes's work has constituted an indispensable point of reference for us in this connection, it should be stressed that his theoretical and institutional project stretches far beyond its currently established interpretations. Our basic thesis is that all of Keynes's work as an economist and reformer is grounded on an idea of money differing radically from 'money as we know it' – to use an expression recurrent in the *General Theory* – in other words, as we shall see, from capitalist money. Well, the key feature of capitalist money is to be a commodity whose price – that is, interest – is determined on the money and financial markets. Therefore what distinguishes capitalism is, first of all, the fact of regarding money as merchandise. It was against this idea of money and in favour of its radical reform that Keynes devoted all his intellectual energies throughout his entire life – and certainly not with a view to a revolutionary overturning of capitalism.

The age we are living in leads us to think that this is by no means a flaw. In fact we do not need a revolution, but something simpler and more subversive. The way out of this crisis is, first and foremost, by *thinking*; and what can make a concrete difference in the mode of thinking about finance is the ability to notice, above all, those differences that usually tend to be taken for mere variations.

The first of these radical differences masked as variations is between capitalism and the market economy. They are *not* the same thing. The market economy will always be understood in this book as the institutional place where markets are *constructed* for the *sole* purpose of making possible the exchange of economic goods and services – and where effort and inventive creativity can therefore be rewarded, labour can be recognized and recompensed in accordance with its dignity, and responsibilities can and must be assumed. Conversely, we shall endeavour to show that, in spite of any form of economicism, capitalism is the *aneconomic* non-place where even what is not a commodity can be traded, and it is therefore possible to reap without having sown and to suffer without being guilty.

In capitalism financial crises are inevitable; in the market economy they are inadmissible. Being truly in favour of the market means starting to depart from capitalism. Departing from capitalism does not, however, mean abolishing finance. What comes to an end in this crisis is the idea of finance grounded in the representation of money and credit as commodities. We have attempted to draw all the conclusions deriving from the end of this representation, with a view to establishing a radically different institutional and theoretical perspective. The basic insight taken as our starting point is that the existence and sound functioning of a credit system capable of supporting real economic activity not only do not depend on, but are also hampered by, the idea of money as merchandise.

This insight also underpins the possibility of imagining an alternative financial system, in which money and credit are not traded and the relations between debtors and creditors are constructed so as to come to an end in payment and to give way to the production and circulation of goods; in short, a form of finance that can truly operate at the service of the market economy, or perhaps of the economy *tout court* – given that a system that can allow itself not to distinguish between what is a commodity and what is not is, quite simply, not an economy but a dangerous surrogate for one.

To conclude, a note about method and an invitation to readers. The fundamental nature of the questions addressed makes it impossible for this book to provide an exhaustive picture of the reforms that any adequate response to the crisis today would require. It has, however, enabled its authors to submit to the judgment of its readers a unifying perspective, both as regards studies already embarked upon by other scholars and with respect to further works intended to address the functioning of the financial system from a critical standpoint. In this sense, our work seeks to provide a seminal contribution, which not only can, but in a certain sense must, be followed up by more detailed studies.

A final note: all the translations of original sources are ours, unless otherwise specified, and all the quotations from works originally written in English are reproduced in their original form.

Massimo Amato and Luca Fantacci

Milan, 6 June 2009

PART I

Phenomenology

1

Do we know what the financial markets are?

The growth of a *doxa* or general opinion increasingly favourable to financial markets and to their unrestricted liberalization appeared to have encountered no obstacles for years, if not indeed for decades. The objections had died down and the number of conversions increased, also and above all on the left. While subtle distinctions were certainly possible as regards allegiance to the new paradigm of financial globalization, that is all they were. The new order reigned triumphant, and any doubt or opposition could easily be branded as failure to keep up with the times.

In any case, the primary virtue of an ideology is to make things awkward not only for its adversaries, who may be numerous but remain captive to a counter-ideology, but also for the few dissidents. Rather than proponents of critical views, these are made to appear as no more than the advocates of a vanquished and outmoded ideology, who should be left to 'gnash their teeth' in silence. If an ideology is to aspire to 'hegemony', it is first of all essential that everything should be presented in the light of ideological juxtaposition. So it was that the collapse of an ideology so opposed to 'the market' as to feel no obligation even to think about it paved the way for a *doxa* so favourable to 'the market' as to feel no obligation to define it. It is within this self-referential dimension that the financial markets were able to find justification in ideological far sooner than in practical terms.

The outbreak of the crisis *momentarily* interrupted this self-referentiality. The ability to say something concrete about finance and its economic meaning suddenly became crucial. Was there any advantage taken of this opportunity to think? Has the crisis helped us to know a little bit more today about what finance is? Can we now claim a better understanding of that particular configuration of finance known as the *financial markets*? In other words, can we, today, base our judgements in this field on more solid knowledge? Nearly two years after the crisis broke out, the answer is no. Why was the opportunity missed? A short chronological history of the predominant attitudes towards the financial crisis can help to find the answer.

The most widespread tendency at first was simply to deny that it was legitimate to talk about a crisis. It was, people said, a 'temporary setback' or a 'technical adjustment' on the part of the markets. 'Come on, let's not get worked up over nothing.' This was the response. There were indeed explicit warnings not to say *too much* about the possibility of a crisis in order to avoid lowering the expectations of financial agents.

In time, this approach gave way under the weight of evidence, but not to the point of complete surrender. The crisis was interpreted as a cyclical phenomenon that was bound to pass, and, above all, as nothing so serious as to call for any rethinking of the ruling model. The crisis was the price to be paid for prosperity, a sort of wildly astronomical telephone bill that *someone* had to pay every so often. But, since there was no certainty that *everyone* would have to pay, the survivors could still hope to start operating again in the best of all possible worlds.

Then came the Black October of 2008. The apologists maintained a sometimes deafening silence, and 'posthumous prophets' made their appearance. It suddenly transpired that everyone had already known that the system was untenable. This is not to say that no authoritative figures had spoken out before the fat was in the fire, to warn against the danger of financial trends that seemed to justify all the trust put in them solely by their apparent capacity for indefinite self-perpetuation.[1] The sudden glut of sages did, however, appear strange, to say the least.

This is, of course, nothing to be too surprised about in a disproportionately media-dominated society like ours, where the moulding of public opinion is no longer even connected with mechanisms of production, but rather with the constant and mobile management of widespread uncertainty – which stems in turn from a growing incapacity to master information that now affects all and sundry, from the simple 'man in the street' to the most sophisticated analyst or policymaker. In this society of pure information and widespread expectations, where what is 'true' tends to be what is regarded as such, there is a real risk of people reinventing their past in a way that becomes all the more dangerous the less it is recognized.

Thus it is that an article of faith can become an object of ridicule overnight and that swings in opinion can suddenly swing back. This is indeed what happened around the spring of 2009, when the G-20 proclamations and the bailing out of banks and of the market prompted a number of observers, sometimes the very ones who were seeing 'the dark side' in the autumn, to glimpse 'signs of recovery' or, more prudently, 'signs that the collapse is slowing down'. Nor did it take long for these signs to become 'green shoots'. Such is the power of springtime. . .

And the media were thus able to take up the visions of the 'springtime prophets' with the same unreflecting thoughtlessness as they had taken up in the autumn the press releases of the posthumous prophets.

In the autumn the much lauded 'financial innovation' had come to be known by the more traditional and sinister name of 'speculation'. Unswerving faith in the 'evident' capacity for self-regulation of the 'market' had given way to an equally 'evident' need for regulation. It was, we were told, necessary to curb speculation, to restrict the endeavours of the financial system to 'make money out of money'. Now the tune changed again in the spring. The voices of those who had undauntedly defended the financial markets even during the stormy weather were to be heard again, not least because what they had to say was extremely reassuring. The crisis could only be short-lived. It was just a question of waiting for the negative trend to reverse, possibly with the 'help' of some public buffering and further financial innovation. There was nothing fundamental to be reformed. The Anglo-Saxon system of capitalism based on financial markets was in any case the best, and therefore not to be relinquished.[2] And, while the need for a revision of the rules was admitted in this context, it was immediately added that there was no need to clamp the innovative potential of finance in the straitjacket of public control, the tendency of which to degenerate into a subordination of the economy to politics had in any case provided the basic justification for the deregulation of previous years. Simultaneously passivist and activist, like all laissez-faire attitudes, this one has a very solid basis, not perhaps in theory but at least in rhetoric. Nor is it at all easy to refute it until the deep roots of its apparent plausibility have been discerned.

It is, however, precisely because of this difficulty that it is worth observing the pendulum of expert and public opinion and to investigate the laws of its motion. The question that arises here in fact is whether all the views that have so far competed for the media limelight have anything in common. One thing they certainly do share is the fact of being ideological stances distinguished by the 'logic' typical of every ideology: either for me or against me. The financial markets have been judged en bloc, and we have thus missed a possibility that is subtler, but not any less crucial as a consequence of that – quite the contrary. We have been so busy taking sides that we have forgotten to ask ourselves what it actually is that we are for or against.

Regardless of whether it proves to be definitive or temporary, the crisis is not in fact only a setback. It is also an opportunity to ask ourselves, at the very point where every opinion enters a state of potential suspension, *whether we really know what we are talking about when we talk about markets and finance, and hence also about financial markets.* There is no need to be foresighted in order to recognize the necessity of the present crisis and of its end. If we are to understand its innermost nature and hence also its rationale, we must instead know how to see, and above all *where* to look.

This is why the book begins with a phenomenology. We need a phenomenology of finance precisely because its underlying features tend not to manifest themselves. Those involved in the general economic discourse – staunch supporters or stubborn opponents, posthumous or springtime prophets – tend in fact not to see what turns finance into something it really should not be. Above all, they are so caught up in the present-day dogma that they cannot even see it *as such.* They are thus doubly blind. This alone is enough to explain why prophets are two-a-penny, not least because their coats are quickly turned, but explanations are still hard to come by.

If what we are seeking is not a new *doxa* but some understanding of a phenomenon that closely affects us, our starting point must indeed be a fact that is as simple as it escapes notice. Financial deregulation has been able to elevate itself, in the past few decades, to the status of a tenet that does not admit refutation and is not even open to being questioned, primarily because the very idea of regulation in the financial field has become so hazy that it no longer has anything relevant and essential to say to anyone, not even to those who believed for an instant that the time for rules had returned with the new crisis.

An example may serve to clarify this specific point, namely the phenomenon whereby the concept of rules has become hazy both for the advocates and for the opponents of regulation. Given that our purpose is not doxography but the detection of dogma, it will not be necessary to report extreme views, but indeed far more useful to refer to those of an avowedly moderate character. This is why we have chosen a book written not under the influence of the present crisis, but with a view to answering the question of the nature of crises in general, and hence also the extent to which they can be avoided or managed. The author, Barry Eichengreen, is recognized as one of the greatest experts on financial systems, and not only as an economist but also as a historian. Entitled *Financial Crises and What to Do about Them* and published in 2002, the book provides documentation, impeccable in its own way, of the dogmatism running right through contemporary economic discourse. What it puts forward with respect to the financial markets is in fact neither a theory susceptible of verification or confutation nor a simple ideology to be espoused or attacked, but a dogma – in other words, something the truth of which cannot be questioned and that is therefore placed above and beyond any ideological endorsement or theoretical proof.

Some months after the end of the Argentinean crisis, at a time when the forecasts admitted the possibility of further crises in peripheral or emerging economies but did not even consider the possibility of the central economies of the world system being affected, Eichengreen wrote as follows:

> The prevailing system may be widely criticized but it is not discredited. The dominant view, to paraphrase Sir Winston Churchill on democracy, is that it is the worst way of organizing the allocation of financial resources, except for the available alternatives.[3]

Since we are not dealing with something said for effect but with the assertion of a dogma, it will be necessary to subject it to precise exegesis, not least with the help of what the author goes on to say.

It is no coincidence that Eichengreen begins with an analogy between finance and democracy. The basic idea is that, just as the last word has been said in politics, the same has now happened also in economics. As Mrs Thatcher said at the beginning of the era of deregulation, there is no alternative to the market.

This reference to Churchill's historical argument is, however, not unattended by dangers today. His remark seemed extremely clear in the context in which it was made. When the West was in the middle of a lethal fight for hegemony between fascism, communism and the nascent mass democracy, it may have made sense, within certain limits, to be blunt about the latter's shortcomings. For Churchill more than anyone else, it was indeed the worst system, but only apart from its available alternatives; and that had to suffice. Those alternatives have now been swept away, however, and all that remains of his comment is 'the worst form of government' – a 'worst form' that nevertheless has the Darwinian merit of being the only one to have survived in the West, and therefore appears capable of making up for any shortcomings of principle with efficiency of fact.[4]

This is not a particularly contorted way of surreptitiously avowing a distrust of democracy.[5] If there is one thing for which fanatical support makes no sense, it is precisely democracy, which exists through criticism. This is the very least that can be said. A democracy that justifies itself simply on the grounds that there are no known alternatives is already on the point of turning into something unnamed and dangerous. The observation we have put forward here is simply necessary to an understanding of the general ideological context in which it was possible for deregulation to be produced.

Under the influence of a Darwinian image of politics that led to talk about the 'end of history', the collapse of communism and of its attendant apparatus of economic planning seemed sufficient grounds in the early 1990s (and indeed from the early 1980s on) to claim that a historical process had come to an end. Capitalism and democracy ceased to appear even remotely antagonistic or incompatible in the West, and it was possible for the spread of capitalism to be presented as the royal road to democratization of the economic and political spheres. The idea that the economic and political development, both of the West and (above all) of the 'emerging countries', had to be accompanied by the rapid opening up of local financial markets to the movements of international capital, including short-term flows, was espoused not only by Margaret Thatcher and Ronald Reagan but also by left-wing reformers, not only by the 'Washington consensus' but also by the European countries, which accelerated the process of the primarily economic and secondarily political unification of Europe in the 1990s. Financial protectionism, to be understood as limitations on the movements of capital, was quickly and rashly equated with commercial protectionism and, ultimately, with 'political protectionism', understood as the efforts of the ruling classes of emerging countries to defend their privileges against any process of democratization. Refusing, or even simply resisting to open up financial markets was *flatly* interpreted as proof of an obscurantist determination to preserve political systems actually constituting the basis of systems of privilege for castes or bureaucracies. Capitalism, and specifically the movement of capital on open financial markets, was regarded and dogmatically imposed as paving the way for democracy.

In other words, the 'financial revolution' of the 1980s and 1990s presented itself as the best and most efficient concentrate of the doctrine of modernization, which was in turn the more or less unwitting heir to the concept of 'permanent revolution'. Financial deregulation was therefore not simply presented in negative terms, as a process designed to eliminate a suffocating system of control, but also as a way of making it possible to establish a 'new world order' based on the indefinite growth of transparency and power, the latter to be understood first and foremost as the constantly increased capacity to improve the performative efficiency of the economic system. This is the basic idea underpinning the construction of the role of finance in the economic discourse of the last few years. Consider, for example, the following extract from a long pamphlet that has enjoyed very broad circulation:

> Because of their role in financing new ideas, financial markets keep alive the process of 'creative destruction' – whereby old ideas and organizations are constantly challenged and replaced by new, better ones. Without vibrant, innovative financial markets, economies would invariably ossify and decline.[6]

Now, despite the apparent disproportion between the vast scale of this project and the apparent sobriety of Eichengreen's text, that text is an expression of this dogma. Let us examine it point by point.

The 'prevailing system' is justified by the very fact of being the only alternative left. While Eichengreen acknowledges that it can of course be 'widely criticized', it is not thereby 'discredited'. The 'system' is above attack in principle by virtue of being irreplaceable in fact. The opposite inference also holds, however: the system is irreplaceable in fact as long as it appears to be above attack in principle. The real is rational. This is how the thinking goes.

It is in any case very important to realize the fact that, in this way, the justification of the system is not required to refer to any of its 'natural' characteristics. The self-regulating capacities of post-Bretton Woods finance have been increasingly understood as being based on its capacity for constant transformation rather than on any presumed 'natural propensity' of the system to converge on equilibrium positions. The permanent revolution has been reworked in terms of 'permanent evolution' or *permanent reform*: 'reform of the international financial architecture is an ongoing process',[7] the nature of which cannot be fitted into the classical categories in which the juxtaposition of state and market is couched. In other words, it is not a matter of seeing the market, and the financial market in particular, as something to be regulated by the state or, on the contrary, as something absolutely not amenable to regulation. From this perspective, the first concept to have changed in meaning is precisely that of 'financial architecture'. What has established itself is something that Eichengreen summarizes very well, and we could sum it up in turn with the expression 'architecture with no architect': 'the system evolves gradually through tinkering at the margins, not discontinuously in response to the radical visions of some financial Frank Lloyd Wright'.[8]

One of the reasons why it proves difficult to discern the peculiar dogmatic structure of finance born out of deregulation lies precisely in its avowedly acephalous condition, which is wholly compatible not only with the permanence, but also with the strengthening of the relations between public and private elements – relations that can, however, never be brought into being in the name of *rules*.

How does Eichengreen actually depict the system?

> The international financial system is a dense network of social, economic, and financial institutions. As with any complex mechanism, there are limits on the feasible changes to any one component so long as the others remain in place. It makes no sense to install a jet engine on a Cessna Piper Cub. The same is true of the international financial system, whose structure is lent inertia by the interaction of its components.[9]

What does the last sentence mean? That the international financial system, made up of elements perpetually adjusting to each other, has no stability other than that deriving from the friction between its components. There is no keystone in this 'system', and hence no architectural principle that can be represented as such, and therefore no *constructive* rule, and therefore no *regulative* rule. Regulation is deregulation in this system.

This proposition is to be understood in the strict sense of dialectical–speculative logic: every thesis is its antithesis, since nothing determined and finite can aspire to full and stable existence but can only foster progress towards the absolute. The phrase 'regulation is deregulation' does not mean therefore that finance is like the Wild West, teeming with outlaws and gunslingers and in need of upright and fearless sheriffs, but that the *operative* rule of the financial system is that every rule, insofar as it is *laid down*, tends to generate its own replacement by its *opposite*.[10]

From this perspective, the present-day irreplaceability of a system that cannot be identified with any of its states actually becomes the way of accounting retrospectively for its historical emergence. The *doxa* that Eichengreen most remarkably illustrates says essentially that the financial systems have been networks of institutions from the very outset and have always evolved 'incrementally',[11] in a process where new elements are piled up on those already existing, thus bringing about an increase in complexity, in the combinations of interactions, and in the evolutionary inertia of the structure: 'The international monetary and financial system has evolved incrementally from the gold standard to the gold-exchange standard, to the Bretton Woods gold-dollar system, and now to the post-Bretton Woods "nonsystem".'[12]

Even the collapse of the Bretton Woods system – the only one established as the result of a pondered decision, as Eichengreen himself acknowledges – is thus absorbed in its acephalous and non-systematic continuation, with no break in continuity. The system 'evolves gradually through tinkering at the margins'.

The only rule of financial deregulation is therefore not so much the absence of rules as the *readiness* of the rules to change in accordance with an *absolute* evolutionary trend. We are reminded of the definition of democracy given in an article in the 1960s, which was significantly reprinted in 1990 by the *Harvard Business Review*: unlike any other political regime, democracy 'attempts to upset nothing, but only to facilitate the potential upset of anything'.[13] There is no better *technical* and *technocratic* definition of the permanent revolution or – as some put it with a not always correct reference to Schumpeter – the 'creative destruction' peculiar to the market as *dogmatic construction*.[14]

In any case, the fact that precisely this is the perspective adopted by Eichengreen – and, moreover, in a book expressly devoted to the problem of 'what to do' about financial crises – emerges clearly from the passage following the one quoted at the beginning:

> How then are we to evaluate what must be done, what has been done, and what remains to be done? My evaluation is predicated on the assumption that crises are an unavoidable concomitant of the operation of financial markets.[15]

That crises are an inevitable concomitant of the functioning of the system does not simply mean that the system sometimes works and sometimes breaks down, that if you want the years of plenty you have to put up with the years of famine. It also means that there is absolutely no way to *distinguish* when it is working and when it is not. It is precisely because the current financial dogma, as deduced from Eichengreen's book, regards the financial system as performing no specific task that it regards the crisis as having no specific meaning, and therefore it also tends to discount any possibility of the crisis acting as an alarm signal and catalyst of reform.

But, even if we do assume that this crisis can be seen as indicative of a need for reform and regulation that cannot be delayed, the question still remains, however, of what the new rules should be like. And, even before this, what is the object to which they will need to be applied? How can we think about a rule and its *adequacy* if we have no idea of what is to be regulated? In other words, the dogma underpinning the representation of the system as architecture with no architect also obscures our vision of the object of the financial market in its specific and possibly problematic nature. Eichengreen attributes the genesis of crises to no concrete and structural element, but rather to the *variability immanent* in the very process through which the system operates:

> Financial markets are markets in information, and information by its nature is asymmetric and incomplete. It arrives on an unpredictable schedule, and when it arrives the markets react. Inevitably, then, sharp changes in asset prices – sometimes so sharp as to threaten the stability of the financial system and the economy – will occur from time to time. They are likely to be especially pervasive in the international sphere, where the transmission of information between borrowers and lenders is complicated by physical and cultural distance and where writing and enforcing contracts that anticipate the relevant contingencies is particularly difficult.[16]

'Financial markets are markets in information.' This is an assertion whose importance should not be underestimated. Nobody could in fact deny that information plays a crucial role in the financial markets, as well as in markets in general – and perhaps even in areas other than markets. Of course it does. It is, however, quite a different thing to assert as an incontrovertible truth that 'information' is the *precise object* of negotiation and trade in the particular market known as the financial market. Moreover, this is information that is 'by its nature [. . .] asymmetric and incomplete' and hence, as we stated at the outset, information that by its very nature makes it difficult not only for the man in the street, but also for the professionally involved to form opinions that may serve as a basis for responsible action.

We should perhaps realize the *extremely hazy* nature of this apparently crystal-clear definition of the financial market as a market of information and seek to formulate a hypothesis that makes it possible not only to understand the reasons for this haziness, but also to begin to dispel it, so as to attain a clearer grasp of our subject.

The hypothesis is this: what 'information' denotes is not so much the *object* of financial contracts as the *measure* of that object and the *guarantee* of those contracts. (As we shall see shortly, this holds also for 'expectations' and for 'trust'.)

If this were so, a market of information would be essentially a *market of the measure that serves to guarantee the market*. If this were so, crises would really be, 'inevitably', the moments in which this institutional impossibility suddenly resurfaces 'from time to time', opening up a void in which it becomes increasingly difficult to ensure a regulated and contractual transmission of information between 'lenders and borrowers' – that is, between debtors and creditors – one that is truly able to 'anticipate the relevant contingencies'. And a void in which the widespread incapacity to *understand* the object of finance returns like a ghost to haunt us.

2

At the root of the possibility of crisis: Liquidity and risk

> Bluffing lies at the heart of the game and dominates it due to the very fact of being permitted. If it dominates, however, it is only *as the shadow of someone absent*. Its actual use *must* be kept negligible. [. . .] Bad players see bluffing everywhere and keep it in mind. Good players believe it to be negligible and primarily follow their knowledge of the means they have at any moment.
>
> Guy Debord, *Notes sur le Poker*

It is not at all necessary to set yourself up as a prophet in order to understand something of what is going on. It is enough to act as a *historian* and start asking whether there were by chance any signs of anxiety present on a large scale, albeit not necessarily understood, even before the outbreak of the crisis. This is in itself enough to provide an *embarras de choix*.

We shall consider three, once again with the proviso that we are not extrapolating from a doxography but endeavouring to highlight the structure of a dogma.

It is early 2007 and the subprime crisis has yet to begin. Moreover, the system of globalized finance has enjoyed fifteen years of comparative calm and a high degree of 'confidence' after twenty years of almost uninterrupted local crises, ending with Argentina's default. The result, to use the relevant jargon, is a market sentiment characterized by high propensity for risk. The basis of this attitude is the liquidity that the Fed has been pumping into the market for five years – since the manoeuvre through which Alan Greenspan successfully engineered a way out of the bubble of the new economy – to the point where it is now over-saturated. The amount of liquidity, *in the sense of readily available money*, is growing all the time. Contrary to what might be expected, however, this generates no inflation. The characteristic feature of Greenspan's manoeuvre is the fact of being inflationary but without inflation. The only prices to rise are those of financial assets, securities and real estate, since the money put into circulation has prompted a growing demand for stocks and shares and homes rather than primarily for consumer goods – where the demand is in any case not greater than the increasing supply, made possible by rises in productivity and by 'new economies'. The result is therefore an increase in the liquidity of the markets *in the sense of an abundance of purchasers for financial assets of every kind* and a resulting rise in the prices of shares and property. While it could be pointed out that this too is inflation, it is of a type that inspires optimism rather than anxiety, because it affects capital goods rather than consumer goods and thus gives everyone the illusion of becoming richer and not of spending more. At least for as long as it lasts.

In any case, for as long as it lasts, the rise in the prices of financial assets – or even just the expectation of their indefinite growth – works in turn to strengthen the propensity for risk, in other words the search for more profitable investment opportunities, even at the cost of high risk. This also explains why the sector of derivatives is decidedly the most 'dynamic' within the context of overall financial growth. Derivatives are in fact instruments that make it possible to increase leverage – and hence also the expected yield – in return for an increase in the level of risk.

The overall effect of this set of factors is clear and unequivocal: you *have to* buy, no matter what. The relevant offices of investment banks are inundated every morning with phone calls from customers whose only concern is to find something to buy.

All well and good, then. Or is it precisely this situation of security and assured growth that can turn strangely into a source of anxiety? The hushed whispers circulating since the beginning of the year seem to be saying: 'It's all going well, too well, *worryingly* well.'

The whispers are truly hushed and, when they do make themselves heard, the tone of voice is very soft. Nevertheless, something is said, as in the 2007 issue of *Financial Risk Outlook*: 'While volatility remains at recent historic lows, the factors that have contributed to it (such as widely available, cheap funding and high risk appetite) could *quickly reverse*, potentially resulting in a deterioration of global financial market conditions.'[1]

The concern goes no further than the statement of a formula: everything could quickly turn into its opposite. Yes, but *when*? When *and how* will this 'when' arrive? Is it possible – for a financial market that not only economic discourse in general, but also the practically unchallenged economic doctrine professed in the world's major universities tend to present as the most efficient way of managing the uncertainty connected with the future, that is, as the *technical centre of forecasting* – is it possible for it to predict *on the selfsame technical basis* the approach of a radical change in direction, of a crisis?

The following observation from *The Financial Times* of 29 January 2007 takes a decidedly negative view:

> The trouble [. . .] is that we do not have the capacity to anticipate the timing and triggers of such a shock – every now and then stuff happens. And if we could anticipate the timing and triggers, the shocks wouldn't happen.

Here we have a statement, made well before there was any pressure to do so, that should *already* have provided food for thought. The market foresees everything except crises.[2] Once again, however, this is not because it is full of shady or stupid people. Finance has attracted the best brains of all the leading schools of economics and mathematics over the last few years. Nevertheless, both the confidence that makes the markets liquid and the liquidity that makes the markets confident seem to be hanging over a void, or at least over nothing other than their simple and indefinitely repeatable reference to each other. There is something, namely the crisis, that appears to be inevitable but at the same time unpredictable, and not because of any negligence but *because this is how the markets work*. This at least is the sense of another statement, made in January 2007 – this time by Jim O'Neill, head of research at Goldman Sachs: 'Liquidity is there until it is not – that is the reality of modern markets.' An utterance oracular more than scholarly in character.

All is well and good as far as oracles go; but oracles 'neither reveal nor conceal'. They indicate. It is therefore a matter of interpreting them, and 'something happens' depending on how this is done. We shall therefore try to interpret O'Neill's remark in two diametrically opposite ways. In actual fact, it either states an inescapable fact about liquidity or it points to liquidity itself as a *problem*.

First interpretation: liquidity is the other face of trust, or rather of the *peculiar type of trust* that must reign in the financial markets. We refer to the trust that lenders – meaning people who buy shares, in the case of financial markets – must feel in their ability to sell what they buy, *at any time and with no uncertainty*. This does not mean that it must be possible to establish the selling price deterministically, in advance. On the contrary, it is clear that the future selling price cannot be known with any certainty on a financial market, or indeed on any other market. If agents are to agree to operate in this aleatory context, however, they must be able to associate a probability expressed in numerical terms with this variable, upon which their gain depends. The trust upon which the functioning of the financial markets rests therefore hinges in turn on the implicit assumption that *all* probabilities can be calculated, that only calculable risks exist, that nothing unexpected can happen, and indeed that nothing can happen at all as long as the period of time taken into consideration is *sufficiently short*.

These are in fact the *assumptions* underpinning the *theory* of financial markets. The markets are effectively 'liquid' as long as they are actually held also *in practice*. When they are instead doubted, wealth begins to be held in the only form that protects it even from imponderable risk. Then, liquidity is no longer a property of the markets but exclusively 'hard cash'. And, in actual fact, even when the situation is 'normal', the monetary interest rate already measures the *degree of distrust in the assumptions* upon which, 'in theory', the functioning of the financial markets is supposed to rest. As Keynes said,

> our desire to hold money as a store of wealth is a barometer of the degree of our distrust of our own calculations and conventions concerning the future. [. . .] It takes charge at the moments when the higher, more precarious conventions have weakened. The possession of actual money lulls our disquietude; and the premium which we require to make us part with money is the measure of the degree of our disquietude.[3]

The crisis of liquidity, or the liquidity trap, is a situation for which the theory fails to account because it is generated precisely when the assumptions upon which it considers the markets to rest are violated.

Buyers are confident when they believe they can sell. Otherwise they do not buy but rather seek to sell what they have. As long as there is confidence, there is liquidity, in other words *money that is spent*. The opposite is also true, however: as long as there is liquidity, in other words *the possibility of selling assets for money*, there is confidence. In this operative framework, information and expectations are nothing but the 'amniotic fluid' in which this intrinsically irresolvable interweaving of liquidity and confidence is as though immersed and from which it appears to be able to draw 'sustenance'. As long as the market works, liquidity thus makes it possible to satisfy both the investors' preferences and the financial requirements of governments and firms. As long as the market works. But how long is that? If we think in these terms, there really is no way of knowing until it is too late, until 'trust' in the full calculability of risk has evaporated, until risk has reappeared in its imponderable nature and the only certainty left is *liquidity in the sense of money that is hoarded, not spent.*

The second interpretation starts from the assumption that this reciprocal support – easy to observe as long as everything works, and inexorably lost when it ceases to do so, but always and exclusively at the level of the individual agent – is instead *problematic* from the very outset, in terms of the *overall set* of operations and agents making up the financial markets. Keynes, now the economist most cherished by the posthumous prophets, stated this clearly in his day, but without being really taken seriously by anyone, not even his heirs. A true prophet. . .

As we read in his *General Theory*:

> Of the maxims of orthodox finance none, surely, is more anti-social than the fetish of liquidity, the doctrine that it is a positive virtue on the part of investment institutions to concentrate their resources upon the holding of 'liquid' securities. It forgets that there is no such thing as liquidity of investment for the community as a whole.[4]

This is not some abstruse idea, but the thinking of an economist – if this is understood as someone whose yardstick of judgement is primarily the *balance sheet.* It is in fact from the viewpoint of the overall set of interrelated balance sheets in terms of which the financial system can and must be considered that Keynes's description of liquidity as a fetish appears, not as a judgement of moral condemnation, but as an observation based on facts of accounting that cannot be easily dismissed. The liquidity of an investment, meaning the prompt and immediate transformability of assets into money, always presupposes the existence of at least one agent willing to buy. What must be possible to take place is the transfer of a *financial asset* from one balance sheet to another. Conversely, from the standpoint of the financial community and hence of investors en bloc – that is, from the standpoint of their consolidated balance sheets – investments are not liquid, since this would presuppose the liquidation of all the economic assets in which financial capital is invested. This is, however, precisely what the crisis is. The objection could be raised that this is not a question of imagining a situation in which everyone sells and nobody buys, but rather one where everyone can sell one asset in order to purchase another. Even on this view, however, the liquidity accorded to securities by the financial markets is by no means a property belonging to the investments that those securities are supposed to represent. A share in a steel mill can be (more or less) liquid, but not so the steel mill. For this reason, an inconsistency must be pointed out between the liquidity of a security (which can be readily sold in order for another to be bought) and the structural non-liquidity of the capital represented by that security (the factory, whose decommissioning and conversion would entail a massive outlay of resources and time). The truth of bookkeeping therefore has real implications.

Seen in Keynesian terms, O'Neill's oracular utterance becomes a theoretical proposition in the sense of being testable. The point is not to make do with a nudge and a wink, 'recognizing' that liquidity – *whatever it may be* – is either there or not there and passively seeing the economic cycle as an inevitable and unpredictable series of ups and downs explicable *a posteriori* in terms of changes in expectations. The point is rather to understand whether what makes crises inevitable is in turn really indispensable, or even just desirable.

Keynes tells us that, precisely because liquidity *does not exist* from the outset – or cannot constitute the basis for the functioning of a system of healthy credit distribution – it can only *exist* as long as no questions are asked about it, or at least as long as we pretend to know what it is. As long as people believe in the fetish, it will dispense its supposedly beneficial effects. When they stop, the fetish is finally revealed for what it has been all along: something incapable of adequately supporting the basic relations involved in finance.

We must now gather together the points for reflection scattered throughout the first section and endeavour to construct a problematic framework of greater clarity, above all with a view to what we will have to say in the following chapters. For this reason it will be best to take as our starting point the ambiguity of the idea of liquidity. In current language, as we have seen, liquidity can mean both money and the transformability of credit into money. The liquidability of an asset can in turn, depending on market sentiment, be such as to delay its liquidation indefinitely or to necessitate it immediately.

This ambiguity can be stated with greater precision by concentrating on the wholly peculiar *relationship* between money and credit precisely where the concept of liquidity reigns, namely in the financial system as we know it:

> in economics, liquidity indicates 'the interchangeability of assets and money'. Therefore, speaking of an asset, liquidity consists in its prompt convertibility into money; whereas speaking of money, liquidity refers

> to its use as an asset, i.e. as a store of value, rather than as a means of exchange. Economic theory has retained from Keynes the conception of money in terms of liquidity – neglecting that Keynes himself regarded it as a misconception.[5]

Why should the conception of money in terms of liquidity be a misconception? Essentially because it yokes together indistinguishably a proper function of money, namely that of being spent, of acting as a medium of payment and exchange, and a function – which is improper but crucial in the system of modern finance – of acting as a store of value, as something that can be kept out of circulation indefinitely without losing any of its value.[6] On this view, money is not only what makes it possible to acquire wealth and to measure its value; it is also wealth itself at the same time.

Why is the function of a store of value crucial to the system of modern finance? If credit is an activity that in any case involves a fundamental uncertainty for the creditor (ultimately, the uncertainty connected with the effective ability of the debtor to honour the debt when it becomes due), money as a store of value constitutes wealth for its holder with no uncertainty whatsoever. This is why the interchangeability of money and securities at a price expressed by the market rate of interest performs a key role in the functioning of finance as we know it: in the form of the *financial market.* Interest must be paid in proportion to the degree to which the security is comparatively less liquid than money and therefore represents a *liquidity premium*, in other words a *compensation* for the loss of liquidity incurred by whoever gives money in exchange for securities. In this configuration of finance, interest is the rate of substitution between an amount of money (wealth) that is present and certain, and an amount of money (wealth) that is future and uncertain. As interchangeability between money and credit, liquidity enables the individual holder of money to *monetize* not only the calculable *risk* but also the *fundamental uncertainty* inherent in credit. It *dissolves* the imponderability of risk, that is, the fundamental uncertainty that characterizes every true operation of credit, and *resolves* it into a quantity with a price – a commodity. In 'normal times', when the risk apparently vanishes, the liquidability of securities is such that it is not only unreasonable to expect them to be liquidated, but it is also possible to expect the overall set of short-term calculations made by professional operators (speculators) to enable the system, in the long run, to supply the productive system with the capital it effectively needs. Speculation and arbitrage, with the gains they involve, are thus presented in general discourse as the requisite for the attainment of the only end that really justifies the existence of a financial market, its only *socially admissible* purpose, namely the financing of what, for the moment, we can content ourselves to call the 'real economy'.

At the same time, following Keynes, we must ask whether a 'market' organized on the basis of liquidity can really work like this *as a whole*. Is it really possible to attribute the 'market' something like a psychology, and to interpret this psychology in exactly the same way we represent the psychology of individual agents? If all agents feel safe from risk and uncertainty on account of the liquidity of their individual investments, is this fact, in itself, sufficient for the overall set of their relations to enjoy the same condition? Practice, meaning crises, says that it is not. Suddenly and unforeseeably, something changes, 'stuff happens', and 'good news' is no longer enough to fuel trust. The agents' expectations are reversed. But then the question we must ask ourselves regards the nature of the system of expectations connected with liquidity and the reason why it is always *subject to sudden swings*. Why can *market sentiment* and *confidence* shift so abruptly? Is not the real economy, upon which the social justification of financial dealings rests, supposed to constitute a 'solid' point of reference for the financial system as a whole?

The chapter in which Keynes describes liquidity as a fetish also says something that can help us to answer this question:

> It might have been supposed that competition between expert professionals, possessing judgment and knowledge beyond that of the average private investor, would correct the vagaries of the ignorant individual left to himself. It happens, however, that the energies and skill of the professional investor and speculator are mainly occupied otherwise. For most of these persons are, in fact, largely concerned, not with making superior long-term forecasts of the probable yield of an investment over its whole life, but with foreseeing changes in the conventional basis of valuation a short time ahead of the general public. They are concerned, not with what an investment is really worth to a man who buys it 'for keeps', but with what the market will value it at, under the influence of mass psychology, three months or a year hence. Moreover, this behaviour is not the outcome of a wrong-headed propensity. It is an inevitable result of an investment market organised along the lines described [i.e. on the operative concept of liquidity]. For it is not sensible to pay 25 for an investment of which you believe the prospective yield to justify a value of 30, if you also believe that the market will value it at 20 three months hence.[7]

Evidently, the opposite also holds. If the market, understood here as the set of the agents' expectations as to what the other agents will do, is inclined to value an investment three months from now at far more than what might appear to be a prudent valuation in view of its long-term yield, it continues to be irrational for any investor to buck the trend by deciding not to buy the corresponding securities. This is what the (few) financial managers fired after the wave of bankruptcies in the first phase of the crisis have continued to maintain: even though I knew that the prices were too high, I bear no responsibility for the decisions taken from one quarter to the next. I was 'just obeying orders'.[8]

The fact that these were orders arriving, not from any recognizable entity, but from an average state of expectations makes no difference. They may indeed have been still less open to question for that very reason. Keynes was well aware of this:

> the professional investor is forced to concern himself with the anticipation of impending changes, in the news or in the atmosphere, of the kind by which experience shows that the mass psychology of the market is most influenced. This is the inevitable result of investment markets organised with a view to so-called 'liquidity'.[9]

While expectations are formed for short periods of time, or indeed with a view to their imminence, the ultimate justification of the financial markets remains one for a process 'in the long run'. These markets must present themselves dogmatically as an efficient forecasting agency, one whose efficiency derives precisely from the mobile correlation of decisions formally taken in autonomy – and on the assumption of personal liability – by a set of individuals guided by the goal of maximizing profit. If these individuals must, however, place their trust in liquidity as the decisive parameter of all their decisions, they become at the same time *something less and something more than responsible and far-sighted individuals*.

Something more in that they must act normally – which is to say, like anyone else.[10] Something less in that they must constantly seek to wrest from others what others could wrest from them. The result is a permanent conflict between their social function and their private practice:

> The social object of skilled investment should be to defeat the dark forces of time and ignorance which envelop our future. The actual, private object of the most skilled investment to-day is 'to beat the

> gun',[11] as the Americans so well express it, to outwit the crowd, and to pass the bad, or depreciating, half-crown to the other fellow.[12]

Acting as they do, normal financial agents seem to play precisely the part of Debord's bad poker player. The game on the financial markets is, however, not the same as poker. Regardless of whether you are a good or bad player, you can never truly rely on knowledge of your own real means. The game you are forced to play seems to allow still less freedom than poker does: a game of chance, true, but first and foremost one of skill.

Immersed in the atmosphere (what we called the amniotic fluid) of expectations they do help to create, yes, but to which they are also subject as to an extraneous power, financial agents do not reduce market swings, which is supposedly their only function, but they tend instead to accentuate them, both on the upswing and on the downswing. And, when they push the market down, *liquidity vanishes*.

If liquidity 'dissolves' the imponderability of risk, as stated above, the disappearance of liquidity, in other words a financial crisis, entails the reappearance of this imponderability. To be still more precise, what reappears with a financial crisis is what Keynes, on the basis of his theory of probability, calls a 'fundamental uncertainty'.[13] Something incalculable returns, and its nature is such as to remove every *degree of relevance* from the calculations that in normal times, and on the basis of a normality hypothesis, make it possible to resolve uncertainty in a distribution of probability, and hence to make the markets work by keeping them liquid.

Disregard for the ineradicable nature of uncertainty provides support for the normal functioning of the financial system but at the same time makes inevitable a sudden departure from normality. This disregard is in fact constantly at work and brings with it the need for a continuous reformulation of short-run expectations or, if you prefer, a fundamental lack of interest in long-run conditions. The future, understood as the moment of truth, is thus constantly postponed, with all its burden of uncertainty. Postponed, but not eliminated. The raising of stakes that serves to delay the moment of truth simply increases cost.

It is precisely the mechanism of ever higher stakes, inherent in liquidity, that makes the system based upon it structurally incapable of fulfilling its purpose – namely to provide support for economic activity. This end is never achieved. We either go too far (boom) or fall too short (crunch) – and by a measure that, in both cases, cannot be assessed. The access to credit granted indiscriminately on the basis of optimistic expectations alternates with the equally indiscriminate refusal to grant credit.

And it should be stated that the end is not achieved because *no end* is really compatible with the relations of debit and credit established by the financial system on the basis of liquidity. As a result of the unconditional convertibility between money and credit entailed by liquidity, the very concepts of credit and money become hazy. Credit can no longer be seen as the act of making a loan that is to be repaid – as an act that does not require something susceptible of constant deferment through reiteration, namely *liquidity*, but instead involves something that has its own rhythm and cannot be indefinitely postponed, like *breathing*. Blocked in its function as a store of value, money can no longer function properly as a way of paying off debts.

The question that imposes itself is: what sort of thing can money and credit be, when their relationship *does not take* the form of liquidity? If it were in fact possible to conceive of other relationships linking money and credit institutionally – in short, if liquidity were no longer seen as the prerequisite for the very possibility of credit – then we could also ask whether the provision of credit, this indispensable element of every economy, must necessarily take the form of a financial *market*.

3

What is credit?

The contemporary credit system is organized in the form of a market, on the basis of the principle of liquidity. This principle lies at the root not only of the recent tendency of the financial market to predominate over banking intermediation, but also of the entire financial system since the beginning of the modern age. Indeed we are not alone in sticking out our necks to claim that the present situation is not simply a particularly intense and prolonged *liquidity crisis*, but also a *crisis of liquidity* as the principle governing the organization of the credit system in the form of the financial market.

It can also be argued, of course – as others do – that this is instead a normal crisis within a business cycle, that we will emerge from it just as we have from previous ones, and that there is no need to call into question the structural elements of the system.[1]

But in any case decisions as to the adequacy or inadequacy of the present system can no longer be taken simply through reference to supposedly incontrovertible 'matters of fact'. If what is really at stake is an understanding and a judgement about the nature of the present financial institutions and their ability to perform their functions, the evidence offered can hardly be limited to pointing out either that they perform well in normal periods or that they are working badly now.

Proof is required at another level. In particular, those who wish to maintain that we are faced with a cyclical downturn within an essentially sound structure will have to show that recovery from the crisis, accomplished with or without the aid of public intervention, will not simply pave the way for another catastrophe, probably worse. On the other hand, those who maintain, as we do, that this is a systemic crisis must be able to provide some term of comparison on the basis of which it is possible to show in what sense the current system *cannot perform* the function desired by all, namely that of supporting production through the supply of credit in all the forms that production itself requires, whereas a differently structured system could achieve this.

The second approach obviously implies that it is possible to speak about credit without identifying it totally and unconditionally with the present form of its provision through the financial markets. The first negative effect of the *fetish* of liquidity is, however, precisely to prevent anyone from wondering whether liquidity itself is not, by any chance, an obstacle to the attainment of the objective for which it proposes itself as a tool.

Is liquidity – the unconditional convertibility between money and credit – the only, or the most efficient, tool that makes it possible to provide credit in accordance with the requirements of the real economy? Or is it liquidity that prevents us from knowing what money and credit really are, precisely because its structural effect is to make them indistinguishable?

If we are not completely wrong to expose liquidity as the problem, it may well be that this effect of impediment is precisely what lies at the root of the marked embarrassment currently characterizing both the attempts to explain the crisis and the attempts to indicate a way out of it.

In the meantime, however, the crisis itself continues to provide pointers insofar as it is recognized as a crisis of liquidity. A liquidity crisis deprives us not only of credit, but also – in a certain sense – of money, in that money is not spent. Above all, such a crisis tends to reveal that we have no clear idea about the relationship that should exist between the two.

If the present crisis has the effect that securities lose liquidity and everybody wants to get rid of them in exchange for money that they will not use, preferring to wait for better times, there is a real risk of these times never arriving *precisely because money is not spent.* If the liquidity crisis has clearly contracted the availability of credit immeasurably, just as the boom expanded it immeasurably, the real problem is that the measure, which would at least enable us to quantify both the excess of yesterday and the deficit of today, is precisely what is lacking when finance is organized as a financial market based on the principle of liquidity. And, for as long as this measure continues to be lacking, it makes little sense to speak of 'corrections' designed to make the economic systems converge – both individually and as an interrelated whole – towards a position of equilibrium and 'sustainable growth' (regardless of whether these are arrived at exclusively through the market and the interaction of private decisions or through the combination of private and public action, for which many are calling again today).

If we are to decide whether to intervene in the market and whether such action should be contingent or structural in nature, we need first and foremost to be clear about a certain number of distinctions, which everyone talks about today but which prove to be hazy both in theory and in practice.

First of all, there is the distinction between the short term and the long term, which involves the possibility of assessing both the legitimacy of speculation and the legitimacy of maybe limiting it, with a view to long-term stability. Then we have the distinctions between finance and the real economy, between speculation and long-term investment, and finally between contingent and 'fundamental' variables.

Well, while it is to be hoped that all these distinctions will be drawn, they prove at the same time impossible, on the basis of the current *doxa* developed in academic and practical economic discourse.

Once again, the fetish of liquidity prevents us from addressing the problem of these distinctions and of their impossibility, precisely because it prevents us in the first place from asking what relations there are between the financial market and credit, between credit and money, and between money as a means of payment and money as a store of value.

What can in fact be said about the financial markets – and what is actually said, if not in order to reach an understanding at least in order to cheer us up – on the basis of an unchallenged concept of liquidity? That they are the markets of that particular commodity known as saved money, which, in return for that particular price known as rate of interest, is loaned by those who earn more than they spend to those who have no money but a very good idea of how to spend it, especially for financing investments. The economic growth deriving from those investments makes it possible to pay not only the wages of those for whom they provide work, but also the profits of the entrepreneurs and the interest of the lenders. In short, the squaring of the circle. Or simply a slightly more complicated version of Say's law, according to which 'supply creates its own demand', and therefore all the income not spent on consumption is necessarily invested in such a way as to ensure that the full utilization of resources always obtains in the system.

This is, however, precisely the 'law' that Keynes calls into question on the basis of the fact that capitalist money can be not only spent or lent but also accumulated indefinitely. We shall return to the possibility of effectively conceiving a form of finance grounded in money that cannot be accumulated when it becomes necessary to speak not only about Keynes's theories but also about his practical proposals with respect to the financial system. For the moment, we shall concentrate on the first part of the widespread view of credit as the loaning of money by creditors who have saved to debtors who want to spend money but have none.

Here we have two elements mixed up with one another, only one of which is really essential.

Credit is a loan. This is the essential point: so much so that, in some ways, nothing else is needed; so much so that no form of economic life is properly worthy of this name without it. Investment entails lending, but then so does professional trading, understood as the dealings of merchants who buy with a view to selling. And for the entrepreneur, in a certain sense wages, too, are an advance against the remuneration for what will be produced within the working relationship established with the employee. In short, no matter how they may be regarded, producers are structurally debtors. It is therefore not only that the innovative ideas of the entrepreneur, the only one capable of creating new wealth, require credit in the form of a loan, but also that economic life as a whole is based in general terms on a dimension of debt that can never be eliminated, but simply has to be faced.

Credit is essential to economic life because it responds to one of its essential and very *real* needs. The economy of producers, what is commonly known as the 'real economy', cannot exist without credit. This has important consequences for the present-day debate on the relations that should exist between finance and the real economy. If it is true that finance can become independent of the real economy, the opposite is not. The structural debt of the producer *must* be able to find an equally structural capacity for lending within the economic system. The basic economic problem is therefore to ensure the correct balance between these two elements.

'Correct' in what sense? What is it that must be loaned? The normal and, so to speak, automatic answer is that what is to be loaned is an amount of money previously *set aside*. This is, however, *one* possible form of credit, not its structural form. It is practically tantamount to saying that a loan is inconceivable in the absence of previously accumulated money, whereas the opposite is actually true. Structurally speaking, there is no need for any amount of money in order to create a relationship of credit. The simplest way to borrow is in fact to *defer payment*, to postpone the settlement of debts. The creditor becomes a creditor quite simply on accepting, from the debtor, a promise.

In order to take place as an anticipation, credit has no need whatsoever of the prior accumulation of money, but rather of *the institution of a shared space of promising and waiting*: a space in which the debtor appears credible and the creditor is prepared to wait; a space where the promise and the waiting can meet at a point in time. The space of the promise can in fact be established *only with a view to fulfilment of the promise at the moment agreed upon by the parties concerned.* As some readers may have noticed, all we have done here is describe one of the most ancient instruments of credit, born in the West under the name of 'bill of exchange' during the Middle Ages and known today as a 'promissory note'. There is no need to represent this form of credit as a trade between present and future money. In other words, it entails no liquidity but simply deferral, what is referred to in economic jargon as 'respite for payment'. This is granted to the debtor solely to the extent that the creditor is prepared to wait – certainly not indefinitely or forever, but for a set period of time. *The granting of credit is essentially an advance against settlement.* Precisely in order to be what it has to be, however, this advance binds the debtor and the creditor jointly within the framework of the promise. Like trade, credit is essentially not a thing but a *relationship*.

This relationship has to be seen in itself, that is, prior to – and independently of – the contractual forms in which it has taken specific shape historically. In other words, the task is to pinpoint its basic economic feature. From the viewpoint of a phenomenology of finance, this is its *intrinsic riskiness*. If it is true that credit has to do with promises, the ability to make and accept promises can never in itself guarantee that they will be kept. The truth of promises runs up against the possibility of non-fulfilment, of the debtor proving insolvent. Once again, this is a structural matter. No debtor – not even one who borrows with a view to production, one *really lacking* what is needed in order to undertake an economic activity – can be totally sure of being able to pay in accordance with the terms agreed upon. The promises accepted by creditors are in fact as risky for them as the economic undertakings made possible by this credit are for debtors. Even if the decision to borrow is made on the basis of the most prudent and realistic of business plans, entrepreneurs can never have completely certain foreknowledge of the economic conditions in which they will find themselves operating once the investments are made. A sudden and unforeseen drop in the prices of the goods they intend to produce could make entirely unprofitable a project undertaken on the assumption – entirely reasonable at the time – that there would be no change in the trend of prices. It should be noted in passing that this is the condition in which producers risk finding themselves *today*.

As has been stated, in paradoxical terms, the only certain way for debtors and creditors to avoid risk is quite simply to borrow and lend nothing at all.[2] Risk is in fact bound up with the very structure of credit. The loan granted now will be repaid at a later date, which means in economic conditions that not only cannot be predicted with complete certainty but also prove radically resistant to exhaustive measurement in terms of probability. Insofar as it involves a relationship with the future of economic relations, credit knows no certainty.

Risk is inherent in the *relationship* because the relationship is structurally suspended over a 'fundamental uncertainty'. Moreover, as it is the relationship itself that entails the risk, this cannot properly be borne by just one of the two parties involved. Debtors must of course be able to anticipate extremely well the conditions of their solvency, just as entrepreneurs are true to their name and truly courageous when they are not afraid to take risks, but at the same time they avoid entanglement in plainly reckless or unrealistic plans of investment. Conversely, shrewd creditors must be able to assess the credibility of those seeking funds. If a bank is to perform its real function as a *financial intermediary*, it must in this sense be capable of 'rationing' credit and of granting it only to those it judges capable of meeting the commitments undertaken, for instance by distinguishing between *prime and subprime borrowers*, more and less safe debtors.

These are, or rather should be, the basic tools of the trade on both sides, and their possible shortcomings are precisely what bankruptcy law has to deal with. Even though each party will obviously be tempted to shift onto the other as much as possible of the burden of uncertainty and thus to make its position more 'sustainable' also with respect to its own errors of evaluation, the fact remains that this burden can never be wholly resolved in a calculation of risk. The burden of the fundamental uncertainty characterizing their relationship is something to be shouldered and borne by the debtor and the creditor together. It is precisely because he did not fail to take all this into account that Keynes was able to identify the relation between debtor and creditor as the very foundation of economic activity,[3] the basis – or rather the indispensable prerequisite – of every real economy. For the same reason, this relation is also the framework within which the necessary relationship between the financial economy and the real economy is established.

We are of course speaking here not about risk but about uncertainty. The difference between the two is one between what can be reasonably assessed and what eludes the effective and concrete possibilities of prediction. Where the calculation of probabilities is possible, *insurance* against the risk calculated in this way is possible too. Also possible is the development of a specific profession, characterized by the ability to assume risk on behalf of others. In this perspective, *and within the limits set by the calculability of risk*, speculation can actually be seen as a form of insurance, and thus as constituting an element of market stabilization and a factor of growth for business transactions. But what are the limits of calculability? The question is highly delicate and calls for close attention on the part of any study of the economy wishing to be regarded as scientific. The ever present temptation is, however, to ignore the problem and to construct credit institutions as markets pure and simple, on the basis of the dogmatic assumption that *everything* can be calculated, and that the interaction of speculative dealings removes all uncertainty from the relationship of debt and credit, at least asymptotically.[4] It is on this skewed plane that liquidity assumes its whole relevance in history. The illusion guiding this dogmatic construction is that of a financial market whose increasing liquidity and completeness – or whose endowment with sophisticated tools for the calculation and the negotiation of every type of risk – is directly proportional to its capacity to *eliminate* uncertainty, first of all for creditors, but then, indirectly, also for the debtors. As creditors who are certain about getting their money back at any time will lend capital more readily, debtors will be able to enjoy increasingly easy access to credit.

This illusion, which goes by the name of the 'democratization of finance', has recently been expressed with a dogmatic forcefulness that leaves no room for doubt. The goal, as some have literally said, is to arrive at a position where credit can be granted also to those who do not deserve it,[5] namely the structurally insolvent, the 'subprime borrowers', also known – improperly – as 'the poor'.

Even assuming that this is not an illusion but an operatively manageable situation, we must, however, ask whether this objective is desirable *economically*, not to mention morally or anthropologically, and whether it really enables the economic system that achieves it to *strengthen its basis*.[6]

A sound economy – probably one capable of less explosive growth than the 'economic miracles' to which we have become accustomed, but also one of less severe and protracted depressions – should perhaps be able to ground itself on the acknowledgement of the *solidarity* that must reign between debtor and creditor. Nor has such solidarity any need of interpretation in 'bleeding-heart' terms, as it is in fact capable of developing, *at a strictly economic level*, in the form of a *sharing of the burdens of adjustment* – which the uncertain change of economic conditions requires towards the effective payment of debts.

Keynes at least thought so, one example being his suggestion that the 'model' for the debtor/creditor relation should be 'marriage', a union from which it is *permissible* to derive all the pleasure possible as long as you are prepared to face whatever fate may bring. To take the metaphor a little further, the radical alternative to matrimony, and one that also offers more 'pleasure' in the short run, is the large-scale orgy – a way of organizing interpersonal relations that is based, let's say, on the fact that they can be broken off at the drop of a hat.

While it would be interesting to see how often the term 'orgy' crops up in relation to the financial markets, we have no wish to trust so completely the evocative power of a metaphor. This is simply a matter of recognizing that the debtor/creditor relationship possesses a basic indissolubility, which no detour through liquidity can really eliminate. It should not be forgotten, however, that the advocates of financial innovation, and especially of derivatives, have maintained precisely this: that there exists, at least asymptotically, a situation of the financial market in which liquidity, by distributing risk through the market, can guarantee something very similar to the disappearance of uncertainty.

Above and beyond all metaphor, what is at stake is actually institutional in character. If the uncertainty inherent in the debt/credit relationship could truly be resolved in a set of calculations, it would then be possible, and indeed legitimate and necessary, to conclude that credit as such is a commodity like all the others, hence one whose price depends exclusively on its conditions of supply and demand. If this were so, the financial *markets* would indeed make the most suitable and the most efficient institutional framework for credit. The interest rate would not be, simply, *a parameter* serving to assess the liquidity of assets, but in all respects *the measure* – that is, the price or rate of substitution – guaranteeing equilibrium between the supply of credit and the demand for credit. And credit would essentially be nothing but an intertemporal trading of actual money. No relationship would survive the possibility of treating credit as a thing. One small problem would remain, however. How are we to explain, without resorting to human frailty and the *virtus dormitiva* of Molière's celebrated physicians, not only the crises that have marked the history of the financial markets ever since their birth in the seventeenth century, but also their increasing intensity and frequency precisely when the dogmatic decision to treat credit as a commodity has swept aside all opposition and the trend is towards the abolition of all restrictions on international capital movements?

Moreover, if credit were, by its very nature, nothing but a commodity, what are we to say about the fact that credit has proved historically possible – and this, even without assigning the interest rate a central and institutional role as the balancing price between demand and supply of money? What are we to say, in short, about the forms of institutional organization of the debtor/creditor relationship, which seem to respect the 'fundamental uncertainty' characterizing it? One way out would be to declare them forms superseded by evolution and innovation – on the wholly unproven assumption that 'innovation' is synonymous with improvement.[7]

What is known as 'Islamic finance' would appear to meet the demand for self-persuasion on the part of the pro-market *doxa*. Islamic finance is supposedly nothing more than a residue of an 'inferior' organizational form grounded on the prohibition of lending at interest, which is in turn grounded on 'moral prejudices' indicative of 'cultural backwardness'. Despite the fact that more than one objection could be raised against this self-serving representation, there is, however, no need to look outside the western economic tradition in order to find forms of credit closely akin to the basic principles of *sharia*-inspired finance. One example is venture capital. In the contractual form of the *commenda*, venture capital (or the partnership between a party with money but no ideas and an entrepreneur with ideas but no money) constituted a formidable stimulus for the recovery of international trade from the thirteenth century on, and at the same time it was judged to be compatible with the legal prohibition of lending at interest. The basic rationale of the contract is simple: the combination between money with no purpose and a purpose with no money makes possible an activity that is intrinsically risky but, for this very reason, also potentially profitable. When venture capital does not take contractual forms so asymmetrical as to eliminate all risk for the creditor – which was always historically possible but not, for this reason, necessary – what is *jointly* shared in a relationship of basic solidarity is both the risk and the gain. The capital makes a profit if the business does, and not independently from it. The parties give each other gratification and support but cannot unilaterally exempt themselves from risk. The formalization of this type of credit relationship owes a great deal to fourteenth-century Franciscan theology.

Multilateral clearing also rests on the same principles of solidarity. To put it very simply (given that we shall return to clearing in Parts II and III of this book), the idea at the root of the principle of clearing is that *liquidity is not necessary*. In other words, there is no need for a predetermined amount of money to be exchanged between debtors and creditors in order for trade and investments to become possible. A clearing system is created in order to meet the need for advances without requiring any previous accumulation of money for this purpose. It simply makes it possible to register (1) a debt owed by someone who is required to make a payment but cannot do so immediately; and (2) the corresponding credit in favour of the party to be paid. This is, however, from the very outset a trilateral rather than a bilateral relationship: both sums are registered as debit or credit *with respect to the system as a whole*. In virtue of its tripartite structure, the system permits the use of credits to make payments also towards third parties. In this way debit and credit are not individual and fungible positions, but acquire their meaning in relation to the entire set of relations constituting the system. Within a clearing system, credit takes the form, not of a bilateral relationship represented by a negotiable security, but that of the net position (positive or negative) of each member with respect to the set of all the others. What ensures the actual clearing, in other words the effective meeting of debtors and creditors, is therefore not a price (a rate of interest) such as to balance the supply and demand of money, but rather the multilateral compensation of profits and losses and the tendency to converge towards parity for all the participants.[8]

Clearing thus ensures all the advantages of liquidity, but without liquidity being taken as the cornerstone of the system of relations.

Far from being a relic of a past evolutionarily superseded by financial innovation, the principle at the root of the above-mentioned operative possibilities, and presumably of others too, is one that still awaits exploration. Above all, it shows that the dogmatic operation of reducing credit to a commodity is neither self-evident nor necessary. And indeed a dogmatic operation it is, both theoretically (Say's law and its possible transformations) and at the level of practice (the organization of financial markets on the basis of liquidity).

Moreover, insofar as these forms of credit provision do not entail the presentation of credit as a loan of previously accumulated money, they raise the problem of the nature of money and of its relationship with credit. But this is the subject of the next chapter.

4

What is money?

In our discussion of credit and liquidity, the identification of saving with investment emerged as the cornerstone of orthodox economic theory, a tenet that Keynes vigorously challenged throughout his career as an economist.

It is indeed an odd identification, albeit one that is always true in a certain sense in bookkeeping terms, since saving is always equal to investment in national accounting, on condition that stocks of unsold goods are also recorded as investment.

Above all, however, the identification is always true *dogmatically*. Not only is it entirely impossible to prove it or to disprove it, but also, when adopted as a term of reference, it makes it possible to represent any deviation from the long-term market equilibrium it describes as being contingent and short-term in character, and for that very reason entirely attributable to the failure of economic actors to adapt to market mechanisms.

This is the reasoning developed, with no real discussion whatsoever, in the most widely circulated manuals of macroeconomics. The dogmatic effect is clear. On the one hand, the market is structurally a mechanism that efficiently sets the real price of every commodity, including credit. On the other, the imbalances and crises in which the inefficiency of the market actually manifests itself at intervals can always be attributed to external factors that prevent the mechanism from functioning correctly. In short, the market always works *well*. When something goes wrong, the cause is not the market, but a failure to adapt properly, in the short term, to its 'long-period' laws.

In a different context – but one that proves in some respects very similar to the one addressed here – Hannah Arendt observed that the hallmark of every ideology and the basis of its apparent and alluring realism is precisely its adamantine irrefutability, which subsists until the unrealistic foundation of its cast-iron logic is called into question. And it is upon this representation of the short period as a deviation from a long-period equilibrium that the theory, practice and ideology of the market have been built over the last twenty years, in an altogether indistinguishable fashion.[1]

The simple fact of casting doubt on the unconditional relevance of the identification of saving and investment therefore implies the need to reconsider the entire doctrinaire framework that has supported and at the same time has been supported by the recent development of the financial markets.

Nevertheless, our task is not to counter the fetish of a – let's say – 'reasonably' doubtful doctrine by using the totem of an economist, namely Keynes, who would instead be 'right' *tout court*. The 'Keynesian revival' of recent times should indeed be viewed with no less circumspection than what is known as 'mainstream economics'. What we have to do is identify the evidence that Keynes took as the basis of his critique rather than repeat what his followers may have deduced. Well, the primary evidence prompting his criticism of the identification between saving and investment was not a theory of economic policy, but precisely the fact that money was then regarded as just another commodity, despite both its peculiar nature and the requirements of the economic equilibrium of full employment.

We have already outlined the reasons why credit itself, in its nature as a relationship, does not appear to be compatible with its representation exclusively as a commodity, and why the expression 'credit *market*' proves misleading, to say the least. But we must proceed further. At the heart of this doubt lies also, in fact, one as to whether the credit market can be represented as the market of money not spent, and therefore *ipso facto* saved.

What we must realize in the first place is that the idea of monetary saving is nothing obvious and natural, but rather an institutional fact – and indeed one of a markedly ambiguous character. Why is it so clear that the idea of monetary saving can be presented as an obvious element, legitimately serving as a starting point in addressing the question of credit?

The answer, if we hold on to the doctrine that we have, however, begun to challenge, is simple. Money can be saved, and its saving can be rewarded with an interest rate set on the market where it is an object of demand and supply, because money itself is a commodity. Money is the very special commodity that *represents* all the others and that can be *exchanged* with each of them but can also be *preserved indefinitely and at no cost*, that is, without losing its capacity to be exchanged with every other commodity at a later stage. Money is purchasing power, or rather purchasing *potential* that can remain indefinitely in the state of potentiality. It is the commodity that can be put aside and kept out of circulation indefinitely because, unlike all the other commodities, which are perishable and can only be stored at the owner's expense, it has no maintenance cost. The idea of monetary saving implies the idea of money as a commodity, and hence of a money market.

All we have done in the previous paragraph is to provide an – as it were – 'literary' reformulation of the definition of money that underpins the whole of mainstream economics. Money is the commodity capable of performing *simultaneously* the three functions of a *measure of value*, a *means of payment and exchange*, and a *store of value*.

The critical discussion of this representation has already been developed in other works, to which the reader is referred.[2] We shall confine ourselves here to summarizing and asking whether this representation really constitutes something self-evident rather than a problem in itself. Is it really necessary that these three functions should be performed at the same time by the same money? At a still more fundamental level, are the three functions all equally essential? In any case, how should they be organized with respect to one another?

In order to perform its function of measurement and make possible the immediate comparability of every commodity with every other, which frees the economic system from the bilateral constraints of barter, money does not even need to be physically minted or issued. I can say that a good is worth €5 a unit without having even €1 in my pocket, just as I can exchange two units of it directly for a good worth €10 a unit without actually being in possession of euros. Nor does this hold solely for Adam Smith's crude and primitive stages of civilization, as is demonstrated by the fact that an international clearing system can effectively work in the same way. The 'Clearing Union' planned by Keynes for Bretton Woods envisaged the use of money existing exclusively in the form of a unit of account, namely the *bancor*, in order to run and finance international commerce.

A bookkeeping system and the system of trade in general can, however, register imbalances at the local level that cannot be rectified through compensation or direct exchange of goods. And in still more general terms, as we have seen, economic life cannot do without structural forms of debt, which money as a unit of account can indeed measure, but certainly not pay. If it is in terms of money as a pure unit of account that debts are reckoned, it is instead with the actual money used as a medium of payment and exchange – the money that passes from hand to hand – that debts are paid. And no reasonably organized economy can do without these two functions.

But only *these two functions* prove indispensable. The third function of money, as a store of value, is definitely not required with the same cogency. Neither trade nor credit necessitates its existence in principle. All that trade requires is money that is spent, in other words a medium of exchange – and a common yardstick of equivalence, so that it can be spent. In its basic form of payment deferral, credit entails a measure with which to specify the debt at the moment when it is incurred and a means with which to pay it when it falls due. In any case, neither as a measure nor as a means is money required to have a value, still less to retain the same value indefinitely. *There is thus no need whatsoever for it to be a commodity*. This is what Keynes suggested in 1923 in his *Tract on Monetary Reform*:

> It is not easy, it seems, for men to apprehend that their money is a mere intermediary, without significance in itself, which flows from one hand to another, is received and is dispensed, and disappears when its work is done from the sum of a nation's wealth.[3]

It is not only that there is no need for money to be a commodity in order to do its job. Looking at the same question from another viewpoint, we can also see that neither credit nor exchange requires what acts as a measure to be the same thing as what functions as a means of payment. When I ask for a metre of material, I want a piece of cloth one metre long, not a metre made of cloth. The same holds in economics, and indeed to a still greater degree. The money in terms of which a debt is denominated is not necessarily the money in which it must be paid. In order to serve its requisite function as a public tool, money only requires the relationship between the two functions of measure and means to be *established publicly and in due time*. This is at least what Keynes wrote in the early pages of his *Treatise on Money*:

> Perhaps we may elucidate the distinction between money and money of account by saying that the money of account is the description or title and the money is the thing which answers to the description. Now, if the same thing always answered to the same description, the distinction would have no practical interest. But if the thing can change, whilst the description remains the same, then the distinction can be highly significant. The difference is like that between the king of England (whoever he may be) and King George. A contract to pay ten years

> hence a weight of gold equal to the weight of the king of England is not the same thing as a contract to pay a weight of gold equal to the weight of the individual who is now King George. It is for the State to declare, when the time comes, who the king of England is.[4]

Keynes's observations of 1930 regarded the gold standard, which explains his reference to gold and his criticism of the identification of the unit of account with a set amount of the same metal. But the substance of what he said then still holds today, when gold has definitively ceased to be the physical basis of our money. What is, in fact, the consequence of the difference between a unit of money whose ability to pay debts is defined once and for all, independently of all circumstances, and a unit of money whose effective ability to perform this function can and must be deliberately redefined according to circumstances and contingencies?

The consequence is that *the former alone* fully performs the function of store of value. Only money in which the functions of measure and medium of exchange are definitively and institutionally combined is, at one and the same time, necessarily and primarily a store of value. Given that there is always a decision, even at the basis of the identification between the unit of account and the means of payment, the stability of a form of money thus constituted coincides with the stability with which it performs the function of a store of value.

But let us ask once again: what does the attribution of this third function mean for money and its relationship with credit? And what effects does it have on the first two functions and on their relationship?

Let us try to answer the first question with a formula: money that is not a store of value is money that *serves for the payment of debts*, whereas money that is a store of value is itself *credit*. In more formal terms, we could say that, for finance, money is a means in the one case, while in the other it is, simultaneously and (above all) indistinguishably, a means *and* also a possible objective or, as one would have it, an end.

If 'store of value' is correctly understood not as a 'reserve' of means of payment, but as the *possibility* of putting aside a means of exchange with the *institutionally guaranteed* certainty that it will preserve its value in the terms of the unit of account (that the king of England will always weigh the same as King George, to use Keynes's image), then this intertemporal cost-free transferability makes store-of-value money the absolute form of every asset and instrument of credit. Store-of-value money is the ultimate *risk-free asset*. For that very reason, it can become not so much the foundation as the starting point in the *two-directional movement* peculiar to liquidity – that is, to the unconditional transformability of money into *credit* or, if you prefer, of money into capital. And vice versa.

Such transformability is, however, operative only within a market whose goods of exchange are money and credit, in their unconditional convertibility, and whose 'price' of reference is therefore the interest rate. Only when money is a store of value does it begin to become indistinguishable from the other assets. Above all, only then is it completely a commodity. From this standpoint, 'capitalism' begins to take shape not as a slightly antiquated synonym for 'market economy', but as that particular form of market economy in which even money is a commodity. This entails a change not only in the meaning of 'money' – which ceases to be a simple means of payment at the service of exchange and lending – but also in the meaning of 'commodity' and 'market'.[5]

The second question remains to be dealt with. Does the addition of the function of a store of value leave unchanged the sense of the first two functions and of their relationship? We now have all the evidence required for a negative answer. The function of a means of payment is hindered rather than facilitated by the function of a store of value. When the unconditional saveability of money is guaranteed by definition, it is always possible for the circulation of money to be obstructed by another potential use of money: that of holding it indefinitely at no cost. The function of a store of value makes money potentially deflationary. This is what we have seen in recent months, when massive 'injections of liquidity' have had little success in restoring liquidity to the markets and in bringing down the interbank rate – simply because the money pumped in by the central banks has been put aside by the banking system itself.

The function of money as a measure of value is threatened perhaps even more directly. When money is also a store of value, money as a measure of value ceases to be something really different from what it measures. To return to our previous image, it can become difficult to distinguish between a piece of cloth that is one metre in length and a metre that is made of cloth, or between intermediation and speculation in non-metaphorical terms.

Furthermore, what, by definition, disappears when money is a store of value is the possibility of determining the relationship between measure and means with a view to the appropriate performance of both functions, and above all to the payment of debts. What appears in place of this *relationship* is a *thing*, namely money as a commodity with a price: the interest rate.

We have thus reached the end of our circular path, where what we find is a problem dogmatically presented at first as something self-evident, namely the fact that the unconditional saveability of money as a store of value constitutes the basis of the legitimacy of the loan at an interest, and hence the legitimacy of the current identification of finance with the present money and financial *markets*. There is indeed nothing at all self-evident about this. Within the present institutional framework, money is what makes it possible for goods to have a price and comparability on the one hand, and something with its own price, namely the interest rate, on the other. But this means that its circulation does not depend solely on its ability to perform the role of a means of exchange and of a payer of debts. That role is constantly threatened by the possibility of money, as an asset, being transformed into less liquid assets. The function of money as a store of value, and hence essentially as a commodity, makes it impossible to think *in concrete terms* about any form of relationship between the real economy and the financial economy, and in this sense it is not at the service of credit. And all of the wholly justified calls for the introduction of new rules will continue to run up against this obstacle until its problematic nature is finally recognized. The only rule to be imposed on money is one enabling it to be *money in the proper sense of the term*.

What we have endeavoured to show can be summed up as follows: money properly called by this name is not a commodity based on the indistinguishability of its first two functions, but an institution designed to determine their relationship with a view to payment.

As we shall see, the basic representation of money as a commodity among commodities has influenced the history of financial markets from their birth as markets of liquidity, all the way up to the present crisis of liquidity.

What we have obtained for the moment through consideration of the nature of money as an institution is the possibility of drawing and putting forward some distinctions, which make it possible to bring to a close this initial phenomenological overview.

Before that, however, it will be worth stating clearly at what level we see the problematic element of the store of value to be situated. There is a real risk that our observations may be interpreted as a particularly elaborate and abstruse variation on the old moral theme of the condemnation of greed and of *auri sacra fames*. Our purpose is not to condemn the accumulation of money, Weber's 'worldly asceticism' of the capitalist saver, in the name of an 'asceticism' with no qualifying adjectives (or rather with all the adjectives – supportive, alternative, anti-consumerist and so on – that the anti-capitalist 'alternativism', internal and subordinate to the triumphant capitalism of the last twenty years, has already coined and will continue to coin). What it means to have an adequate relationship with needs, and whether 'capitalism' constitutes a real and humanely practicable answer to the human problem of the relationship with needs – these are two authentic *political* questions in all respects. What we are saying about the potential danger of money as a store of value and as a commodity has, however, an *exquisitely economic* foundation.

That the problem is not moral in nature emerges from a simple fact, which tends to be overlooked precisely because of its simplicity: there is no need whatsoever for saving to take place in monetary form in order to be economically significant. The fact of making it impossible to save money *indefinitely*, in other words the fact of ending its function as a store of value, in no way implies that one intends to make it impossible to save, but rather, perhaps, that the time has come to ask what saving really means *from an economic viewpoint*.

On the contrary, the institution of money as a store of value makes it possible for saving to be entirely unconnected with concrete goods and to take place rather through the constant and indefinite accumulation of abstract purchasing power, in the precise sense of *power independent of the fact of being concretely exerted* – so independent as to jeopardize the very possibility of its being exerted. It is the institution of money *as liquidity*, of which its function as a store of value constitutes one of the fundamental pillars, that makes crises *of liquidity* possible.

5
Finance starting from the end

Our observations concerning money as a store of value have shown the possibility and the utility of certain distinctions that are not generally drawn. Above all, they have left us with the need to decide whether what Keynes often refers to as money 'as we know it' – the money upon which the financial markets are based, money as a store of value and a commodity – is also money 'as it ought to be' – in other words money capable of performing the function required of it in an economy where credit is truly at the service of labour and production.

In some respects this is not just *a* decision, but *the* fundamental decision, to which we are led today not only by logic and a sense of responsibility, but also by the circumstances. If the present crisis is interpreted as a crisis of liquidity, then it is necessary to be consistent. Even more than the economy, what is today in a state of crisis – in the literal and etymological sense of being *subjected to judgement* – is precisely the representation of money as a commodity. And if the underlying message of the crisis is that this representation is untenable in theory and in practice, then what will accompany it in radical collapse is clearly the *economic* validity of representing the relationship between money and credit in terms of liquidity, that is, in terms of interchangeability, and hence of representing finance as a *market*.

At the same time, however, there is nothing to support the idea that *the* market would then have to be reorganized in favour of its control by *the* state. The possibility that emerges throughout this crisis is rather that of an alternative, located within the economic dimension – in terms of which the question of the relationship between state and market, too, can (and indeed must) be reconsidered.

This alternative is by no means purely theoretical. It has a history, not only because it has a past but also because it has a future. Money as a commodity was born in England at the beginning of the modern era, out of the abolition of the European system of 'imaginary money', based as the latter was on a separation of functions – that of measure and that of means of payment.[1] It is important at this point to underscore the fact that money 'as we know it' was born historically, out of a decision that marks a watershed in the history of western money. If we keep this fact firmly in view, the first important consequence is that our monetary and financial history cannot be read purely as an evolution from less efficient to more efficient structures.

What the decision involves cannot in fact be represented solely as the evolutionary strengthening of the means at the disposal of finance, but must also be seen – in fact seen above all – as a change in the relationship between finance and *its economic purpose or end.*

The decision whether to assign or deny the function of a store of value institutionally to money is by no means neutral. It involves the possibility or impossibility of regarding money as a commodity and therefore it affects the plausibility and the institutional legitimacy of the financial markets as an efficient and rational means to achieve the very purpose of finance, namely to support the real economy.

As regards our future in terms of the subject matter of this book, the 'new rules' that the present crisis of liquidity seems to require cannot even be sketched out unless all the possibilities offered by our monetary history are explored, if only because there is nothing natural and inevitable about the 'paradigm of liquidity'. It is not even the worst system (apart from its no longer available alternatives), but rather the result of a historical decision that can be called into question and reversed at any time. It must be assessed in terms not only of the undeniable increases in power it has brought, but also of the ever increasing power of the crises it has constantly generated.

The common feature of all these crises has been in fact the resurfacing of the institutional untenability of liquidity as the cornerstone of the financial system. We shall demonstrate this, just as we shall demonstrate that the responses given so far to the financial crises – which have constituted apparently inevitable concomitants of the functioning of financial markets – have been an attempt to resolve an institutional shortcoming through an operative strengthening by means of constantly raising the stakes, which has paved the way for the constant reappearance of the crisis. In other words, it has been decided from the very start not to decide as to the nature of finance, and utter confusion has been engendered precisely where the faculty of distinguishing should have been exercised – not just for the sake of drawing distinctions, but as a preparatory step towards decision-making.

The first decision concerns the status of money. Is money the object of finance or a tool at the service of the economy? Is it an instrument of credit, to be exchanged with other instruments of credit on the financial markets, or the means of payment for the settlement of every kind of debt? Is it a commodity created so that it may be accumulated indefinitely, or something that must be created so that it may 'disappear when its work is done from the sum of a nation's wealth'[2]?

Anyone asking for an answer would most probably have no hesitation in opting for the second alternative in each case. Money is a pure medium at the service of the exchange of goods. It is a tool for the payment of debts, given that these must be paid. It is something that, in itself, counts for nothing – a mere veil, and not a form of wealth. In short, as they say, 'money can't buy happiness'.

Nevertheless, the first alternative is the one that holds, implacably, for money as we know it since three hundred years ago, when it first appeared as paper money issued by the central banks: money is a commodity; it is a debt, constructed so as not to be paid and so as to make always possible the consolidation of any debt, or the deferral of its payment; it is something that is multiplied and accumulated indefinitely – even though it still can't buy happiness, especially at times of crisis.

Jokes apart, why does money as we know it work like this? Even though the subsequent historical section will be entirely devoted to tracing all the phases in the genesis of money as we know it, it is well worth mentioning in advance some of the essential features, which have proved particularly striking over the last forty years. Ever since 1971 the central banks have continually endowed the economic systems with a means of payment that, in bookkeeping terms, is nothing but their own debt – but a debt created not in order to be paid, but rather to remain in circulation indefinitely. Not being required to pay their debt, the central banks are technically in a position to decide not to make their own debtors pay, thus acting as lenders of last resort, with no restrictions on their ability to create money. The creation of this money is structurally unrestricted precisely because its purpose is to act not only as a medium of exchange for the purchase of goods and services in the real economy, but also as a commodity on the very particular markets known as financial markets. Moreover, this money can be a commodity, and a very peculiar one indeed, precisely because it is created so that it may be accumulated indefinitely and may thereby meet the unique need for accumulation in the most absolute way. In short, constantly torn between two competing functions, this money ends up not performing the one function it is primarily called upon to perform, namely that of making it possible to borrow and to pay debts.

To put this assertion immediately to the test, we can refer to the widespread use of the practice known as 'lender of last resort', correctly employed to designate operations like the Paulson Plan, the bank nationalizations of the Brown government in Great Britain and the repeated and indiscriminate 'helicopter drops' of money into the economy carried out by Bernanke (whence his nickname 'helicopter Ben'). This practice is nothing but a concrete manifestation of the only principle that seems to underpin the present monetary and financial system, namely the systematic deferral of payment.

There is something – the state, or rather the self-supporting complex of state and central bank – that cannot go bust and can therefore decide to extend this singular economic status also to other bodies, and especially to the very peculiar enterprises known as banks. The temptation could thus arise to declare the market, or rather the financial markets, to be exempt from bankruptcy as well. Presented by the economic *doxa* as an 'infallible' mechanism as regards its ability to organize forecasts, the market is thus made infallible also in the sense that it cannot become insolvent and *close down*.

From a hyper-liberal standpoint this could be regarded as frankly excessive, and many have indeed evoked the spectre of 'socialism' in connection with the Paulson Plan. The hyper-liberal criticism of this approach fails, however, to see that the state is already necessarily present in the financial markets, regardless of whether or not it decides to perform the function of a lender of last resort, and thus to prevent private concerns from bankruptcy by 'socializing the losses'. The question of the relationship between state and market arises in fact *before* this point and regards the role that the former can actually play with a view to the full existence of a market economy that is private and really independent of the public sector.

What is this role? What must it be restricted to? There are essentially two *public* economic functions that should be carried out by the state. The first is to set up and make operative the legal framework within which contracts are performed. The second, which is actually prior to this, is to define what can serve as a unit of account and as an instrument of payment, as well as the relationship that must exist between the two. This is at least the sense of the continuation of the passage from Keynes quoted in the previous chapter:

> The State, therefore, comes in first of all as the authority of law which enforces the payment of the thing which corresponds to the name or the description in the contract. But it comes in doubly when, in addition, it claims the right to determine and declare *what thing* corresponds to the name, and to vary its declaration from time to time – when, that is to say, it claims the right to re-edit the dictionary.[3]

It is worth noting that in this case the term 'state' is in no way necessarily associated with the idea of an 'interventionist state', which owns and suffocates the market, but rather with the function of determining *in advance* [*ex ante*] the conditions for the performance of contracts, which Barry Eichengreen, too, describes – in the presentation of international financial markets quoted in Chapter 1 – as something of which such markets are hardly capable.[4] *In advance*: that is, before the market starts to make its calculations and *in view of the fact that* it can make them effectively and freely, thus leaving the possibility of individual bankruptcy intact. If the principle that debts must be paid on pain of bankruptcy is to hold with no exceptions allowed for private concerns – since a system based on the private appropriation of profit and on the socialization of loss is simply an iniquitous system, regardless of any alternative – then the *public principle* that the debts must be *made payable*, even if this entails *joint* redefinition of the terms of payment, is a necessary prerequisite.

Well, money as we know it prevents any such redefinition precisely because, as we have seen, it incorporates both the measure of debts and the means for their payment. In point of fact, our money crystallizes this impossibility in that it involves the state in any case – and not in order to redefine *each time* the relationship between means and measure with a view to payment, but in order to define money, *once and for all*, as the fusion of means and measure, in other words as a store of value.

The 'mixed economy' begins here – long before the state nationalizes or privatizes, regulates or deregulates, intervenes or refrains from intervening – precisely when the state relinquishes its only true economic function as guarantor of the payment and of the payability of debts. The state thus puts into practical effect the dialectical proposition that may have startled the reader at the beginning of Chapter 1: regulation *is* deregulation. The only thing the state has firmly guaranteed for some three hundred years is that it will never assume the role of impartial guarantor, although this is the first role to belong to it rightfully. Even before the dilemma of state or market ('how much state and how much market?' 'the market, yes, but with rules that have certainty!') begins to fuel all kinds of ideological controversies, the state is *already involved in* the financial markets in the ambiguous role of a guarantor that is, at the same time, a *debtor* (insofar as it issues public debt bonds). And what does it guarantee? That what it should establish as a measure for *the* markets that make up the real economy is at the same time the commodity of *a* market, namely the financial market.

This opens up the possibility of a distinction that is even less perceived. Both the champions of the free market and the advocates of the need for regulation normally go on failing to distinguish between one market and another. The market is seen en bloc by both. Take it or leave it. But how can we fail to recognize that there is also a difference between markets of goods and markets of capital – between markets for the supply and demand of a commodity that does not depend on their existence and *markets for the supply and demand of a commodity that does depend on their existence*?[5] In actual fact, the distinction is possible and has been drawn – and not only recently,[6] but also at the dawn of modern economics, by Adam Smith:

> A positive law may render a shilling legal tender for a guinea, because it may direct the courts of justice to discharge the debtor who has made that tender. But no positive law can oblige a person who sells goods, and who is at liberty to sell or not to sell as he pleases, to accept a shilling as equivalent to a guinea in the price of them.[7]

How can we fail to see a very close connection between what Smith attributes here to the law and what Keynes assigns to the state as a task? Above all, how can we fail to see that Smith still maintains a distinction between the exchange of goods and the debtor/creditor relationship?

If all this has any meaning, it may actually be possible to draw a distinction between capitalism and the market economy without raising the spectre of an 'alternativism' as absolute as it is incapable of proposing economically practicable alternatives.[8] In the light of this distinction, capitalism would be seen for what it is: a market system, of course, but one whose markets also include what could and should instead be excluded, namely money, not on moral or ideological grounds but simply because, if money is to be at the service of credit, it must be organized in such a way as not to constitute a commodity.

But this brings us back to the fundamental alternative. Suggesting that it is possible for money to be stripped of the character of a commodity in no way implies a need or a desire to abandon finance, but perhaps, quite simply, that we should finally start to ask about its nature and about the purpose it serves.

Let us begin with an anecdote set in France during the 1950s. Being required by the regulations to write a short thesis on political economy, a young doctorate student of law decides to turn for help to Jacques Rueff, the 'guiding light' of French liberal economists. With all the ingenuousness of a neophyte, he asks the scholar for something that economists always find it hard to give in their treatises, namely a definition of the economy. The answer is memorable: 'Economy is the meeting of all the debtors and all the creditors.'

In addition to being memorable, it goes right to the heart of the problem. There is no economy without credit, simply because there is no real economic activity that does not involve debt. There is no creditor without a debtor and vice versa. Of course. But, as is clearly indicated by Rueff, the central and vital point about the debt/credit relationship is *the relationship itself.* And if meeting is a relationship, not every relationship has the form of a meeting. The meeting must be organized. In other words, things must be arranged so that debtor and creditor *really* do meet. Otherwise neither of them *actually* exists. This meeting is in fact not to be envisaged as the effect of interaction between 'debtors' and 'creditors' as such, either individually or as a whole. Debtors and creditors really exist if and only if a space for their meeting has been set up in advance.

Rueff's answer offers us an authentic cornerstone for the understanding of finance. *Finance has to do with the creation of the structural conditions of possibility for a meeting between debtor and creditor in which the payment of debts can take place.* Only if payment can take place is it possible to make loans with a view to payment or settlement. Finance has to do with settlement, the end of the transaction. The end of finance, understood as its purpose, is a meeting between debtor and creditor in which their relationship can come to an end.

This is indeed the very meaning of the word, especially at the beginning of its history. In the Latin of the late Roman Empire, *financia* meant in fact the 'amicable settlement of a dispute'. It is, however, not termination that comes to mind when we think of finance today. If anything, it is growth. But the growth of what? The etymologist to whom we owe this information wrote as follows under the heading 'finanza':

> from *the amicable settlement of a dispute* (from *FINÀRE, for FINÍRE, *to terminate*, *conclude*, or from FÍNIS, *end*, *conclusion* [. . .]) the word came to mean pecuniary service, money [. . .], used for business in

> general. In Provençal and Old French FIN meant end, liquidation, settlement. Today [in the late nineteenth century] it means money and state revenues; administration of the same; pecuniary resources, personal wealth.[9]

The etymologist summarizes a history characterized by the fact that it involves the loss of the original meaning of the word. Finance has ceased to refer to a situation in which a payment in money takes place in a suitable amount, at the due time, and becomes simply money! We could almost say that the history of the word is the history of the transformation of a means into an end, but this would be saying little in concrete terms. We cannot in fact content ourselves with fourth-hand sophisms and embark on a critique of 'modernity' and its 'instrumental reason'; we must rather try to see whether this transformation of meaning involves not so much the replacement of the end with the means as the loss of a medium and the end in the sense of conclusion.

If there is to be a real *definition* of the relationship between debtor and creditor, which is risky and easily gives rise to controversy, and if this definition is to be *amicable*, not involving hostile relations between the participants, then there must be (1) a shared end, in the sense of a conclusion; and (2) the possibility of mediation with a view to the attainment of that end.

1 All debts are and must be *for a set period of time*. A debt with no set term for repayment is humanly unacceptable, either because it can never be paid off, thus making the debtor a slave, or because its payment cannot ultimately be enforced. In any case, what is lost in human terms is something precious, namely the possibility of assuming responsibility for one's actions. Debts are for a set term, and this term must not only be known in advance but also chosen in relation to the type of credit requested, which depends in turn on the end or purpose for which the loan is requested. It must be possible to establish a relationship between the incurring of short-term or long-term debt and the type of activity for which financing is requested. The loan is made with a view to an end in the sense of a conclusion.
2 When responsibly agreed upon and accepted, this end is something that *liberates*, in the sense that it makes the parties involved truly *free* to undertake mutual *obligations*, i.e. to assume all the responsibilities that derive from the obligation. The first of these is the obligation for both parties to work together so as to arrive

at the end or conclusion. That end is payment. Paying originally means 'making peace' or 'placating'. On being paid, the creditor releases the debtor from his obligations. As every responsible debtor knows, however, payment gives peace both to the creditor and to the debtor. The ability to pay is indispensable for those who do not want to live on credit. For those who do not want to live on unearned income, in other words *solely on the labour of others*, it is important to ensure that the others can pay, even at the cost of some personal loss. Debtor and creditor enter into a joint obligation to attain the end or purpose of finance, which is to bring their relationship to an end. And this holds not only at the anthropological and individual level but also at the economic level, both national and international. This was also Keynes's view when he made the following observation in connection with the reconstruction of the international monetary system at the end of the Second World War, and hence with the role of the United States as net creditor at the time:

> a country finding itself in a creditor position *against the rest of the world as a whole* should enter into an obligation to dispose of this credit balance and not to allow it meanwhile to exercise a contractionist pressure against the world economy and, by repercussion, against the economy of the creditor country itself.[10]

The creditor's obligation has nothing to do with the individual decision 'to feel morally obliged', but rather with the *political* decision to institute an intermediate space or *medium* for the settlement of mutual obligations. This medium is finance, on condition that it is equipped with suitable money to perform its task of mediation.

What are the prerequisites of a kind of money capable of performing the function of mediation? It must ensure that what is shared first of all is the risk inherent in the debt/credit relation, since this alone provides access to the mutual advantages offered by the relation.

The idea of a credit devoid of risk – once again, the basic idea of money as liquidity – can be seen from this perspective as being wholly incompatible with the end or purpose of finance. As we shall see in the next chapter, however, it is not incompatible with the peculiar *absence of ends* that characterizes capitalism. Liquidity and the financial markets are incompatible with a type of finance that can be organized with a view to an end in the sense of termination of the debt/credit relations initiated through it.

It remains, then, to see whether capitalism is a system capable of meeting this need. For this purpose, however, we need a definition of capitalism as seen from the viewpoint of payment. In short, what form of payment is structurally inherent in capitalism?

Keynes said that liquidity – and the elimination of risk that it appears to permit in normal times – does not exist for a community. This means that no community, and still less the financial community, can ever eliminate the risk connected with its existence as a community. The objection might, however, be raised that, while it cannot of course eliminate this risk, it can try to 'quantify' and 'sell' it. But at what price? At what price can risk find a price? At the price of indefinite postponement of the end – that is, of the moment of payment. The price of this procrastination is a constant increase in financial activity regardless of the economy's actual need for funding. This increase is based on the possibility, apparently always available in normal times, of avoiding liquidation by bolstering confidence in liquidity.

In the light of our foregoing observations, however, the confidence corresponding to liquidity is simply the *deferral of a lack of confidence* on the basis of *expectations* concerning the system's short-term growth and *faith* in its virtues of stability over the long term. But what faith and, above all, what long term are we talking about? In the long run, as Keynes remarked, are we not all dead?

6

Capitalism and debt: a matter of life and death

> – Baron, it's high time you paid up . . .
> – What! Are you insinuating that I don't mean to pay? Watch your step, young man!
> – But yesterday you said, 'I'll pay you tomorrow.'
> – And tomorrow I will. I always keep my word.
> – But you said 'tomorrow' yesterday!
> – Young man, if I said 'tomorrow' yesterday then I'll pay tomorrow.
> – But 'tomorrow' is today!
> – No, today is today and tomorrow is tomorrow, two very different things. I said 'tomorrow'? Right then, I'll pay you tomorrow.
>
> Totò, *Signori si nasce*, 1960

'In the long run we are all dead.' Keynes made this remark in the context of a discussion of the 'quantitative theory of money', in his *Tract on Monetary Reform* (written in 1923). This is the only theory truly compatible with money as a commodity, as it states in its simplest formulation that, other things being equal, an increase in the amount of money generates a decrease in its price, as measured by the rise in the level of the prices of goods in terms of money. Keynes obviously had grave doubts as to the plausibility of the assumption that these other things (namely 'the habits of the public in the use of money and of banking facilities and the practices of the banks in respect of their reserves') can in fact remain equal. He also admits that the direct proportion between quantity of money and level of prices can instead obtain in the long run.[1]

It was at this point that Keynes wrote one of his most famous and frequently quoted remarks – which is not to say that it is read with due attention, and still less that it is really understood:

> But this *long run* is a misleading guide to current affairs. *In the long run* we are all dead. Economists set themselves too easy, too useless a task if in tempestuous seasons they can only tell us that when the storm is past the ocean is flat again.[2]

How is this passage interpreted in the almost unchallenged climate of opinion that has established itself? More or less as follows: Keynes is an economist who 'does not believe' in the long term, and *therefore* he is a short-term economist who sees economic policy as the use of public action (taxes and spending) *with no delay*, perhaps accompanied by inflationary monetary policies, to compensate for the shortcomings of market performance, with a view to achieving 'full employment' *at all costs*. All these forms of intervention constitute the 'Keynesian policies', and their underlying philosophy can be summarized as follows. What does the long run matter? Life is short and tomorrow uncertain. 'Gather ye rosebuds while ye may' and let the future generations look after themselves. Up with life and down with death.

Thus restricted to the short period, Keynes's economic theory has been absorbed into the 'neoclassical synthesis' as the particular case in which the laws of the market are hampered in their operation by various forms of interference (ideological, political, and perhaps even 'human'[3]) and 'everything goes wrong', but all this happens within a long-term framework in which the same laws continue to operate undisturbed and 'everything will be all right'.

But in fact it is this very juxtaposition of the short and the long term that Keynes criticizes. He says: '*this* long run is a misleading guide.' It is misleading precisely for the 'current business', in which we are, all, constantly involved and often absorbed to the point where we can no longer see the very elements that should guide us *also and above all* in current business, and hence we fall back on that surrogate guide, 'market sentiment', which is the average level of expectations. Nor do we realize that this 'trust' simply makes it still more difficult to remember that current transactions need a guide that does not confine itself unreflectingly to reflecting feelings, but is capable of directing them.[4]

Trust in what? What should be our guide? A genuine rule, or maybe what the agents, caught up in their operations, take as a plausible representation of one? The now ingrained habit of basing the stability of markets on the 'trust' demonstrated by investors has the result that, in times of 'euphoria', the mere fact of mentioning rules causes irritation and exposes anyone who calls for their introduction to accusations of defeatism, if not indeed of 'statism'. In times of 'depression', on the other hand, any regulatory expedient involving palliatives for the most superficial effects of the crisis generates on the markets wholly disproportionate reactions, which, however, soon fade away when the placebo effect typical of antidepressants wears off.

What should be our guide? Certainly not, in Keynes's view, the assurance that everything comes to an end sooner or later, even crises. This would hardly give economists and economic policymakers any reason to feel satisfied with their work. So what, then? What indeed, if not a long term, correctly understood? In actual fact, all we have to do is read correctly. The text does not say 'we *will* all *be* dead' in the future, which is how Piero Sraffa thought it could be translated into Italian. It says 'we *are* all dead'. The tense of the long run is the *present* for Keynes. To put it another way, when we are out on the stormy sea of credit, our only pole star or compass is the degree of certainty with which we can, *from the very beginning, anticipate something like an end.*

Let's take it from the beginning. If we really want to start thinking about the future, we cannot content ourselves with recalling the fact that we will all die sooner or later, albeit not just yet, and perhaps cross our fingers. We should pay heed to the fact that, in order to preserve intact the possibilities held in store for what economists call the 'future generations', each generation must bow out with dignity, after shouldering its responsibilities *as well as possible.* We should know this, and we should prepare ourselves accordingly *during life.* The long term is not something that will arrive 'later', when we are all dead. It arrives *all the time*, or rather *from time to time*,[5] whenever the time comes for each one of us to do his or her duty. This is the first thing we must all know if we want to live *responsibly.*

In economics, the question of time is primarily bound up with the relationship that must be able to exist between the short and the long term. Correctly understood, the long run, unlike the one that left Keynes rightly dissatisfied and critical, cannot be something that comes after the short run. If we see it in those terms, we will keep it from ever arriving, and, above all, from ever providing us with guidance, as a point of reference. We will live in the short run, but with no compass and no truth.

Contrary to the current interpretation of his thinking, Keynes saw the long run as the moment of the end and of the truth. The hiatus between the short and the long run is not simply chronological. The long run is not an indefinitely long period of time, but the time when a *long-awaited* truth arrives – that is, a truth awaited *all along* the period of time that this very awaiting opens up. In this respect the long run is the time of a measure, which is given precisely in order to measure the contingent situation, and in this sense it is a time that precedes the short run and guides it.

Whether you believe that death has nothing to do with you or you pay heed to it makes a great difference to the way you live. Above all, you live more responsibly in the second case, and perhaps, quite simply, this is when *you do live*. Life is not a business that always ends in loss, as Schopenhauer described it, thus displaying a limited grasp of economics (and perhaps also of philosophy). Paying heed to death does not mean expecting it to come at any moment as a definitive and inevitable loss, to the point where you are disheartened by its 'expectation', but rather bearing it in mind as something that puts into proportion the *fundamental uncertainty* of life. The uncertainty of life can be faced with neither fear or fearlessness, but with a reasonable degree of courage. The 'animal spirits' referred to by Keynes are not blind and 'irrational' drives but the vivacity, backbone and self-control with which it is possible and desirable to look to the future, not least in economic enterprises.

> It can be confidently stated that enterprise, which depends on hopes regarding the future, benefits the community as a whole. Individual initiative will, however, only be adequate when reasonable use of calculation is backed up and supplemented by animal spirits. In this way, the thought of definitive loss that often discourages pioneers – as current experience unquestionably suggests to us and to them – is put aside, just as a healthy person does not dwell on the expectation of death.[6]

While this discussion may have taken up some time, it enables us to provide a clear exposition of a thesis that Keynes never expressed in these terms, but with which we are certain that he would agree fully: *the long run is the moment of the payment of debts* – the debts that fall due *then*, but whose date of settlement was *previously* set by common accord between a debtor and a creditor: their point of reference and orientation, right from the initial stage of negotiating the terms of their relationship, was the moment in which that relation would come to an end. There is no 'today' without a 'tomorrow'. Totò was well aware of this too, as his ability to make us laugh by simply reversing the relationship between these adverbs clearly shows.

It is, however, precisely *this* long run and its relationship with the short run that both the theory and the practice of the modern financial markets now prefer to ignore, confining themselves to the assertion that the long run is the state of stability around which the volatility of prices in the short run – those prices set on the financial markets through the interaction of the decisions of the agents – is distributed equiprobably – that is, in accordance with a normal distribution.

These decisions are taken, not on the basis of what is held to be the long-run trend of the market but rather on the basis of trust in today's general opinion of tomorrow, and essentially on the basis of trusting that this trust can be shared. This is why the thing 'to which practical men always pay the closest and most anxious attention'[7] is the 'state of confidence' rather than the object of that confidence. The financial markets are dominated by long-term expectations that are constantly reformulated in the short, if not indeed the very short, term, as Eichengreen reminded us back in Chapter 1. 'Rational' is the adjective that the economics of the last few years has tacked onto these expectations in order to parry Keynes's objections. These still stand, however, as is shown by a careful reading of what he wrote in the *General Theory* precisely with respect to the temptation of rationalization:

> How then are these highly significant daily, even hourly, revaluations of existing investments carried out in practice? In practice we have tacitly agreed, as a rule, to fall back on what is, in truth, a convention. The essence of this convention – though it does not, of course, work out quite so simply – lies in assuming that the existing state of affairs will continue indefinitely, except in so far as we have specific reasons to expect a change. This does not mean *that we really believe that the existing state of affairs will continue indefinitely*. We know from extensive experience that this is most unlikely. The actual results of an investment over a long term of years very seldom agree with the initial expectation. *Nor can we rationalise our behaviour by arguing that to a man in a state of ignorance errors in either direction are equally probable, so that there remains a mean actuarial expectation based on equi-probabilities. For it can easily be shown that the assumption of arithmetically equal probabilities based on a state of ignorance leads to absurdities.*[8]

These 'rational' expectations simply *rationalize* something unpredictable. There is, however, nothing inherently reasonable about the peculiar rationalization upon which rational expectations are grounded. Like the rationalization of which psychoanalysis speaks, it is rather the ultimate expedient employed by neurotics to avoid facing what they fear. Yet neurotics are essentially afraid of life itself, as well as of the imponderable dimension of the future, which life brings about and which calls upon us to take *responsibility* for our actions without having any certainty that we will be able to avoid mistakes.

The rationalization that lies at the root of financial neurosis – which is characterized, like every other neurosis, by the pure alternation of euphoria and depression – has taken the form of the Black-Scholes formula for calculating the price of derivatives: its structural foundation is 'a mean actuarial expectation based on equi-probabilities', in other words on 'normal distribution', despite the fact that 'it can easily be shown that the assumption of arithmetically equal probabilities based on a state of ignorance leads to absurdities'.[9] It is tacitly but incessantly decided to maintain a convention essentially based on the optimistic view that – to paraphrase an observation by Marc Bloch to which we shall be returning later – it is possible to discount the profits of the future, thus *repressing* its precariousness. The effect on the financial markets is the reciprocal dependency of trust and liquidity seen and described above. The effect on the relationship of the financial markets with the real economy is the illusion that they are really at the service of the real economy and of the long term precisely by virtue of their short-term structure:

> investment becomes reasonably 'safe' for the individual investor over short periods, and hence over a succession of short periods however many, if he can fairly rely on there being no breakdown in the convention and on his therefore having an opportunity to revise his judgment and change his investment, before there has been time for much to happen. Investments which are 'fixed' for the community are thus made 'liquid' for the individual.[10]

A touch of erudition is, however, still required in order to add the last ingredient needed if we are to understand the structure of the secret of the market economy 'as we know it' and of its peculiar interpretation of the relationship between the short and the long period. From the perspective of the *real* economy, the only concept of 'the long period' was developed by Alfred Marshall, according to whom, *in a market economy*, the short period is one in which firms meet the demand for their goods relying on a given endowment of *fixed capital*, whereas the long period is one in which they can modify their endowment of *fixed capital*: this is the moment when they start to borrow and to ask for credit in order to make investments that *are fixed for the community* precisely because they are connected with fixed capital.

What happens then, if this demand for credit finds response in a financial market that is structurally based on the short term and on the regime of expectations characterizing it, whereas the long term is simply regarded as a period long enough for the attainment of equilibrium? In a nutshell, *the market economy is surreptitiously and unexpectedly transformed into a capitalist economy.*

We must, however, move beyond formulae and try to state in positive terms what characterizes a capitalist economy and what distinguishes it from a strict market economy. We need some sign, capable of showing *both* the difference between the market economy and capitalism *and* the tendency for the latter to be taken for the former. Help is provided by Marc Bloch, a historian who wrote about money in the same period as Keynes, albeit without having read him at the time. Bloch discussed credit and its role in the modern capitalist economy in 1935, during a course devoted to European monetary history – a context in which he also spoke about the end of the monetary system based on the distinction between unit of account and medium of exchange, and about the emergence of a system grounded in the notion of money as a commodity and in the stabilization of its purchasing power. He clearly saw the role of credit as crucial; and in a certain sense he also saw credit as capable of substituting money. The appearance of forms of credit based on commodity money and at the same time capable of replacing it – in short, the birth of the financial markets – contributed to what he calls the 'euphoria' of the eighteenth century, the era of the industrial revolution and of the 'birth of capitalism'. His discussion continues as follows:

> Delaying payments or reimbursements and causing such delays to overlap perpetually with one another: this was in short the great secret of the modern capitalist system, which could perhaps be most precisely defined as a system that would perish if all the accounts were settled at the same time. This system is fuelled by an optimism that constantly discounts the profits of the future, its eternal precariousness [*un optimisme qui, sans trêve, escompte les profits de l'avenir, son éternel porte-à-faux*].[11]

Commenting on this observation in another context, we said that it 'is not so much a definition of capitalism as an intuition of the *secret* that silently underpins the relationship between credit and money in that system'.[12] A secret that is hidden all the better as it appears to be something self-evident and unproblematic. A system that *would perish* in the long run if all the accounts were closed at the same time is in fact a system that lives systematically in the short period of their constant overlapping.

Nothing could be more pragmatic, one might say, or basically more in keeping with economic life itself, provided that this is a process in which the end of one debt is invariably accompanied by the beginning of another. The financial markets would thus simply *adapt*, with the greatest desirable flexibility, to the requirements of an economic life in constant motion. In this sense it is not strange that, precisely by virtue of its capacity for systematic overlapping of the debts handled by the financial markets, capitalism should be seen by some not only as fully synonymous with the market economy, but also, and above all, as 'the most effective way to organize production and distribution that human beings have found'.[13] In order to go on being optimistic, all we have to do is go on discounting, *uninterruptedly*, the profits of the future, or making constantly possible their anticipatory monetization.

This secret is more of a secret the less it is known. The less it is known, however, the riskier it becomes, precisely because it can induce people to think that every risk is calculable in the economic sphere, even the risk that is inherent to the future. *In actual fact*, however, the profit deriving from production is not, as such, susceptible of anticipatory monetization. As accounting tells us, profit is the firm's income. This is calculated at the end of production and sales, and only then can it give rise to the payment of dividends – which are socially justified *precisely as the reward for exposure to a fundamental uncertainty, which cannot be calculated in advance but must simply be accepted.*

What is indeed susceptible of monetization – and made so by the financial markets themselves – is the credit granted in order to finance the firm, which can be made liquid before it falls due. It is precisely this possibility of monetization – liquidity as the interchangeability of money and credit – that makes the credit market 'safe' and thus, as long as the optimism lasts, facilitates the financing of the fixed capital required in the long run (in Marshall's sense of the phrase) by the real economy, in order for it to grow.

The secret that silently underpins the capitalist system would therefore be precisely the relationship between money and credit embodied by liquidity and by the rate of interest, the operative parameter or *rate* whereby the future is made present, in other words is *discounted*.[14] The real but future profit that *may* derive from the immobilization of the resources and of the labour in which real investment consists would therefore be compatible with the financial but present 'realizability' of the credit that makes it possible.[15] As markets of liquidity, the financial markets are *markets of maturities*.

On the basis of this secret, the long-term real objectives of growth and the short-term financial volatility would be wholly 'synergetic', at least 'in the long run'. The financial markets would thus be 'an extraordinarily effective tool in spreading opportunity and fighting poverty'.[16] In short, a perfect tool to address the primary poverty of the economy, that is, the poverty of credit, that is, the producers' structural condition of debt. A tool without which 'economies would invariably ossify and decline'.[17] Work and unearned income, matrimony and the orgy, would thus be reconciled.

It is, however, precisely the way in which the financial markets support the other markets that makes not only possible but also *perilously probable* the simultaneous closing of all accounts in the shape of a liquidity crisis. Given the liberty of creditors to withdraw from the relationship before its agreed maturity, if a large number of them stop being 'optimistic' and exercise this capacity by selling (or even if they only fear that others may sell) their credits, preferring to obtain a guaranteed store of value, this very fact will cause a rush to pull out, and hence a crisis. When this happens, the overlapping of maturities will no longer be sufficient to ensure recovery. It will become necessary to delay payments to the point of *eliminating all maturities*.

As Bloch glimpsed it, this is what capitalism lives on: the attempt, constantly perpetrated on the financial markets, to avoid compliance with the real maturities that capitalism carries with it as a market economy. In other words, it cannot comply with what is a prerequisite in a market economy, namely the payment of debts. Therefore it cannot meet a requirement that it must, in any case, claim to wish to meet – since this constitutes its sole economic justification: the requirement that the way in which credit is granted correspond adequately to the dimension of debt in which human beings live, and hence that the forms of the granting of credit meet the borrowing needs of producers.

Ever since the birth of the financial markets, capitalism has tended to generate what would cause its death, namely the simultaneous settlement of accounts, and has therefore been obliged in actual fact – so as to avoid killing itself, or to 'save capitalism from capitalism' – to delay *all maturity* and payment.

Nevertheless, even if it can indefinitely postpone the closing of the accounts, it cannot actually abolish it – simply because it cannot abolish time, the end, and death. If nobody ever died, it would be better. If humans were not mortal – finite beings called upon to assume their responsibilities – this way of organizing the relations of debt and credit really would be perfect. But people do die, and it is for this very reason that they have an economic life in which they are required to live on the fruits of their labour, and not on unearned income; to pay their debts and not to make the payment of other people's debts impossible; to face risk and not to avoid it; to think about the future and not to discount it.

Let us try to restate this in more technical terms. Capitalism is a historical manifestation of the debt/credit relationship characterized by the fact of removing from this relationship, *on principle*, what makes it humanly bearable, namely the end. The credit it provides is not linked to the shared certainty of a maturity agreed upon from the outset, but to the constantly renegotiated uncertainty of its indefinite prolongation. This credit thus tends to lose any *real* connection with investments and results – any connection with what credit should make possible from an economic point of view, and with what should impose, on credit, the structure of its maturities – and is replaced by a continuous and alternating process in which credit is either provided excessively and out of all proportion or denied indiscriminately – hence, always out of all proportion. We thus have a process called upon to last indefinitely and in which crises become a necessary concomitant of the normal functioning of the markets.

It is from this perspective that the long term necessarily becomes, for capitalism and for the prevailing economic *doxa*, the moment in which we will *all* be dead, a moment that is completely unreal and ahistorical and, above all, completely irrelevant from the economic viewpoint: a sort of 'end of days' in which there is no longer any link between today and tomorrow, between present and future generations, in which the death of all is also the survival of all and, as Rabelais humorously put it, 'everyone becomes his own heir', in which all debts can finally be paid with no effort at all.

Part II will now try to show that, unlike a market economy, capitalism has lived historically, from its very first steps up to the present crisis, by postponing the moment of payment through the creation of debtors who never pay because they never die, and who never die because they never pay: first of all the states, with their public debt as a guarantee of their *fiat* money; but now perhaps also the financial markets themselves, which are currently requesting, and in most cases obtaining, from the states all the liquidity they believe to be necessary, not in order to pay the debts but rather to restore the liquidity of credit and thus to continue the never-ending process by which they live.

But at this point we, too, have all the elements we need not only to lay bare the difference between a market economy and a capitalist economy, but also to understand where the present crisis has come from and *what it is a crisis of*. In the end, we may even be able to understand all the reasons why this crisis – regardless of the fact that it can be 'resolved' with expedients that will probably do nothing but pave the way for the next – may prove an opportunity to see how it is effectively possible to maintain the market economy but to jettison capitalism in the name of a sound and responsible foundation for the economy.

For this very reason, however, it will be best to start from the event that testifies most openly to this age-old tendency of capitalism to postpone the moment of truth. The present crisis was triggered by the collapse of the market of subprime mortgages, a market constructed programmatically on the assumption that the important thing about a debt is not its 'payability' but its 'liquidability'. It is from this, from the most recent and intense manifestation of the postponement of the end, that our exploration must start. Only by working slowly backwards, through the course of a history normally recounted in terms of innovation and evolution, shall we be able to ask what has come to grief with this crisis and what direction our thinking must take if we are to avoid a situation where its end inevitably coincides with the beginning of the next.

PART II

History

1

From credit risk to liquidity risk (2008)

The summer of 2007 saw the outbreak of a crisis whose eventual outcome is still unforeseeable. What is more, the outcome will depend on the ability of those whose task it is to see what exactly is at stake, and so to distinguish between rough and ready remedies and appropriate reforms. Before we can say, on due reflection, what we may reasonably expect and what direction the political and economic responses should be taking, we need not only to understand the present situation in the light of the factors that have made it possible, but also to consider whether this situation is the result of an ineluctable train of events, or whether it may prove to be the upshot of decisions and directions that were far from inevitable.

A point that should begin to emerge fairly clearly already in this chapter is that even the most recent innovations are no more than the latest version of a way of thinking and practising financial relations that has been in currency, in all sorts of forms and places, for at least thirty years. This way of conducting finance had in turn been made possible by the existence (or rather by the lack) of an institutional framework that did not begin with the end of the Bretton Woods system but dates back to the beginnings of the western financial system. We will work our way gradually back to those beginnings in the following chapters, setting out to see not only what the consequences are of this way of conducting finance, but also what historical decisions and institutional transitions have led to it. The process will shed yet more light on the fact that we are not facing here the outcome of an evolutionary process without alternatives, but the product of precise decisions, taken more or less wittingly. This will also help us to adumbrate, in the light of the historical alternatives and principles in play, the alternatives that are possible in the present; these will come under closer scrutiny in Part III.

But let us take things in order, beginning from the end.

Even before coming to an end, the crisis under way has already taken on a distinct identity – for the media at least, if not for history – as the 'subprime crisis'. If the name is anything to go by, it all seems to have started with a particular financial market: the subprime mortgage market, which came into its own only recently. So recently, in fact, that news about this type of instrument began to circulate, even in the specialized financial press, only after it had come into crisis.

In less than two years, the crisis of a market that represented only 15 per cent of the American mortgage market – which in turn represented only 15 per cent of Wall Street's fixed-income investments – brought about losses for financial institutions throughout the world, losses, according to the latest International Monetary Fund estimates,[1] of over 4,000 billion dollars, which rapidly began to translate in terms – all too real and tangible – of bankruptcies, layoffs, plunging income and rising unemployment. What was it that sent the subprime mortgage market hurtling into crisis? And why did a crisis in what was, after all, only a small sector drag with it the financial markets and economic systems *of the whole world*? To answer both of these questions, it is necessary and, in certain respects, sufficient to begin from a description of these instruments.

Subprime mortgages are granted to people who have no access to ordinary credit, being unable to offer adequate guarantees in terms of income or property already in their possession, or because there is evidence that they have not been able to meet their debts in the past.[2] These mortgages are granted on more onerous conditions than those reserved for the borrowers who, on the contrary, have shown evidence of being solvent and reliable (the 'prime borrowers', as they are called).

Anyone who has a healthily naïve idea of the banker's profession, imagining that his task lies in lending money to those who may reasonably be expected to pay it back, might make do with this definition to account for the subprime default. If I can lend 100 to a trusted person on the reasonable assumption that he/she can pay me back 110, why should I expect *more* of someone who is *less reliable*?

With hindsight, we can see the writing on the wall for every crisis, bursting like a bubble that was bound to burst. However, our task would be all too easy, and indeed useless, if we simply concluded that all bubbles burst sooner or later: we need to be able to explain how each particular bubble was able to appear without any of the agents involved getting wind of it – or even being able to get wind of it – as such. So, with the soul of simplicity, we must ask: how on earth could credit have been supplied to debtors who, by definition, could never have been eligible for it on the basis of the traditional, prudential criteria? Whence came the possibility for these instruments to sprout and burgeon so plentifully for over a decade, to the extent of reaching an overall volume of 1,300 billion dollars of credit supplied on the eve of crisis?

The supply of subprime mortgages was made possible through the development of a financial practice that has ancient roots, but only from the beginning of the 1980s was it technically adjusted into the form under which it is familiar to us today: securitization. The characteristic feature of this way of organizing financial relations is that the credit granted is not entered into the balance sheet of the bank issuing it (and kept there until it is fully paid back), but transformed into negotiable securities: in other words it is 'securitized'. The securities produced through this system are in turn sold to other investors. In this way, on the one hand the bank issuing them can immediately collect the entire sum of the credit supplied, plus a commission charged for the operation, which is often proportionate to the sum of the loan. On the other hand, the bank is in no way exposed to credit risk – the risk, that is, of the debtor proving insolvent. Any such risk is passed on to the purchasers of the securities.

The latter, however, need not wait until the credit matures, facing the risk of non-payment in the meantime. The securities they have purchased are in fact negotiable; they can be resold on the market at any moment. Thus the investors benefit not only from the returns on the securities (in other words, from interest on the credit supplied, which is particularly high for subprime mortgages), but also from capital gains, if they manage to sell the securities at a higher price than the one they paid for them.

Expectations of such gains were fuelled by the rise in real estate market quotations, which in turn buoyed up through the expansion of credit that had been enabled by securitization – in a system of circular causation, which from the very outset had rendered unnecessary and, ultimately, impossible any reference to fundamentals. On top of the quantitative burgeoning of securities there also came a qualitative advantage for investors in the variety of securities issued, which were supplying various combinations of risk and returns to meet all sorts of preferences.

Such were the advantages for the creditors. But for the debtors, too, the advantages of the subprime mortgages could appear, at least to begin with, quite obvious and, above all, irresistible. Here were debtors who, by definition, would never receive any credit from a traditional bank but who, thanks to securitization, had access not only to residential mortgages, but also student loans, auto loans and credit card debts. In fact, the securitization carried out by the banks also extended to these types of debts. Thus securitization generated a huge increase in the number of people with access to credit, gathering in vast quantities of money from investors all over the world, to be placed at the disposal of workers who lacked job security, of ethnic minorities, of the marginalized and, in short, of the vast ranks of the 'poor' to buy a house, pay for tuition or meet any everyday expense. Hence securitization was seen as a particularly worthy financial innovation carried out in the interest of the 'democratization of finance' – much like microcredit, but on a larger scale and with incomparably greater expansive capacity.[3]

By now we have enough evidence to understand the extraordinary expansion of subprime mortgages. All the agents involved – banks, investors and borrowers – derived tangible advantages from using this instrument. It looked like an exemplary case of successful financial innovation: a new form of intermediation, offering undreamed of possibilities to match credit seekers and investors in search of remunerative opportunities. It could be hailed as a simple and entirely positive evolutionary fact, a 'paradigm shift' for the global banking system, which entailed transition from an 'originate and hold' model, in which the supplier of credit enters it in the balance sheet accepting the risk, to an 'originate and distribute' model, in which the supplier of credit distributes it, selling it on the market together with the associated risk in the form of securities[4] (See Figure II 1.1).

Moreover, this innovation did not seem to benefit debtors, creditors and intermediaries alone; the beneficial effects cascaded over other agents – in fact over the entire economic system. The generous supply of mortgages buoyed up housing demand, fuelling an unprecedented rise in real estate prices, which in turn boosted the building sector. Similarly, the expansion of consumption credit kept up demand and, with it, the income for firms and employment. The overall advantages were not only economic, but also social. How, indeed, could one deny that buying a house to live in and accessing higher education, especially for the less privileged classes, constitute decisive contributions to the enhancement of social cohesion? And again, if, between 1998 and 2006, a million and a half Americans became owners of the houses they lived in, this is thanks to subprime mortgages.[5]

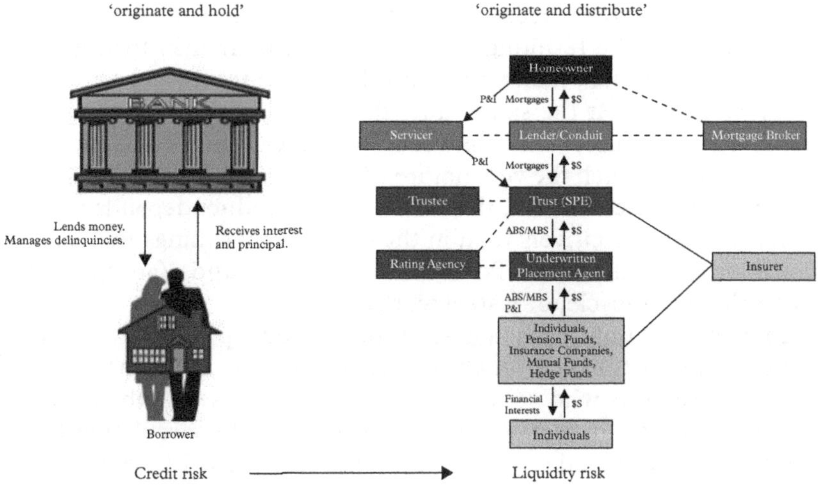

Figure II 1.1 The change of paradigm

Source: NERA Economic Consulting, *The Subprime Meltdown*, NERA Insights Series, 21 June 2007

So what went wrong? Why did the mechanism eventually seize up? In a recent study dedicated to the subprime crisis, Robert J. Shiller – an expert in real estate markets and the deviser of the first and most important index to measure housing prices (the Standard & Poors/Case-Shiller index), who is acknowledged as one of the few to have foreseen the real estate crisis – argued that this was a matter of faulty application of a good idea and that securitization as a means to democratize finance is a step in the right direction, since 'by spreading risk, it places economic life on a firmer foundation'.[6]

And yet, if we have outlined the situation aright, then there is very strong evidence pointing to the exact contrary. Securitization *undermines* the foundations of economic life, for it changes that fundamental economic relationship which is the link between creditor and debtor, making it not more solid but, literally, *more liquid.* As we have seen, in fact, securitization transforms relations of credit into negotiable – and thus liquid – securities that can be passed on from hand to hand indefinitely. Creditor and debtor are no longer bound together in a stable relationship, which traditionally lasts for as many as thirty years in the case of a mortgage, but are separated by an indefinite chain of legal and economic transactions.

Securitization generates a sort of 'long value chain' in the production of credit, as compared with the 'short value chain' of the traditional mortgage. Here, too, extension of the value chain finds justification in the resulting economies of scale thanks to which, in turn, prices can fall, making the 'product' (the mortgage) accessible to more people. At the same time, the lengthening value chain also eliminates the direct link between 'producer' and 'consumer' (of savings) upon which the very nature of the 'product' (credit) depends – and, in the case of credit, the nature of the product depends on that link even more decisively than in the case of other things that can be considered 'products' on far more concrete grounds (an apple, for example, or a bicycle, or a steel works).

In fact, not only does the securitized credit pass from hand to hand countless times, through transactions on the secondary market between creditors who no longer have any relations with the debtors; but even before circulating, and to ensure that the circulation be as fluid and widespread as possible, the credit must be transformed into negotiable, fungible securities. Subprime mortgages have been allocated in funds, grouped according to risk, classified by the rating agencies, and even insured by specialized companies against the risk of insolvency. In this way, through a series of contracts and legal fictions, personal credit to individuals could be bundled together and then redistributed in the form of standardized, transferable securities – prêt-à-porter, as it were, albeit differentiated so as to cater for a wide range of investment profiles. The personal link between creditor and debtor is severed in the name of liquidity.

The implications of this severance also run diametrically opposite Shiller's indications. If it is true that the risk is distributed, through securitization, in a quantity and variety of securities traded throughout the whole world, this very distribution depends crucially on the liquidity of the securities themselves. Loss of liquidity in the securities means the immediate resurgence of the risk that seemed parcelled away – risk that is now out of all proportion and incalculable. People who had acquired these securities in the conviction that they faced no risk of debtor insolvency, being able to resell them on the market at any moment, suddenly find out that they are equally likely not to find any purchasers for such securities. Only then does it become evident that securitization, far from sharing out the risk and making it bearable by diluting it until it virtually disappears, transforms credit risk into liquidity risk. Or, to be more precise, *the liquidity risk emerges as a consequence of a stratagem to get around the credit risk.*

In fact, thanks to securitization, credit can be supplied without any consideration for the debtor's effective capacity to pay it back, or at the best by making do with a rough estimate of the credit risk.

Repentant brokers recall how they scoured the outskirts of major US metropolises to induce people on low incomes, and often the jobless, to accept a loan to buy a house, luring them on with concessional rates[7] and encouraging them to make false income declarations if they did not come up to the requisites, lax as they were. The most striking aspect of these accounts, however, lies not so much in what was done without regard for rules and laws, not even in the fraud and enticement involved, as in the fact that the securitization rules themselves made all this possible, and indeed desirable. Those brokers were *justified* in lending money to people who would clearly be unable to repay the debts on their incomes, since the debts would be resold as securities and, as a whole, the price of the securities would be sustained by the increasing value of the real estate behind them. That housing prices could only go on increasing was the *common opinion*, apparently borne out statistically by a ten-year record of rising prices. And for the brokers, whose sole aim was to maximize the number of mortgages supplied over the short period to their own advantage and to the benefit of their firm and of society as a whole, being able to lend meant having to lend.[8]

Fraudulent practices are in no need of ethical judgement; they are simply to be prosecuted. What does come in for judgement, and on economical grounds even before we bring in ethical considerations, is the justification of a form of loan that does not require the borrower to be solvent, nor therefore the lender to be able to assess solvency. If, with the introduction of this instrument, financial intermediation is relieved of this responsibility, this is not to be blamed on the agents who practise it and, reasonably enough, profit from it, whether small brokers or managing directors of big banking groups. Nor is it a matter of limiting bonuses: if the job is to sell, better results are obtained by paying a commission on sales. The question we should be asking is whether the banker's job is in fact to sell anything at all, or whether it should not rather be to bring together creditor and debtor.[9]

What merits indictment, not primarily as a personal fault but as a systemic flaw, is the legal invention of a financial instrument that preventively relieves debtor and creditor of all personal liability for the payment of the debt. Debtors can and must take on personal responsibility for the payment of their debts; on the other hand, they can have no responsibility for the fact that the securities based on those debts are acquired on the market. Creditors can and must be considered responsible for the assessment of the borrowers' solvency: significantly, the procedure involved in assessing the firm's assets for the purposes of acquisition is traditionally called *due diligence*. On the other hand, creditors cannot be held responsible for the fact that the securities they have acquired lose their liquidity. Solvency is a responsibility shared by debtors and creditors alike, playing antagonistic, but, for this very reason, complementary roles. For liquidity, all and none are responsible, for it depends on collective behaviour to which each contributes in part, but none decisively.

The essential difference between credit risk and liquidity risk is also manifested in the way risks materialize, generating their effects. In the introduction we quoted Bloch's definition of capitalism as 'a system that would perish if all the accounts were settled at the same time'. We also saw that this is far from implying that capitalism is bound to collapse through some immanent necessity, but rather that it seeks to avoid simultaneous settlement in such a way as to make it, nevertheless, somewhat probable. As long as the accounts reflect credit *relationships*, and hence they take the form of long-term contracts or at any rate of contracts with a set maturity, simultaneous settlement remains *systematically* impossible. But when any creditor is systematically granted the option to withdraw from any relationship at any moment, such simultaneity becomes not only possible but highly probable, although unforeseeable. In fact, as we observed earlier, if an appreciable number of creditors within a particular market withdraw, selling their instruments of credit (or even simply fearing that others may do so), this will in itself suffice to start a run for closing the positions.

Transforming the credit relationship into a liquid security means entrusting the market with an evaluation of the debtor's soundness. All the information is encapsulated in the price: it is 'priced in'. But if a security loses its liquidity, in other words its negotiability, it no longer has a price. Consequently, all knowledge of the debt represented by that security, of the debtor's solvency or profitability, is suddenly blanked out. Even now, for many derivatives, there is no longer any price; for there is no market and there are no purchasers. The central banks and governments themselves hesitate to buy 'toxic' securities, their toxicity depending on the fact that they represent incalculable costs – there is no knowing how long they will have to be kept or how much they can be resold for.

The lack of a market price for these securities is producing particularly problematic effects due to the 'mark-to-market' accounting standards, by which funds are required to enter their financial assets into the balance sheet at market prices. If there is no market price, then the holders of these securities have no way of quantifying their assets, and their creditors, effective or potential, are in turn unable to evaluate their solvency. As a result, the market freezes still further, not only for those securities but also for other forms of credit between the agents involved. One consequence was, for example, a freeze on loans between banks in the early stages of the crisis. And, more generally, this explains how the crisis was able to spread through an ever vaster and more varied range of markets, agents, economic sectors and national economies.

So far we have considered the early manifestations of the crisis under way and the factors that unleashed it. We must now take a step back to inquire, over and above the more immediate causes, where the crisis that broke out in the summer of 2007 came from. Would it have been possible without the rising tide of liquidity in the global financial market that we have witnessed over the last few decades? How exactly does this crisis depend on liquidity – liquidity understood not only in quantitative terms, but as a way to conceive of, and to structure, financial relations?

2

The globalization of capital (1973)

The supply of subprime mortgages by means of securitization is a recent and limited practice. Over the last ten years it enjoyed its heyday, above all, at the outskirts of various American metropolises; but when it crashed it dragged down with it banks, insurance companies and big corporations, flooding over geographical and sectorial frontiers, to overwhelm entire countries and to provoke generalized recession on a global scale. How is it that an apparently circumscribed crash was able to swell up into what has been called a 'financial tsunami', with effects that proved all the more devastating the further they reached from the epicentre? How could the default of a very small proportion of borrowers (of whom, moreover, nothing had ever been expected) lead to the failure of one of the oldest and greatest investment banks in the world and to the urgent need to rescue half of the British banking system? The scandalous proportions of the contagion unleashed a manhunt for the spreaders of infection. And yet the spreading of the crisis, like its inception, depended not so much on breaking the rules that had allowed for the previous growth, as on their actual application.

Effectively, even more than the crisis itself, its *spread* is to be imputed not to contingent circumstances, but rather to structural conditions. To begin with, these conditions are to be found in the very rules of the new financial paradigm – which, just as it 'originates and distributes' credit, so it generates and distributes the corresponding risk. What opened the way for the crisis to spread was precisely the distribution achieved through securitization: people all over the world who had acquired the securities, and had gone on making capital gains as long as demand and prices grew, suffered often literally incalculable losses in the same way when prices began to fall and trading was suspended.

It would, however, be wrong to impute the virulence of the crisis solely to the proliferation of innovative financial instruments, the toxicity of which would be lurking behind acronyms that were often indecipherable even for the managers of the banks trading in them. Securities that, until the outbreak of crisis, had been blindly welcomed as a sort of manna were as blindly cast aside as toxic refuse once the crisis broke out. It is all too easy for repentant bankers or politicians to turn round and deplore the excesses of the financial innovations, calling for stricter rules to clamp down on them, as if the securities placed on the market until last year (like the cylindrical hats rashly acquired by a character in Borges's tale 'The Zahir') were merely the fruit of greedy speculators' wild fantasies, and it was up to some authority in Paris to decree that, far from being securities (hats), they were 'arbitrary and unauthorized *caprices*'.[1] On the market, however, the only goods are the ones that sell. Asset backed securities (ABSs) and collateralized debt obligations (CDOs) were created to meet the demand of investors all over the world. It was the demand that generated the supply. Incriminating and banning the subprimes, therefore, is hardly going to help us with understanding how the crisis spread and with getting to the roots of it: what we need is to identify and, if possible, to remove the factors that led to the emergence of subprimes.

Now, if we approach the question from the demand side, it is evident that, without a great many risk-prone investors, these instruments could never have been thought of, let alone traded. And without an increasingly deregulated movement of capital they could never have spread so copiously. The inextricable combination of these two characteristics – a fair amount of money available for financial instruments and the lack of legal restrictions on the reciprocal exchangeability of securities and money – constitutes what is commonly called the 'liquidity' of a market.[2] The liquidity of global financial markets constituted the right condition for the development and diffusion of subprimes. In this sense, we may even say that the crisis was due to liquidity.

This, however, is an observation in sharp contrast with the economic theory that teaches us to consider liquidity to be a positive and desirable feature of financial markets; therefore it must be qualified. In order to attempt to vindicate, at least in part, the merits of liquidity, one might be tempted to specify that it constituted a necessary but not a sufficient condition for the bubble and its implosion; in other words, it allowed for, but did not dictate, the provision of subprime mortgages. In practice, however, empirical evidence suggests exactly the contrary: the international capital market, liquid and integrated, did not serve for the poor of America's outskirts to seek money overseas, but it did serve for the money of savers from all corners of the world *to come looking for them*. Why should thousands of brokers have invaded America's slum areas with 'predatory practices',[3] had they not been riding a tide of liquidity running after returns?

This is, indeed, the most disruptive aspect of the new global finance paradigm: credit is not created on request, by the debtor, to meet particular needs for financing, but on the insistent, often underhand and occasionally fraudulent proposal of people bent on loaning at all costs – to the extent that it is more appropriate to call it, as in fact is the case, 'originate *to* distribute'. Credit is originated solely for the purpose of distribution, the supply of loan serving the sale of securities, and not vice versa. The possibility of distribution constitutes the actual motive behind the operation, and not simply the opportunity for it.

Thus, we may argue, if the crisis comes from the subprimes, the subprimes in turn come from liquidity. Without the increasing liquidity that has characterized financial markets over the last few decades, subprimes would never have been feasible, nor even conceivable. The liquidity of the global financial market not only provided a channel for the transmission of the crisis, but constituted the condition that made it possible.

Now, the liquidity of the international financial relations is not a fact of life or a permanent feature of human economic structures, but has a history of its own, which began not so long ago. The growth of liquidity, understood both as the liberalization of capital movements at the international level and as the potentially unlimited increase in the quantity of money available for those movements, *had its beginnings in the mid-1970s*. It was then that subprimes began to be possible. And the most telling proof lies in the fact that the subprime crisis is not the only one of its kind. Many other bubbles and crises punctuated this period with unprecedented frequency, from the South American debt crisis to the crisis of the US savings banks and to the currency and banking crises that shook Southeast Asia.[4] In general the tendency is to point out the peculiarity of the present crisis, marking it out from previous occurrences, but there are in fact strong grounds to argue that all these crises show features creating a marked family resemblance in terms of procedures for the constitution and, above all, resolution of debtor/creditor relations.

Let us therefore extend our horizons over the last thirty years. From the end of the 1970s on, the volume of capital movements, in particular towards developing countries, has increased exponentially. This, too, is a phenomenon that can be described in terms of increasing credit accessibility for agents who belong, in this case, to whole countries, geographical areas or economic sectors previously excluded from the international financial system: we might call them the 'planetary subprime borrowers'. Just as unprecedented volumes of money could be channelled towards the outskirts of America's metropolises thanks to the securitization of mortgages in the 1990s, so staggering volumes of investments were able to find their way to the far-flung outskirts of the world thanks to the liberalization of capital movements and growing integration of the financial markets in the 1970s and 1980s.

Portfolio investments made a far greater contribution to the volatility of capital movements than foreign direct investments did.[5] The difference between the two types of investment corresponds to the difference between a securitized mortgage and a traditional one. Like a traditional mortgage, direct investment binds creditor and debtor together over an extensive set period that corresponds to the time horizon of the investment, which is usually dedicated to financing the construction of a productive plant or infrastructures. Like a subprime mortgage, portfolio investment is made through the acquisition of financial instruments that can be resold at any moment on the market, and it is therefore driven by the liquidity of the instruments and possible capital gains to be made on selling them rather than by the profitability of the capital goods that the instruments represent, more or less directly. And, like subprimes, portfolio investments can be withdrawn just as rapidly as they have been conferred. The virtuous circle, with its rising stock market trend that attracts ever more investments and fuels expectations of further rises, can reverse overnight into a vicious circle, in which even the simple expectation that the upward trend might come to an end generates a sudden reduction of positions, and consequently a drop in rates – which simultaneously confirms and reinforces bearish expectations. The inflow and outflow of capital, equally rapid and indeed equally favoured by the liquidity of investments, underlay the bubbles and successive crises that hit the developing countries over the last few decades, regardless of the specific reasons that triggered the reversal of expectations: from Mexico (1995) to Southeast Asia (1997), from Russia to Brazil (1998), and from Turkey to Argentina (2001).

Much the same applies to an apparently very different bubble, which blew into the air from the 'new economy'. Again, financing was granted to people who would never have had access to traditional credit, in order to set up companies that were meant to (and for a time effectively did) reward the lender with handsome capital gains by listing the new company on the market, often without actually making a profit. And in this case, too, aggressive investors, confident of returns and heedless of risk, opened up new investment frontiers – not geographical but technological[6] – for even more blindly confident and unwittingly reckless savers.

Such cases not only show marked analogies, but are in fact closely connected. The apparent succession of cycles that gathered momentum over the last thirty years can actually be seen as one single wave generated by a mass of liquidity that, pursuing the most profitable investment opportunities on global financial markets, flowed into one market, boosting returns and attracting new investments, only to pour out even more abruptly and flood other markets, opening the way to the next crisis.[7] Or, to change the metaphor in order to reflect even better the volatility of these investments, one might picture a bubble in an only partially inflated air mattress, shifting this way or that under the weight of the crisis. It is precisely the severance of the creditor/debtor relationship (severance that characterizes both portfolio investments and securitization) that allowed for such rapidity in the shifting of money through forms of investment that are ever more varied by area, sector or instrument.

However, it is highly debatable whether the net effect of the inflows and outflows of capital proved positive. In other words, it is not clear whether, over and above the fluctuations caused by the capital movements also in such real variables as GDP and volume of foreign trade, a positive trend can be established for these variables clearly attributable to the financing made available through the liberalization of financial markets. In the case of subprime mortgages, the net real effect, in terms of first house ownership, has proved negative: while 1.4 million people were able to buy houses thanks also to subprime mortgages between 1998 and 2006, 2.4 million came in for foreclosure by failing to keep up with the repayments. Even before the crisis broke out there were nearly 1 million fewer homeowners.[8] As for the capital flows towards countries, the positive effects of portfolio investments are more open to questioning, although the negative effects of disinvestment are all too evident. Nevertheless, the suspicion remains that other forms of financing, such as direct investments, might offer more certain and reliable advances, even if occasionally rather more slender ones.[9] The same consideration applies to investment in the emerging sectors: it is true that innovation calls for financing, but must it really take the form of IPOs (initial public offerings) and LBOs (leveraged buy-outs), or can it bind creditor and debtor together in a long-term relationship?[10]

The task of weighing up alternatives of this kind awaits us in Part III of this book. In the meantime, having yet to arrive at a conclusive and agreed assessment of the contribution made by financial integration to the state of health of the global economy, we must at least acknowledge that the question remains open.[11] Nevertheless, we cannot help wondering how it is that, historically, the liberalization of capital movements has been so strenuously enforced over the last few decades, despite all the doubts raised on various sides and yet to be convincingly allayed.

Various explanations have been advanced. Some see in growing financial integration the inevitable result of technological progress, in particular in the information and communication sectors. This point of view is eloquently summed up by Walter B. Wriston in an article published in *Foreign Affairs*, which echoes Eichengreen's evolutionary argument in resounding tones:

> Today we are witnessing a galloping new system of international finance. Our new international financial regime differs radically from its precursors in that it was not built by politicians, economists, central bankers or finance ministers, nor did high-level international conferences produce a master plan. It was built by technology. It is doubtful if the men and women who interconnected the planet with telecommunications and computers realized that they were assembling a global financial marketplace that would replace the Bretton Woods agreements and, over time, alter political structures.[12]

Others, by contrast, hold that the liberalization of capital movements came about solely for ideological reasons of neoliberal origin, following a bias in favour of opening up the markets for the (presumed) benefit of creditors more than of debtors. This is, for example, how Jagdish Bhagwati wrote in the same journal, after ten years fraught with banking and currency crises in the emerging countries:

> And despite the evidence of the inherent risks of free capital flows, the Wall Street-Treasury complex is currently proceeding on the self-serving assumption that the ideal world is indeed one of free capital flows, with the IMF and its bailouts at the apex in a role that guarantees its survival and enhances its status. But the weight of evidence and the force of logic point in the opposite direction, toward restraints on capital flows. It is time to shift the burden of proof from those who oppose to those who favor liberated capital.[13]

Perhaps, rather than being self-interested, the assumption is frankly dogmatic, as we had occasion to remark in relation to the formulation of neoliberal theses accomplished by Rajan and Zingales.[14] In a study addressing the issue systematically, in a historical perspective, Eric Helleiner reviews a series of political and institutional factors beside technology and ideology – which, naturally, are not excluded – on the evidence of which he is able to demonstrate the crucial role played by states in the creation of global finance. As Helleiner points out, far from failing to resist the spontaneous tendency of the financial markets to integrate, the states played a decisive role in adopting explicit deregulation measures from the mid-1970s on, dismantling the controls over capital movements that had been introduced in the aftermath of the Second World War. Moreover, the states intervened even more decisively to prevent liberalization from collapsing under the weight of its failures; they did this through an unflagging activity to forestall and address a series of international crises, and in particular by taking on the function of lender of last resort. Thus the path was cleared for the systematic elusion of the problem of imbalances in the balance of payments of major countries, and in particular of the accumulation of debts on the part of the USA and complementary accumulation of dollars in other countries, beginning with the countries that benefited from the 1973 oil shock.[15]

Helleiner's argument thus seems to bear out the thesis that regulation and deregulation are two sides of one and the same process in the contemporary world. And yet the question remains: why have so many states opened up to the free movement of capital, while at the same time clamping down on the free movement of goods? Helleiner attributes this to the 'unique mobility and fungibility of money', which would have called for a virtually impossible degree of international coordination to contain the flows.[16] This, however, is an explanation that could detract from his thesis. If, in fact, mobility and fungibility were intrinsic characteristics of money, or qualities acquired through technological process in electronic payment systems, then the political aspect would once again have proved decidedly marginal. However, precisely this definition of money, and in particular of money as a mobile and fungible commodity at the international level, can by no means be taken for granted. Indeed, looking at the concrete realities, we must recognize that it depends precisely on those political factors pointed up by Helleiner, and in particular on the need to perpetuate financial imbalances in order to avoid political frictions and avert economic crises.

Where, after all, does international liquidity come from? What is the source of this superabundance of money, which, to find some remunerative use, must always seek out investment opportunities, invent ever new 'subprime markets' throughout the whole world? The answer, basically, is very simple: ultimately the money comes from those who 'produce' it. And in the modern system the creation of money is subject to a monopoly regime. The primary source of liquidity is the central bank.

In this respect the present crisis is emblematic: it was the monetary expansion implemented by the Fed, after the crisis of the new economy and with the deliberate intention of mitigating its depressive effects, that led to this overabundance of liquidity, which eventually sought an outlet in subprime mortgages. And this was no exceptional episode: adopting an expansive policy as an anti-cyclic measure has been a regular feature of the Fed over the last twenty years. Ever since the first crisis he had to address, namely the Wall Street crash of 1987, and on through the Russian and Brazilian debt crises, the busting of the NASDAQ bubble, the apprehensions for the millennium bug and the trauma of 9/11, Greenspan always set out to prevent possible market downturns, and, when they nevertheless occurred, to see to them with expansive manoeuvres. The banks coined the expression 'Greenspan put' for this strategy, since the effect was comparable to a 'put option': in practice the Fed set a limit to the possible losses of financial agents, as if the agents had acquired from Greenspan (and, what is more, acquired without even paying the premium) an option that offered them the possibility to sell their financial assets at a set minimum price.

Reassured by an increasing series of encouraging precedents, investors could expect the Fed to step in whenever financial asset prices sank, either by lowering the target rate or by increasing the quantity of money, thereby helping them to back up once more. A marked correlation between share index trends and expectations of a cut in the Fed funds rate had been noted as early as December 2000 in *Financial Times* (see Figure II 2.1).[17]

The Fed injections of liquidity acted like 'injections of optimism', like administrations of antidepressant drugs, reducing the agents' perception of risk, thereby inducing them to take on ever greater risks, ever more unwittingly. So much so that, when asked about the causes of the crisis, eighty-year-old Peter Bernstein, who literally wrote the history of finance both as an investment manager and as a successful author of books, could only answer, laconically: 'The bad news grew out of too much good news.'[18]

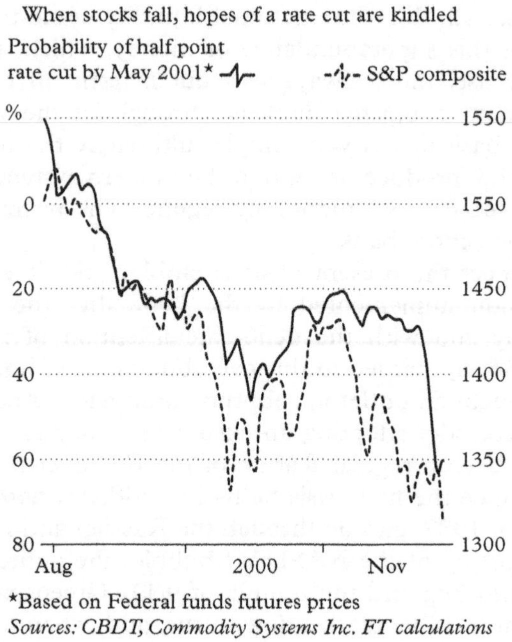

Figure II 2.1 The Fed is our friend
Source: 'The Fed Is Our Friend', *Financial Times*, 8 December 2000

Thus it was precisely the way the monetary policy had helped through the previous crises that created the conditions for the present crisis. The unprecedented reductions of interest rates and injections of liquidity that have been applied to tackle the latest crisis, and not only by the Federal Reserve, hardly bode well. Despite repeated warnings alerting against the consequent moral hazard, the function of lender of last resort has been exercised with increasing nonchalance. All this has been justified through the need to address the most immediate risks and losses, with scant consideration for the consequences entailed for a future that could be surprisingly near.

In this way, it was the very institutions that bore responsibility for the stability of the currency, and hence of the relations between creditors and debtors, *that catalyzed the transformation of credit risk into liquidity risk*. Here eloquent proof is to be seen in the fact that in the United States the concerted action of the authorities through emergency funds was not designed to make the debtors solvent, but to endow with liquidity the securities that represented their debts. Indeed, as the name given to the plan makes it clear (TARP,

Troubled Assets Relief Program), the 700 billion of the Paulson plan were allocated by the government not to help troubled families to pay back their mortgages, but to help troubled securities to regain liquidity. Both options were on the table: Congress favoured the former option, but the latter was chosen thanks to the opposition of Fed governor Bernanke and Treasury Secretary Paulson, who were against public money being used to help debtors. Thus the idea prevailed that it was not justified for the state to intervene so as to allow debtors to pay their debts, but it was fully justified for it to intervene so as to allow them not to pay indefinitely. The rationale for payment gave way to the rationale for consolidation.[19]

It is worth noting that, despite the rhetoric that often accompanies it, the latter was by no means a choice against the state and in favour of the market, regarded as an efficient mechanism for the allocation of financial resources. On the contrary, on this approach state and market are brought together as recipients of potentially unlimited funds designed to ensure that they function properly. The only debtors too big to fail are in fact the state and the financial market:[20] the central bank rescues the market with the government's bailout plans, just as it supports the state through the market or, more precisely, through open market operations.

Although there is no (longer any) obligation for central banks to lend to governments in most systems, public debt securities are again beginning to represent one of the most substantial forms of assets of the issuing institutes and a precise measure of the degree of support that governments receive from them. And yet, precisely because they take this form through acquisition of government securities on the open market, loans made by the central banks are not meant to allow governments to pay their debts, but rather to endow with liquidity the securities representing these debts.

In order to cope with the subprime crisis, the same principle that had hitherto applied solely to the safest of securities – government securities – was also extended to securities that were by no means as safe. Thanks also to the coverage offered by the TARP, between December 2007 and November 2008 the Fed constituted a great many funds endowed with some hundreds of billions of dollars, to offer loans in exchange for securities that nobody wanted any longer, with the declared intention of restoring liquidity to the respective markets.[21] The irredeemable debts of state and market thus piled up side by side as assets of the central bank, which agreed to finance them indefinitely. Thanks to the financial support of the central bank, state and market were able to consolidate their position as the only agents never required to pay their debts and that in consequence *never die* – not only legally but also economically.

But where does this unlimited lending capacity of the central banks come from, in turn? Who lends to the lender? The most immediate answer seems to be – no one. This is why the central banks are said to play the part of lender of last resort. The central banks create money through '*fiat*' and have no need to borrow it. And yet, how do they create it? It was Alan Greenspan himself, Fed governor for much of the period in question, who spelled out just what the exercise of this function implies, namely nothing less than the ability 'to induce market participants to employ one's liabilities as a money'.[22] In other words, the central bank is a legal entity that has the option not to pay its debts, putting them into circulation as money. Thus it is above all its own debts that the central bank is able to make irredeemable, on the strength of their liquidity, or on the strength of the fact that there are market actors ready to accept them.

For as long as he was in office, Greenspan played the part of central banker, and hence also of lender of last resort, not only for the United States but for the rest of the world, too, inasmuch as he was able to go on inducing the world's market actors to use his debts – his dollars, that is – as international currency. The point is, however, that these actors will not necessarily go on letting themselves indefinitely led to accept American debts as money, above all in view of the fact that a growing proportion of the debts are not circulating at all, but for some time now have been piling up in the reserves of foreign central banks, and notably in certain countries in the Middle and Far East.[23] If America's debts should cease to circulate as money, they would once again become simple debts, and the solvency of the American debtor would again become a matter of importance. And if the entity exercising international seignorage with the *consensus of the other countries* were to lose this consensus and to be seen again as a simple debtor, the question would then be for how long the creditors would be prepared to go on financing it – also taking into account the consideration that their very position as creditors depends increasingly on their willingness to go on holding unpayable credit.

One solution might be the transference – gradual and negotiated – of the function of lender of last resort, and thus of the centre of the global financial system, somewhere else. There appears to be some evidence in support of this idea, suggesting that the United States' trade deficit is getting increasingly difficult to finance. Whereas in the first months of the crisis private agents continued to take refuge in America's public debt securities, driving returns down to a minimum and contributing to dollar revaluation, US Treasury Department figures now reveal that, for some months, foreign authorities have been selling off long-term US securities.[24] Here the increasingly frequent and explicit appeals made by the West to the East for help and collaboration have been of little avail: take for example the need to open up the global economy summit from the G-8 to the G-20 to include the major foreign holders of dollars (in addition to Japan, bringing in China, Saudi Arabia and South Korea). In the meantime China has begun to supply huge yuan-denominated loans, not only to countries in Southeast Asia but also to trading partners as far-flung as Argentina.[25] These may perhaps all be signs indicating that the place of the global lender of last resort has already changed – at least inasmuch as the US government can afford to extend credit to American banks and firms that are in difficulty only because there is someone who, in turn, continues lending to it.

Perhaps, however, even before asking who is performing the function of lender of last resort or where it is shifting to, we might well ask ourselves whether the existence of a global lender of last resort is really necessary and desirable. The question is well worth raising, and we will return to it in Part III. Suffice it here to ask when it came into existence in this form. How long have there existed debts that need not, and indeed cannot, be paid? This is the story that we will be recounting in the following chapters – a story that had already come to a fundamental turning point about thirty-five years ago – significantly enough, coinciding with the initial burgeoning of capital movements at the international level and the ensuing crises.

3

'*Fiat* dollar'. And the world saw that it was good (1971)

On 15 August 1971, addressing the nation in a speech broadcast at nine o'clock at night on radio and television, President Richard Nixon announced *urbi et orbi* – to America and the entire world – that he had given instructions temporarily to suspend the convertibility of the dollar into gold. Thus was born the nonconvertible currency – pure and simple paper with no intrinsic value, which could be created by the Federal Reserve in potentially unlimited quantities, through a simple decree. Aptly, therefore, it was called '*fiat* money': money created from nothing, by the sheer force of a demiurgic word.

Actually every currency owes its existence to a '*fiat*', a sovereign act. The only way for a currency to come into circulation legitimately is through the sanction of an authority. To become a currency, gold itself has to be minted; all the more, a banknote can only circulate in representation or substitution of gold if it bears the seal and signature of the issuer. It was not, therefore, as a sovereign act that Nixon's decision created a new currency. Rather, a radically new turn was taken with his decision to leave the paper circulation system intact while removing the grounds of its legitimacy – namely a rate of convertibility to a quantity of gold. Nixon's command was not 'let there be money', but 'let there be no payment'. The first effect of this order, before creating a new currency, was to eliminate the old one. In fact, with Nixon's declaration, what had been, up until then and from times immemorial, the currency par excellence – gold – lost the major prerogative of money, which is to pay debts.

In the performance of the very act with which Nixon, somewhat unwittingly, put an end to 2,500 years of history, a new era was ushered in, and a new currency: from now on the currency, the legal means to pay debts, would no longer be gold but another debt. A particular type of debt, which is at the same time money, and in consequence irredeemable. An unpayable, indeed, immortal debt. A consolidated debt. A debt transformed into paper, into a transferable security, destined to circulate indefinitely – a securitized debt. Nixon's act was the mother of all securitizations.

The speech with which Nixon inaugurated a new monetary regime bore the ambitious and promising title 'The Challenge of Peace'. The declared aim, also to be served by the suspension of dollar convertibility, was to promote growth and peace, bringing in a 'new prosperity without war'.[1] One might be tempted to interpret these declarations as pure rhetoric underpinning a decision that was difficult to understand and accept at home, and even more so abroad. And yet, as we shall see, Nixon's decision might have seemed to make real the dream of an economy where everyone gained and nobody lost – the dream of an economic growth able to smooth away all political friction. Of course, the dream came at a price, which would remain overshadowed as long as the illusion lasted: the loss of the standard – a 'shadow price' that would materialize with crisis.

In fact Nixon's decision, however unwittingly, had disruptive effects on the very nature of money. Three distinctions that had hitherto remained – albeit with increasing vagueness – at the basis of the international monetary and financial system were abruptly and definitively wiped out: the distinction between money and credit; the distinction between national and international currency; and the distinction between money and commodities. It was from these institutional suppressions that stemmed the successes and imbalances of global finance accumulated over the last few decades, with the explosion of the American debt, the corresponding and equally problematic growth of dollar assets abroad, and the volatility of the currency and financial markets. The implications of all this, both institutional and practical, are worth examining point by point.

1 The first implication we have already mentioned. As long as a banknote can be converted into gold, it is not exactly money, but rather a credit instrument payable to the bearer on demand. US law still defines the Federal Reserve notes as credit instruments: 'The said notes shall be obligations of the United States [. . .] They shall be redeemed in lawful money on demand at the Treasury Department of the United States, in the city of Washington, District of Columbia, or at any Federal Reserve bank.'[2] Up to the 1963 issue the greenbacks were clearly presented as promissory

notes, bearing the legend 'The United States promise to pay to the bearer. . .'.

No sooner is its convertibility suspended than a banknote becomes 'forced circulation' currency, that is, credit whose payment is temporarily deferred, acceptance of which in the meantime is enjoined by the law for every payment with full redeeming power, like good money. Beginning with 'obsidional coins' – made of base metal or even of leather and paper, and issued as long ago as the sixteenth century by cities under siege, in order for them to be able to continue paying the troops despite the lack of precious metal – states would occasionally fall back on forced circulation as an expedient related to the finance of war. In comparison with these precedents, however, the post-1971 dollar has certain particular features that change its nature completely.

To begin with, forced circulation is by definition a temporary measure. The suspension of dollar convertibility was also meant to be temporary at the outset – a temporariness, however, that, like eternity for Woody Allen, tends to be very long. . . especially towards the end. The forced circulation brought in by Nixon was *the first one in history to assume a permanent character*.[3] As long as forced circulation remains a temporary measure, banknotes continue to represent credit instruments whose payment is simply deferred; but, when it becomes perpetual and payment is indefinitely deferred, those credit instruments become money for all practical purposes. The new monetary regime brought in by Nixon consisted in putting into circulation the central bank's debts (or the government's debts issued by the central bank, to put it another way) *as if* they were money. The exercise of monetary sovereignty *now* consisted in identifying debt with money.

Today this identity is sanctioned by the US law in force. Already in 1968, an act of Congress had abrogated the provision obliging the Federal Reserve to hold gold reserves for a value corresponding to at least 25 per cent of the banknotes issued.[4] However, it took six more years after Nixon's declaration for the legal obligation of gold convertibility to be lifted in 1977. Yet this was achieved not through a new definition of money, but through a new definition of conversion: 'The United States Government may not pay out any gold coin. A person lawfully holding United States coins and currency may present the coins and currency to the Secretary of the Treasury for exchange (dollar for dollar). . .'. Exchange for what? For '. . . other United States coins and currency (other than gold and silver coins) that may be lawfully held.

The Secretary shall make the exchange under regulations prescribed by the Secretary.' [5] Thus runs the totally self-referential '*fiat*' implied by '*fiat* money': money is defined solely in terms of convertibility of money into money. Rather than being an institutive act, this reads more like a transposition of the famous lines by Gertrude Stein ('Rose is a rose is a rose. . .') into an axiom of the form 'Dollar is a dollar is a dollar. . .'.

Needless to say, changing one banknote for another is neither the most significant nor the most frequent operation performed at the Federal Reserve banks. What characterizes a central bank as such is the operation through which banknotes are handed over in exchange for credit instruments, exchanged not at an equal rate (dollar for dollar), but at a discount (a dollar's worth of credit instruments for a dollar's worth of banknotes, minus the discount).

Now, the central bank's practice of the discount certainly did not begin in 1971; it began with the foundation of central banking with the establishment of the Bank of England in 1694. Until 1971, however, the difference in value between what the bank gave and what it received, in other words the discount, was justified by the fact that the bank obtained a credit that was payable only on a given maturity, but it handed over ready money (gold) or a credit payable *on demand* (a banknote). With the suspension of convertibility, however, a banknote is no different from any other credit instrument, which should mean that there is no reason for a discount. If, say, banknote convertibility were suspended for a period corresponding to the duration of the credit instrument, then exchange should be at par, which would cancel out not only the central bank's gain but also the advantage for the bearer of the credit instrument.

Hence the expediency, and not only for the bank, of suspending convertibility *sine die* and of letting banknotes circulate like money. In this way the bank can go ahead with its discount practice, with the benefit of seignorage, and the economic system can have a continuous supply of money, no longer limited by gold reserves. Thus '*fiat* money' came into the world, not through an act of force or abuse of authority, but for the common convenience of the various users.

By now it is clear that the new monetary regime is not one of forced circulation, which would imply that the deliberate will of some was imposed on others, but one of voluntary circulation, which implies, by contrast, a collective will in which all, in their different ways, are *willing participants*. Greenspan was rightly able to claim, as a prerogative of the bank as issuer of money, its capacity to *induce* – and not to *oblige* – 'market participants to employ one's liabilities as a money'.[6] Moreover, what marks this regime out from all previous ones is not the fact of creating money from nothing through a sovereign act, but being able to do so for the first time and institutionally, with no limitation beyond the pure *will* to create it.

With the suspension of dollar–gold convertibility the Fed was apparently able to match up in the best of possible ways to the institutional task it had been entrusted with from its foundation, namely 'to furnish an elastic currency'.[7] Now the power to create money from nothing, with no backing, and gainfully was entrusted upon America's central bank, in the interests of the community, with a threefold objective in view: stability of prices, stability of employment and stability of the financial system.

All three objectives should set a limit on the otherwise unlimited exercise of this prerogative. In practice, however, it is only the objective of price stability that sets a limitation on what is being issued. The other two could not only allow, but even require, as indeed has been the case since 1987, that the Fed should 'serve as a source of liquidity to support the economic and financial system'.[8] In other systems price stability constitutes, perhaps more appropriately, the unique objective with which the central bank is entrusted.[9] In any case, however, not even this criterion can suffice to limit paper issue as long as it is confined to consumer prices alone, without considering the increase in share prices, the proliferation of financial instruments, the rising real estate prices, the bubbles in commodity futures markets, and so forth.

In fact, as long as the liquidity created by the central bank finds an outlet on Wall Street, boosting asset prices, and not on Main Street, consumer and wholesale prices signal no danger of inflation. If the price of bread increases, everyone feels a bit poorer. On the other hand, if the price of General Mills shares rises, everyone – certainly everyone who holds them – will feel richer. The problem is that both increases could depend *solely* on an increase in the quantity of money. However, while in the first case the responsibilities of the central bank are evident and people talk of inflation, in the second case the loss of proportion is concealed in the guise of growing wealth and financial democratization, fuelling the illusion of prosperity without social conflict.

2 Approached in this way, the international implications of Nixon's decision become clearer. In fact, the suspension of dollar convertibility found more immediate application abroad than in the US. From 1971 on the Fed debts became international as well as national currency. The same decision that could appear to be an arbitrary act at home could look rather more like an act of hostility abroad. And yet it was eventually accepted – and not imposed – as being mutually advantageous, with a view to a 'new prosperity without wars'.[10] The exercise of American hegemony in the form of soft power, theorized by Clinton's advisers at the beginning of the 1990s precisely as a way to preserve an apparently declining power, actually had its origins in the 1970s.

> A country may achieve the outcomes it prefers in world politics because other countries want to follow it or have agreed to a system that produces such effects. In this sense, it is just as important to set the agenda and structure the situations in world politics as it is to get others to change in particular situations. [. . .] The ability to establish preferences tends to be associated with intangible resources such as culture, ideology, and institutions. This dimension can be thought of as soft power, in contrast to the hard command power usually associated with tangible resources like military and economic strength. [. . .] If it can help support institutions that encourage other states to channel or limit their activities in ways the dominant state prefers, it may not need as many costly exercises of coercive or hard power in bargaining situations.[11]

It seems surprising to find formulations so reminiscent of Gramsci's way of thinking underlying the theories of neoliberal leadership. But perhaps it is not so surprising after all. One cannot help thinking that Giorgio Gaber's popular parody of the intellectual could apply to these theoreticians as well as to Nixon himself: 'for now I'll put off suicide / and set up a study group / the masses, the class struggle, the texts by Gramsci, / pretend to be sane . . .'.[12]

Irony apart, it is clear that, in order to legitimize Nixon's decision to continue exercising powers of mobilization by other means, claims were made on behalf of the American 'ability to establish preferences' in the matter of peace and freedom. And yet if, as the etymon suggests, paying is a way of making peace, then it is hard to see the suspension of payment decreed by Nixon as a response to the challenge of peace. Effectively, Treasury Secretary John Connally talked more like a cowboy – which he was – than like a diplomat. As he famously put it, in presenting the matter to the European creditors, the dollar 'may be our currency, but it's your problem'. Fewer people may have heard the franker version he reserved for the American public: 'Foreigners are out to screw us, our job is to screw them first.'[13]

In any case, as is also explicit in Nixon's speech, this was not a matter of making peace, but of continuing to wage war for the purpose of 'defending freedom around the world', albeit with different means and a different distribution of burdens among the allies. It was a matter of allowing the United States to regain international competitiveness and, at the same time, of making the allies bear the corresponding burden, as a fair contribution to the common cause.[14]

In itself, this objective would have called neither for the suspension of convertibility nor for the adoption of flexible exchange rates; it would have sufficed to reset the dollar exchange rate with the other currencies. The problem is that the Bretton Woods system prevented by statute the United States, and only the United States, from doing what all the other countries could do, namely devalue their currency unilaterally. A crucial aspect of the Bretton Woods system lies in the ambiguous and problematic way in which parity was defined in 1944, a point we will be returning to later on. For the time being, to convey an idea of the asymmetry that tied Nixon's hands in 1971, it will suffice to recall the definition, inadequate but prevalent, of the monetary regime that came to an end that year: a system in which, it was said, 'the United States was the only country to peg its currency to gold; most other countries were pegged to the US dollar'.[15] Clearly, then, with a system of the sort, the only way to devalue the dollar was to revalue all the other currencies. Thus the United States found itself compelled to appeal to its creditors, forcefully, while eschewing force, to revalue their currencies.

Actually the suspension of dollar convertibility was not meant to be a permanent measure to begin with, but a stratagem to reinforce the United States' bargaining power. At the Cabinet Council held on the morning of 16 August, Secretary Connally himself expressed his awareness that the declaration of the day before could generate instability, but had been necessary in order to bring the United States' creditors to the negotiating table.[16] In other words, it was a matter of demonstrating in concrete terms that, since the Second World War, the United States had taken upon itself the responsibility for growth and stability for the benefit of all, but was no longer prepared to bear the resulting costs in terms of diminished competitiveness.

Effectively, the suspension of convertibility brought in a febrile season of international monetary negotiations. That hectic autumn of the currencies settled down, or so it seemed, with the Smithsonian Agreement, signed in Washington on 18 December by the Group of Ten, which determined dollar devaluation by about 10 per cent and a broader fluctuation band for the exchange rate. Nevertheless, although President Nixon hailed it emphatically as 'the most significant monetary agreement in the history of the world',[17] the realignment proved insufficient to iron out the imbalances in international payments and, on the other hand, extraordinarily effective in fuelling expectations of further devaluations. So it was that repeated attempts at correction over the following two years had the sole effect of encouraging flight from the dollar until, in March 1973, the principal currencies were left free to fluctuate. This in practice put an end to the Bretton Woods system.

According to the logic of the system itself, to be credible and thus stable, the redefinition of currency parity was to be such as to restore the structural equilibrium of the external accounts of the country in question. Unfortunately, as we will see, the Bretton Woods agreements had made no attempt to explain what exactly was meant by *structural* equilibrium.[18] Nor was any attempt made to do so between 1971 and 1973, when evidence of a disequilibrium became undeniable, despite the worries that had for some time been expressed by economists of the calibre of Triffin and Rueff.

Correcting the disequilibrium *structurally* could only mean one thing: to put the United States in a condition of being able to pay back its debts, in other words to restore dollar–gold convertibility. Any such action was, however, completely out of the question, and it is not hard to see why. As we will see, a substantial proportion of those debts had not been contracted with a view to paying them back. Moreover, devaluing the dollar so as to ensure its convertibility was not even in the interests of the creditors, who would find their competitiveness seriously impaired. Thus, once again, the rationale for consolidation prevailed over the rationale for payment: debtors and creditors came to terms, not on a parity that would allow for the payment of debts, but on an indefinite procrastination in that direction.

What eventually settled all contrasts was the decision not to decide. As far as tackling dollar convertibility was concerned,

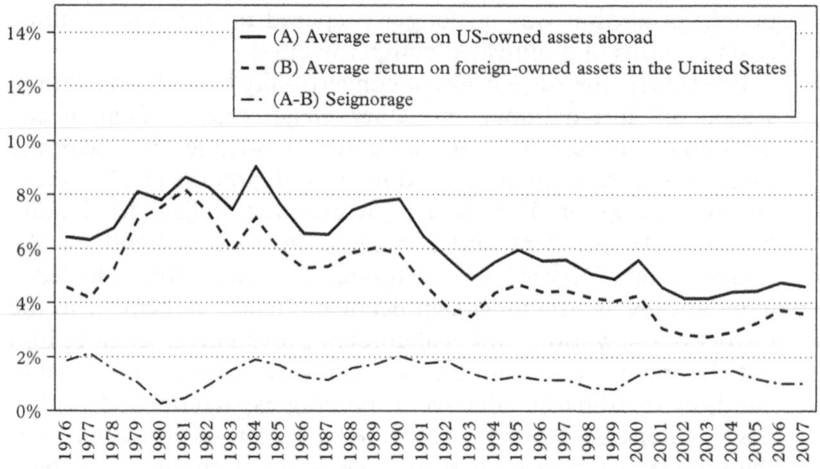

Figure II 3.1 US international seignorage

Source: Our processing of data from the US Department of Commerce (Bureau of Economic Analysis, www.bea.gov)

procrastination *sine die* was the magic formula to go on fighting a common war with no sacrifice for any of the allies, and so with no quarrelling. The United States failed to draw its allies into a redistribution of the costs of maintaining world order and had to go on bearing practically the whole burden. By way of compensation, it was now able to do so with uncovered cheques.

Thus, with the willing consent of the other industrialized countries, the United States retained the faculty to exercise seignorage on a global scale, even when the principle of responsibility on the grounds of which that faculty had originally been granted, the convertibility of the dollar into gold, had fallen off. Henceforth the dollars circulating outside the United States would be, at one and the same time, an American debt and an international currency.

Consistently with the above-quoted definition of seignorage, which we owe to Greenspan, through the exercise of international seignorage the United States obtained an income that 'reflects the return on interest-bearing assets that are financed by the issuance of currency, which pays no interest, or at most a below-market rate, to the holder'.[19] In other words, the United States gained from its international investments returns that were on average in excess (by nearly a third) of the payment it had to make on its international debts, a substantial proportion of those

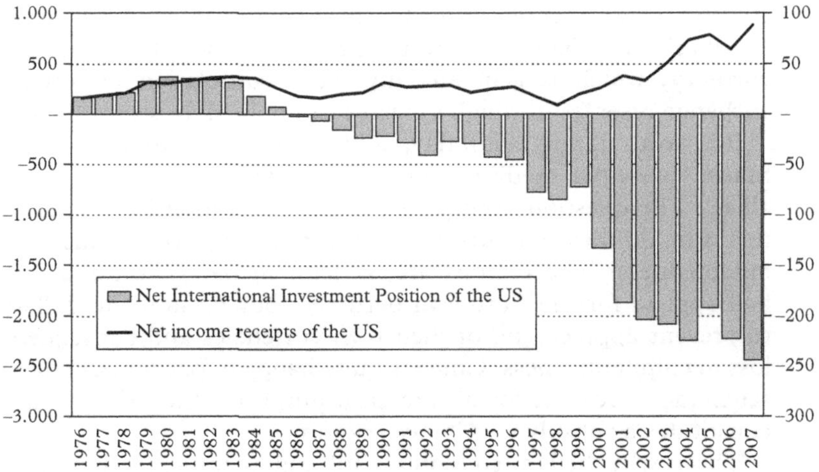

Figure II 3.2 How to live as a rentier on one's debts

Source: Our processing of data from the US Department of Commerce, Bureau of Economic Analysis, US International Investment Position (version issued on 27 June 2008) and US International Transactions Account Data (version issued on 17 September 2008). The data are available at http://www.bea.gov/international/index.htm

debts circulating as currency, and so being free from any interest. Figure II 3.1 shows the average returns of external assets and liabilities for the United States and the difference between the two, providing a measure of the United States' international seignorage.

Figure II 3.2 shows how, thanks to seignorage, the United States has continued to reap positive net investment income although its external net credit position had reversed as early as the mid-1980s to a debit position, now touching on 2,500 billion dollars. Basically, for twenty years the United States continued to live as a rentier, earning income. . . *on its debts*!

As the graphs show, the 'peace' inaugurated by Nixon, based on non-payment, still constitutes the shaky foundations of relations between the United States and its creditors even today. In fact, as the US external debt grows, currency reserves are accumulated, still mainly in dollars, by the oil-exporting countries, by Japan and, above all, by China. These are the countries bearing the burden of the seignorage gained by the United States, insofar as they accept to hold their dollar assets in the form of US Treasury bills or deposits with low returns. Indeed, accumulating currency reserves entails a loss for those countries that, like China, 'sterilize' the inflationary effects of the excess supply of national currency, which is generated by the accumulation of foreign exchange reserves, through the issue of public debt securities.

It is worth noting that today, unlike forty years ago, the United States' principal creditors no longer include only its 'natural allies'. The question prompted by this observation is, of course, this: why do these countries accept to pay the price of American indebtedness? The reasons are, at least in part, the same that had applied for the European partners: they accumulate dollars to prevent appreciation of their own currencies and consequent loss in competitiveness. China is quite happy to pay for American seignorage because, for all practical purposes, the price it pays constitutes a subsidy for Chinese exports.

This is why the United States is still calling for a redefinition of exchange rate parities, in particular that between dollar and yuan, with sharper appreciation of the latter. The alternative remains the same as the one that faced the United States at the beginning of the 1970s: either negotiate the conditions for payment, that is, for the reabsorption of America's foreign debt and trade deficit, or postpone them indefinitely. For the time being the latter continues to be favoured: solidarity between debtor and creditor forms with a view not to payment, but to deferment, in the hope that either side might thereby continue to grow indefinitely.

3 By now it should be clear how much all this actually costs. The price to pay is the final disappearance of an appropriate standard for international payments. At Bretton Woods the dollar had been chosen as the international currency in virtue of its stability. This stability was sanctioned by convertibility into gold, which in turn was guaranteed by America's ample gold reserves. In 1971 the gold anchor was lifted. In 1973 parities, which had hitherto served as a measure for international trade, began to fluctuate. Thus transition came about from a regime of set exchange rates to a non-regime of flexible rates.

This transition was granted legal sanction with the second amendment to the International Monetary Fund (IMF) Articles, which was approved in 1978, after years of negotiations launched with the first G-7 summit held in the November of 1975 at Rambouillet. The crucial step was to go from the system of stable exchange rates instituted in 1944 to 'a stable system of exchange rates'.[20] As has been pointed out, 'no one has been able to give operational meaning to that phrase, but the agreement to put the word "stable" in an unnatural place played a key role in defusing the conflict between American and French views about the future of the monetary system'.[21]

In fact, from the beginning of the 1970s, exchange rate volatility saw a huge increase. What made this possible was the fact that, at the level of the law, the task of defining parity between currencies, and thus the yardstick for international trade, was transferred from the political sphere (the IMF member countries) to the economic arena (the foreign exchange money markets). And yet – a point that needs stressing here – this abdication of all rights to decide publicly on the standard could only be accomplished through a public decision. Abnegatory as it was, the new 'Constitution' of the international monetary system could not evade the task of providing a new definition of money, in other words of what is to be accepted as legal tender in international payments. With gold abandoned, the new means for international payments consists in *freely usable currency* – that is, 'a member's currency that the Fund determines (i) is, in fact, widely used to make payments for international transactions, and (ii) is widely traded in the principal exchange markets'.[22] Thus the new international monetary law recognizes as money whatever the market defines as such: money is money is money. . .

In practice, however, with the international monetary system that took shape with the second amendment and is still in force, exchange rates are neither fixed by decree nor left free to float on the market. According to IMF taxonomy, what we should rightly speak of is 'managed floating'. But managed to what end? What are the aims that the national authorities have in view when they intervene on the exchange market to set limits to its functioning? What, ultimately, sets the standard for international trade? By now the answer should be self-evident: not balance of payments equilibrium, but rather sustainability of global disequilibria.

Again, how did we get into a situation where payment is impossible? Granted that the ultimate responsibility lies with the ambiguity and limitations of the Bretton Woods agreement, much also depends upon the way the agreement has been interpreted. Before reappraising Bretton Woods, therefore, we should take a look at two institutions that, far more than the International Monetary Fund and despite the intentions of its founders, effectively provided a means for international payments in the 1950s and 1960s, namely the eurodollar market and the European Payments Union.

4

The Eurodollar chimera (1958)

How did the dollar turn into paper? Up to the day Nixon suspended convertibility, a dollar had been a certain quantity of gold. Thus it had been defined by law ever since 1833. And this quantity remained extraordinarily constant – about one twentieth of an ounce, with one adjustment made just a century later. Since then and until 1971, banknotes denominated in dollars were convertible into gold at the new parity of thirty-five dollars per ounce. With the Bretton Woods Conference, convertibility into gold at the same parity was extended to the dollar reserves held by foreign central banks as coverage for their banknotes, while the convertibility of the dollar into gold was guaranteed by the United States' gold reserves.

Now, since the Second World War until 1971, America's gold reserves saw a steady dwindling, while the dollar reserves abroad – for which the gold was to stand as guarantee – showed an equally steady increase (see Figure II 4.1).

The factors underlying both trends were pointed out by Nixon himself in his speech announcing suspension: in twenty-five years the United States had donated $143 billion for the reconstruction of Europe and had borne tremendous costs 'defending freedom around the world'; it had spent out equally for war and for peace, for world warfare and for world welfare. It also saw a growing balance of trade deficit, accepting to keep dollar parity unchanged in the face of increasing competitiveness from the European countries – which was also achieved thanks to the aid granted and to the devaluations permitted by the USA. By 1959 America's gold reserves were sinking below the level that was needed to cover the other countries' dollar reserves, and by 1971 they were, by a large margin, insufficient to guarantee an effective conversion (even without taking into account

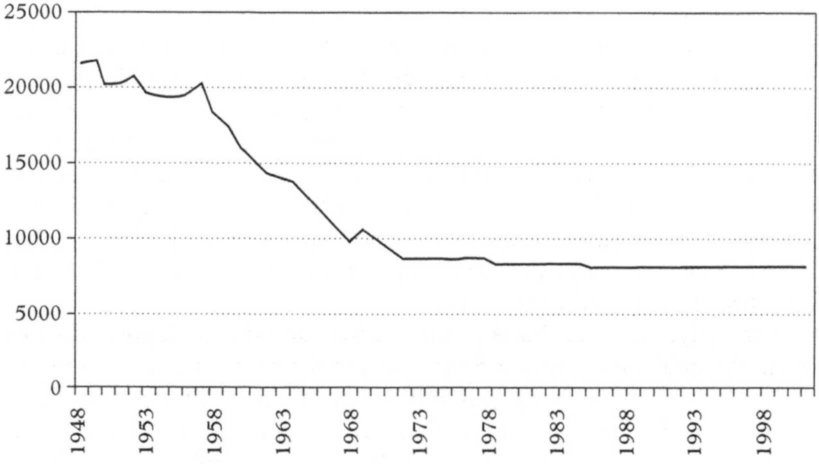

Figure II 4.1 US gold reserves (tonnes)
Source: World Gold Council

the fact that the same reserves were also to serve for coverage and conversion of the dollars circulating within the country).[1]

In the light of these data and facing an ever-growing demand for conversion from the major dollar holders, starting with France, the United States quite clearly found it impossible to stick to its commitment to guarantee dollar convertibility at the parity fixed and sanctioned by the Bretton Woods agreements. In the previous chapter we considered the solidly pragmatic reasons why not only the debtor, but also the creditors found it expedient to accept indefinite suspension of payment, in other words conversion, as the least taxing way out of the impasse. Allowing the United States to settle its balance of payments deficit in dollars that are declared to be unconvertible *sine die* means in effect ensuring an uninterrupted source of liquidity for expanding trade and investments on the international markets, with no corresponding loss in liquidity on the US market.

However, the solution was not adopted for reasons of expediency alone. There were also points of principle, on the basis of which the US President could judge it legitimate to suspend conversion. Actually, not all the dollars held outside the United States were issued by decision or under control of the Fed. An appreciable, growing and, above all, indeterminate quantity of dollars consisted of what, from 1958 on, had gone under the name of 'eurodollars'.

What are eurodollars? In short, they are credit in dollars held outside the United States, not in the physical form of metal or paper money, but in the form of *bank money* – in other words in the form of deposits in banks, which are outside the United States, and are not subject to US jurisdiction, even though they operate in dollars: 'Eurobanks', as they are called. The original depositors were big commercial banks, multinationals, central banks and international financial institutions. The depositors also included countries belonging to the Soviet bloc that preferred to hold their assets in dollars outside the United States, for fear of a deposit freeze like the one that hit the Arab countries involved in the 1956 Suez crisis and led such countries to proceed in this manner.[2]

Naturally, the Eurobanks that receive dollars in deposit do not normally hold them among their assets in the form of cash or reserves at the Fed but use them, possibly through other intermediaries, to finance the final users, namely firms engaged in productive or commercial activity at the international level. The Eurobanks are linked up through a network of interconnections that benefit also from technological innovations in the field of telecommunications but owe their existence, above all, to consolidated relationships and acquaintanceships among financial institutions accredited at the international level. By virtue of sharing information and reciprocal accreditation, the Eurobanks are able to combine in performing intermediation activity – that is, in 'making' the eurodollar market.

Constitutionally, this market has enjoyed the distinction of being free from restrictions and regulations from the very outset. By right, in fact, it can be considered the first deregulated form of international financial market, just as its growth can be seen as the first wave – little more than a ripple to begin with – of what was to be, in the 1980s and 1990s, the rising tide of free capital movements at the global level.

For all practical purposes, it amounts to a market *constructed to be deregulated.* In fact, the banks operating on the eurodollar market are not subject to reserve obligations and are free to offer deposits at very short maturity.[3] Consequently they have lower costs to bear than the banks operating on the national markets and are therefore able to offer higher interest rates on deposits.[4] The higher interest rates attract growing volumes of deposits, thereby contributing to the growth of the eurodollar market. In turn, as the market grows, the investors' perception of risk diminishes, and they are even more easily persuaded to hold their assets in this form rather than in other, less remunerative forms (such as certificates of deposit in American banks). If it is to be judged by its effects, the circle thus created can only be described as a virtuous one: effectively, it afforded the eurodollar market growth from 20 to 1,200 billion dollars in the twenty

Table II 4.1 Growth of the eurodollar market (compound annual growth rates in percentages), 1964–1985

	1964–72	1972–80	1980–5	*1964–85*
Net eurodollar market[a]	33,6	26,7	12,9	*25,8*
Gross eurodollar market[b]	34,0	28,6	10,8	*26,1*
International trade[c]	12,0	21,2	0,4	*12,4*
World production[d]	9,6	15,0	4,7	*10,4*

Notes

[a] Excluding re-deposits between Eurobanks (BIS data).

[b] Including interbank redeposits (Morgan Guaranty data).

[c] International trade in goods and services, excluding the Soviet bloc (IMF data).

[d] Global GDP, excluding the Soviet bloc.

Source: S. Battilossi, 'The Eurodollar Market and Structural Innovation in Western Banking, 1960–1985', in D. Ross and M. Pohle Fraser (eds), *Investment and Savings: Historical Perspectives*, Aldershot and London: Ashgate 2009, vol. 1, Table 1.

years spanning from 1964 to 1985, which corresponds to an average annual compound growth rate of 26 per cent (see Table II 4.1).

The diminishing perception of risk as the market grew was also reflected in the procedures followed by the Eurobanks in supplying credit. If, to begin with, this was essentially a matter of commercial credit, effectively guaranteed by the commodities whose circulation on the international market this credit was to facilitate, subsequently such credit was supplied regardless of purpose or provision of guarantees, simply on the strength of the *name* of the intermediaries involved and of how readily they could refinance themselves. But in reality invoking the 'name' is a way not to hold anybody to account for anything: on the eurodollar market, Einzig declared, 'no questions are asked, no information is given'.[5]

This is not to say, however, that the market took shape and grew spontaneously, solely on the initiative of private agents. Here too, deregulation is inextricably associated with a form of regulation. Suggestive as the idea may be of a market that is free and thriving precisely because it is unconstrained by tiresome regulations and by the influence of 'politicians', politics did have a decisive role to play, at least in this case, in creating the conditions necessary for eurodollars to exist and prosper.

In fact, the regime of exemption from reserve obligations and interest ceilings enjoyed by the Eurobanks was not only tolerated, but actually made possible and encouraged by the British authorities, eager as they were to attract funds to the London market, with the explicit aim of making it the hub of a vigorously expanding market and of reasserting London's position in the international financial system in this way. On the other hand, the US authorities, too, were not unhappy to let banks under their jurisdiction escape restrictions on capital movements and evade the tax originally brought in to curb the outflow of dollars, by operating on the eurodollar market. Indeed, for both countries this market afforded the opportunity to favour the interests of their respective financial lobbies, while at the same time keeping control over capital movements and thus retaining an autonomy in economic and monetary policy that was now deemed inalienable.

This, be it noted, was not simply a matter of window dressing, formally upholding regulations and prohibitions while turning a blind eye in practice. On the contrary, it was precisely in virtue of the totally free space reserved for capital movements on the eurodollar market that it was possible to prevent them from generating pressure on balances of payments and hence on the national currencies, at least as long as that space remained separate from the national monetary and financial systems. On this condition – which, however, remained implicit and problematic – the eurodollar market can be considered an autonomous monetary area with its own currency.

That this was so for the British is fairly obvious. Pound parity was finally fixed, together with the parity of a large proportion of Europe's currencies, in 1958. Now, if capital movements were free, defending the exchange rate would mean, for the UK, having to apply economic and monetary policy with extreme rigour, to avoid sudden outflows of capital or currency crises, as in fact befell in 1957. On the other hand, the British government was certainly not willing to forego construction and defence of the welfare state nor, in general, its political autonomy. Thus it found itself in an impasse – the kind of situation that Robert Mundell summed up at the time in his 'trilemma' theory, according to which it is impossible to reconcile fixed exchange rates, free capital movements and autonomy in monetary policy: in any given country, at least one of the three has to go.[6]

In keeping with an approach shared and sanctioned by the Bretton Woods agreements, the United Kingdom decided not only to maintain, but indeed to tighten restrictions on capital movements, even after restoring current account balance convertibility in 1958. This meant, among other things, that pounds sterling could be exchanged for foreign currency only to finance the foreign trade of the United Kingdom – and not, as had happened on a large scale before the war, to finance international trade between other countries. In other words, the United Kingdom waived the possibility of restoring to the pound the role it had enjoyed for over a century as international currency. In doing so, however, it also risked sacrificing the central position of London as international financial market, and with it the income it brought in for the banks and, indirectly, for the British economy as a whole.

Against such a background, it is not hard to understand why eurodollars must have looked like a *deus ex machina* opening up a way out from the trilemma. 'The London bankers found they could satisfy this demand [for international credit] by offering dollar loans against their dollar deposits of overseas residents'.[7] The example was rapidly followed, albeit less successfully, by the bankers of other important markets such as Zurich, Luxembourg and Tokyo. By virtue of operating in dollars, they were all able to operate with a perspective of increasing activity in international financial intermediation, without breaching the restrictions raised in defence of national economic interests.

Actually this was by no means an absolute innovation: in the Renaissance the major financial communities (or 'nations', as they were then called) had accumulated their fortunes on a system that, as we shall see, *distinguished* national currencies from the international currency, reserving the latter for the activities of the financiers in support of long-distance European trade. If anything, the peculiarity of the new international currency, rediscovered five centuries later, is that, for one country, this international currency *coincides with its national currency.*

The country in question is, of course, the United States, and it is therefore useful to view the eurodollar market from that country's point of view. Thus we can see how this market constitutes for the USA, too, a monetary space cut off from the national sphere, able to ease tensions on the balance of payments and to offer a way out from the trilemma. At first sight, in fact, eurodollars do not appear to constitute a currency distinct from the US currency. If they are, in fact, dollars deposited outside the United States, then there is nothing to stop them from going back there in principle. And, as long as dollar convertibility holds, this could also entail an effective demand for conversion with the consequent outflow of gold.

Thus the growth of the eurodollar market eased off pressure on the US balance of payments only insofar as the dollars flowing out of the United States were destined *not to make their way back*.[8] The United States, too, could consider eurodollars an international currency only on the assumption that the conversion of dollars into eurodollars was in practice irreversible. The suspension of dollar convertibility was therefore already implicated, as an implicit but imperative option, by the very notion of the eurodollar, even before the growth in the volume of international Eurodollar market beyond the limits of the US gold reserves began to point in that direction. The Eurodollar can be considered an international currency distinct from the dollar only as long as it is not seen as American debt, bound to be paid.

From this perspective, the eurodollar market as such could already be seen to stem from a coalition between debtors and creditors formed to avoid payment rather than to allow for it, well before the suspension of dollar convertibility, which would sanction its implicit logic. Here, too, we see a blurring of those distinctions that were indicated in Part I of this volume as essential for a proper monetary and financial system: on the eurodollar market, the distinction is lost between national and international currency, and indeed between money and credit.

The distinction between money and credit is in fact crucial to any banking system. What matters is not so much precisely where the line of demarcation is drawn, but the fact that it *is* drawn.[9] The possibility to regulate the monetary base and, through reserve obligations, the volume of deposits created by the banks is something that the central bank owes to the fact of money being unequivocally defined, and defined as distinct from credit. The obligatory reserve is nothing but the quantity of *money* that every bank is required to hold against the quantity of *credit* its depositors can lay claim to.

No reserve obligation applies to the eurodollar market, which means that no clear-cut distinction between money and credit holds there. This had much the same practical consequence as would later derive from the cancellation of the distinction between money and credit implicit in the suspension of dollar convertibility, namely the possibility of unlimited multiplication of international liquidity. Significantly, this possibility was seen as a real danger even by such a staunch advocate of deregulation as Milton Friedman, and indeed by such a convinced upholder of this market's basic soundness as Paul Einzig.[10]

On the other hand, no such apprehension of the dangers that lay in constituting a deregulated international money market seems to have troubled the central banks, which opened the way to the development of the eurodollar market not only passively, through a particularly accommodating approach, but actively, through their reserves:

> Possibly some Central Banks or Treasuries are to this day blissfully oblivious that, for the sake of a relatively modest additional yield on their dollar holding, they have greatly increased the difficulty of their own main task of defending their currencies and of controlling their money markets and their domestic credit structure.[11]

On the evidence of empirical studies that suggest a creation of liquidity not exceeding one dollar for every five dollars deposited in the Eurobanks, other authors have questioned whether the multiplication of liquidity did in fact occur on a significant scale.[12] The more long-term investment the banks make with the short-term deposits they have collected, the more liquidity they create. Now, as these authors point out, although the Eurobanks are exonerated from reserve obligations, their balance sheets show no more pronounced a maturity transformation between assets and liabilities than those of the normal commercial banks.

Nevertheless, these authors cannot ignore the fact that there is

> a group of banks that have indeed engaged in massive maturity transformation. These are the central banks. Whenever a central bank invests dollar holdings in 3-month Eurodollars, it creates liquidity for the nonbank sector in the same way as the Federal Reserve buying 3-month treasury bills in the open market.[13]

The most substantial creation of money takes place, therefore, not *within* the eurodollar market but *in the transformation* of dollars (for example, dollars held in reserve by the central banks) into eurodollars.

Nowadays this situation tends to be interpreted in one way alone: the function of the eurodollar market is seen to lie not so much in the *creation* of international liquidity as in its *allocation* at the global level.[14] Following this approach, the existence of a eurodollar market would appear to be attributable solely to the function of efficient allocation of demand and supply of *given* resources.

And yet, what we ought to be asking ourselves is *how* these resources are given; after all, we are talking about money and not any run-of-the-mill product. Then, if the eurodollars are not created by the Eurobanks, where do they come from, if not from the United States or, better still, from its deficit? There can be no getting away from the fact that the very reason given in support of the idea of efficient allocation – the decidedly limited creation of money within the eurodollar market – could be interpreted precisely as a sign of the fact that the growth of this market was driven by the international *supply* of dollars implicated by US deficits far more than by effective *demand* for dollars to finance international trade. Thus we can hardly help but see the eurodollar market as a way to create a growing reservoir of liquidity in order to absorb the increasing outflow of dollars from the United States, thereby allowing the American foreign debt to circulate indefinitely as international currency.

Whatever the extent of eurodollar *multiplication* may have been on the international market, the fact remains that these dollars were *created* starting from the dollars initially deposited in the Eurobanks, and not within the US banking system. This very fact should imply the need to establish the degree of liquidity (or, as it is put even more significantly, the degree of 'moneyness') of eurodollars as compared with that of dollars. In other words, it ought to be possible to tell, with all due certainty, whether eurodollars are money or credit. As long as they are spent or lent outside the United States, continuing to circulate on the eurodollar market, they can be considered money. On the other hand, the (apparently only theoretical) dilemma as to whether they are really money or a debt that needs to be paid could grow into a dramatically concrete problem should the holders of eurodollar deposits wish to cash them in, converting them into dollars and eventually into gold.

This is why the countries most implicated in the matter eventually agreed to intervene, through the Bank for International Settlements, as lenders of last resort, to prevent the system from imploding. Insofar as the US deficits were not reabsorbed, and the US debt therefore went on growing, the eurodollar market could only go on growing in turn. It was *condemned to grow*, and preventive intervention was agreed upon to ensure that the growth was not interrupted. The market was completely free, and yet the system of countries participating in it remained the guarantor for its functioning, albeit a rather particular guarantor: in fact, its sole function was to guarantee against any form of regulation or intervention, except to endow the market with liquidity, should this prove necessary.

From the mid-1980s on, the eurodollar began to decline in importance, but not because the demand for international liquidity was waning or the eurodollar market was no longer able to satisfy it, but because international finance began to prefer the intermediation of the financial markets to that of the banks. Gradually the banks came to be replaced by the stock exchanges as vehicles for international capital movements – if the idea was to provide liquidity, the stock exchanges were more efficient. Precisely because it marked an initial, decisive step in the direction of adapting the western financial system to the demands of providing liquidity, the eurodollar market was doomed to decline as securitization came under way.[15]

Eurodollars had begun to appear on the scene when the Bretton Woods system came into force as a fixed exchange rate regime (1958), which means that the system never functioned fully in respect of the Articles of Agreement, except in the years that saw the emergence and full development of the eurodollar market. One cannot help thinking that the system could never have functioned without this market – and that ultimately, therefore, it had never constituted a proper system. Effectively, the eurodollar market represented at the same time a means to enhance the Bretton Woods system and a means to elude it: it enhanced the possibility of maintaining stable exchange rates, but it did so by eluding those restrictions on capital movements for which the system formally made provision. And, on the other hand, in a less evident but perfectly complementary manner, that market could exist only as a systematic elusion of the rules that were there to ensure not only limitation of capital movements but also reabsorption of trade balance deficits. Far from bringing grist to the mill of deregulation, bearing out the idea that the market is too powerful a force to be reined in by politics, the moral of this story is that the financial markets, with their corollary of deregulation, live on a muddying of the very concept of rules.

Thus the eurodollar market constituted an initial form of subterfuge in the search for a way out from the trilemma. Alas, no more than a subterfuge. The trilemma was to open up only fifteen years later – and in part due to imbalances aggravated by the growth of the eurodollar market – when the abandonment of stable exchange rates left the world without a reliable standard for international investments and trade.

Is it possible to reconcile the maintenance of a standard with the objectives that it is supposed to allow for? On the evidence of the story we have followed here, apparently not. In reality, however, the answer is unequivocally affirmative, provided that the standard is not reduced to an irrevocably fixed exchange rate and international investment to a commodity to negotiate on the market. Eloquent evidence of this possibility is offered by that international financial system which, albeit only for a limited area, preceded the institution of the eurodollar market, namely the European Payments Union.

5

The European Payments Union (1950)

The invention and growth of the eurodollar market, the suspension of dollar convertibility and the liberalization of the international financial markets all contributed, each in its own way, to maintaining a growing volume of dollars in circulation beyond the borders of the United States. Even the present crisis, at least in its early days, helped to sustain international demand for the dollar, simply by changing its function and form; for, even as the contraction of international private investments and trade led to a fall in dollar assets held abroad for such purposes, foreign investments in US government securities showed a corresponding increase.[1]

The stability of the dollar exchange rate at the beginning of the crisis bears out the fact that, despite the marked increase in international dollar supply, which corresponds to the US balance of payments deficits, the international demand for dollars continues to grow, absorbing it completely.[2]

Harking back to the distinction Keynes introduced in his *General Theory*, we might speak of a fall in the demand for dollars for speculative and transactional purposes, as against an increase in the demand for precautionary purposes. Albeit with some growing – and perfectly understandable – hesitation, the dollar continued to be treated as a refuge currency. This could have been the practical effect of a 'symbolic capital' as yet not completely exhausted – but not, for this reason, inexhaustible.

As we have seen, over the last fifty years world financial history has been characterized by a growing flood – overflow upon overflow – of liquidity in dollars outside the United States. This liquidity brought with it growth and, at the same time, instability: *effective* growth in international trade and *potential* instability, potentially growing, in balances of payments and rates of exchange. What is more, this liquidity allowed for stability only in the form of a continuous, unconditional, unlimited and unsacrificeable growth, both in the economic systems and in the expansive policy interventions designed to support them. Liquidity calls for ever more liquidity, as can also be seen in the case of the recent rescue plans – which, viewed from the perspective of the last half century, really do look like 'irrigation plans during the flood'.[3]

We have already looked into the reasons why, once the production of liquidity in the form of dollars had been launched, it had to be continually relaunched; and we will look further into this matter later on. First, however, we must consider a very basic question: why, and how, did this apparently ineluctable process get under way? What was the magic word, the spell, that stirred the broom of the sorcerer's apprentice to life? When did the apprentice start playing with power and liquidity? To approach that seminal moment, that odd run of unwitting decisions that led to identification of the dollar as international currency and, as a consequence, made the United States a measureless source of liquidity, we must take yet another step back in history.

In fact we need only go back a decade or so to find a totally different financial climate. In the aftermath of the Second World War the basic problem for international payments lay in what was then called a dollar shortage – a chronic shortage of dollars experienced by economies worldwide, and in particular in Europe. What was it, then, that brought about this international dollar 'drought'? How was it variously tackled? And by what turn of events, without even going through a midway point of equilibrium, did drought reverse into the flood that now threatens to submerge the global economy? Such are the questions we will have to address in this chapter.

The devastation left by the Second World War was seen at its most formidable in the damage to the infrastructures and productive plant of the warring countries, in Europe and Japan. And yet the post-war economic difficulties were not due so much to material damage as to the collapse of that delicate financial equilibrium upon which the national economies, with their various interconnections, had rested until war broke out. If military destruction (and also, perhaps, military production, since its sole purpose is to destroy) entails a loss of wealth, the needs of reconstruction and post-war conversion of industry could in themselves act as a factor boosting the production of new wealth, insofar as they buoy up the demand for goods. For this to hold, however, the demand must be satisfied by adequate supply, and so there must also be a monetary and financial system able to match demand and supply.

The basic economic problem besetting the countries hardest hit by the war, in particular in Europe, was not so much the general and widespread state of need generated by five years of devastation as the risk that this need might not be able to be satisfied, for lack of money and credit.[4] The problem arose on two partially interrelated fronts of the international economic relations: those between Europe and the United States on the one hand, and those amongst the various countries of Europe on the other. We should take these two aspects separately, since the same problem was addressed through diametrically opposite approaches in the respective cases.

The United States emerged from the war with its productive system practically intact, and indeed reinforced. In fact, it was able to return to full-scale operation after a decade of underemployment precisely, and *only*, thanks to the armaments supplied to the Allied governments, which gave a powerful boost not only to production but also to technological innovation. With peace restored, the crucial problem facing the US economy was to go on finding adequate outlets for an unprecedented and unparalleled productive capacity. Thus it was for economic as well as political reasons that the United States seemed to be the ideal partner for the countries of Europe drained by the war effort. The sale of goods from one side of the Atlantic to the other appeared to be the best solution for both sides, but it immediately raised another problem – the problem of payment.

The war had left Europe with greater needs for consumption goods and for means of production, but also with a reduced capacity to finance their purchase. The prospects of paying for imports with the income from exports were jeopardized by the loss of colonial market outlets and by the dismantlement of civil production, which meant less competitiveness by comparison with the American counterpart. Moreover, the decline in competitiveness was aggravated by the loss, now looming close, of cheap supply markets, not only in the colonies but also in eastern Europe, which had gone (or was on the way to going) communist. At the same time, the European balance of trade deficit could not be offset by capital gains either: the war effort had overturned the net credit position of Europe's strongest economies, now burdened with huge war debts due to the United States.

The one source of financing, at least for the more urgent import of staple goods, thus lay in the gold and currency reserves of the European countries. Already sorely depleted by the expenses of war, these reserves were rapidly exhausted, as indeed were the slender lines of credit made available by the World Bank and the International Monetary Fund.[5] Further credit and aid could only come, and indeed did come, from the United States. At the same time, the US Congress was becoming increasingly reluctant to grant loans and contributions, in the endeavour to fill in the dollar gap – a gap that threatened to open out into a bottomless abyss.

In any case, if the only way to recovery for a Europe already burdened with debts lay in increasing them yet further and extending their maturities, the American creditor's decision to go on lending could only be conditional upon reasonable expectations that recovery would effectively take place. The fact was that, despite massive aid granted during and immediately after the war, Europe's economies were still limping along throughout the whole of 1947. What was the matter with them?

The financial straits that Europe as a whole was caught in reflected the dire conditions of individual countries. In certain respects, each one found itself, on a smaller scale, up against the same problem that weighed on the entire European economy, namely the difficulty of financing a – temporary but inevitable – balance of payments deficit caused by the need to import consumption and capital goods. Such goods were sorely needed in order to get back to work – to produce and eventually to export, thus rebalancing the external accounts. In short, not only in trade with the United States but also in their own trade relations the countries of Europe *had no more money, and needed credit.*

There is, however, a substantial difference, and not simply one of scale, between the position of the European countries taken individually and as a whole vis-à-vis the United States, and the position of each of these countries in relation to its neighbours. Given its ample resources in gold (and its more ample ones in dollars), the United States could also grant credit to another country in the form of a loan in international currency. By contrast, the countries of Europe, having exhausted their gold (and dollar) reserves, could only grant one another credit in the form of a deferred payment for the goods traded. Now, while the former type of credit places at the disposal of the debtor a certain amount of international currency that, by definition, can be spent to settle up with any other country, and so to fuel a chain of multilateral trading, the latter form of credit is nothing but a bilateral relationship between the debtor country and the creditor country. This sort of relationship is opened with the transference of goods from the latter to the former and closes only when an equivalent transfer is made in the opposite direction.

The first bilateral trade agreement of this type had already been signed between the governments of Belgium, Holland and Luxembourg, in exile, in October 1943, when war was still raging. The following four years saw the signing of over 400 bilateral agreements following the same model, which prompted a comparison between European trade and 'a spaghetti bowl'.[6] Drawn up in response to the lack of international currency, these agreements sought to reproduce its functions on a bilateral basis, so as to find application at least between the signatories and for the duration of the agreement. To begin with, therefore, for trade over the borders, a unit of measurement had to be defined in the form of a fixed exchange rate between the currencies of the two signatory countries. As there was no common standard of exchange that could cross national borders, payment had to be made in two stages: the importers paid the due sum in national currency, to their central bank, while the exporters received the corresponding sum from their central bank, in their own currency. These operations gave rise to debts and credits between the two central banks, which were settled on a periodic basis. At the end of the set period the balance due would be paid or refinanced in compliance with the procedure established in the agreement.[7]

Clearly enough, while they afforded more breathing space than simple barter, these bilateral credit agreements seriously limited the scope for expansion in European trade. To begin with, they compelled each country to maintain a balance-of-trade equilibrium *with each of the other countries*. In other words there could be no question of *offsetting* a deficit vis-à-vis one trading partner with a surplus in relation to another. On top of this already severe limitation was the fact that a country holding a credit position in relation to another would tend to favour imports from that country, thereby reducing its exposure in that direction, while taking an obstructive line with all the others. Thus, as a sort of corollary to the countless bilateral agreements, as many restrictions, tariffs and discriminatory/protectionist practices were added, ultimately stymieing intra-European trade and in consequence heaving an insurmountable obstacle in the way of recovery for the production upon which trade depended.

Thus the two facets of the post-war financial problem appear to have been connected in a relation of reciprocal dependence that risked spiralling into a vicious circle: the need for money to finance transatlantic trade could be satisfied, it seemed, only on the basis of recovery of trade and production in Europe; but this, in turn, appeared to depend crucially on American imports and on the possibility of financing them.

The importance and innovative force of the Marshall Plan lay, even beyond the scale of the aid offered, precisely in the fact that it constituted an endeavour to address the two facets of the problem *at the same time*, combining concession of contributions on the part of the USA with explicit coordination among the European countries, with a view to causing an upturn in trade and production in Europe – while Europe as a whole was to stand as a credible trading partner for the USA. Unlike all the plans drawn up at the time, or in the immediate aftermath of the war, the Marshall Plan made the supply of contributions conditional upon the drafting of a plan by all the European governments in concert – a plan for the distribution and utilization of the funds. European response was immediate: less than six months after Marshall had formulated the idea of the plan in a celebrated speech at Harvard University in July 1947, the governments of western Europe, coming together in an organization that would subsequently become permanent, the Conference for European Economic Cooperation (CEEC), drew up and agreed upon a four-year plan. Thanks to the pains taken to achieve coordination, the proposal won the approval of the US Congress, and in April 1948 it became operative under the constitution of the Economic Cooperation Administration (ECA).[8]

The dollars granted as part of the Marshall Plan were, as ECA director Paul Hoffman succinctly put it, *double-duty dollars*, serving to finance imports from the United States and at the same time the recovery of European trade.[9] In fact, contrary to widespread opinion, the United States did not require aid to be used solely to pay for its own supplies, but allowed for, and indeed encouraged, its use also as a means of payment for intra-European trade. This was, after all, perfectly in keeping with the interests of the USA as a creditor to create the conditions for the debtor to get back to work, produce goods, therefore income, and eventually pay back the debts.[10]

Despite its good intentions, the Marshall Plan failed in its endeavour to make of Europe a trading partner for the United States, in that country's own image. The US expected the concerted planning for the allocation of aid to be the prelude to a broader and fuller economic collaboration on the part of Europe. Just a year later, however, it was precisely the allocation of funds that became a bone of fierce contention; in the meantime, massive as it was, the aid granted had failed to foster significant growth in European trade. It was becoming increasingly evident that one had to tackle head on the crucial problem created by the tangle of bilateral agreements that hamstrung trade between the European countries. In other words, awareness began to dawn that the revival of European trade did not depend so much on *injections of liquidity* in the form of dollars, which could always be put in reserve (as was in fact the case) and cease to circulate, as on the institution of a common standard and means for the denomination and payment of debts. What European trade really needed was certainly not more money, but a *currency*.

Answering to this need was the European Payments Union, conceived in December 1949 by the ECA and launched, after a mere nine months' 'gestation', with an agreement signed in September 1950. As was appropriately pointed out by Robert Triffin, an economist who dedicated all his energies to the problem of constructing a true international currency between the 1930s and 1960s, this was indeed 'a remarkably clean and simple document, embodying sweeping and precise commitments of a revolutionary nature, which drastically shifted overnight the whole structure of intra-European settlements from a bilateral to a multilateral basis'.[11] Essentially, the Union made provision for each country to have, rather than as many bilateral accounts as it had trading partners, with separate records of the credits and liabilities deriving from trade with each of them, *one single account* held at a 'clearing centre' in which the position was recorded as a *net position* in relation to the clearing centre itself, and thus as a multilateral position in relation to all the other countries. Balances were calculated at monthly intervals: as its debt increased, each country was to pay in gold an increasing fraction of its negative balance while, correspondingly, with the increase of its credit, each creditor country had the right to payment in gold of an increasing fraction of its positive balance. Debtors paid interest on the uncovered balance and the creditors reaped it.

A quota was set for each country corresponding to 15 per cent of its trade with the other countries of the Union, as registered in 1949. The rules of the Union state that the credit or debit balance must not exceed the respective quota. Thus the system not only set a limit to the accumulation of debts with the Union, but also, through reimbursements in gold and passive interest, provided debtors with an incentive to emerge from their debit positions and to converge towards equilibrium.

On the other hand, despite the credit interest gained on positive balances, there were in practice, *also for the creditors*, strong incentives to emerge from their credit position and to converge towards balance. In fact, the reimbursement conditions for any surplus in excess of the respective quota were to be negotiated by each country, with the directive counselling of the Union. Thus the Union was empowered to exert strong pressure on the creditor country to liberalize trade and reduce restrictions, so as to raise imports and cut the surplus. However, even before hitting their quota, the countries with a surplus found that it was in their interest to reduce their position within the Union insofar as they could make more profitable use of their assets elsewhere, investing them at higher interest rates or trading with countries outside Europe. Eloquent evidence of this expediency can be seen in the fact that, in order to reduce their surplus, some creditor countries went as far as liberalizing trade with the other member countries well beyond the requisites set by the 'Code of Liberalization' adopted by the Union.[12] Thus the European Payments Union functions in such a way as to establish the balanced budget as the only economically admissible position – the position, that is, towards which both creditor and debtor countries would find it expedient to converge.

With this set of provisions, the European Payments Union succeeded where every previous plan had failed. It provided for a multilateral, intertemporal clearing for European trade,[13] an extraordinary export-driven growth in production, in Germany and Italy in particular,[14] and the liberalization of trade not only with the countries of Europe but well beyond, and in particular with the United States (see Table II 5.1). Thus trade in Europe did not recover *at the expense* of trade with the rest of the world. The Union was not a means to protect a non-competitive economic system, but a way to regain a degree of competitiveness sufficient for it to stand up to international competition *without protective measures*.[15]

In 1958 the European Payments Union was closed down, not because it did not work, but because it worked so well that the purpose it had been created for was now fully achieved. With production revived, trade relaunched and equilibrium restored in their balances of payments, the countries of Europe were at last able to fix a stable rate of exchange for their currencies, finally gaining full access to the international monetary system instituted at Bretton Woods. As we will see in the next chapter, the system had left ambiguously open the possibility of defining parity in terms of dollars or gold. In principle, given the fixed parity of dollar–gold convertibility, there should have been no difference between the two options. In practice, however, the option taken by the countries of Europe in 1958, to anchor their currencies on the dollar rather than gold, sanctioned the role played by the US currency as international money, thereby setting global trade on foundations that were diametrically opposite to those upon which European trade had been conducted under the Union.

Table II 5.1 The European economy before and after the EPU

Economic indicator	Unit of measurement	Before EPU	After EPU	Percentage increase
Liberalization of intra-European trade	*Percentage of private trade*	56	89	
Liberalization of trade with the dollar area	*Percentage of private trade*	11	72	
Intra-European trade	*c.i.f. imports, monthly averages, millions of dollars*	845	1.943	130%
OEEC exports to North America	*f.o.b., monthly averages, millions of dollars*	144	441	206%
OEEC imports from North America	*c.i.f., monthly averages, millions of dollars*	324	508	57%
OEEC exports to the rest of the world	*Volume*			85%
OEEC imports from the rest of the world	*Volume*			75%
Employment	*monthly averages, millions of people*	101	111	10%
Gross domestic product	*Real*			48%
Industrial production	*Real*			65%
Gold and currency reserves	*Billions of dollars*	9,9	20,5	107%

Source: Our processing of data from J. J. Kaplan and G. Schleiminger, *The European Payments Union. Financial Diplomacy in the 1950s*. Oxford: Clarendon Press, 1989, p. 343.

When parity was fixed in terms of dollars for a currency, it was a matter of indifference for the central bank issuing that currency whether it held gold or dollars to cover it and defend the fixed parity. Nevertheless, insofar as the central banks of Europe and the whole world were ready to go on accumulating dollar reserves indefinitely to stash their surpluses, the United States gained the corresponding right to accumulate debts against its deficits. Unlike the European Payments Union, the system set no limits to increases in credit or debit positions and no incentive to curb them. The contrast could hardly be more radical: in the Union, commercial credit was granted freely, but always with a view to clearance or reimbursement, which was guaranteed by the *clearing* principle; in the financial system that came under way after the Union had been dismantled, credit took the form of unrestricted, unlimited increase in international *liquidity*, consisting of dollar balances that were never to be reabsorbed. Moreover, with the asymmetrical relationship established between the dollar and all the other currencies in 1958, the *multilateral* creation of credit characteristic of the European Payments Union gave way to the *unilateral* creation of liquidity – in other words to the exercise of international seignorage on the part of the United States.

Thus were laid the financial foundations for American unilateralism, by no means to be seen as a warlike stance, but rather as a *de facto* position, equally indifferent to peaceful and warlike uses of liquidity. The fact is that the adoption of the dollar as international currency 'produced the secret of a deficit without tears. It allowed [the US] to give without taking, to lend without borrowing, and to acquire without paying'.[16] Thus Jacques Rueff, former French finance minister and economic advisor to de Gaulle, characterized the dollar-based system – but by no means with the intention of stigmatizing an American privilege. Rueff recognized that this system had 'created the right conditions for that great change that introduced into international traditions the policy of giving', and that 'the US balance-of-payments deficits over the past decade [1951–61] have been outweighed by the grants and loans they accorded with unprecedented generosity to nations that experienced a foreign exchange shortage at the end of the war. But', Rueff concluded, 'the method of giving is no less important than the object of the gift itself, in particular when it is likely seriously to affect stability, and indeed the very existence of the receiving and donor countries alike'.[17] The 'original sin' of the new international monetary system was not being biased in favour of a country (also because this bias, as Rueff points out, can favour all, indiscriminately), but toppling the very mainstay of the balance of international payments.

What, we might ask at this point, is the moral of the story? And, all things considered, in this case the word 'moral' is in fact rather apt. The history of the European Payments Union is, effectively, the story of the implementation of an institution designed to favour the *virtuous economic behaviour* of all its participants. We can read in this light Triffin's observation on the *nature* of the liberalization of trade that the Union enabled: 'Discrimination and bilateralism in intra-European trade were not merely outlawed. They became technically impossible to implement.'[18] In other words, the Union did not simply prohibit, but actually set about making pointless, for any single member, whatever might be pointless for the community of traders as a whole. Protectionist policies designed to accumulate trade surpluses and reserves were rendered at the same time technically impossible and economically insensate, there being no 'money-or-credit' – no liquidity, that is – within the Union that could be accumulated indefinitely.

Precisely because the European Payments Union was not based on liquidity, the *quantity of money had no role to play* in it. The success of the Union demonstrates in concrete terms the theoretical arguments set out in Part I: credit, that is, the advance granted as a necessary, preliminary condition to be able to work, produce and trade, does not depend upon the availability of a quantity of money set aside in advance, but upon an opening where it is possible to promise – that is, to supply or apply for credit. The Second World War left Europe with no money, no gold and no currency reserves. And yet the extraordinary recovery of the European economy in the 1950s is attributable not so much to the injections of American dollars, massive as they were, as to the introduction of a European multilateral credit and clearing system, again, promoted and enabled by the United States – acting, *in this case*, truly as a *third party*: not as a lender of last resort (which actually amounts to being a creditor, and thus an interested party), but as a *guarantor* of the meeting between debtors and creditors.

The twenty-year span we have traversed in this chapter and in the previous one shows, in the concrete reality of the historical process, two alternative ways of organizing the international monetary system, which are based on two radically different principles: liquidity and clearing. It also shows how the former eventually came to prevail. But how and when were the foundations put in place for the system that was to come fully into force in 1958? Wouldn't it have been possible to devise and implement a different system, extending on a global scale the very mechanisms that had been seen to work so well in the European Payments Union? In order to answer these two questions we must take yet a further step back and 'return to Bretton Woods'. In fact, the two alternative plans that came into competition there, and which will be dealt with in the next two chapters, supply the respective answers. There was the American plan, which, with certain decisive modifications, came to form the basis of the system that was effectively adopted at Bretton Woods, one founded on the principle of liquidity; and then there was Keynes's plan. With this plan, rejected at Bretton Woods, it would have been possible to organize the whole of world trade on the basis of the clearing principle.

6

Bretton Woods: The plan that might have made it (1944)

The year 1944 marked a crucial transition in the history of the international monetary system. July of that year saw delegates converging on Bretton Woods from forty-four countries that were beginning to see signs of an Allied victory bringing the war to an end, in the not too distant future. Weighing on their shoulders, and indeed on those of the whole world, were not only five years of war, but also ten years of equally worldwide depression, plus another ten years of speculative and inflationary excesses and turmoil – generated, in turn, by the contradictions that had emerged in the wake of the First World War. The stakes were dauntingly high: the mistakes made at the end of the First World War were to be avoided at all costs; the curtain was to be brought down on thirty years of hostility and purblind nationalism, also at the economic level; and the foundations were to be laid for the rebuilding of international trade, so as to usher in a new age, one of peace and prosperity, comparable with the image still cherished by all – that of the thirty-year period preceding the assassination at Sarajevo. The response proved as historic as the task ahead: the Bretton Woods Conference was the first and, so far, the only occasion when the rules for international payments were expressly agreed upon and established by common consent.

As we have seen in the foregoing chapters, the results fell short of the noble ambitions. The Bretton Woods system was to last a mere twenty-five years, from the Savannah Conference of 1946, which ratified the agreements, to the speech delivered by Nixon in 1971, which effectively brought them to an end. But not even those twenty-five years ever saw the system fully in force: the fundamental rule of convertibility was at last adopted by most of the countries only when – and thanks to the fact that – another fundamental rule, providing for controls over capital, was effectively bypassed, with the emergence of the eurodollar market. Nevertheless, those were, at least, twenty-five years of prosperity, if not of peace – now not only regretted as a sort of second *belle époque*, but actually stretched out into 'the Glorious Thirty'. Historians concur, however, in attributing the economic growth of this period to the financial flows running *outside* the Bretton Woods system, along the channels mapped out in the two preceding chapters, far more than to the financing mobilized by the World Bank and the International Monetary Fund – precisely the institutions designated at Bretton Woods with the purpose of promoting reconstruction and revival of trade.

The aims of the new system were set in the first article of the agreement, in these precise terms: 'to facilitate the expansion and growth of international trade, [. . .] to promote exchange stability, [. . .] and lessen the degree of disequilibrium in the international balances of payments of members'.[1] And yet the path effectively taken, on a global scale, over the following years – that of bypassing the rules laid down by the agreements through massive capital movements denominated in dollars – did in fact lead to the objective of growth, but at the expense of the other objectives. Over the same period, the European Payments Union testified to the possibility of supporting the free expansion of international trade by radically different means, thanks to which it was feasible not only to *maintain* the convertibility of exchange rates together with the equilibrium in the balances of payments, but also to achieve these two objectives starting out from a situation of marked instability and disequilibrium.

One cannot help wondering whether it wouldn't have been possible to devise a system of regulations on the model of the European Union of Payments, but permanently and on a worldwide scale, thereby avoiding the need to resort to that source of liquidity and of disequilibria opened up through the adoption of the dollar as international currency. Actually, a system of the sort not only could have been devised, but effectively was devised, with the precise purpose of drawing up the economic rules for the post-war years. This was the International Clearing Union, engineered by Keynes on behalf of the British government in the course of the bilateral negotiations with the United States that began in 1942 and culminated with the Bretton Woods Conference.

As we know, it was, however, the American plan that found its way into the final text of the agreements. We also know the reason customarily invoked to explain why this was so: at the end of the war the United States was so powerful as to be able to bring its own interests to prevail, not only over the countries that were eventually defeated, but also over the countries that, thanks to US intervention alone, had emerged victorious. And yet, in the light of the course of events that followed, we cannot but wonder whether American policy was long-sighted enough *to be able to weigh up* the country's real interests: in 1947 US unilateralism might have been worth the 4 billion dollars a year of the Marshall Plan; but, over sixty years later, is it still worth America's 800 billion dollars a year current-account deficit?[2] Or had such a price actually been anticipated?

Keynes's plan merits revaluation, not by the yardstick of British interests, but in the prospect also of America's real advantage. It was in fact in the interests of the United States that Keynes urged the need for a clearing system: only with a system conceived in these terms would it be possible to answer to the interests of both the creditor and the debtor countries, setting in motion a mechanism that would literally bring them to converge towards a common position of equilibrium. Before examining this mechanism in detail, it is worth rereading the passage quoted in Part I, where Keynes describes its advantages:

> A country finding itself in a creditor position *against the rest of the world as a whole* should enter into an obligation to dispose of this credit balance and not to allow it meanwhile to exercise a contractionist pressure against the world economy and, by repercussion, against the economy of the creditor country itself. This would give, and all others, the great assistance of multilateral clearing. [. . .] This is not a Red Cross philanthropic relief scheme, by which the rich countries come to the rescue of the poor. It is a piece of highly necessary business mechanism, which is at least as useful to the creditor as to the debtor.[3]

According to Keynes, the international payments system should be constructed in such a way that the international creditor position of one country – that is, a *credit* – be bound together with an obligation – literally, a *debt*. This debt consists in the duty, incumbent on the creditor country, to dispose of its credit, not allowing it to accumulate indefinitely – which would mean removing the means of trade from circulation, with deflationary effects harmful to the whole system and so, ultimately, to the creditor country itself. We might describe it as a matter of moral duty, in the sense we used the term in the previous chapter: what this duty implies, in the first place, is not promoting *good behaviour* in respect of a given rule, but introducing a good rule – a rule, that is, drawn up in such a way as to render any legitimate choice made by a part compatible with the soundness and integrity of the whole.

In fact Keynes immediately went on to point out that the reference here to the creditor's debt had no implications in terms of individual morality: it was not a matter of appealing to the *goodness of an individual* creditor country (for example the United States) to agree to reduce its credit by an act of unilateral generosity (for example through an aid plan) inspired by some philanthropic or humanitarian aim (for example 'to defend freedom around the world'). What was at stake was the institutional viability of the international monetary system as a whole: it was a matter of guaranteeing the *soundness of the system*, or its capacity to bring the legitimate national interests of each country to converge with the common interests of international trade. To achieve this, the system was to be constructed in such a way that creditor countries would not expect to be thanked for lending, but rather would have a concrete interest in doing so. But how could such a system be put together?

Keynes's proposal revolved around the institution that gave its name to the plan – the International Clearing Union. It was conceived of as a clearing house, much like the European Payments Union, but on the global scale. Each member country was to hold an account with the Clearing Union that would be denominated in an international unit of account, instituted for the purpose and called *bancor*. The national currency of each member country was to have its parity fixed in terms of the *bancor*. The initial balance of each account was to stand at zero.[4] Every commercial transaction was to be recorded with double entry: credit would be entered on the side of the exporting country, while the corresponding debit would be recorded for the importing country. But this was not to be a bilateral debit/credit relationship between the two countries: in fact, both debit and credit fell to the Clearing Union as a whole. This meant that the exporting country could use its credit to pay for imports at any time and from any other member country, while the importer could pay its debts with the proceeds from exports made at any time to any other member.

Thus the Clearing Union would provide for continuous multilateral and intertemporal clearing of credit (exports) and debit (imports) postings. For each country, the balance would always correspond to its net overall balance of trade (positive in the case of surplus, negative in the case of deficit), while the balance of the Clearing Union as a whole would *always remain at zero*. For this reason, the Clearing Union has in principle no need of any initial endowment of money (in the form of deposit, capital or reserve).

So far, however, there seems to be little to distinguish the Clearing

Union from a bank. Indeed, in describing the system, Keynes made it quite clear that his source of inspiration lay in the mechanisms for the creation of bank money. Just like a bank, the Clearing Union created money at a simple stroke of the pen, offering advances that were not necessarily covered by an equivalent amount of deposits. Indeed, having no deposits or reserves in any form, the Clearing Union would supply credit without any monetary base, and it could be said to create money from nothing. This is why many critics denounced Keynes's proposal as inflationary. It is a charge that merits serious attention, not because it is well grounded but because the many objections that can be raised against it bring to the fore as many characteristics peculiar to Keynes's plan.

To begin with, it is well to clear the field of any idea that Keynes might have been ideologically in favour of inflation regardless. That his recommendations were mainly of an expansive nature is unquestionable, but this was only because he was living in a period marked by deflation, which he set out to tackle by every means that might serve the purpose. Keynes waxed sarcastic against the dogmatism of those who made monetary rigour a matter of orthodoxy: 'To be sometimes in favour of dearer money and sometimes in favour of cheaper money seems to them like being sometimes a Protestant and sometimes a Roman Catholic.'[5] The line to be taken in monetary policy was, for Keynes, a practical choice that depended on the circumstances. In the years that saw him drawing up his plan for Bretton Woods, his main preoccupation was that money might be wanting after the war, and not abounding. It was for this reason that, unlike Rueff, Keynes opposed any return to gold, no matter what form it might take. It was not an inflationary consideration that guided his plan, but an anti-deflationary one – which, moreover, he made perfectly clear: 'The plan aims at the substitution of an expansionist, in place of a contractionist, pressure on world trade.'[6]

More precisely still, for Keynes the purchasing power to be put at the disposal of trade was to be neither great nor little, but commensurate with the availability of goods to be traded at any given moment. Hence in his project he pegged the creation of international money on the commercial transactions effectively undertaken, which meant that the money Keynes had in mind was not created 'from nothing', but *followed upon trade in goods*. At the same time, and precisely for the same reason, the money created as *bancor* asset in favour of a country in surplus is by the same token destroyed whenever that country reduces its credit position by importing. In accordance with the definition Keynes had already provided twenty years before, the money created in the Clearing Union 'is a mere intermediary, without significance in itself, which flows from one [nation] to another, is received and is dispensed, and disappears when its work is done [from the accounts of the Clearing Union]'.[7] If every country were to bring its balance of trade to equilibrium, then every balance would return to zero, the creation of money being entirely reabsorbed, having served solely to provide for the transfer of goods among all the participating countries – in other words for an increase in real wealth.

Within the Clearing Union the balanced budget was not to be a merely ideal situation that could be departed from indefinitely by accumulating increasing credit and debit balances, as was feared by critics, who read an intrinsic inflationary bias in the proposal. On the contrary, the balanced budget was to be the concrete situation from which the members of the Clearing Union set out to begin with, from which they could not depart beyond certain limits and to which, above all, they were constantly led back. The countries in deficit would certainly not be entitled to go on piling debt upon debt indefinitely, but they would have to contain the debt within the quota set for each country in proportion to the volume of its foreign trade. Moreover, within these limits countries would also have an incentive to reduce their debit position, being subject to a charge proportional to their debt. With the Clearing Union debts can be run up freely, but not free of charge, nor without limit, nor indeed for any purpose whatsoever.

Nevertheless, the mechanisms we have so far described for the Clearing Union still resemble those of any commercial bank. Unlike a commercial bank, on the other hand, the Clearing Union still shows what appears to be a shortcoming, making provision for no form of reserve or guarantee. But what should the Clearing Union guarantee to its creditors? Unlike the depositors of a commercial bank, the creditor countries of the Clearing Union have no right to draw anything from their accounts. On the other hand, however, they have made no deposits either. Their credit has matured within the Clearing Union through the trade that the latter has enabled them to perform, and in consequence of their decision to import less than they have exported. Moreover, the countries in surplus are free to make full use of their assets and can decide to spend them however they like and whenever they like: they come up against no restrictions to their purchasing power and they run no risk as long as there is something in the world to acquire. For all these reasons, there is no need to protect or compensate the creditor countries in any way. The need is, rather, to prevent them from carrying on piling up assets indefinitely, thereby exerting contractive pressure on world trade. This, in fact, is why assets are subject to the same limitations and charges as apply to liabilities in the Clearing Union: credit and debit alike are subject to the same 'negative interest'. In either case, interest is paid to the Clearing Union as a management charge.

This symmetrical charge, on debit and credit alike, was actually the most original and significant feature of Keynes's entire plan. At the institutional and at the operational level, the charge was justified by the need to ensure that the aim of each country would converge with their collective goal (in other words, with the aim of the Union), which was to bring the balances towards equilibrium (in other words, towards Clearing). If balance of payments equilibrium was in fact the sole *economic* criterion, then the countries in surplus would be in a position of disequilibrium no less than the countries in deficit and, like them, should be led to correct it. This equal treatment of credits and liabilities is the only guarantee the Clearing Union needs. It is in fact a stronger guarantee than any reserve constraint that might apply to the creation of money through leverage and liquidity. In fact, thanks to the equal distribution of charges between creditors and debtors, all the money created in the Clearing Union with a view to international trade not only can, but indeed must eventually be reabsorbed, bringing all the credit and debit balances back towards zero thanks to further trading.

Despite all the provisions we have so far described, the case could still arise in practice of a country persisting in balance of trade disequilibrium. To cope with this eventuality, should a country's deficit or surplus exceed a certain threshold for a certain period of time, then the rules of the Clearing Union would grant the country in question the faculty to adjust its exchange rate within a 5 per cent limit. Thus, for example, a country showing a sizable chronic deficit would be able to devalue its currency against the *bancor* so as to regain competitiveness and bring its external accounts back to equilibrium without having to resort to deflationary measures, and thus with no prejudice to its internal equilibrium. In this way, thanks to the distinction between national and international currency, it would be possible to adjust the rate of exchange between the two, and with it the ratio between the internal and the external purchasing power of each currency. And, given the possibility to adjust this ratio, equilibrium could in turn be pursued in the internal economy and in foreign trade at the same time, eliminating any contrast between the two objectives, which would thus prove compatible. Moreover, with the unequivocal definition of disequilibrium in external accounts in terms of a significant and persistent departure from equilibrium, and with the precise measurement that could be made of this disequilibrium on the evidence of the Clearing Union accounts, there would be no risk of arbitrary use of the scope for regulation offered by the system of 'adjustable exchange rates'.

On the strength of this consistent set of rules, the Clearing Union was conceived of as a financial instrument for international trade, eminently apt for the fundamental task required of credit as defined in Part I, namely to provide an advance against future payment. Having now looked into the essential mechanisms driving it, it is worth recapitulating at this point the implications of the Clearing Union for the fundamental components of the financial relationship, as they emerged in Part I: (1) the connection between advance and settlement; (2) the relations between the monetary functions; (3) the distinction between money and goods; and (4) the connection between national and international economy.

1 The Clearing Union is geared, entirely and solely, towards providing overdraft facilities for trade in goods between countries against future settlement. Balance of trade equilibrium is central to the Union as its starting point and constituent law: it is this rule that makes it into a Clearing Union – literally, that is, a union for the balancing of all accounts, the clearing of all positions.[8] In virtue of this rule, the Clearing Union was to take on the form of an international economic space created to enable, according to Rueff's formula, the 'meeting of all the creditors with all the debtors'.

Precisely because it was to be made the governing principle of the Clearing Union, balance of trade equilibrium could also be identified with the long-term tendential equilibrium seen not as the *ex post* outcome of short-period interactions, but rather as the horizon towards which they would be moving. For a system of regulations governed by the Clearing Union provisions, balance of trade equilibrium was to constitute a point that, in physical terms, could be defined 'stable' and 'attractive': within this system each country's balance of trade, like a ball rolling about in a bowl, is inexorably drawn towards the central point of gravity.

If this is in fact the case, then there can clearly be no question of attributing an intrinsic inflationary tendency to the Clearing Union. Inflation implies creating money in excess of the goods it can buy. In the Clearing Union each country creates money whenever it sells goods to another country, but in the very act of creation it also undertakes to destroy it, acquiring goods from any other countries so as to bring its balance back to zero. Thus, far from being inflationary, the Clearing Union takes on the form of a system in which the quantity of money does not count. As Keynes himself put it:

> The peculiar merit of the Clearing Union as a means of remedying a chronic shortage of international money is that it operates through the velocity, rather than through the volume, of circulation. [. . .] The C.U., if it were fully successful, would deal with the quantity of international money by *making any significant quantity unnecessary*.[9]

The same idea was reasserted by the British economist D. H. Robertson, who answered to the Fed directors' fears during Anglo-American negotiations by pointing out how the tasks of monetary authority would change within the framework of the Clearing Union:

> It is arguable that the proudest day in the life of the Manager of the Clearing Union would be that on which, as a result of the smooth functioning of the correctives set in motion by the Plan, there were no holders of international money – on which he was able to show a balance sheet on both sides of the account.[10]

2 Moreover, the Clearing Union was designed in such a way as to dispense with the supply of a quantity of money from the outset. It is enough to consider its architecture to see that there is clearly no need for any preventive allocation of money (of a fund) for advances in order to finance the temporary balance of payments deficits: it is not necessary to have money to provide credit, or in any case to have money in the form of a currency reserve. What is needed, rather, is an international unit of account corresponding in no way to any national currency, for the denomination of the debits and credits generated by trading transactions between countries. Precisely for this reason, the fundamental mainstay of Keynes's proposal was the *bancor*, i.e. *international money of account*, purely abstract, immaterial (or, to use the terminology of a very old system to which we will be returning later, 'imaginary'). The second mainstay is the *overdraft facility*: *credit as pure and simple advance* – not a loan of money previously allocated, but breathing space granted to importers so that they can, thanks to their imports, produce and export in turn.

On the one hand, then, the credit granted by the Clearing

Union to its member countries depends upon this money as international unit of account. On the other hand, however, the credit can be spent at any time and for any end, and is therefore, to all intents and purposes, money, in the sense of a means for international payment.

Thus the money created by the Clearing Union, consisting of credit balances in *bancors*, could be considered and used as a means for international trade, but not as a currency reserve; for it could not be conserved indefinitely. Ultimately, payment must be made with goods, and with goods alone. Anyone holding money in the form of credit balances in *bancors* is under the obligation to spend it. This money, therefore, given the rules that govern its functioning, incorporates the most fundamental characteristic of money: it is money made to be spent, bearing with it the constant reminder to those holding it that they must spend it, and thereby representing in concrete terms Keynes's idea of the 'creditor's debt'.

The country holding credit with the Clearing Union has a duty, not a right. In particular, it can claim no right of ownership, full and exclusive, over its credit balances in *bancors*. In this respect, in the Clearing Union no one is 'owner of international liquidity'. Anyone holding money in the Clearing Union would be 'at the mercy of his neighbours', as Keynes aptly put it in describing the peculiarity of money in a manuscript note to the *Tract*.[11] The country holding *bancors* is in fact beholden to the other countries as a whole, depending upon them to transform that credit into goods.

3 The *Clearing Union* project incorporates all the more or less explicit indications that can be drawn from Keynes's theoretical work, spanning the twenty-five years from his first publication on the faults of the monetary system 'as we know it' and on the characteristics of a monetary system 'as it ought to be'. It is beyond our scope to trace out in detail the theoretical foundations of the Clearing Union in the corpus of Keynes's writings,[12] but there is at least one element worth mentioning here. In chapter 17 of the *General Theory* Keynes compares money and goods as alternative forms in which wealth can be held, pointing out that money enjoys an advantage in that holding it, unlike holding goods, entails no costs due to storage or deterioration. It is also on account of this advantage that money can take on the function of store of value: it can in fact be withdrawn from circulation indefinitely, with

consequent deflationary pressure on trade and production. To avoid this risk, Keynes went as far as to take into serious consideration the idea of introducing 'artificial carrying costs' for money, to ensure that it be spent and not withheld *beyond the lapse of time required by trade.* In the closing chapters of his major work, Keynes again raised the possibility of such a scheme as a decisive step towards exit from crisis, praising the heterodox economist Silvio Gesell, the first one to have devised and experimented with forms of 'stamped money' (*Schwundgeld*).

The costs borne by the Clearing Union creditors can be understood in the sense of a charge for holding wealth in the form of an international currency. Given these costs, the *bancor* is in fact money subject to artificial carrying costs, that is, money that cannot be held as store of value. It has to be spent within a certain period of time, and insofar as it is not spent it is 'destroyed': the unutilized credit balance of the creditor country diminishes periodically by a sum corresponding to the charge fixed by the Clearing Union. Thus the international currency ceases to enjoy the dubious advantage of being non-perishable, and the country will prefer to acquire goods rather than going on accumulating trade surpluses indefinitely.

Nevertheless, the *bancor* would still have an advantage over a stock of goods: the advantage of not being subject to variations in price and of being immediately transformable into any commodity. This particular advantage, which Keynes called 'liquidity', constitutes the second reason for preferring the currency to goods as a way of holding wealth. And this, too, Keynes set out to avoid: the same years that saw him working on the proposal for the Clearing Union also saw Keynes airing a plan for the international stockpiling of raw materials and agricultural produce. The idea was to endow commodities with the liquidity they lack, exploiting them as means of reserve that could even replace gold as the basis of the monetary system.

The idea behind the *two integrated plans* was to encourage the holding of commodities rather than the accumulation of money, and the circulation of goods rather than of capital. This may have been the reason why Keynes placed less emphasis than the drafter of the American plan, H. D. White, on the expediency of bringing in restrictions on capital movements. His aim was not so much to bar capital movements (that is, movements of money as capital, liquidity, asset, store of value) as to make them less advantageous than the purchase of goods.

4 The institutions that Keynes projected for the post-war period were also specifically designed to make national economic and monetary policies as independent as they could possibly be of the exigencies of the external account. Here he seems explicitly to have come down in favour of one of the horns of Mundell's trilemma at the expense of the other two: for the sake of national autonomy he was apparently ready to forego both fixed exchange rates and international capital movements. At this point, however, we have enough evidence to be able to see just what this 'renunciation' meant and the peculiar form it took.

Fixed exchange rates and capital movements are not ends in themselves. The former serve for international trade, ensuring firm standards of measurement, the latter serve for investments. Clearly, Keynes had no intention of limiting international trade or investments. In fact he did not look to a flexible exchange rate system, but rather to one of fixed but adjustable rates, departures from the fixed rates being justified precisely by the need to guarantee equilibrium in trade. Similarly, far from hampering international credit, his idea was to facilitate it, under the form of commercial credit granted by the Clearing Union and under the form of foreign direct investments, monetary transfers being associated with transfers of goods, consumption or capital. On the other hand, what the Clearing Union was decidedly closed to were portfolio investments – in other words transfers of money as assets against negotiable securities.

All this seems to have been quite masterfully designed and, above all, designed to serve the purposes of all. So the question arising here, even more forcefully than before, is this: if the Clearing Union was such an expertly devised system, why wasn't it adopted at Bretton Woods?

7

Bretton Woods: The system that found implementation (1944)

The international monetary system launched in 1944 bears only a remote and decidedly superficial resemblance to the Clearing Union. The Bretton Woods system was no offspring of Keynes. Only a perfunctory reading of the history could suggest attributing paternity to him. Not one of the mainstays of Keynes's proposal, reviewed in the previous chapter, was left in place after two years of negotiations and a conference lasting twenty-two days.

The first, fundamental element without which the Clearing Union could not have been conceived was the international unit of account (*bancor*). The Bretton Woods agreements envisaged no such thing. Indeed, they did away with the international standard hitherto respected – gold – irrevocably bestowing this role to a national unit of account: the dollar. Just why the participants fell in line with this solution is a matter we will be looking into later on. To begin with, however, let us focus on the various implications this decision held.

The most immediate implication was that the system had to do without the second pillar of Keynes's plan, namely the *overdraft facility*, which granted the opening of credit. Of course, it is always possible for one country to open credit to another, denominated in the national unit of account. However, such credit cannot be spent in a third country – it remains bilateral, not multilateral credit. Unlike *bancor* balances, credits denominated in the currency of a country can be used by the creditor to purchase goods from that country alone. In other words, if there is no international unit of account, neither is there a means of international payment in the form of multilateral credit, and thus spendable in all directions.

And if this is in fact how things stand, then we have to face the fact that the Bretton Woods agreements instituted *a monetary system without money*. To be even more precise, they instituted an international monetary system without an international currency, which meant that the denomination and payment of debts could only be achieved by resorting to national currencies: country A has to pay for its imports from another country B, by using the latter's currency. If no agreement has been come to, then A should obtain the necessary currency with a corresponding volume of exports to B. In practice, however, this would imply bilateral equilibrium in the balance between all the countries, which would eventually snarl up the whole of international trade. To avoid this constraint, provision is made in the Bretton Woods agreements for the country in deficit to be able to acquire the currencies it needs in order to pay its creditors from an institution designed for the function, namely the International Monetary Fund. This is in fact quite literally a fund – a stock of national currencies collected for the purpose of facilitating international trade.

The Fund was constituted with the initial contributions of the member countries. Each country paid its quota, partly in its national currency, partly in gold. With this endowment the Fund is able to provide countries in deficit with the specific currency they need in order to pay off their trade debts to the creditor countries. This does not take the form of a loan, however, for in that case the country in question would have to repay in the same currency as that of the loan: the country would benefit from a certain breathing space, but would still be bound by the need to balance foreign trade on a bilateral basis. So the country in deficit obtains the foreign currency from the Fund not *on loan*, but *on sale*, for a corresponding sum of its own currency, calculated at the prefixed rates.

And yet this would seem to be a decidedly odd sort of sale, costing the purchaser nothing, since, by paying for foreign currency with its own, it would find itself in the curious situation of being able to bear potentially unlimited balance of trade deficits, having the option to produce a potentially unlimited quantity of national currency. International trade would end up being financed entirely through uncovered cheques issued by the most thriftless countries. Insofar as it is an institution given the task of creating currency, the International Monetary Fund must, no less than the Clearing Union, cope with the risk of a possible *inflation drift*, and has therefore to adopt due limitations so as to avoid generating too much, and to destroy any excess. Effectively, what qualifies a monetary institution is precisely the criteria and the procedures by which it regulates the issue, the circulation *and the destruction* of money.

Within the terms of the Bretton Woods agreements, the creation of money takes place when, and to the extent to which, the Fund sells foreign currency to a member country in exchange for its national currency. No creation of an international currency is involved, but rather the transformation of one national currency into another in order to enable an international payment. For the country in deficit, the operation entails the transformation of national purchasing power into international purchasing power. Obviously, such a benefit cannot be granted without restrictions; otherwise there would be no incentive for any country to settle its deficits. This is why, unlike a normal sale transaction, the purchase of foreign currency from the Fund does not release the purchaser from the seller, but entails a number of constraints. In particular – to begin with the most substantial one – the purchaser is committed to buying its currency back from the Fund in exchange for gold or convertible currency, so as to keep the share of its currency, which is held by the Fund, tendentially within the limits of the initial endowment, corresponding to the country's quota. To reinforce this constraint, a country in deficit is liable to pay a charge that increases with the increasing quantity of its currency held by the Fund in excess of its quota. Finally, every purchase of foreign currency from the Fund is subject to a commission, which means that, in practice, the purchaser pays a higher price than the one determined by the prefixed parity between the currencies.

As a result of these various provisions, what the agreements describe as a purchase actually has for the purchaser the effects of a loan. The purchaser receives foreign currency in return for his national currency, but the latter is seen by the Fund not as a means of payment that releases the purchaser, but rather as a debt that binds him. Moreover, given that it is national paper money, it is after all only right that it should be seen, at the international level, as a debt on the part of the issuer.

Re-examined in this light, the Bretton Woods agreements appear to treat the countries in deficit in much the same way as the Clearing Union had envisaged. In practice, these countries are granted by the Fund temporary access to foreign currency to settle their deficits vis-à-vis a country, and at the same time they are given the opportunity to readjust to the limits of their quota through deferred payments, in gold or any other currency, and thus on the strength of the surpluses they may have vis-à-vis any other country. In practice, therefore, the Fund offers an advance with a view to payment, allowing for an intertemporal, multilateral transformation of purchasing power. And yet one cannot help wondering why this objective, which is no different from that of the Clearing Union, should be pursued in such a lumbering way, through continual exchange of national currencies treated like debts, and not by instituting an international unit of account and a clearing system.[1]

If we are to explain the rationale behind this choice, we must turn to consider what happens, within the terms of the agreements, to a country in surplus. In this case, too, beside the quota initially contributed, the country in question sells the Fund its currency to finance its imports and buys it back through the proceeds on its exports (or will have it acquired directly by the recipients of the exports). As it is a country in surplus, however, the balance of Fund transactions in its currency will be negative: if a country exports more than it imports, the other countries' demand for its currency will exceed the supply, and the Fund will have the task of making up for the difference, selling its reserves in that particular currency. Should the surplus prove persistent, sales could be protracted to such an extent that the currency in question would eventually become 'scarce'.

This is a situation that can in fact arise, since in the Bretton Woods system, unlike in the Clearing Union, a surplus does not automatically give rise to a multilateral credit. The only automatic consequence of a surplus is an outflow of the currency in question from the Fund's reserves. When the currency comes close to running out, the time is ripe for Article 7 of the agreements – the 'scarce currency' clause – to be applied.

It has often been pointed out that this clause has failed to find application.[2] Yet, we should ask, why hasn't it been applied? Is this a simple matter of fact, or does it reflect something lacking at the level, not of facts, but of rules? Effectively, reading the clause through, we find no prescriptive content. What it states is that, if reserves of a particular currency are running out, the Fund is empowered to: inform the member countries and issue recommendations (section 1); seek a loan in the currency concerned or buy it for gold (section 2); and, finally, should the scarcity persist, authorize member countries to impose limitations on exchange operations in the scarce currency (section 3).

These provisions might be seen as a sort of crescendo in forms of intervention by the Fund. And yet, without dwelling on its role as dispenser of advice sought or unsought – and in any case certainly not binding (section 1) – we must observe that the solutions offered to the problem of scarce currency depend, not upon any exercise of sovereignty by the Fund, but rather on abdication of sovereignty. The first line of intervention (section 2) depends, not on the activity of the

Fund, but on the international monetary and financial markets – the very mechanisms whose role was supposed to be reduced through the institution of the Fund itself; while the second line (section 3) means adopting protectionist policies and thereby flying in the face of the free market principle, which constitutes the ultimate aim legitimizing the existence of the Fund.

While the scarce currency clause sees the Fund abdicating its prerogatives, it also implies, literally *a fortiori*, powers devolving to those who are directly called by the clause to make up for the shortcomings of the Fund – in other words to the countries in surplus. Thanks to the mechanism envisaged by the scarce currency clause, ultimate sovereignty appears to go, not to the regulator of debtor/creditor relations, but to the creditors themselves, directly. In practice, the clause grants countries in surplus greater bargaining powers than those conceded not only to the countries in deficit, but indeed to the Fund itself: once the currency of the country in surplus with respect to the quota has been used up, anyone in need of it has no choice but to buy it for gold or to borrow it, paying interest.

We have now assembled enough evidence to be able to compare the Clearing Union and the Fund, and thus to assess in more concrete terms what these two *alternative* configurations of the centre of the international monetary system actually imply. On the surface, the Fund may look rather more solid than the Clearing Union on the strength of its initial endowment, and hence precisely in virtue of its specific identity as a fund. In practice, however, once its reserves – meagre enough from the outset – have been drained, the Fund finds itself in a rather weaker position than the Union. While the idea of the Clearing Union was that the centre would provide credit to the member countries without any need for it to borrow in turn, in the case of the Fund it is the countries in surplus that supply credit to the Fund for the loans that, in this way, the Fund will be able to make in its turn.

There are various consequences to be reckoned with. For example, a country whose currency came under fairly strong demand from the others would in fact find itself in a position to exercise international seignorage. Thus, in practice, the 1944 agreements bestow international monetary authority not on the supranational organism instituted for the purpose – the Fund itself – but on the national members that find themselves in a position of surplus – or, in concrete terms, on the United States.

One might object – also in the light of what we have seen in previous chapters – that any such transference of international monetary sovereignty could take place only insofar as the resources of the Fund proved insufficient, and thus as an exception – if not to the letter, at least to the spirit of the agreements signed at Bretton Woods. Actually, however, the transactions performed through the Fund already entail a radical asymmetry between countries in surplus and countries in deficit. While it is in fact true that the former receive no interest on the currency placed at the disposal of the Fund within the limits of their quota, the latter, on the other hand, face increasing costs if they wish to draw on the supply. Thus we have an asymmetry that, far from favouring a return to equilibrium on both sides, tends rather to aggravate disequilibria. On top of all this is the fact that, unlike Keynes's plan, the Bretton Woods agreements provide no clear definition of the state of 'fundamental disequilibrium', which makes it difficult to apply the exchange rate adjustments that might be made to correct any such disequilibrium. Finally, the Fund's initial endowment was set at the very modest level of 8.8 billion dollars.[3] This happened at the insistence of the United States, which was pursuing the calculated aim of limiting its exposure and of making it a matter of necessity for countries to negotiate any concession of dollars over and above this meagre limit.

For all these reasons, it was *inevitable* that the Fund's resources prove insufficient to support a significant share of international trade; all too soon the need arose to make up for this by using unilateral supplies of dollars from the United States, as a loan or as a donation. Despite the fact that they lay down explicit limitations on capital movements, the Bretton Woods agreements delineated an international monetary system that, in practice, made these movements indispensable. At this point we can see how the Bretton Woods agreements opened the way both to the post-war 'dollar gap' and to the subsequent international 'dollar glut', the consequences of which we are still paying for.

Having now taken the full measure of the distance between the Clearing Union and the International Monetary Fund, we can return to addressing the previous question: what is this distance due to? Why did the Anglo-American negotiations lead so far from Keynes's vision? The answer seems obvious and hard to get away from: the United States was stronger, and so it could not, nor could it even wish to, accept a monetary architecture that placed it on the same plane as other, less powerful countries. On closer consideration, however, this answer does not appear quite so self-evident. To begin with, if it is true that the Clearing Union was to start literally from scratch, taking no account of the existing power relations, Keynes was not so ingenuous as to fail to reckon with the past. He did not expect to make a clean sweep of the economic and financial relations as they stood at the time, nor did he imagine creating a new currency through the simple elimination of the old one, without allowing for its conversion. In particular, it would have been unthinkable for him to fail to take into account the gold already accumulated by the individual countries and, as it happened, mostly by the United States, which held over 90 per cent of the world's gold reserves at the end of the war. Keynes envisaged this gold as being deposited in the Clearing Union, thereby boosting the owner's balance in *bancors*. Perfectly natural, one might say. And, effectively, failing to admit this possibility would have shown a sadly deficient sense of reality (and of power).

Nevertheless, there were strings attached. Keynes envisaged the convertibility of gold into *bancors* as a *one-way* option: while gold could be converted into *bancors*, the balance in *bancors* could not be converted back into gold. So what was the motive for this? It was not only that, from a practical point of view, reconversion would have offered countries in surplus a loophole to save their assets from the costs imposed by the Clearing Union, but also that, as a matter of principle, exchanging an old currency for a new one can only imply a one-way conversion.

Why, then, did the United States reject this solution? Here again the answer seems obvious. The United States had practically all the gold in the world, and could keep it at no apparent costs. Keynes was asking the country to cede it in exchange for credit – and a credit not remunerated, but subject to various charges; moreover, a credit to be spent at all costs. To all intents and purposes, it would have seemed like a compulsory sacrifice. But what exactly was being sacrificed? To be precise – as precise as the case demands – not a *quantity* of wealth (unless, of course, like King Midas, one equates gold with wealth), nor the goods that the gold could buy, but rather a *definition* of wealth in terms of an indefinitely conservable store of value.

Keynes's plan was not rejected because it would have ruled out taking due account of the effective power relationships. Conversion of gold into *bancors* would have allowed for the effective distribution of the existing wealth to be reflected perfectly in the initial accounts of the Clearing Union. The objection raised by the United States had nothing to do with the physical question of how to distribute wealth, but was directed at the metaphysical question of how to define it; the United States did not object to the initial distribution of monetary endowments, but *to the rules* of the international monetary system proposed by Keynes.

Having made this point, we can now reformulate the original question: why were the rules established at Bretton Woods so radically different from those Keynes had proposed in his plan? In these terms, too, the answer seems fairly evident: the Americans had their alternative plan, and they had every interest in seeing the rules and principles it incorporated duly upheld. In fact, the same years that saw Keynes drafting his plan for the Clearing Union also saw Harry Dexter White at work drafting the plan of the Fund for the United States. Authoritative versions of the story describe the Bretton Woods agreements as a compromise between the two plans, with the balance in the favour of the American one. Nevertheless, in terms of the two fundamental characteristics, White's plan seems far closer to Keynes's plan than it was to the agreements that were eventually and definitively approved. Both plans made provision for an international currency and for controls over capital movements, and in this respect, therefore, the rejection of Keynes's plan also implied rejection of White's. Thus we have further proof of the fact that, if we want to form some idea of what really happened at Bretton Woods, we must move on from the plane of pure and simple relationships of power. If both of the two major powers designed a post-war monetary system displaying the same two distinctive features, why on earth was a system eventually launched *that excluded both of them*? Effectively, the agreements did not bring in an international currency and went no further than admitting capital controls on the initiative of individual countries, without any system of coordination and with manifold exceptions. Viewed in this light, the outcome of the negotiations looks rather less straightforward.

So, if it was not the American plan that won out over the British plan, what was it that finally triumphed over both? To answer this question, we must give closer consideration to the two cornerstones dislodged from the construction of the post-war monetary architecture, in order to assess the implications and possibly find some clue as to who could have had an interest in removing them. And *in the name of what.*

The international unit of account as distinct from national currencies is clearly a peculiar characteristic of the British plan. Nevertheless, it also appears in certain versions of the American plan, going under the name of *unitas*. Moreover, the first version of this plan, where it makes no appearance, was accompanied by a long note on 'a new international currency'. In this note White recognized the possible expediency of granting the new international organism the faculty to create money in order to make up for the insufficient and potentially deflationary gold reserves, 'and at the same time help correct the maldistribution of gold' at the global level.[4] In such an eventuality, what unit of account was to be chosen to denominate the newly issued currency? White came up with an answer that should have served as a warning, but was totally disregarded at Bretton Woods:

> It would be preferable to adopt a new unit. The adoption of a new international unit of currency of account [*sic*!] would probably meet with little opposition, whereas an attempt to use any one of the existing currencies, such as dollars, sterling or francs for that purpose would be opposed on the grounds that it would seem to give the country possessing that currency some slight advantage in publicity or trade.[5]

Having now traced the story thus far back, it may be superfluous to point out that it was eventually the United States that induced (and with scant opposition) the rest of the world to use its currency, thereby obtaining 'some slight advantage' – not so much in terms of publicity or trade as (more precisely) *in terms of seignorage*. As we noted in describing how the Clearing Union functioned, the adoption of an international unit of account would not only have made it possible for all countries to compete on an equal footing; it would also have dispensed with any need to bring into being international liquidity and to grant short-term loans in order to finance temporary balance of trade deficits.

For this reason, having finally abandoned the idea of an international unit of account, White had no choice but to stress the need to limit capital movements, and in doing so he went even further than Keynes.[6] In particular, he was aiming at controlling short-term movements, in other words portfolio investments, so as to counteract the destabilizing effects of sudden outflows of capital on balances of payment and on rates of exchange. The point at issue here was precisely to get to grips with the liquidity of international investments – that is, with the immediate and reversible convertibility of money into securities. As White put it: 'control means, however, less freedom for owners of liquid capital. It would constitute another restriction on the property rights of this 5 or 10% of persons in foreign countries who have enough wealth or income to keep or invest some of it abroad'.[7]

It was thus White himself who, with surprising frankness, pointed out the various interests in play without mincing his words: if it was true that limitation of capital movements was called for in the general interest of trade – both US and world trade – it was also true that a small part of the global population would be penalized. The existence of an international unit of account makes capital movements useless, while its nonexistence makes them indispensable. It takes no great effort of the imagination, therefore, to guess which of the two options was preferable for that '5 or 10 per cent of persons' who lived on international capital movements.

An article published in the *New York Times* on 1 July 1944, the day of the inauguration of the Bretton Woods Conference, made very clear what the financial community of Wall Street expected from the agreements: the introduction of an exchange system firmly anchored on gold, which would thereby drive the countries concerned in the direction of fiscal rigour and open up the movement of capital. Were the fixed exchange rates to guarantee the stability that international capital movements required, or were international investments to impose the fiscal rigour that the maintenance of fixed exchange rates required? Whatever the answer may be, the solution was not to be in the first place a matter of setting mechanisms moving. The *anonymous* author of the comment had no doubts:

> Any machinery that is set up will be of secondary importance for world recovery *compared with ideological reforms*. Each nation should abandon the fallacious idea that is to its own advantage to [. . .] forbid its own citizens to export gold, capital or credit.[8]

Even reforms of an ideological nature still need the support of the law. However, they need a law constructed in such a way as to entail resort, in the final instance, to an unwritten dogma to the effect that money, even when it serves as a unit of measure, is above all wealth – is indeed the immediate and absolute form in which to hold it. And if you want it, you must pay for it. This is why the 'ideological reform' was to find concrete expression at the institutional level in the cancellation of the international unit of account from the text of the agreements. It was still there when the article was written, and in the most traditional form – gold. But before the conference was over, the dollar was surreptitiously and ambiguously added. Article IV, section 1 reads thus:

> The par value of the currency of each member shall be expressed in terms of gold as a Common denominator or in terms of the United States dollar of the weight and fineness in effect on July 1, 1944.

It was only *in the final version* that the mentioning of the dollar found its way into the text of the agreements. Furthermore, although the conference took longer than expected to arrive at its conclusion, when the time came to sign the agreement complete copies of the articles had yet to become available.[9] The all too imaginable consequence was that Keynes, too, had to forego perusal of the complete text. As he acerbically remarked:

> We, all of us, had to sign, of course, before we had had a chance of reading through a clean and consecutive copy of the document. All we had seen of it was the dotted line. Our only excuse is the knowledge that our hosts had made final arrangements to throw us out of the hotel, unhouselled, disappointed, unanealed, within a few hours.[10]

Thus the interests that each of the countries had in the liberalization of trade gave way to the interests of the respective financial lobbies. The United States preferred to dig itself into a position where it had to hand over huge sums of money – even to give it away, as it would do with the Marshall plan – rather than surrender to the creation of an international currency.

At the same time, however, a point that needs to be made clear is that the decisions made at Bretton Woods, far from proving the (inevitable) triumph of the market rationale over the logic of intervention, showed the demands of finance prevailing over the needs of trade. Bretton Woods represents no attempt to enmesh the market in regulations that the post-1971 deregulation was to lift; it represents, to all intents and purposes, the victory of capitalism over the market economy. At Bretton Woods the drive towards consolidation prevailed over the criterion of settling accounts.

In the light of these considerations, the canonical explanation, which has it that the 'law of the strongest' prevailed at Bretton Woods, simply won't do. If things had really gone like that, there would be little point in historical investigation. If the widely acclaimed and often invoked 'law of the strongest' simply meant the factual predominance of whoever should at any time appear to offer the most effective support to power, there would be no need for international agreements, and certainly no need to study their history. If, on the other hand it refers – as is indeed quite possible – to the law dictated by the strongest in the name of sheer strength, the law of the strongest nevertheless remains a law, and is to be judged as such. But how is it to be judged, and by what standards?

It is not strength in itself that plays the dominant role, but a conception of strength or, even better, of power, which gives rise to a peculiar conception of finance. The preference shown by the United

States for liquidity reflects not so much the concern of the American administration, reprehensible or justifiable as it may be, for the unearned income of the dominant financial lobbies, as, at a deeper level, an unconditional and unwavering bias in favour of power – a bias which, being expressed in these terms, is neither blameworthy nor commendable but stands literally beyond good and evil. The bias in favour of power that lay behind the Bretton Woods decisions was such as to reflect the need, inescapable for any power-serving policy, not to separate the financing of trade from the financing of war. In fact, while the Bretton Woods negotiations saw the beginning of the end of one waged war, a new war (cold, admittedly, but nevertheless financially demanding) was looming on the horizon against the other candidate that upheld the power imperative, namely the Soviet 'superpower'. It was a war that, perhaps even more than the war then coming to an end, involved the demand for a liquidity that would be unconditionally available and capable of being created at will.

And yet this unconditional option in favour of potentially unlimited liquidity was not seen for what it was, but rather as a perfectly reasonable way of organizing economic and political relations in the West, in the name of freedom and growth.

What was it, then, that made this misleading appearance so convincing? The fact is that weighing on Bretton Woods were two centuries of monetary history tending – with practically no deviation – in the direction of making of liquidity not a problem, but a plain fact of life upon which to construct theories and monetary institutions.

This is why it is not enough to go 'back to Bretton Woods' – not even from the point of view of a historical reconstruction of the origins of the present crisis. In fact we are now faced with the task of tracing the history of a phenomenon that exploded like a sort of financial atomic bomb in the mid-twentieth century, but had already begun to gather momentum in the early days of the modern age. This will be our task in the next five chapters.

Exactly why liquidity and its enhancement seem to be the only possible form for the international financial system is an issue that will come fully to light only at the end of this second part of our exploration.

However, one question does arise immediately, and here it is. If the form had long been decided upon, why was it felt necessary to call for reform and convene an international conference for the purpose? Why, at the end of the Second World War, did the major powers of the West – which were also the leading economies, including notably the United Kingdom and United States – feel such an urgent need to sit down together and thrash out the rules of the international finance game?

Perhaps because, although the form was basically beyond discussion, the financial system had gone through years of evident malfunctioning. The crash of 1929 and its political and economic outcomes were still a painful memory. There was, at the very least, a state of disorder that needed putting aright without more delay.

This, in turn, prompts another question: what exactly was this state of disorder, from which one had to take one's distance when constructing the new post-war international monetary order? Again, to answer this question we must take yet a further step back, returning to the aftermath of the First World War and the financial imbalances that marked it so deeply. Analysis of these events, and of how they were interpreted and addressed, will help us to appreciate not only the concerns that motivated the architects of Bretton Woods, but also the reasons why no more than the façade of the building they had designed was eventually completed.

8

The standard crisis (1929)

The financial pattern that emerged at the end of the Second World War was largely dictated by the intention to avoid the errors made in the aftermath of the First World War and all their dramatic consequences, on the conviction that never so much as in this case would it have proved diabolical to persevere. Did this eventually turn out to be more than just a good intention? For sixty years one might have thought so. Today, however, in the face of a crisis that, as it deepens and spreads, brings 1929 ever more imperatively to mind as a historically comparable precedent, it is worth considering the question afresh. If, as we have sought to demonstrate in the preceding chapters, the origins of the present crisis can be traced back to incongruities in the system launched at Bretton Woods, then we may feel that the financial system might perhaps have been set on rather more solid bases on that occasion. Effectively, as we shall see, the errors made in the aftermath of the First World War were not corrected in the aftermath of the second: the approach was simply reversed. Economic nationalism was replaced with internationalism, deflation with inflation, and a 'loser pays all' with a 'winner pays all' principle.

While the interwar years had been plagued by nationalism – including economic nationalism – which took the form of increasingly violent mercantilist clashes in defence of national trading and production interests, and indeed of gold reserves, the Bretton Woods Conference came up with the primary commitment, as stated in the first point of the first article of the agreements, to 'promote international monetary cooperation through a permanent institution which provides the machinery for consultation and collaboration on international monetary problems'. If the deflationary pressure generated through the need to defend gold parity was a fundamental cause of the interwar depression, all the financial instruments adopted in the aftermath of the Second World War, within and outside the Bretton Woods system, were geared towards opening the way for an expansion of credit able, in turn, to fuel expansion in world trade. If, at the end of the First World War, the idea was to place the entire financial burden of reconstruction on the shoulders of the major defeated power, the Second World War ended with the major victorious power taking on the financial burden of recovery.

There can be no doubt about it: these various reversals of approach combined to open the way, at least for the first twenty-five years of the new system, for widespread economic growth, in stark contrast to the general stagnation of the preceding twenty-five years. Nevertheless, the risk is that the accolades generally attributed to these changes may cover up a feature that, by contrast, spans the two periods seamlessly – and that is, in a word, non-payment.

At the financial level, the settlement of both wars entailed – albeit in different ways – debts destined *not* to be paid. Despite the fact that the costs of peace were allocated according to diametrically opposite approaches, being nominally borne the first time round by the defeated, next time by the victor, in either case neither eventually paid. The international payment system brought in at the end of the First World War, like the system introduced at the end of the second, had rather all the appearances of a 'non-payment system' – a system, that is, in which accounts cannot be settled, or else the system itself would collapse; a system in which, if the demand for payment implies crisis, the impossibility of payment entails the impossibility of peace. Let us retrace the principal stages in the development of the international financial system between the two wars, highlighting those particular elements that lay behind both the Great Depression and the strategies adopted to address it.

At the end of the First World War, the terms of international financial relations were dictated by the Treaty of Versailles. The underlying principle was very simple: since all responsibility for the outbreak of the war was imputed to Germany, the entire cost of the war fell on its shoulders too. The reparations Germany was to pay to the victorious powers were to cover this cost, thereby enabling the Allies, in turn, to pay their war debts, contracted mainly with the United States. In this way the entire burden of adjusting the post-war financial imbalances was made to fall on the shoulders of the defeated country.

Attending the Versailles Conference as a young member of the British delegation, Keynes was severely critical of this approach.

Unable to change the course of negotiations, he resigned, and from the independent position thus gained he published a scathing indictment, in a pamphlet entitled *The Economic Consequences of the Peace*. For Keynes, this book marked the beginning of public recognition and, above all, of that quest for a rule to regulate international financial relations that he was to pursue for twenty-five years, culminating in the Bretton Woods Conference (which was to be for him, after Versailles, a second crushing defeat).

Keynes indicted the Treaty on the grounds that it was both unjust and inapplicable. It was unjust because, with the armistice that brought the war to an end, Germany had taken on the commitment to pay for war *damage*, whereas now, with the peace treaty, the country was compelled to pay all the *costs* – not only the cost of the destruction wrought by German attacks, but also the cost of the Allied attacks on Germany. The difference was enormous, both in quantitative and in symbolic terms. Moreover, Keynes saw the unilateral alteration of conditions previously agreed upon as a cynical violation of the sacrosanct status of international agreements, in the name of which the Allies had declared war on the invader of neutral Belgium.[1]

As pointed out above, Keynes found the Treaty not only unjust, but also inapplicable, since the sum demanded of Germany as reparation was discussed *without the least reference to the country's effective capacity to pay it*. Ultimately, any capacity that Germany may have had could only derive from a healthy balance of trade. Keynes's doubts about Germany's chances of accumulating even the slightest surplus were in fact well founded: even before the war Germany had been looking to a deficit, and the war effort, combined with the unfavourable conditions for peace, had seriously depleted the country's productive capacity. According to Keynes's calculations, the reparations demanded of Germany exceeded by far the most optimistic expectations for the recovery of German competitiveness.

Worse still, the actual sum of the reparations remained undecided, while a special commission had been set up to establish the terms of payment. This commission was formally invested with the prerogatives of an arbitrator; its task was to settle all the questions left pending by the treaty, but it was effectively constituted by representatives of the victorious countries, who defended their own interests.[2] Entrusting the interested parties with the execution of the treaty and hence with the definition of post-war financial relations, was hardly likely not to compromise the ternary structure required in order not only to pass impartial judgement, but also to guarantee that relations between debtors and creditors are settled on fair terms of payment. Thus, already in 1919 (as was to happen also in 1944 and 1971, from what we have seen), despite the common etymology, the idea was to secure *peace* without creating the conditions for the due *payment*.

While continuing to pay lip service to the wisdom of von Clausewitz, the Treaty of Versailles implied a radical inversion of his celebrated maxim: the peace treaty was a continuation of war by other means – not diplomatic, but financial. The economic consequences of the peace contributed to ensuring that the 'war to end all wars' would be but the beginning of an endless series of wars. War knows no end until a way is found to peace. And peace would require that the opposing parties be able to reach a settlement *at the financial level, too*, in the form of a possible payment.

What interest could the victorious countries possibly have had in devising and imposing an impossible payment and an unfeasible peace? One motive was certainly the spirit of revenge, which animated in particular the French delegation led by Clemenceau: he set out to humiliate the defeated enemy by having the treaty signed in the same Hall of Mirrors where Kaiser Wilhelm had received the imperial crown at the end of the Franco-Prussian War. The 'Carthaginian peace' denounced by Keynes appeared to have the deliberate aim of destroying the Central Powers, cancelling them from the political, if not from the physical map of Europe. Moreover, for both the French and the British governments, *révanche* was the way to accomplish the explicit electoral duty of making Germany pay for the war and for reconstruction, thereby keeping power at home.

However, there were also considerations of international finance that counted as much as, if not actually more than, national policy. In fact the war had left the victorious countries, too, with a heavy burden of debts, particularly to the United States (see Table II 8.1). Since the US was not ready to forego repayment of its credits, which accounted for about a half of the total, the European Allies regarded German reparations as an indispensable source of income towards meeting their commitments.[3] The issue of reparations was thus doubly bound up with the problem of inter-Allied debts, which meant that the whole picture of post-war financial relations had to be viewed in terms of settlement not simply between the victorious and the defeated, but, more complicatedly, between creditors and debtors.

Table II 8.1 International debts at the end of the First World War (millions of pounds sterling)

Creditor country:	United States	United Kingdom	France	Total
Debtor country:				
United Kingdom	842	–	–	842
France	550	508	–	1058
Italy	325	467	35	827
Russia	38	568	160	766
Belgium	80	98	90	268
Serbia and Yugoslavia	20	20	20	60
Other allies	35	79	50	164
Total	1900	1740	355	3995

Source: J. M. Keynes, *The Economic Consequences of the Peace* [1919], in *The Collected Writings of John Maynard Keynes*, 1971–89. London and Cambridge: Macmillan and Cambridge University Press, vol. 2, p. 172.

The huge mountain of international debts appeared, at least to Keynes, as the potentially explosive, destabilizing legacy of the war, and it had to be defused. The solution he favoured entailed lightening the burden of debts, and this was to be achieved in the least unfair and indiscriminate way possible:

> The war has ended with every one owing every one else immense sums of money. [. . .] A general bonfire is so great a necessity that unless we can make of it an orderly and good-tempered affair in which no serious injustice is done to any one, it will, when it comes at last, grow into a conflagration that may destroy much else as well.[4]

Keynes also suggested a possible way of lightening the debts, so as to make them payable: not through partial cancellation, but through an adjustment of the purchasing power of the unit of account that would allow for them to be paid entirely.[5] In other words, to lighten the burden of the debts to be paid, it would have sufficed for the unit of account in which the debts were denominated to be set so as to correspond to a lesser quantity of goods. In some notes of a historical nature penned in the same months, Keynes observed that this change might be achieved in two alternative ways: either through an inflation of the means of payment or through a variation in the legal ratio between the unit of account and the material support of the means of exchange.[6] In the years immediately after the end of the First World War, the widespread inflation in many countries of Europe, which produced dramatic peaks of hyper-inflation in Germany itself, would show how tremendously and indiscriminately destructive the former option was. In his treatise on monetary reform of 1923, Keynes himself, having described the dire economic and social consequences of inflation, had no hesitation in recommending the second option, in the hope that the regulation of the value of money be subject to deliberate decision on scientific bases, rather than to chance fluctuations and traumatic upheavals.[7]

In the following chapters we will see that it was precisely the regulation of the ratio between the unit in which debts were denominated and the means for their payment that constituted the essential prerogative of monetary authority before the gold standard was brought in.[8] We will also see, however, that, from the moment of its identification with gold, the monetary standard could no longer be considered a variable to be decided upon, regulated as a matter of policy, so as to allow for debts to be paid. In the immediate aftermath of the war the major concern of all the industrialized countries was rather to restore as soon as possible a fixed parity of their unit of account in terms of gold; they wanted to bring back convertibility, which had been suspended on the eve of the war, in the hope that a return to the gold standard would set the global economy back on the path of integration and growth, which it had steadily pursued during the preceding period.

Ironically enough, however, the return to gold after the war proved more of a hindrance than a factor of expansion. The countries of Europe set about stuffing their coffers and this reduced the amount of gold available for world trade and for international investments. On the other hand, the demand for international loans had grown, not only to finance reconstruction but also to refinance war debts, and this contributed to keeping interest rates high in Europe. With the waning of the initial drive towards reconstruction, which had afforded ample returns, the high level of interest rates discouraged new investments, and the gold standard ended up by generating structural deflationary pressure on trade and production.

Chronic shortage of international currency was the constitutional weakness that marked both post-war periods; as the second was afflicted by a *dollar shortage*, so the first had suffered from what we might call a *gold shortage*. The solution to the problem, too, was analogous: in both cases the idea was to boost the monetary base by swelling currency reserves. In the interwar years, however, when the revival of the gold standard was a dominant theme, this meant making explicit exception to the technical principle and symbolic dogma of gold reserves. The way was opened with the 1922 Genoa Conference: Resolution 9 established that, in order to save gold and replace it in the reserves, the central banks would be allowed to hold foreign currency to cover their respective national currencies. Thus the foundations were laid for the gold exchange standard – a system based on gold and foreign exchange ('exchange' referring here to foreign exchange).

With the gold exchange standard in place, national currencies convertible into gold could be used for reserve purposes, and thus as international currency. This not only answered to the problem of lack of international currency, but actually opened the way to multiplying it, and potentially with no limits. With a system based on gold the quantity of international currency is theoretically limited – at least over the long period – by the quantity of gold available. Every payment or loan from one country to another would entail a corresponding flow of gold in the same direction. Insofar as the rule implicit in the gold standard is respected, the result is a zero sum game: the second country gains what the first country loses. With the gold exchange standard, however, a country receiving a loan or a payment from another can accept the latter's currency without requiring its immediate conversion into gold, but redepositing it as reserve in the issuer's central bank. In this way the monetary base of the country at the receiving end increases proportionately to the increase in its currency reserves, *but with no reduction in the monetary base of the other country*. With the gold standard, international currency can only be transferred from one country to another through movements of gold, whereas under the *gold exchange* standard international *liquidity* can be created *ad libitum* through capital movements.

Given the superior competitiveness of the USA and the weakness of the European economies, drained as they were by war, the capital movements necessary for post-war recovery were largely from the USA to Europe. So here we have a further strand of continuity: in the aftermath of the First World War, as of the second, exchange rate stability and balance of payments equilibrium were ensured not so much through gold as the international means of payment of last resort as through the supply of US loans. Just like the Bretton Woods system, the interwar gold standard (with the little prosperity it brought) was made possible (for the little time it lasted) thanks solely to transatlantic capital movements.

Here, however, a point needs to be made clear: 'capital *movements*' is actually a misleading expression. Thanks to the gold exchange standard, the capital flowing into Europe was not in fact flowing out of the United States, but rather going through a process of duplication, which made it possible for the European recovery and for the US boom to be financed together and indiscriminately.[9]

The gold exchange standard endows the precious metal with the gift of ubiquity. At last the international currency could abound everywhere, giving rise simultaneously to the 'roaring twenties' in the United States and to the *goldene Zwanziger* in Germany. This was possible because, on the gold base it formally maintained, the gold exchange standard built a house of cards. In reality, the 'golden twenties' were paper years – years that saw growth secured only through a supply of credit as unlimited as it was unconditional. On a tiny pivot of gold, the new-found optimism pulled the credit lever.

Thus the economic growth of the 1920s spread on a wave of liquidity. Optimistic expectations appeared to be justified and reinforced by the recovery and growth that credit had fired. Technological progress and mass production held a promise of affluence that knew no limits and no borders. Finance itself was renewed and democratized. In this respect there can be no doubt about the absolute relevance of a comparison between the 1920s and the 1990s.[10]

Then as now, the extraordinary expansion – not only financial, but also real – afforded by the growth of liquidity tended to hide the ambiguity of the monetary system upon which it was built. Indeed, it thrived on this concealment. But, now as then, the question remains: how was it possible that the same monetary system could have been underlying both the expansion of the 1920s and the depression of the 1930s? This, in effect, is the paradox we must address and bring to light, by reading between the lines of a book by Barry Eichengreen, *Golden Fetters*, considered fundamental on this period: from 1929 on the gold standard became a 'golden fetter' that played its part in aggravating and propagating the crisis, and yet until then it had been serving as a growth factor. 'So long as American lending continued, the gold standard remained viable and did not pose a threat to prosperity.'[11] But how can a source of prosperity also be a factor in bringing on crisis?

Let us briefly outline Eichengreen's reconstruction: the gold exchange standard, he argues, is expansive as long as the emphasis is placed on *exchange*, and assets in foreign currency – dollars and pounds sterling, in particular – are accepted as means of payment and as international reserve; on the other hand, it proves restrictive when the stress falls on *gold*, and no currency is accepted other than gold.

So we come back to the basic question: how and when does the reversal take place? When and how does liquidity dry up?[12] If the event proved unexpected and inexplicable for contemporaries, historians should ideally be able to get a better grasp on it. It simply will not do, especially in the course of historical reconstruction, to settle for a mere chronicle of the events. The point that needs to be brought out is that prosperity can only reign at the expense of stability, which is tantamount to saying that crisis is *preceded* by loss of equilibrium. In other words, what needs to be brought into focus is the intrinsic instability of a system that, in phases of expansion and contraction alike, finds support in a self-referential circularity.

In the gold exchange standard, gold and currency reserves – *gold* and *exchange* – were bound together in a *circular relationship*. This is the crucial point. Gold could remain at the base of the national and international monetary systems only by virtue of a surrogate in the form of reserves in foreign currency, made available in turn through capital movements. At the same time, these capital movements were themselves made possible only through their anchoring on gold, which protected international financial relations from exchange rate risk and encouraged the accumulation of currency reserves. The currencies' gold parities were at the same time the condition for, and an effect of, capital movements. It was, therefore, precisely thanks to the strange 'equilibrium' implied by the gold exchange standard that financial investments could flourish without a base – that is, without any reference to fundamentals: in short, with no possibility of distinguishing between good and bad investments. Even before leading up to the crisis itself and to the consequent depression, the gold exchange standard was therefore responsible for the speculative bubble that preceded and opened the way to it. As Rueff remarked: 'the gold-exchange standard was one of the major causes of the wave of speculation that culminated in the September 1929 crisis'.[13]

Giving due account to the self-referential structure of the system, it is in fact hardly surprising that the causes of the crisis *coincided* with the causes of the boom. The year 1929 was not only the year of the crisis, but also the year between the two wars that saw the greatest number of countries subscribing to the gold standard in one form or another.[14] In the expansive and in the implosive phases alike, the problem was not so much gold in itself as the loans supplied on the basis of the gold clause implicit in the gold standard. The conditions for crisis to break out and spread on the global scale were created by inflation in the international and national means of payment, which, paradoxically, was made possible by what should have prevented it: the identification of money with gold.

Just as it acted in the expansive phase, so the multiplying effect of the gold exchange standard also acted at the beginning of the recessionary phase. It took no more than a minor adjustment of US monetary policy, which became restrictive in 1928, to bring on the collapse of the delicate financial relations upon which the previous expansion had been built: with the sudden contraction of credit, the speculative bubble on Wall Street shrank abruptly; attempts by the producer countries to make up for the reduction in foreign loans through an increase in exports sent the prices of raw materials plunging; and the US capital invested in Europe returned home. The crisis arose from the impossibility of regulating, with just one lever – the interest rate – three markets – of credit to internal production, of credit to financial investments and of international credit – since interest rates could not be maintained at differential levels given the mobility of capital.

As soon as the restrictive policy began to have effect – and, let it be noted, the *desired* effect, deliberately pursued by the US monetary policy authorities, of putting an end to the apparently excessive increase in share prices – the wave of falling prices inexorably rolled and swept everything, from the financial sector to the real sector, from one country to another, knowing no limits or borders. Share price inflation instantly gave way to generalized and equally inordinate deflation:

> The immediate causes of the financial panic – for that is what it is – are obvious. They are to be found in a catastrophic fall in the money value not only of commodities but of practically every kind of asset – a fall which has proceeded to a point at which the assets, held against money debts of every kind including bank deposits, no longer have a realisable value equal to the amount of the debt. We are now in the phase where the risk of carrying assets with borrowed money is so great that there is a competitive panic to get liquid. And each individual who succeeds in getting more liquid forces down the price of assets in the process of getting liquid, with the result that the margins of other individuals are impaired and their courage undermined. And so the process continues [. . .] The competitive struggle for liquidity has now extended beyond individuals and institutions to nations and governments.[15]

The effects of the credit freeze proved every bit as transmissible and indiscriminate as the effects of expansion had been. In either case it was the liquidity of investments that set off the chain reaction.

Deflation was able to spread from one sector to another only because falling prices prompted the immediate sale of assets, and so only because these assets were held in liquid form; in other words, they had been acquired *only because they were saleable*. The national monetary freeze was transmissible on the international scale only because the hike in the US discount rate brought capital flowing back from Europe, and therefore only to the extent to which capital movements took the form of short-term or portfolio investments and not of direct investments during the boom.

If the immediate causes of the crisis are to be attributed to deflation, the remedies to which the countries hit by it made immediate resort were worse than the problem, only contributing to exacerbate it. Just as the financial agents who sought to defend their portfolios by selling securities, anxious about their possible depreciation, eventually brought about a general collapse in their prices, so the states that sought to defend their credit and trade by adopting restrictive monetary policies and protectionist trading policies eventually triggered a general contraction in global finance and trade.

The first faltering steps out of the maelstrom were taken only with a later and decisive turnaround, by responding to deflation with reflation (although it was only through rearmament that real recovery got under way). From 1932, one after another, all the countries that had subscribed to the gold standard over the previous decade abandoned it and, having thrown off the 'golden fetters', were able to stride along the road leading to monetary and fiscal expansion. Nevertheless, here again, switching direction did not mean correcting mistakes. Behind the apparent discontinuity there lurked two fundamental features that continued to characterize the financial system structurally, regardless of the cyclical fluctuations it generated.

The first feature of the financial system that characterized not only the whole of the 1930s (and quite obviously so), but also reached back to the 1920s and remains a fact of economic life even now, is the *contraposition* between national and international interests. Although lifting the anchor from gold freed the various states from the need to defend their gold reserves, the transition to expansive policies did not entail a slackening in international economic contrasts. The competition in hoarding gold was over, but competition went on even more keenly for the control of supply and outlet markets. The standard for measurement had changed, but not the basic drive: growth remained the one essential condition for the stability and survival of the national economic systems. As the decade rolled on, expansive policy increasingly took the form of rearmament policy. The way out of the financial crisis led to war finance. From this point of view, continuity with the successive bids for peace in the course of the twentieth century appears perfectly seamless: just as the New Deal was the prelude to war finance, so Bretton Woods was the prelude to cold war finance, and the end of Bretton Woods was the prelude to global preventive war finance.

The second permanent feature of the financial system, from the crisis of '29 to the present crisis, is liquidity. The interwar years showed liquidity in all its possible guises: inflation, hyper-inflation, credit and financial inflation, generalized deflation and reflation. Over and above all the differences in terms of effects, inflation and deflation, growth and crisis, at this point appear simply as *the two faces of liquidity*. Within this perspective, all the stages we have so far covered by moving back from the present crisis can be seen as a unique attempt to avert the crisis by continually raising the stakes, in what appears to be mounting waves of liquidity: eighty years of crisis management, from 1929 to 2009, without ever arriving at a real solution.

It should by now be clear that, whatever the immediate and circumstantial causes may be, in every crisis that takes the form of a 'liquidity crisis' a far deeper cause is at work, without which no such crisis would be possible. In fact, if there is to be such an abundance or such a scarcity of liquidity as to give rise to a bubble or a crisis, the prime condition is *that there be liquidity*. A liquidity crisis can only arise where there is liquidity.

The catalyst for the 1929 crisis and the channel for contagion is, beyond doubt, the gold exchange standard, as Eichengreen argues – but not on account of the gold; rather the effect was due to the capital movements it enabled, which at the same time supported it. The problem with the gold exchange standard was precisely the relationship between *gold* and *exchange*, in other words between two standards meant to cohere through convertibility, which were in reality competing through liquidity.

One might, of course, argue that the gold base rests on credit, in the form of international capital movements. On the other hand, however, had it not been for the public declaration identifying the monetary standard with a quantity of gold, the capital movements could not have taken place.

If this is the way things stand, then we must make the hypothesis that there is no discontinuity, on this plane, between the pre-war and the post-war gold standard. This supposition contrasts with the well-established idea of the gold standard as a system firmly anchored on the gold base, and hence immune to all the forms of instability related to '*fiat* money'. But was the age of the gold standard truly the golden age of money?

9

Orchestra rehearsal. The international gold standard and the dissolution of gold (1871)

The story is well known, or so it seems. The gold standard saw the light of day, almost by chance, in the United Kingdom at the beginning of the eighteenth century, and for a century and a half remained a national peculiarity of the British economic system; a peculiarity, moreover, thanks to which Great Britain was able to build up an 'avant-garde' financial system, at least in the sense that it was able to finance, simultaneously and inextricably, the country's economic advance and the military construction of its empire – in a word, to underpin the engineering of its hegemony. From the 1870s, the gold standard became the international monetary system through which the first western, colonial and Eurocentric globalization reached the threshold of the first globalized war (Figure II 9.1).

Beginning with Germany, in 1871, the major European and extra-European countries subscribed to the gold standard one by one, committing themselves to immutable gold convertibility for their units of account and thereby giving rise to a system of fixed exchange rates; in practice, this meant attributing gold with the function of unit of measure, means of payment and *international reserve*.

Unlike its attempted reincarnations after the two world wars, the 'classical' gold standard was at that time a system based *officially* on the prompt and direct convertibility into gold of *all* the currencies of the countries subscribing to it. This, too, is well known, or at any rate it seems to be. Had this been the actual state of affairs, we would have had a monetary system able to provide a means of international payment of last resort for all debts: in other words, a system designed to make the payment of debts possible, and therefore a system that retained the distinction between money and credit. Had it been so, we would have to conclude that the financial markets that were built

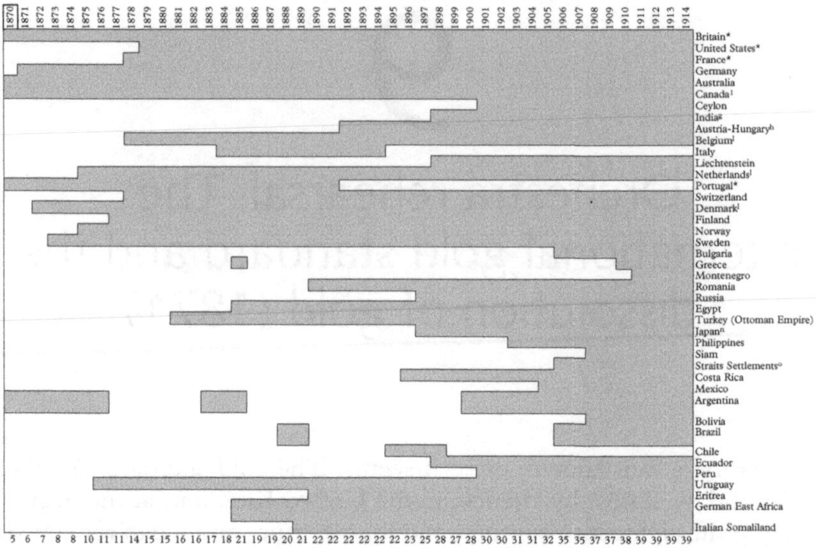

Figure II 9.1 Chronology of accession to the gold standard

Source: L. H. Officer, 'Gold Standard', in R. Whaples (ed.), *EH.Net Encyclopedia of Economic and Business History*, available at http://eh.net/encyclopedia/article/officer.gold.standard (accessed 14 May 2011)

on the foundations of the gold standard as international monetary system and that opened the way to what has been called, with good reason, the first globalization were not really based on the principle of liquidity that we have seen at work so far, the ultimate effect of which was to preclude settlement between debtors and creditors, the end of finance. It would then have been true that, as Rueff argued, with the gold standard every disequilibrium must be paid for by an effective transfer of gold.

And yet it seems to be equally well known that the international gold standard was *at the same time* a 'sterling standard',[1] in other words a system in which all countries were, of course, obliged to ensure convertibility of their currencies into gold, but provision was made for different ways of doing it depending on whether their currency was the sterling or not.

The sterling was in fact not only the British national currency, but also the currency normally used in international transactions. This meant that it was also held by non-British agents outside the United Kingdom, not so much in the form of banknotes or gold coin as in the form of bank deposits denominated in sterling, held by foreigners in

British banks. Thanks to this twofold position of the sterling, which reflected the hegemonic, economic and imperial position of Great Britain, the country was able to cope with the deficits that might arise in its balance of payments not in a state of passive acceptance of the outflow of its own gold, as the rules would have required, but actively, by adjusting the Bank of England discount rate so as to attract larger volumes of deposits. Thus, while all the other countries had to possess gold to make up for their deficits, as long as the gold standard was in place the United Kingdom enjoyed the possibility to borrow gold from other countries, or at least to avoid its outflow from the Bank of England coffers by raising the discount rate – in other words by adjusting the financial parameter par excellence, the rate of interest. So it was that the 'gold-sterling standard' took the form of a game that admitted exceptions to the rules – exceptions granted, precisely and indeed only, to the regulator of the game, in the name of the credibility and centrality that the regulator had acquired and that, as long as everything worked, tended to reinforce each other reciprocally.

'Exception: Say that it confirms the rule. Do not venture to say how.' Thus wrote Flaubert a few years before the birth of the international gold standard. Nevertheless, it would be useful to be able to say how; for, while the plain fact of the exceptionality represented by sterling is generally recognized as such, it still remains to be seen how this fact relates to the golden rule. Despite the dispensations from gold backing granted to the sterling in certain circumstances, the latter still had to have its gold convertibility guaranteed if the system was to survive, and yet this convertibility could not be sustained without continual and increasing recourse to dispensation.

In short, not only did the gold money system enjoying official sanction have an unofficial *alter ego*, but what emerges strikingly at a closer look into how the system actually worked is the impossibility of distinguishing, at the practical level, between official façade and dispensation.

The gold standard was effectively to last as long as the guarantee offered by sterling convertibility was held credible. In this sense the sterling standard 'was', to all intents and purposes, the international gold standard from 1871 to 1914. But what did this credibility rest upon? Certainly not the volume of Bank of England reserves, which were traditionally slender and grew increasingly poorer as the years went by. What, then?

The question is usually settled thus: rules are respected over the long period but broken in the short. Such is the interpretation suggested, by way of identifying a sort of middle ground between spirit of compromise and dialectical approach, for example by Charles Kindleberger, and readily embraced also by Barry Eichengreen:

> Central banks could deviate from the rules of the game because their commitment to the maintenance of gold convertibility was credible. Although it was possible to find repeated violations of the rules over periods as short as a year, over longer intervals central banks' domestic and foreign assets moved together. Central banks possessed the capacity to violate the rules of the game in the short run because *there was no question* about obeying them in the long run.[2]

A fair explanation, perhaps, but it holds good only if the relationship linking the long and the short term is known – a condition that, in the specific case of Eichengreen and Kindleberger, we may reasonably doubt. The odd situation that emerges is, in fact, that of a long period growing ever longer, reaching out to the time when the faith invoked by Eichengreen, finds its reward – if not in eternal life, at least in gold conversion. . .

It was in connection with this odd situation, in which the exception seems to confirm the rule only as long as the dogmatic conviction persists that it must sooner or later (preferably later) confirm it, that Keynes first introduced – with a touch of irony, actually – the expression 'rules of the game'.[3]

And what game was the gold standard playing? Could it have been a game that consisted in managing not to apply the rules upon which it was based, while making it look as if they had been respected? In any case, if this was the game, the need would have been not so much for a master (at that time Great Britain was the greatest colonial power in the world) as for a *leader*, or, to take another image from Keynes, a 'conductor of the orchestra' who may lead all the others through this score and, above all, provide the appropriate indications for what *cannot be written* in it. And yet, to follow through with the metaphor and to look beyond it, in the case of the gold standard there is a difference; it is as if, in the very act of projecting the 'symphony' from the printed score, the conductor – the Bank of England – were to throw awry the very conditions for the orchestra to produce a sound: at some point everything begins to 'sound strange'. As in Fellini's *Orchestra Rehearsal* [*Prova d'orchestra*] (1978), the members of the orchestra begin to play on their own: the cacophony grows, and the conductor becomes increasingly groggy. Above all, at the end something happens that has nothing to do with the old order and ruins any chance of its being restored.

But let us take things in the right order. The first question to address is this: what made the countries of Europe adopt the British national system as the international system? There are reasons that had to do with British hegemony in the fields of international trade and finance. Until 1851, and in some respects until the 1870s, Great Britain was the locomotive to the economy of the western world. But, as it came to maturity in the mid-nineteenth century, certain undesirable effects began to be generated. The British balance of trade became structurally negative and was to remain so until 1914 (and after). At the same time, however, British financial capacity went on growing, and capital that was now finding its rewards dwindling at home started to seek new outlets abroad, mainly in the form of direct investments and in the financing of international trade, in particular trade in raw materials. At the same time the countries of Europe to begin with, then certain extra-European countries, notably the USA and Japan, set off on a road of no return, from their traditional economic systems to industrialization. As a result of the changes that modernization brought to these countries, their economic stability came to depend on growth, and growth depended increasingly on their capacity to find outlets for trade abroad.

Effectively, having been liberalized in the years before the adoption of the gold standard and subsequently subjected to ever stronger protectionist measures from the 1870s on, international trade went on growing, and with it technology transfers through foreign direct investments. Given this state of affairs, in which the wealth produced by one country was very often sold beyond its borders while for the emerging countries the conditions for such production depended increasingly on international loans, the whole business of the international transfer of trade surpluses and capital gains generated the need for certainty in the measurement of these transfers. The need was for an exchange rate system characterized by certainty; and it seemed then that only fixed rates could ensure this certainty. Thus, in the current realities and power relations, given the initial British gold standard option and a British banking system able to underpin the expansion of trade and international finance, it seems natural enough for the convergence to fixed exchange rates to have been based on gold at the expense of silver – the other traditional money metal. With the progressive abandonment of silver, in which Germany led the way, the price of this metal dipped in favour of gold. This rendered bimetallic systems – which were based on a gold/silver conversion ratio fixed by law and hence were always inclined to rate gold below its commercial price – always more exposed to gold shortages. The upshot was that, without any international conference to establish it, convergence on gold won the day. Not only the industrial world and its colonial ramifications, but also the emerging extra-European countries became gold monometallists.

As historians unanimously recognize, short of the discovery of new gold deposits, the effect of such a convergence should tend to be deflationary. Having become the currency of the planet, gold should tend to come short of the volume of payments it was required to sustain. Thus the structural effect of the gold system should, according to the quantity equation of money, be a price deflation – above all, if gold were used unconditionally, as means of payment of the last resort. However, as Keynes pointed out, this structural and purely quantitative effect can be countered by the ways in which money is or is not spent, in other words by 'the habits of the public in the use of money and of banking facilities and the practices of the banks in respect of their reserves'.[4] Effectively in this period the commercial banks reduced their gold reserves, relying on the respective central banks for their financing needs, while one central bank – the Bank of England – operated in such a way as to reduce its gold reserves to a minimum. If the problem about the gold standard was its deflationary tendency, the function of the banking system, and in particular of the British system hinging on the regulatory role of the Bank of England, was, as Marcello de Cecco points out, 'to retard rather than enhance the functioning of the free gold market, to "put sand in the wheels" of the international gold standard'.[5] We can get a better idea of this with the help of Figure II 9.2, which illustrates international clearing, in millions of pounds sterling, among the participants in international trade.

It was precisely the equivalence, decreed and unconditionally promised, between sterling and gold that made it possible to substitute, for gold, the promise of gold, in other words the sterling. What was taking shape on the basis of the United Kingdom's hegemonic position was the possibility of securing a global sustainability of the British structural trade deficits through their financing by means of credit instruments, hence by avoiding payment in gold, as the rules would have officially required. In this way the United Kingdom, in permanent trade deficit but richly endowed with capital, whether (increasingly less) its own or (increasingly) borrowed, was able to become the pivot in the triangulation illustrated in Figure II 9.2. The trade credits of the countries from which it imported most were not paid in gold, but took the form of assets in sterling deposited in the City. Thus the City had enough money at its disposal to finance

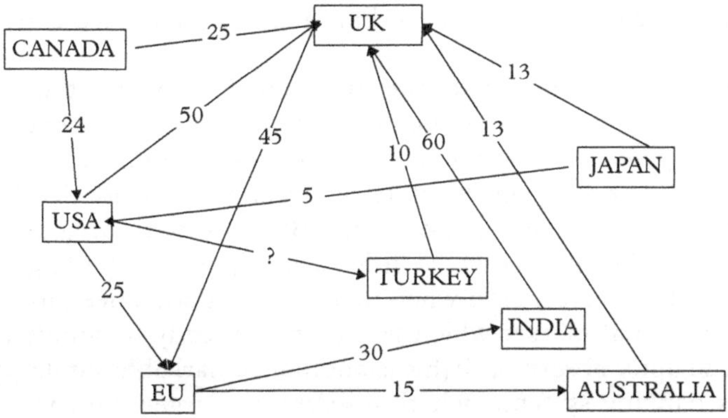

Figure II 9.2 Triangulation of international payments
Source: M. de Cecco, *Moneta e impero. Il sistema finanziario internazionale dal 1890 al 1914.* Torino: Einaudi, 1979, p. 35.

both the international trade in raw materials and the long-term direct investments in the 'emerging economies'. This financing generated for the United Kingdom a financial income in excess of the interest it had to pay on the borrowed funds – in short, it enabled the UK to exercise international seignorage. Thanks to this seignorage, the United Kingdom was able to even out its imbalances: the countries it financed obtained the sterling they needed for repayments from the proceeds from trade with countries that had a positive balance of trade with the United Kingdom. The triangulation was thus completed, as shown in the figure.

In this way, thanks to the overall equilibrium in the British balance of payments, the sterling maintained a credible convertibility. At the same time, however, this equilibrium held only as long as the sterling assets were not effectively converted into gold. Thus sterling convertibility was structurally based on its non-conversion.

It was on this ambiguous basis that the financial powerhouse of the British Empire was able to guarantee international liquidity in sterling as a surrogate for gold. The sterling was a surrogate of gold not simply in the sense of *temporarily* substituting it until conversion, but rather as a permanent surrogate, and as such *not structurally limited* by the quantity of gold effectively held in reserve in the Bank of England coffers. What we have already seen in the case of liquidity (the fact, that is, that when expectations are favourable the liquidability of the securities makes their liquidation inexpedient and disadvantageous), we see here at an even more elementary level:

trust in the convertibility of sterling makes its effective conversion useless.

In this way the squaring of the circle – in other words the completion of the accounting triangulation – creates the practical possibility of a *global financial lever* anchored on Britain's official commitment to guaranteeing the convertibility of sterling into gold. As the gold standard became a global system, the British system became 'highly leveraged and came to own as little cash as possible, finding it more convenient to borrow cash when there was a sudden need for it from an international market which was ever less ready to supply it'.[6] As de Cecco aptly observes, '[t]his is another remarkable similarity with today's banking systems, where reserves are largely borrowed from the market'.[7]

Just why the international market was to grow increasingly reluctant to grant this type of loan is a point we must return to later on. However, we already have all the evidence we need to understand the rationale for that exception, so fundamental for the gold standard, represented by the Bank of England discount rate manoeuvre. Insofar as sterling systematically leveraged the gold that was supposed to cover it, the possibility arose that in certain circumstances the lack of overall coverage might suddenly emerge, in full view, as potentially unsustainable; for example, if foreign holders of sterling assets in the City called for them to be converted, as they had every right to do – say, to pay creditors no longer prepared to accept sterling. In this case the British response was, systematically, a hike in the Bank of England discount rate. Right up to the '80s – as long as France retained the bimetallic system, and hence was more readily inclined to lend quantities of gold that it could make up for internally through increased recourse to silver – even a fairly modest rise in the British discount rate could rapidly lead to a shipment of gold, possibly quite substantial, from France to Great Britain. In part this was due to the mediation of the Rothschild House, which presided over the international gold market and had branches in both countries.

At least at the beginning, the credit 'sand' thrown into the gold standard's monetary works did not jam the mechanism but, on the contrary, allowed both for trade and capital movements to expand and for stability to be maintained.

So, was it all hunky-dory? If we take it to have been so, we are immediately faced with the problem of trying to understand why this system could not go on indefinitely – why, indeed, it came to an end *before* the war made the unofficial suspension of gold convertibility politically acceptable. In the contrary case, the problem is to explain how it could have lasted so long. How can we get round this dilemma? Perhaps simply by recognizing that the question is not framed in the right terms. Before any possible judgement on the 'soundness' of the system, what needs to be addressed is the formidable question of the relationship between the rule and the exception that it incorporated. We must ask in the first place whether the system might have been able to function only by *systematically eroding* the foundations of its functioning, and by opening the way, *already* as gold standard, to that blurring of distinctions between money and credit that came about, through the historical sequence of events we have retraced, in 1971, with the final demonetization of gold.

What, after all, was the gold standard? Was it a monetary system designed to make payment possible, or a credit system designed to make it deferrable? Or was it neither of these, but rather a system that began, on the sly and in spite of the mystique of gold, to reshuffle the cards, literally mixing gold and paper together?

In more technical terms, the problem raised with the word 'paper' here is not so much one about using paper money as a substitute for gold in national circulation, as one about the *status* of foreign deposits in sterling in the City. What are they to be seen as, money or credit? And, in the latter case, whose credit? Given that '[t]he City had traditionally worked on borrowed funds, which its specialised intermediaries transformed into instruments of international trade and finance',[8] we can only say that the foreign assets in sterling are, simultaneously and ambiguously, debts of Great Britain, international currency and the basis upon which the credit supplied by the British banks is constructed.

The more global the system becomes, the more the costs of its ambiguity emerge; insofar as it functions, it attracts new partners without any need of formal agreement, but to the extent that the system attracts new partners, switching between rule and exception under the counter becomes increasingly difficult for the 'conductor' to pull off:

> British relative industrial and agricultural decline in these decades is well known. Much less known is the challenge the adoption of the Gold Standard by most advanced and developing countries represented for Great Britain. That is considered by most monetary historians as a positive step towards world monetary equilibrium. But was it really positive for the world and for Great Britain?[9]

We can answer de Cecco's question with another observation of his, although we will have to go rather deeper into it:

> The rise of organized finance in the rest of the modernized world thus enlarged *but also reduced* Britain's capacity to 'conduct the international orchestra' as it was supposed to do, *just in those years when such an orchestra was supposed to have played at its best.*[10]

If the gold standard was the measure, the countries subscribing to it had to commit themselves to convertibility for their currency, which meant taking it upon themselves to accumulate gold as a monetary base. At the same time, however, they should also be committed to selling it *on credit*, in response to rises in the Bank of England discount rate in support of sterling convertibility as the international currency.

And yet the fact remains that credit can be granted as an economic operation only as long as the conditions for its repayment are still within sight.

It might be argued, at least theoretically, that, insofar as the British interest rates proved *equivalent* in the long run to the *effective returns* on the investments thus financed, they could constitute the basis both for the stability of the gold standard and for the expansive capacity of the sterling standard. And yet, by its very definition and the way in which it was fixed, the discount rate could not reflect *real* returns, but only the extent to which Great Britain was compelled to attract funds with a view to the exercise of its global *financial* function.

Starting from the years that were to have seen the gold standard triumphing, what we actually see is the difficulty the British had in attracting funds. This difficulty was due to the very fact that the emerging economies subscribing to the gold standard were of necessity compelled to accumulate reserves sufficient to sustain their economic development without compromising the solidity of their credit systems or the stability of their exchange rates. The effect was that the only rules that were to be respected – the rules of the gold standard – tended to make the system implode on itself.

The example of United States is representative enough for all. This was an emerging economy or, to be more precise, a competitor accumulating positions of advantage over Great Britain. It was from this position that, from the 1870s onwards, the USA set about more and more systematically to drain Great Britain of its gold and, above all, to hoard it, thereby making it necessary to raise the discount rate progressively in order to make it flow back to London. The credit exception to the monetary rule became increasingly important.

In its efforts to stem the flow, Great Britain could seek temporary relief by resorting to an exception that could no longer be seen as economic, but was *blatantly colonial*: the exploitation of the subordinate position of India. This colonial possession was compelled by the British to remain on a silver footing. Thanks to the competitive advantage of a silver rupee, which was subject to continual devaluation as a result of the free fall of silver prices, India was able to accumulate huge trade surpluses, which were promptly translated into gold and equally promptly piled up in London in the form of bank deposits and state securities. And even where relations were not, strictly speaking, colonial, as was the case with Japan, the 'task' unofficially assigned to the country in question was to 'buy pounds sterling' through export of its products and to redeposit them in London – in return, for example, for British support in the war against Russia.

On the whole, however, given that the British satellites could only be squeezed so much and no more, it was the implosive tendencies that eventually won out. From the 1890s, deposits had to be attracted from other countries as well – countries not driven by colonial power relations but pursuing market interests against the tide of worsening diplomatic relations between the countries of Europe.

As the other central banks were growing ever more loath to lend to the Bank of England, the discount rate could increasingly be seen for what it really was: a purely self-referential variable, which served the sole purpose of permitting the system simply to *continue*. In other words it was to perpetuate the ambiguous relationship between gold and sterling, but at the cost of its *stability*, which implied nothing more – but also nothing less – than the fact that gold could effectively serve as means of payment. The gold standard – a system *based on gold* – could remain viable only if gold departed ever further from its position as base.

Thus emerges, *in statu nascenti*, a tension that, as we have seen, was to pervade all the subsequent systems: the tension between the imperative of growth and the imperative of stability. If it had actually played its monetary role to the full, gold would have had a deflationary effect; by supplying the international offer of money and credit and by exceeding the quantitative limits imposed by the physical supply of gold, the gold-convertible sterling made it an increasingly chancy undertaking to guarantee the conditions for stability, which, in the case of the gold standard, meant the conditions for its own convertibility – or, in the last analysis, the conditions for the doctrinal and institutional foundations on which the entire system was built.[11]

The crises that began to punctuate the final phases of the gold standard in the early years of the twentieth century, and in particular the crisis of 1907, only brought to light the fundamental instability underlying the system, which appeared now as the inevitable concomitant of a system that lived on the erosion of its own foundations.

These crises took the form of a 'competitive struggle for liquidity', and, in a system officially founded on the identification of money with just one metal, this translated into a *competitive struggle for gold.* When crisis broke out, gold suddenly appeared to be no longer substitutable with assets denominated in sterling; by the same token, and no less suddenly, sterling ceased to be seen as a substitute for gold. Such was the case in 1907, and all the more so in the crisis that broke out in the early days of the summer of 1914, when war still seemed far from inevitable. Still enjoying the status of long-term net creditor, in the short term London was, however, a creditor only for New York, but a debtor for the rest of the world. A stock exchange crisis on the continent raised the need for the funds deposited in London. London tried to cope with the situation by closing its New York positions but, faced with the moratorium announced by Wall Street, the City could only respond, in turn: 'The Gold Standard thus ended *before* war broke out, with a decision to *postpone payments* which was equivalent to a *suspension of convertibility*, even if the latter was never officially declared.'[12]

On the strength of this observation we can look to the future developments in our history, also tying in the points made in the previous chapters; at the same time we can also look still further back, raising a number of questions that will have to be answered in the following chapters. The leitmotif underlying these observations is the *relationship between finance and war.* Naturally, this does not mean conjuring up the cynical figure of the financier who sees war as something 'bad' only when it does not 'pay'. Nor does it mean, on the other hand, overlooking the fact that, where finance is constituted on the basis of the liquidity principle, the financial system is constructed in such a way as not *to be able to distinguish between war finance and peace finance.*

The tendency has always been to represent the end of the gold standard as a *consequence* of the outbreak of war. It was, as the story goes, the need to finance the war that dictated the declaration of *fiat* currency – as had happened at the dawn of the gold standard era in Great Britain, during the Napoleonic Wars. And it was, again, for this reason that, once peace was secured, the drift of common opinion was, as we have seen, to 'bring back gold'.

Things were, however, rather more complicated. *Well before* war broke out, the implosion of the gold standard was catalyzed by the *expectation* of war, which loomed ever more ominously from the end of the first decade of the twentieth century. In fact the countries of Europe tended to see in gold the only possible source of financing for the probable future conflict, and they set about piling it up *as such.* While the adoption of the gold standard has been seen, traditionally (but on the whole still widely), as a choice in favour of 'soft trade', a peaceable sort of choice, when war is impending gold comes to be seen not as a mere means to expand trade but as a *reserve for war*, or, better still, as a reserve of power.

The fact is that the gold-sterling standard opened the way to unprecedented financial integration. The international orchestra was able to play increasingly complicated scores, every member of the orchestra being able to count on every other. But now each one wanted to play his/her own music. It is in fact quite possible that the run towards gold, within such a closely interconnected system, contributed to the rapid deterioration of diplomatic relations that led to war. Financial interdependence could, on the one hand, lead to the indefinite maintenance of a state of peace, but it could also lead down a slippery slope to war, insofar as a competitive struggle for liquidity might become necessary, be it only at the level of probability. It was precisely this contention for gold that progressively undermined the system. By the summer of 1914 the shortage of gold to sustain the British financial lever had become chronic, and the official gold standard was no longer an unofficial gold-sterling standard but effectively no more than a sterling standard – while sterling had lost all *credible* appearances of being convertible.

The markedly Eurocentric and hierarchized world order was in fact the same political–financial 'order' that had promoted 'peace' and globalization throughout the nineteenth century, but that, in the same span of time, also produced a potentially explosive combination of conditions, apt to spark off global war in the form of class struggle, countries fighting for survival and, finally, contention between ideologies of survival and ideologies of power.

And yet, from a financial point of view, that very war was to disprove the

> pernicious proposition [. . .] that a people cannot take to war to achieve a just and sacrosanct national cause if it has not first put together a substantial war budget and if it does not belong to that group of rich countries said to have inexhaustible resources of money to draw upon.[13]

The paper debts that were decided upon, after the first few months, in order to finance a war of position and attrition *pulverized* gold and the importance of gold reserves in wartime, bearing out Einaudi's argument. This war was to reveal unprecedented relations with finance; described by Ernst Jünger as a 'total mobilization', it entailed the *possibility of indebtedness beyond all measure*, and thus the effective accumulation of that unprecedented mass of debts that, as we have seen, lay at the origin of the problem of reparations.

If war itself became a more likely prospect – since it was also being prepared for through financial manoeuvrings designed to amass gold with a view to warlike ends – the fact remains that, just as technology and industry opened the way to a highly interrelated and rapidly responsive financial system in the late nineteenth century, in the early twentieth century they rendered war largely independent of any preventive, calculated mobilization, to give it scope in the form of total mobilization. So much for gold! And so, while the idea of a *Blitzkrieg* rapidly faded away, the German general staff could flaunt the motto *Geld spielt keine rolle* ('Money doesn't matter'), and the director general of the bank of Italy would be able to proclaim in 1917: '[The bank] has shown awareness of the necessity, in the interest of the state, to produce banknotes with as much verve as the manufacturing companies have shown in producing bullets.'[14]

Apparently more 'rigorous' and 'sound' only in comparison with the systems that were to follow it, the gold standard nevertheless proved to be itself the source of its *economic* unsustainability, not so much because it provided for exceptions to an officially rigorous rule as, more precisely, because it constituted a system structurally incapable of distinguishing clearly between rule and exceptions.

The gold standard tended to erode the institutional conditions in terms of which it functioned as a monetary and financial system. On closer examination, the faults that Rueff tended to impute to the gold exchange standard and to the dollar standard, interpreted as a breach of the gold standard rules, were there right from the beginning, part and parcel of the very functioning of the gold standard.

So, how could this come about? Wherefrom did the impulse come that drove the gold standard, not so much to degenerate into something other than itself as, ultimately, to blur the distinction between its regular functioning and degeneration? On the basis of the points made so far, the perspective we must now take on the situation is twofold: on the one hand, the nature of money, and on the other hand the relationship between money and credit. There are, then, various other questions to be answered. How did that currency at the root of the gold standard – the gold currency – actually get constituted? What are the implications of identifying the currency with one single metal? And, finally, what was the currency like before the gold standard?

10

Money before and after the gold standard (1717)

The official birth of the gold standard dates to 1821; but in practice the standard had been around for over a century in the United Kingdom at that date. It was in 1717 that Sir Isaac Newton, director of the Royal Mint since the end of the preceding century, established the ratio on the basis of which the mint would convert ingots of gold into money and vice versa. This ratio was given in terms of a parity between the pound sterling and a quantity of gold – a parity that remained unchanged until Great Britain finally abandoned the gold standard in 1931.

However, rather than from dates, it is more useful to start from an incontestable fact and its corollary. What marks out the gold standard is the fact of its being the first entirely monometallic international monetary system in history. And, being based on one single metal, it was also the first monetary system that precluded a distinction between internal and international currency.

Both within the economic systems and in international trading relations, gold was *the* currency. This is a generally recognized characteristic; but, let it be noted, it is by no means tantamount to saying that *gold coins* constituted *a* means of payment.

The historical novelty of the gold standard lay in the fact that that with which debts were paid was no longer metal coins, normally minted in different metals, but *a quantity of gold equivalent to the debt* according to the predetermined parity. This historical novelty also implied a structural novelty, which was to prove more lasting than the gold standard itself. The fixed, immutable parity between the unit of account and its equivalent value in gold meant that, with the gold standard and only from its introduction, the functions of medium of exchange and unit of account were combined. Thus, underlying the empirical identification of the currency with gold, there was the structural and far more permanent identification of the unit of account with the means of payment.

While the gold standard currency was the first currency to be able to fulfil the function of reserve with no restrictions, thanks to the combination of the first two functions, the combination itself was destined to persist even when gold ceased to have a monetary function. The post-1971 *fiat* money, perhaps even more than the gold standard currency, actually *needs* to be a store of value and thus requires the identification between the functions of unit of measurement and medium of exchange.

However, the corollary needs to be interpreted in structural terms too. It is not simply a matter of making do with the conclusion that, for a certain period of time, gold was able to serve as both national and international currency. Given the structural identification between unit of account and medium of exchange, with the gold standard it was impossible to see the international currency as a pure and simple unit of account, distinct from each of the national currencies.

So here we have the twofold novelty. But the question arising at this point is: what did this novelty contrast with? What was the monetary system that preceded the gold standard? Where was the point of no return between the traditional monetary architecture and the new architecture embodied by the gold standard?

Let us begin with the change that occurred in the relationship between the unit of account and the medium of exchange. With the economic recovery that took place in the Middle Ages, from the thirteenth century on, gold coins, which had disappeared with the Barbarian invasions, were once again being minted and circulating in the West. However, their debt-paying power was not engraved on them. Coined in public mints, they had their debt-paying power decided upon by a local public decree called 'tariff' and measured in a local unit of account that had no fixed parity with any metal. The unit of account was an immaterial or, as it was also called, an 'imaginary' money, impossible to use as a means of payment simply because it was never minted. In this way, within the monetary space delimited by the unit of account, the minted coins could enjoy a debt-paying power susceptible to adjustments – certainly not 'at will', as it were, but equally certainly *at the discretion* of the local monetary authorities. The distinction between money minted as means of payment and the unit of account that determined the degree of debt-paying power of the minted money was based on an *institutional division* between the functions of unit of account and medium of exchange, and thus on the exclusion of the *store of value function*.

The specifically public aspect of the imaginary money system lay precisely in the task of establishing, *at the right moment*, the ratio between the unit of account and the actual money, with a view to ensuring that the debts be *payable*. This task corresponds perfectly to the task that Keynes assigned to the state in the passage of the *Treatise* quoted and commented upon in Part I.[1] What, in western monetary history subsequent to the introduction of the gold standard, has always been left *ex post* to the market, namely the conditions for acceptance of money as means of payment of debts, was, in the system of imaginary money, the statutory prerogative *ex ante* of the monetary authorities.

On the strength of this observation we can go on to make a precise identification of the fulcrum around which all that system's money management activities revolved, and at the same time we can attribute a positive meaning to a term that has not enjoyed a good reputation and that, above all, saw a radical change in meaning after introduction of the gold standard – namely *seignorage*.

Thanks to the tariff system, coins could be valued, and thus endowed with a debt-paying power *other than* the commercial value of the metal they contained. In other words, the 'intrinsic value' – the metal content of the minted coin – was publically, *openly*, distinguished from its 'extrinsic value', set by the public tariff. The difference between the debt-paying power of the coin and the market value of the metal it is made of constitutes, by definition, the seignorage generated by the monetary authorities, the 'lord' (in Old French, the *seignor*, from which the term originated). Anyone taking metal to the mint would normally come away with minted coins that contained a smaller quantity of metal.

At the same time, it was precisely thanks to seignorage that a distinction was made between the metallic means of payment and the metal it was made of: accordingly, the metal ceased to be a commodity, to become a means of buying other commodities. Thus the minted metal became, not by chance but by design, a medium of exchange of no value in itself, simply to be accepted and spent because it circulated independently of the value of the metal it was made of. By the same token, however, the coin could no longer serve as store of value. If the debt-paying power of a single piece of metal could vary as the law decreed, then it made no longer any economic sense to store it so as to conserve its value indefinitely.

With the coin given free circulation, this system of seignorage ensured a *public gain* with *no corresponding private loss.*[2] While the mint deprived the possessor of a certain amount of metal, it gave him/her, in exchange, something that was wholly money – a coin that lacked nothing to perform its task of purchasing goods and of paying debts.[3] Thus the system of seignorage took the form of a preventive distribution of loss among all the potential users of the coin, in other words of the cost that was to be borne *before* having the use of (indeed, in order *to be able* to have the use of) a medium – publicly accepted for the exchange of goods – which, while having material substance, was not identified with that substance. Seignorage dematerialized the coin while leaving it incorporated in tangible material. This was quite a different sort of dematerialization from the one that is generally claimed to be an exclusive prerogative of today's money, but it, too, had significant consequences.

To begin with, the separation of the minted coins from the metal they were made of permitted changes in debt-paying power of the means of payment available, and means of payment could be created and destroyed *quite independently of the effective availability of the metal.* This perfectly legitimate faculty to change served the purposes of internal monetary policy: it afforded a direct regulation of the value of the currency in order to adapt it to the exigencies of domestic trade, thereby preventing deflationary pressure on prices and production.

This was not the only function of seignorage, however. Marc Bloch pointed out another significant implication of 'monetary mutations', namely the possibility to decree the redefinition of the debt-paying power of the effective money thanks to its non-coinciding with the money of account. For the purpose of ensuring that debts could be paid, the burden of payment could be redistributed between debtors and creditors, with appropriate variations. When the debt-paying power of the coins was increased, debts denominated in units of account could be paid using a smaller quantity of means of payment. Debts were still paid in full, but with fewer metal coins, thereby holding off the risk of insolvency – not that of the individual debtors, which could happen any time, but that *of the entire class of debtors.* However, given that the debtors are essentially the producers, as we saw in Part I, what can be avoided with the help of these mutations are situations in which the proportion of financial gains exceeds the productivity of the effective investments.

So far we have discussed the system of imaginary money as if it contemplated only the existence of gold coins, differing from the gold standard only by virtue of the separation between the functions of unit of account and medium of exchange. However, things were a bit more complicated. In fact, while the separation was crucial to this particular monetary architecture, it also created the possibility of minting coins out of a variety of metals, allowing for their specialization. Insofar as it did not coincide *quantitatively* with any real metal coin, the unit of account could measure the debt-paying power of *qualitatively* different coins, which could thus be put to different uses, circulating in different areas. So, while gold coin was specialized as a means of payment for international trade, coins of silver or of other, less 'noble' metals served for internal circulation. Separate regulations of the debt-paying power of coins of different metals could be made through the public tariff. This meant that the debt-paying power of the internal currency could vary without bringing about any variation for the international currency. Indeed, in a money of account system, the variations in the debt-paying power of metal coins produced by changing their rate value left their international debt-paying power quite unaffected. Nothing – literally no *public* instance – can stop coins from being accepted on the basis of their metal content in a private and international area of exchange that, by definition, is not subject to national and public decisions, although of course these coins come back under the national monetary law when they are really spent in areas of the national economy. It is precisely this further degree of freedom that was exploited by merchant–bankers in the sixteenth century, to establish at Lyon a private *clearing* system independent of any state requirement, for the financing of international trading activities.

On the basis of these considerations, it was not only unnecessary to settle on one single metal, but in certain respects this would have limited the degrees of freedom, too. Above all, it would have precluded the degree of freedom that consists in the possibility to distinguish the domestic currency from the international currency.

Therefore the difference between the gold standard and the imaginary money is by no means simply the difference between a monometallic system and a bimetallic system. Einaudi himself, who championed unlimited credits in 1915, had by 1936 rediscovered the system of imaginary money as a historian and published a celebrated article on it. He returned to the subject later on, proposing it no longer as a simple historical curiosity, but in a theoretical exercise to construct a 'managed currency' able to distinguish internal monetary transactions from international uses of money. Significantly, his work was published in *Essays in Honor of Irving Fisher*; for in the early years of the twentieth century Fisher had come up with a similar proposal, which went by the name of 'compensated dollar'.[4] In continuation of this same tradition, our present considerations on the system of imaginary money aim to concentrate not so much on its historical specifics[5] as on the *virtual* aspects of its functioning and on the possibility it offers to put the gold standard in an adequate historical perspective – through closer examination not only of the circumstances of its inception, but also of what was actually *at stake* in it.

If by 'gold standard' we understand a monetary system that bestows on gold the role of medium of exchange but not of unit of account, then we have to recognize that a real and true international gold standard was possible only within the system of imaginary money. And yet the latter system was abolished with the establishment of the gold standard – which meant the institutional identification of *gold* with the unit of account, *the standard.* With the imaginary money system, from the thirteenth to the seventeenth century, gold coins of 'weight and fineness' that remained practically unchanged for centuries (in Italy, the Florin and Sequin) were able to circulate throughout Europe without, however, obstructing the circulation of silver and copper coins within the national monetary areas. Precisely because it was not identified with either, imaginary money was able to play the role of public guarantor of their possible different forms, effectively preventing them from being considered as *substitutes* for each other. Gold was the metal of international transactions, just as silver and copper served for national transactions, on the basis of a *public* guarantee – not, primarily, to be understood in the sense of a 'state' guarantee, but rather as a guarantee that *gave way to no* private instance and so, by definition, untouched by bargaining on the money markets. The economic origins of this money are simple: *markets* need *goods* and a measure for the bargaining and the exchange of goods. Since, however, the measure is not identified with anything negotiable and hence is not a merchandise, money markets have no *reason* to exist.

As long as the possibility remains to establish the relationship between unit of account and medium of exchange according to circumstances, modifying the debt-paying power of the currency is an internal matter for any given monetary area. There is still the possibility of distinguishing internal currency from external, not only on the basis of metal, but even more on the basis of the fact that, within each monetary area, the purchasing power of this metal is the result of deliberation. This deliberation is a matter of placing trust, on due consideration, in the possibility for the minted metal to make all exchanges practicable and all debts payable.

Unlike the systems based on liquidity, this way of organizing relations between money and credit has the advantage that errors in monetary policy can be traced with a fair degree of certainty to the people responsible for them. And, at a more basic level, the relations of trust that must be in place when money and credit are at stake can be established along different lines.

Actually money has always been a matter of trust, in that it has always depended on the trust placed in assertions that what is being used can effectively release from debt and make exchange feasible. Furthermore, this trust must be shared if the aim is to bring all creditors together with all the debtors. The important point here, however, is to see how this trust is built. It seems quite probable that what differentiates the gold standard from the earlier system is the different kind of trust implied by the monetary institution.

The gold standard rose from the dismantled structures that had supported the system of imaginary money. Therefore it was not a matter of evolutionary transition from bimetallism to monometallism, but the establishment of a completely new identification of money as measure with money as means of payment, which in turn underlies the possibility of identifying money with credit; and this is where the source of the liquidity problem lies. From the imaginary money perspective, the emergence of the gold standard can no longer be seen simply as a rational solution to the alleged inefficiency of the bimetallic systems, which continued to thrive throughout the first half of the nineteenth century, but rather as a radical redefinition of the role played by metal in a monetary system, and thus, basically, a radical redefinition of what money is supposed to be in the first place.

However, since the standard criticism brought against nineteenth-century bimetallism – which underlies the interpretation of the gold standard in terms of evolution – is still widely accepted, we must take it into serious consideration. Basically, this criticism says that, insofar as a bimetallic monetary system has the ratio of equivalence between gold and silver – that is, their relative prices – established from above, variations in the prices of these precious metals on the international markets open the way to arbitrage. The effect would be to remove from circulation the species of the metal whose market price exceeded the official price. And the ultimate effect would be to reduce the countries that had opted for the dual circulation of gold and silver to an effective monometallism – unless, of course, the authorities were continually to adjust the legal ratio to the market ratio, which would also imply constant re-minting of coins in both the metals. And even if it obtained the best possible results along these lines, keeping up with the ceaseless pursuit, the system would still be over-complicated, achieving with considerably less efficiency what monometallism, in the sense of the gold standard, permits to achieve far more directly.

However, there is something in this reasoning that remains implicit, taken for granted, and this is precisely the identification of the unit of account with the equivalent metal value. This is a mistake, and in fact the monetary system based on imaginary money by its very nature ruled it out. As Einaudi pointed out, if the money of account is not identified with the effective metal money but merely measures its debt-paying power, then there is no fixed connection between the coins actually minted in the different metals, and variation can be decreed in the bimetallic ratio without any need for re-minting, the coins in the two metals being in variable relation with the unit of account and neither of them incorporating it. Moreover, there is no good reason why the tariff should follow the relative prices of the metals on the international markets. As long as bimetallism applies, it is rather the demand for metals for monetary uses that affects their prices.[6] Indeed one of the main causes of the fall in the price of silver in the second half of the nineteenth century was its demonetization, and not the other way round.

On the other hand, should identification of the unit of account with the medium of exchange be not only taken for granted but actually desired as a matter of principle, monometallism will inevitably win out over bimetallism, making it impossible to keep in circulation coins in different metals. It is only if the aim is for both metals to represent the standard, in the form of minted coins containing the unit of account, that fixing the ratio between gold and silver becomes necessary – and at the same time problematic. But, with bimetallism conceived of in this way, there is risk of a 'limping' system, as the phrase went, since it can give an advantage to choosing which of the two types of metal to use in each country on the basis of the bimetallic ratio adopted. The only solution would be a universal bimetallism, all the countries adopting the same bimetallic ratio. In fact France eventually attempted to impose a system of the sort, through the constitution and extension of the Latin Monetary Union; but the attempt foundered on the hegemony of the United Kingdom, which had long committed itself to monometallism.

Where identification holds between unit of account and medium of exchange, in other words where the institutional architecture based on imaginary money is abandoned, bimetallism is doomed instead to disappear. For, if the standard is effectively to be incorporated, then the incorporation must clearly be unambiguous. However, incorporation of the standard implies identification of the unit of account with the medium of exchange, and the store of value function falls into place. This is the only necessity entailed by the gold standard, and it is in fact the same necessity we had also noted in another, apparently opposite case: in 1971, when the problem arose of a choice between gold or paper as incorporations of the standard. Thus we see an odd sort of continuity taking shape: just as gold put an end to silver, so paper eventually put an end to gold. Here, perhaps, we may begin to find a key to the paradox described by Robert Triffin in relation to the gold standard, which he himself called the 'euthanasia of gold and silver moneys'[7]; for, paradoxically, a system that is supposed to be based on the identification of money with gold tends progressively to substitute paper for the gold in circulation, even to the extent of eliminating any relationship with it. In either case, in fact, the complete substitution of one currency with another is accomplished on the basis of one assumption – the assumption that the currency represents an identification of the unit of account with the medium of exchange.

And yet the question remains: why is this identification necessary, and indeed far more necessary than the identification of the standard with a metal? To answer this question we have to take yet a further step back in time, from the date of the official introduction of the gold standard, 1717, to 1694 – the years that saw the creation of the Bank of England and the somewhat surreptitious beginning of '*fiat* money'.

11

Money for nothing: The invention of central banking (1694)

We are now arriving at the beginning of a story – the story of liquidity – which, as we have been able to reconstruct it retrospectively, shows no 'evolutionary' development, but rather one fundamental point of rupture, followed by a sort of repetition compulsion. The one factor making any difference in this structure is the gravity – the scale and intensity, that is, and thus the dangerousness – of the crises to which it progressively leads. This is one way of looking at it. On the other hand, taking into account all the evidence we have reviewed on our journey in time, from the most glaring examples of present-day securitizations to what, retrospectively, might seem no more than the proper functioning of austere and rigorous systems, we can in fact find all the danger already concentrated at the inception of the system.

So far we have seen this danger taking the form of an ambiguity: the gold standard, seen as the identification of money with gold would appear to be one of the conditions for the emergence of paper money, which progressively ousted gold from its role as sole representative of monetary measure. *Fiat* money thus appears to have come on the scene only in 1971, at the end of the degenerative process that afflicted the gold standard as a system of *commodity money*.[1]

In reality, however, the dates belie this historical reconstruction. If precedents have a sense – if chronology is not a mere matter of opinion – then we must recognize the fact that the introduction of a national paper currency in the United Kingdom, in 1694, *preceded* the establishment of a metal standard, whether silver (1696) or gold (1717).

Not by very much, it is true, but long enough to make it imperative to take a different view of the connection between the two events, departing from the customary approach. So, how are we to take it?

The system of imaginary money and mutations came to an end, according to Bloch, in the late seventeenth century, when concern waxed, pressing for a way to defend creditors' positions systematically. This he sees as being closely tied up with capitalism in the particular sense he attributes to the term: the system, that is, that would die if all *accounts* were settled at the same time and lives therefore by *counting* on being able to *count everything*, which is to say by *discounting* future profits. As long as they are institutionally practicable, mutations make it impossible to consider credit as equivalent, not only to a quantity of metal, but especially to a definite quantity of money. This makes it impossible for a credit transaction to be represented as buying and selling money, and for interest to be represented as the price of that transaction – which means that, while credit is possible and practicable, a credit *market* is neither possible nor practicable.

The separation between unit of account and medium of exchange is incompatible with a credit market. On the other hand, Bloch argues, the possibility of putting an end to mutations arose with the emergence of a credit market, which took on the task of supporting monetary expansion with a method very different from mutations.

What credit and what monetary expansion are we talking about, then, when we refer to capitalism in the sense attributed to it by Bloch? Here we have credit and money serving both private and public requirements. This credit must be supplied in such a way as to take account of the twofold need arising when politics and the economy appear ever more closely bound together in their ends. In a European context characterized from the very beginnings of the modern age by the twofold need for *enhancement* of the national states and for *growth* in *international* trade, it became vitally important for military expansion not to be pursued at the expense of economic growth, and vice versa. Real power, the only power that can grow indefinitely, lies in the balance between the two *dynamics*. The 'global power circuit' that Europe explicitly entered in the early days of the modern age calls for the mutual support of state and market. To this mutual support we can apply the historical term 'mercantilism', but we must avoid reducing this concept to a mere nationalistic defensive option. In the seventeenth and eighteenth centuries the fierce pursuit of national interests was attended by a growth in international trade. This pattern not only characterized the classical gold standard period and the first globalization, but remained as the background to all monetary and financial history up to our own times.[2] Indeed, now more than ever, the currency we make use of is a *money of power* and its relations with the globalized credit market are the major obstacle in the way of any thoughts about possible alternative ways of organizing economic relations, both national and international.

Let us return, however, to the United Kingdom of the late seventeenth century. The important point about the credit system that so much effort was going into constructing at the end of the seventeenth century was that the public debt should not crowd out (as the economists put it) the private credit to investments: it was not to hamper economic growth. The growing financial requirements of the states had to be fed without robbing private activity of its resources. From a monetary point of view, this was a matter of activating mechanisms that would enable the creation of money 'at will', independently of the physical availability of the metals. From the point of view of credit, the need was to create a new trust in the system of loans. A way had to be found to implement a system that would attract private funds but allow for them to be negotiated freely, with a view to alternative uses. In short, if some general compatibility was to be achieved among these imperatives, what had to be constructed was, *precisely, a market.* A liquid credit market or, as it has also been termed, a *cash nexus* had to be instituted.[3]

Imperative as this objective was, how far could the traditional tools of monetary policy serve to achieve it? Not nearly far enough, as it turned out, unless they were to be irreversibly impaired. Throughout the sixteenth and seventeenth centuries, the new states emerging all over Europe increasingly bent the tool of mutations to their financial needs, eventually finding themselves with an unmanageable instrument, a currency that had lost credibility and whose credit was more and more seriously undermined. The paradigmatic case was that of Spain: clearly, a mutation increasing the debt-paying power of the minted coins could work to the advantage of the state insofar as it was debtor of a public debt.[4] Equally clearly, however, in this case the state had an interest in what it was to regulate, and could hardly go on being a disinterested party in the role of guarantor of the mutations. Seignorage would increasingly be subordinated to the purpose of increasing state revenue, and would therefore be less geared to the need to supply a stable measure and a medium of exchange sufficient for private bargaining. The old tool of a monetary policy consisting of mutations proved to be superseded, not in relation to a new, more efficient tool to apply to the customary purposes, but in relation to a new purpose – the purpose of making available unlimited resources for the power politics of the states.

In the late seventeenth century Great Britain devised a method more apt to the purpose. This consisted in opening the way to forms of public debt that could guarantee not so much the payment as *the service* of the debt. But it also had to be able to ensure, for the private creditors as a whole, general returns on their investments – if not certain, *at least calculable* returns, both in terms of the interests they could yield and in terms of their negotiability as securities on a secondary market. It was, in short, a matter of having a currency compatible with all this.

Behind the British endeavour lay over a century of European contrivances to finance the public debt, more or less refined but, on the whole, unsuccessful or only half-successful (which ultimately amounts to failure, too): public banks on the one hand, recourse to international loan systems on the other. These systems proved, respectively, too feeble and too unstable, for they both had to play the roles of monetary tools distinct from the national currency. The banks' money of account differed from the national money of account, and assets held in the banks could therefore not be spent in the ordinary circuit of internal exchanges. Moreover, international debts were denominated in a metal-based international coin, the *écu de marc*, which, however, had *no stable relations with the national currencies*.

The British novelty lay in the fact that the 'financial revolution', which was to lead to the constitution of a liquid secondary market for public debt securities in Great Britain, at the same time took the form of a *monetary revolution*.[5] This twofold revolution was led by three protagonists, namely the state, the bank and the financial markets. To begin with, let us consider the bank, for it is here that the financial and monetary ambits had coincided since its foundation.

From the year 1689 Great Britain enjoyed a constitutional monarchy. In his public function, the sovereign could not run up debts without having first received the authorization of Parliament and specified the fiscal revenue that would be used to pay the debts. However, the sovereign also had the prerogative – or, in those years, the obligation – to wage war against any country that threatened British power. The problem was, then, how to finance war without draining the country's commercial and productive capacities, or how to reconcile political *warfare* with economic *welfare*.

By 1694 the solution was ready, although in the beginning it took the form of a temporary expedient. When the need arose to supply a million and two hundred thousand pounds sterling to the crown, which was at war with Spain, it was decided to take a path that looked quite familiar, but that would lead into hitherto unexplored territory. On the model of the public banks, a private bank of public interest was instituted, endowed with capital corresponding to the figure to be financed. It was rapidly subscribed by private investors, in *tranches* of metal coin amounting to 10,000 pounds sterling. The capital raised was immediately loaned to the crown at an interest of 8 per cent per annum, for twelve years, at the end of which the crown undertook to repay the loan and the bank undertook to close its books, returning the capital to investors. In the bank's assets the metal capital deposited was immediately replaced with state debt securities for a sum amounting to the capital – naturally, denominated in money of account.

So far the operation was simple and not particularly innovative. A sort of closed-end investment fund was constituted to finance the state for a limited term. The problem that still remained to be settled here was that the capital loaned to the crown was removed from the productive uses of private investors. Had this been truly no more than a closed-end investment fund, the bank would have had no way round this problem. But – and here lies the innovation – the bank was granted the power not only to lend money to the state, but also to issue banknotes, for example by commercial discount operations, *up to the amount of capital deposited by subscribers*.

Here, however, arose a dilemma upon the solution of which depended the effective capacity of the new financial institution 'to serve two masters', the state and the market. If, in fact, the issue of paper currency were to have depended on the presence of metal currency in the bank's assets, seeing that all the capital had in fact been loaned to the crown, the bank would have been able to issue absolutely nothing, unless more metal came in. Otherwise the paper money would not have enjoyed the full support of metal currency, but rather of what had taken its place in the bank's assets, namely the public debt, or further debts acquired through paper, in discount operations.

In the former case, the paper would simply have represented, on a temporary basis, the gold placed in reserve, but in the latter case it would be a substitute for it *sine die*, representing an addition. In the former case, the convertibility of paper into gold would have been so certain as to make the banknotes simply stand-ins for the gold, while in the latter case, although remaining formally convertible, the paper money would have a life of its own. More importantly still, in the former case the money loaned to the state would have been removed from internal circulation, insofar as the crown spent it abroad to finance the armies and, supposing that 1.2 million pounds accounted for 5 per cent of the British metal currency, this would have amounted to no small loss. In the latter case, however, there would actually be a *potential duplication* of the sum deposited, which would contemporaneously support, in the form of gold, the sovereign's military outlay, and, in the form of paper, commercial transactions at the private level.

Clearly, therefore, while there would have been nothing particularly new about the former case, the latter would amount to an authentic 'financial innovation': literally, it would be a *securitization* of the public debt. In fact, hitherto the state debt was originated by the creditors on the basis of bilateral relations with the crown, and was to be held by them until maturity. With the Bank of England, the debt originated by the bank in favour of the crown was distributed to the public in the form of negotiable securities against paper currency on the secondary market.

Corresponding to this change in the nature of credit, there was a similar change in the public nature of the currency. Inasmuch as the bank was authorized to issue, as currency, a debt on which it paid no interest – banknotes – against credit, state securities and trade bills upon which, however, it received interest, the bank exercised a novel form of seignorage.

Such, in essence, was the innovation that the bank introduced into western monetary and financial history. And precisely because the object of innovation was the very nature of money and credit, and how they related to each other, it required no less than a charter. But, alas, the charter was rife with inconsistencies, inaugurating a tradition that would continue up to Bretton Woods: 'What the Bank could do, as a corporate body, once the Charter was granted, was nowhere made clear in that turgid document.'[6]

Thus, exploiting the obscurities of the charter, the bank immediately set about issuing banknotes not only against the public debt, but also by discounting trade bills for quite considerable sums. In this way it rendered liquid not only the public debt securities, but also private credits. The overall effect of this *modus operandi* was an extremely slender coverage in gold, which in 1696 arrived at the minimum quota of 2.7 per cent. In other words, there was, to all effects and purposes, a duplication of the quantity of money: 2.4 million had been made with the original 1.2 million, bringing the Bank of England a profit of 8 per cent, at least for the duration of the bank's privilege.

The positive effects of this mechanism seem quite obvious, and they would have sufficed had it been a matter of financing the state temporarily for a certain specified need. On the other hand, they could certainly not suffice if what the state required was not simply to finance a temporary deficit, but to find access to potentially unlimited financing without subtracting funds from production and trade. We may well wonder, then, why a term was initially set for the bank. Presumably its shareholders would not have been too happy about making a permanent subscription. The fact remains that, once this operation was launched, the bank demonstrated that all its very particular and most thoroughly innovative potential depended solely on getting rid of its temporary status. Indeed, the question arising at this point is this: once the mechanism was set in motion, *could it afford to stop*?

Had the bank closed, it would have had to return the capital to its shareholders and reimburse the banknotes to the bearers. Given such debts, the bank would have had to be able to count, with all certainty and immediacy, not only on repayment of the public debt, but also on payment of all the private debt previously discounted. In other words, closing the bank would have meant closing all the accounts opened with a view to the operation. This, however, was a consummation nobody wished for. Certainly the state did not wish for this outcome, since it was in fact exploring paths to boost its borrowing capacity – permanently, and in excess of its capacity to pay. Nor did the private clients: thanks to the bank, they were able to *transform ad libitum*, into *money*, credits entailing some risk vis-à-vis other private parties.

For all these reasons, the institutional experiment launched by the Bank of England, which was now beginning to show the permanent advantage represented by the liquidity with which it endowed all the debts it handled, was bound to achieve permanent status. It had to be able to perpetuate itself. And the means of perpetuation was, after all, quite simple: it was a matter of renewing the temporary concession to the bank whenever the time came, so that the concession could appear to be permanent. For the state, the advantage was obvious and, above all, highly desirable: a debt contracted to be paid became unredeemable. But there was also benefit for the private clients, who could finance the state without undergoing any restrictions, and indeed with prospective increase in the means of payment at their disposal.

In short, war could go on being waged 'in peace'. In fact,

> during the eighteenth century the Bank's future was never determined during a period of long-term peace or stability. On several occasions

> the pressures and demands of hostilities were such that new bargains were struck with the bank, *despite existing agreements having some time to run*, with the result that the Charter was always renewed either when the nation was at war or when it was just emerging from it. [. . .] This brought a particular pattern of development to the Bank that was ultimately dependent upon the rhythm of war and peace.[7]

Given that, with a view to strengthening positions, war is not only hotly fought combat but also cool, constant preparation, the very pulse of power rendered the bank essential even for the mere survival not only of the British state, but also of its market. The point was immediately taken by the shrewder politicians. In 1781 the prime minister, Lord North, addressed the House of Commons thus:

> from long habit and the usage of many years [the Bank was] part of the constitution [or,] if not part of the constitution, at least it was to all important purposes the public exchequer.[8]

What had effectively been brought into existence was an indissoluble bond between state and bank. And the bond offered great potential for development precisely because it had been sealed, never to be undone. When the government of William III received the initial loan from the bank, at the same time

> it gave them a power to issue bills of credit equal to that sum, making itself the security for all those who thus far trusted the Bank, [so that] by virtue of that privilege they [the Bank] have *a further power of issuing what further credit of theirs now passes amongst us*; and all this passes currently upon the bottom of public sanction and security.[9]

Given the relationship between public debtor and bank creditor, a power line never to be lessened or severed, but always extended, the bank was in turn able to become a perpetual but credible debtor towards all those who henceforth were ready to use its debts as money. The more closely this debt resembled reliable currency, the less it could be perceived as debt – as something that had in turn to be paid. On these conditions the economic agents were able to enjoy the use of all the money and credit they needed: quite literally, it was theirs 'at will' or, better still, by '*fiat*'.

As long as this triangulation between state, bank and market worked, its benefits could be enjoyed by all. Freed of concern about repaying its debt, the state could go on expanding its borrowing capacity, proportioning it in terms no longer of repayment, but of debt service. The bank was able to issue debt on which it paid no interest against credit upon which it received interest, benefiting from a seignorage commensurate with the discount rate. Moreover, this debt could be issued not in the certain, 'physical' measure of its metal resources, but according to the probabilistic measure of the effective conversion of the notes. Finally, the holders of the notes were able to enjoy the use of a medium of exchange that proved all the more acceptable as it was unconditionally perceived not only as convertible into gold at the bank, but also as readily retransformable into instruments of credit on the financial market – in a word, as *supremely liquid.* The upshot was that, the more openings paper money found on the financial markets, the less did convertibility into gold seem to matter. *As long as the triangulation worked*, paper money could at the same time enjoy the status of currency – that is, means of payment – and asset – in other words a perfectly safe and liquid form in which to hold wealth.

Precisely because it *also* has to serve as store of value, paper money needs this identity between unit of account and medium of exchange *far more than metal money* does. Unlike the deposits in public banks, which from the fourteenth century managed the business of public loans, banknotes, being credit and money at the same time, simply have to be denominated in national units of account.

Naturally, of course, the climate of trust in which such a currency circulated was radically different from that upon which the imaginary money system depended. If the pound must always be neither more nor less than a pound, then the traditional seignorage, exercised through the determination of a monetary tariff, could only disappear. And yet the seignorage that disappeared from the tariff immediately reappeared in the bank in a new form, which already fitted Greenspan's definition, namely as the difference between the interest I do not pay on my debts and the interest I receive by using my debts to buy other people's debts.

This, however, helps us to bring an important point into sharper focus. In neither case does the problem of seignorage have to do with its alleged 'arbitrariness', for in neither case does it take from anyone anything that really belongs to them. In both cases, indeed, it continues to represent a gain for some, with no corresponding loss for anyone. What changes is the effect of the subtraction. While the old seignorage deprived the currency of its characteristic as a commodity, this seignorage unconditionally and indelibly attributed that particular quality to it.[10]

With the currency now endowed with the quality of being a

commodity, a radical change in the fiduciary underpinning became inevitable. One had no longer to trust the fact that money could be passed from hand to hand, received and spent – a matter of trust precisely because money had no value in itself – but rather the fact that it would retain its value indefinitely, even if only in nominal terms.

The transition was not marked by any technological progress or scientific discovery, but by a dogmatic option. The question is, however, this: *when* did liquidity appear to be such as no longer to admit of an alternative, even a theoretical one – to the extent, indeed, that its destructuring effect, consisting in perpetually deferring settlement of accounts, *came to be seen as a natural requirement of finance*? From a historical point of view, the answer is simple enough: as soon as the public and private debts floated on the financial markets reached a 'critical mass' such as to make positively *suicidal* the very idea of putting an end to relations binding together state, central bank and financial markets – in other words, when the complex of these three components seemed '*too big to fail*'. It was then that a system, initially conceived of as provisional and exceptional, became in every sense of the word permanent, living on the eternal deferment of a final settlement.

There is, however, more to it. Insofar as the two debts, of the bank and the state, while remaining redeemable, are not redeemed – insofar as the banknotes *continue to circulate* and are not cashed in, the debt continuing to be renewed – the bank can remain a free-flowing source of liquidity. This is not, however, a liquidity created for any precise economic purpose; on the contrary, it has to be constantly put back into circulation *regardless of any given economic end*. The blurring of distinctions between peace finance and war finance, and indeed the independence of the monetary system from any anchorage on gold, which we came across at the end of the chapter on the sterling standard, occurred already with the establishment of the Bank of England, and hence *before* the birth of the gold standard.

What was brought into the world in 1694, surreptitious as it may have been, was not the remote future possibility but the effective and powerful reality of *fiat* money. Paper currency did not come in when the gold standard ceased to be the norm. *Fiat* money saw the light of day before gold currency. And it came as a currency of potentially unlimited growth, no matter how it was subjected to regulation. This potentially unlimited growth represented at the same time a condition for the expansion of the credit market, whether for production or destruction. It was, from the very outset, the money of power.

Ultimately, moreover, this money of power was indeed money *of power for power*. Hence it could bear no limitation, whether natural, economic, legal or moral. Rather it enlisted every end, with a view to enhancing, unconditionally, the feasibility of anything. The finance of this money was literally a *finance with no end*, in every sense of the word.

From the traditional historiographic point of view, it has aptly been remarked that

> The British Public Debt was considered as *a prime strategic weapon* by British and foreign observers alike, such as David Hume and Immanuel Kant. It allowed the British to wage war with borrowed money, while other states had to keep a physical war chest that was unutilized except in times of war. The British used the borrowed funds to subsidize allied armies on the continent, sparing them the cost of a standing army. Thus they could maintain and increase a huge fleet to blockade the Continent and defend the empire, including the enforcement of the Monroe doctrine on behalf of the United States, which for a long time had a very small fleet.[11]

When one's own debts can be paid with one's own debts, it becomes relatively *easy* to build up a position of power, for the latter can be fuelled by a *primary lever*, opening up a supply of currency able to mobilize resources. Moreover, not only can the resources run beyond the limits dictated by preventive accumulation or by the subsequent capacity to pay up, but they can be mobilized *regardless of any particular end*. With this currency Great Britain was able to build an *empire*.

However, what this work of construction brought into existence was not only a historically determined political, military and economic empire, but also a dogmatic–metaphysical empire, whose subjects we more or less unwittingly remain, and which does not even appear to need a dominant country to be able to 'evolve incrementally'. While every geopolitical position of power is from the outset doomed to decline (historically, we have witnessed the decline of the British Empire, and now, after the collapse of the Soviet Union, we are seeing the first signs of decline in the American empire), what was destined never to see decline with the empire that rose on British institutional manoeuvring at the end of the seventeenth century was, precisely, the *power imperative*.

Such sway is held by this imperative that even forms of empire ideologically, politically and economically opposed to the institutional format brought in with the British reforms have had to respond to it. In February 1918 the newly constituted Bolshevik government decided not to take on the financial commitments of the previous regime. This was by no means the first time that a western government had failed to respect an international treaty; moreover, the Bolsheviks were able to 'justify' repudiation of the debts by taking due distance from the old regime, 'of the Russian landlords and Russian bourgeoisie'[12] as it was. What ultimately motivated them, however, was their claim to the unconditional right to violate any contract *whenever it proved expedient.*[13]

Today, of course, the doctrine of an 'efficient breach of contract' *in the name of capitalism*[14] is widely professed in US faculties, steeped as they are in economic liberalism; but in those days the Bolshevik action met with an outcry from all the liberals, who denounced the violation of the elementary principles upon which contracts rested. And yet, what they failed to see was that the Bolsheviks had merely taken off their gloves to bang their fists better, but there had long been a clenching of fists. The sacrosanct nature of contracts professed by the West, first Roman–Christian (it is to the canonists that we owe the brocard *pacta sunt servanda*), later on secular and liberal, was in fact violated at the very beginning of the modern age, through the act that constituted the monetary system upon which capitalism and its peculiar finance were to be based.

Taking a broader and deeper look into western history, Martin Heidegger wrote that what the Bolsheviks did, well into the twentieth century and 'without scruple, but not without a general reference to the happiness of the peoples', was accomplished in Great Britain in the seventeenth/eighteenth century with 'gigantic dissimulation in the guise of morality and civilization [so as to make] every deployment of power [appear] harmless and obvious'.[15]

Heidegger actually went as far as to assert that the British state in the early modern age was 'conceived in its essence, independently of the forms of government, society and faith that characterized it historically, exactly like the State of the Union of Soviet Socialist Republics'.[16] This is a surprising assertion. On a first reading, and possibly even on a second, it looks far-fetched, hard to justify and, moreover, open to suspicions of being politically incorrect. And yet we might get a glimpse of the element of truth half-hidden here if only we try to take seriously the enormity of founding a system that proclaims the sacrosanct nature of contracts on a debt designed never to be paid. The 'Bolshevism' that Heidegger attributed to the British ruling classes is not to be taken in the strict sense of an ideological position, anachronistically attributed by Heidegger to the British liberal élites to belittle them, but in the broader, more precise and profound sense of a *metaphysical option*. This can be seen also to have inspired the operation of creating a currency and a finance constitutionally devoid of any limit or end. Metaphysically speaking, Bolshevism is, simply, an unconditional assent to the performative rationale of empowerment. *Nothing* needs a foundation or an end. Suffice it that *it all works*. The metaphysical basis of Russian Bolshevism, but also of capitalism, is, despite all the *evident* differences in their *modus operandi*, one and the same; and its proper name is *nihilism*.

Given, however, that the highly radical nature of this option eludes, or possibly daunts, the interested parties, British institutional nihilism has to go under the guise of an operation of moralization. It was again Heidegger who wrote that nihilism celebrates its supreme triumph when it can pass itself off as a 'defender of morality'. It was precisely this dissimulated morality that underlay the operation through which the subversive potential of the money of pure power that came into being in 1694 was passed off as a moderate and sober reform of public finance.

In 1696 Locke was given the task of publicly asserting the identification of the monetary measure with the metal. With the conviction that in so doing he was advancing the cause of mandatory realism and naturalism, and perhaps without even thinking he might be being used for quite opposite ends, Locke chose silver, calling in the metal coins that had been circulating in fiduciary conditions under the regime of the imaginary money, so that they could be minted anew, on the basis of an equivalence between standard and metal established once and for all. Given the scarcity of silver in Great Britain, the potential effect of this re-minting operation was a massive deflation: the silver currency plunged from 6 to 4 million pounds sterling, and thus the monetary mass contracted by 33 per cent. Such contraction was contained *thanks only to a massive recourse to paper money*. As we have seen, in 1696 paper circulated with hardly any coverage, taking its place alongside silver as surrogate national currency. The year 1717 saw a yet more decisive advance: the preference accorded to gold since 1696, with the decision of the Parliament and crown to overvalue gold in terms of silver with respect to international markets, was fixed on Newton's decision, and the demonetization of silver came under way. Great Britain embarked upon a monetary regime that, while using gold and paper side by side, was also tending to remove gold currency from circulation.

Viewed from its beginnings, the gold standard may indeed be seen as no more than mere institutional window-dressing – a moralistic veil drawn over a currency that was essentially fiduciary, simply to make the operation look less violent than it really was.

On the other hand, the role performed by the metal money reforms that attended upon the birth of paper money was of a *dogmatic* significance. The identification between standard and gold, in other words between the measure and the material made to incorporate it, was in fact a stratagem by which money as a standard was institutionally replaced with a currency that ultimately amounted to no more than a commodity.

This was the fundamental institutional and dogmatic transition. Subsequent to this transition, the currency was no longer, primarily, a measure: at best, it was the commodity that *conventionally* served as measure. On this foundation, liquidity-based financial and money markets could be built. Indeed, liquidity could also be made to appear an essential characteristic, not so much of money as we have known it to be since then, but of *money as such*.

This identity dominated to such an extent as to render unthinkable any alternative way, past or future, of constituting the currency and its relation with credit. With that dogmatic stratagem, and on the basis of the moral pretensions with the help of which it was accomplished, imaginary money, and with it the virtual status it occupied, were relegated to the museum of historical relics. Here it was catalogued as a tyrannical attempt, downright immoral in this case, to deprive money of its characteristic as commodity and, indeed, of its liquidity: above all, it was denounced as an obstacle against the development of credit, with all the corollaries of growth and 'public happiness' that it entails.[17]

Now, at this point of our story, we may have the hindsight and the understanding required for questioning this historical and ideological representation. We can ask what kind of relations there may be between money and credit, and between national and international currency, if money is conceived as something other than a commodity. The possibility was there, in the past, in the times of the imaginary money, and there is nothing to stop it from appearing as a future possibility, apart from our fear of thinking. Before looking to the future, however, we must take one further step back to see how the system of imaginary money functioned historically, also at the level of international economic relations, and what led to its disappearance.

12

The international currency of the trade fairs (1579)

The birth of the money of power in late seventeenth-century England marked at the same time a watershed in the history of credit, of money, and indeed of the relationship between credit and money. With the founding of the Bank of England and subsequent monetary reform came the financial markets – that is, markets for credit, for money and, even more importantly, for the continuous interchangeability of credit and money.

The importance of this turning point is certainly not overlooked in the standard reconstructions of western financial and monetary history. However, it tends to be interpreted in terms of a necessary stage in evolution, ultimately justified by the need to give greater scope to credit. In fact, the birth of the 'modern' financial and credit markets is normally seen as one of the essential preconditions for the Industrial Revolution – the final transition of the real economy from an essentially reproductive type of organization to one geared to growing surplus and real wealth, especially thanks to the innovations that credit opened the way to.

Nor do these reconstructions attempt to gloss over the risks and complications implicit in the institutional solutions that led to the new configuration. And yet the conclusion they generally draw can be summarized thus: although the approach to the modern financial and monetary reforms was undertaken somewhat blindly and even carelessly, it did eventually lead, beyond a formidable impasse, to an unprecedented and cumulative expansion in the supply of money and credit, and this formed the basis both for increased public spending and for an overall growth in a market-based economy. All the theoretical and ideological labours of eighteenth-century Enlightenment and nineteenth-century liberalism concentrated on drawing a 'moral' line to the excesses and instability of the system, in the form of a doctrine limiting state influence over monetary and financial matters in favour of the self-regulating capacities of the system. The course seemed to be set until, over a period spanning from the 1930s to the 1970s, the applecart was overturned by a burst of state regulations culminating in the so-called 'Keynesian' economic policies, only to be overturned once again in the late twentieth century and at the dawn of the new millennium, in a spate of alternating phases of deregulation and re-regulation.

While the relative clout attributed to state and market changed over the centuries and with the varying ideological climate, what was no longer called into question was their relationship, as it had formed from the outset. Behind this historical alternation between regulation and deregulation, whether effective or only preached, lay an initial, structural deregulation that coincided with the new connection between state and market, which had opened the way to the very existence of financial markets.

Far more than any creed of economic liberalism or statism and any fallout they might have had on the institutional order, it was the act of instituting money itself as a commodity and as a lever of power that saw the inextricable bond being tied between state and market. And, without immediately showing it, this structural inextricability led to what we called in Part I a blurring of the rules. We have seen some of the consequences in our own times, in the form of a dialectical–speculative concurrence of regulation and deregulation. The effects were also to be seen in the age of the gold standard, in the form of an irresolvable ambiguity yoking together rule and exception at the heart of the system. And we have just seen it emerging, inchoate and primordial, when the identification between the medium and the measure of exchange opened up the possibility of a *market for the measure itself*; for the financial markets that came into being with the reforms of the late seventeenth century amounted to nothing less.

Of course, all this created scope for the birth and development – occasionally rampant – of new and powerful forms of financing, both national (the public debt and the fractional-reserve banking systems) and international (the capital market); but it nevertheless remained something that lived by confounding the rules underlying its constitution.

The view normally taken of all this evolution is to see it as a transition from a monetary economy to a credit economy,[1] reflected at the institutional level in the concession of a respectable status to the interest rate, with a progressive slackening of the dogmatic anathemas and legal interdictions on usury. And yet there is enough evidence to question just how obvious this linear, evolutionary reconstruction is, going as it does from a system incapable of generating credit to a system based on a virtually unconditional supply of credit – to the extent that the problem of regulation today is to draw a limit to the system's capacity for expansion. Contrary to the dominant representations, credit was institutionally possible also before the birth of commodity money, and precisely on the basis of the separation between the unit of account and the medium of exchange.

In particular, commercial credit could be had on the basis of an international money, not identified with any national currency, and therefore acting as a pure multilateral measure of the shifts in wealth resulting from movements of goods. Moreover, it worked on the basis of respect for, and not evasion of, the ban on interest-bearing loans.

There existed a pre-capitalistic – or, better, historically non-capitalistic – financial system characterized by the fact that it was based on an international currency that was *measure and nothing but measure*:

> the history of money does not consist of a linear evolution toward dematerialization, state control, and internationalization. The mid-sixteenth century had a modern money based on the unit of account, on the relationship between public and private spheres, on the integration of the European area.[2]

Thus was the situation outlined, firmly and clearly, by the three French economists to whom we owe the most complete and convincing reconstruction of the sixteenth-century system of Lyon trade fairs. Between 1533 and 1575 – that is, for a period lasting longer than both the international gold standard and the Bretton Woods system – the Lyon fairs were the centre of a financial system based on money of account that was *immaterial*, in the specific sense that it was not anchored in any quantity of metal; *non-statal*, in that it performed a public function but was managed by a private, international corporation; and *universal*, being purely a currency for international trade.

Thanks to this system, which was completely private in that it was subject to no form of state interference, it was possible to hold a 'common European market' without requiring any sort of 'convergence' among the European economies, which meant not only leaving the countries of Europe recognized margins for internal monetary policy, but actually resting upon the recognition of this autonomy. This was a monetary and financial system that served as support for international trade – and hence provided an outlet for national productions – without asking for any capital movements across international markets for the demand and supply of currencies. Metal money and capital movements came onto the scene not as an evolutionary development, but as the result of a radical departure from the principles of the system that would often lapse into outright degeneration, in the sense of estrangement from its authentic economic aims. So let us take a look at the basic features of this financial system, beginning with its relations with the real economy and the monetary and credit instruments that cemented these relations.

At the time, European international trade was conducted by specialized private agents – the international merchants – who acted as intermediaries for the movement of goods produced locally throughout Europe. They were organized into 'nations' – the term used in those days – operating at the international level on the entirely privatistic basis of the *lex mercatoria*.

By virtue of their method of operation, they were structurally *debtors*: they bought to sell, in other words they contracted debts preventively, by purchasing goods, in order to settle their accounts by selling them. For this operation they needed credit in the form of deferred payment – the commercial breathing space thanks to which they could honour their debts from the proceeds of the subsequent sales, when the agreed term came.

However, this breathing space could not be granted on the basis of bilateral relations between debtor and creditor. Each of the merchants would buy from and sell to different merchants, which brought about a dissociation between purchase and sale, in other words between import and export, with the effect of weaving a web of multilateral relations. The credit one needed had therefore to be multilateral; and one also needed to be able to denominate the complex of debit and credit positions thus generated in an international unit of account.

The money of the fair, the *écu de marc*, was the tool that could be used to build a multilateral system of deferment, clearing and payment. And this was achieved without linkage to a metal equivalent. The international money *of account* made it basically superfluous to move *real* money from one monetary area to another, functioning preventively as standard within a *clearing* system. Indeed, what was accomplished in sixteenth-century Europe in this respect was essentially identical with the achievement, at European level, of the European Union of Payments, and with what could have been achieved worldwide if the International Clearing Union had been approved at Bretton Woods.

It is, however, worth moving on from these analogies, strong and striking as they are, to see if we can draw some structural indications from the organization of the Lyon system. International trade involves the problem of exchange: in fact, each of the merchants borrows in the money of account of the place of purchase, and receives credit in the money of account at the place where the sale is made. The commercial breathing space implies recognition of a debt in one money of account and payment of the debt in another money of account. This is why the instrument with which such a debt is formalized is called a *bill of exchange*. Instead of paying the supplier immediately in gold coin, the merchant substituted a 'letter' for 'money': he acknowledged a debt in money of account, undertaking to pay, through a representative, not the supplier but a representative of the supplier, in a different place and at a subsequent date.

This was the simplest case, known as 'forced exchange'. But suppose payment was to be made at once. In this case the merchant could approach a third merchant, who served as 'merchant banker', supplying him with the money he lacked to make the payment. And in this case, known as 'exchange *per arte*', the credit relationship is established with a bill of exchange, too. Here, once again,

> the bill of exchange concerns two moneys, occurs between two places, and concerns four people [. . .]. At place 1, the 'deliverer' (of the money) hands the money to the 'taker'. The former is said to 'give this money for exchange' or 'lend it for exchange', and the latter 'takes it for exchange'. The taker signs for the deliverer a bill of exchange which he draws on a person of his choice in favor of a 'payee' named by the deliverer. At place 2, and on a fixed date, the payee hands the drawee the bill of exchange he has received from the deliverer by courier, and the drawee, if he accepts it, pays him the stipulated sum in the other money. [. . .] As an instrument for the execution of a contract, the bill of exchange contains in its wording both an order to pay and the description of the transaction.[3]

Just as in the case of paper money, apparently, here too paper substituted gold. Actually, however, this is an entirely different form of substitution. Here the substitution was for a *fixed term*, and implied *destruction* of the 'liquidity' thus created. Once paid, a bill of exchange had no longer any reason to exist, and it was destroyed. Failure to pay implied protest and, in the last resort, bankruptcy for the debtor. This is why there was not, nor ever should have been, any relationship between a paid letter and one newly issued, or between the settlement of one debit relationship and the opening of a new one. There was no question of refinancing the same debt: a new position would be opened, one business cycle following another. The cyclic character of the successive openings was far from implying – in fact it ruled out – the possibility of cumulative debt, which, by contrast, underlies the modern financial markets. Behind every bill of exchange there was a movement of goods, and it was *that* movement that it financed, by moving the date of payment further ahead, according to the distance between the two places involved.

In this way the guarantee for the complex of debit positions entailed by the letters of exchange was the trade itself, in other words, the real goods that were being exchanged. Or, to put it the other way round, behind the debit relationship represented by the letter there was never a quantity of money supplied or demanded *per se*, unrelated to any *real* operation. The credit represented and attested by letter never took the form of purchase and sale of money, not even when 'forced exchange' – an exchange between merchants that was necessitated by a deferred payment for a commodity – was combined with 'exchange *per arte*' – an exchange between a merchant and a merchant banker. Here again, far from being independent of the use it was put to, the issue of liquidity was totally determined by it. And the merchant–banker lent not on *interest* but on *exchange*: he would be paid through a beneficiary of his, in another place and in another currency – and the place would be that which saw the conclusion of the commercial operation for which money had been advanced. Thus the same instrument could be applied both for very simple commercial breathing space and for the supply of money, but always on the basis of an effective commercial transaction.

Moreover, seeing that the giver – the merchant–banker – granted credit in place 1 but was paid in place 2, and given that it was in place 1 that he wanted to be able to spend his gains, he had to arrange to have the payment returned to the original place. This could be achieved in various, more or less complicated ways. In the simplest way, the first bill of exchange would be followed by a second one, originating from a connection with another merchant, who needed money in place 2 and was prepared to pay in place 1. But the merchant may also have been prepared to pay in some place other than 1, and the route back to place 1 could therefore run through a number of markets.

The bill of exchange was able to answer to these needs. However, having described the instrument, we have yet to consider the institutional scope that gave it multilateral application. To ensure that the debt represented could be duly honoured, the bill of exchange worked on the assumption that an exchange rate was fixed between the two units of account inevitably involved in this type of deed. Now, considering that the letters of exchange issued or accepted by any giver or taker could be drafted in terms of all possible combinations of national units of account, the only institutional procedure that made economic sense was to institute a unit that did not enter into any pair of local units. Thus was born a universal unit of account (universal in relation to all the markets systematically engaged in international trade), which at the same time rated the local units of account (of the individual markets) without being rated by them, but by remaining on a different plane.

In turn, a universal, independent currency needed a place that was equally universal and independent of all the local markets. Thus were created the exchange fairs, designed to meet these specifications. Originating in the thirteenth century, also as *lex mercatoria* tribunals, they had enjoyed extraterritorial status from the very outset.[4] This meant that, while Lyon was literally in France, the Lyon fair was not. The only sovereign act conceded to the king of France was to refrain with sovereignty from exercising his authority in the building where the fairs were held for three days every three months. The international currency could exist only for those three days and in that place, and the purpose it served was but one, namely to make all the debts and credits that had accumulated on the commodity markets comparable and clearable, with a view to trade. Thus organization of the institutional area of exchange by bills entailed two interrelated requirements: all the due dates of all the letters of exchange were to be made to coincide on the quarterly editions of the fairs (a perfectly reasonable time, given the seasonal nature of the commodities that were traded); and the Lyon fair was to be included as a third place in every letter. This meant, for example, that a letter from Florence to Antwerp had to be split between an 'outward journey' from Florence to Lyon and a 'return' from Lyon to Antwerp. In this way Lyon could stand as *middle term*, by virtue of which exchanges of all the letters could be expressed as an exchange *to* Lyon or *from* Lyon. This in turn meant that the exchanges would be expressed either as from the local unit of account to *écu de marc*, or from *écu de marc* to a local money of account.

Thanks to the quarterly centralization of payments at the fair, an international rate could be fixed for the exchange of the money of the fair into all the other currencies, thereby harmonizing all the debt/credit relations of the quarter specified in the letters in terms of the fair currency, regardless of the different places involved.[5] In this way, from the very outset, all the individual relations were included within a *multilateral clearing* network, without any reference to the effective currencies, or indeed to the effective availability of gold. The merchants were thus able to settle their debit positions vis-à-vis their creditors as a whole, paying them with the credits accumulated vis-à-vis their debtors as a whole.

If this is indeed how things stood, then we may say that the *theoretical* aim of the gold standard – general balance of payments equilibrium, according to Hume – was in fact achieved at Lyon, but this happened precisely because it did not work as an *effective* gold standard, that is to say, it did not entail financing balance of trade deficits with capital movements. This is why the business of financing international trade need not entail an interest rate: no movement of capital is necessary where positions are interconnected in a multilateral *clearing* scheme. This credit system was not based on liquidity, and therefore it implied no need for money to have a reserve function. No sum of money needs to be placed in reserve to guarantee the credit operation, and the credit operations themselves do not take the form of matching money demand and supply:

> The man of business who dealt in exchange from then on ceased to be the financial intermediary who borrows at a center against a sale of foreign currency abroad, pledging to mobilize the funds he possesses over there [. . .] or else to transport them there. He now becomes a buyer of bills of exchange and supplies money against a promise of payment abroad, made by a merchant who pledges to transport and sell his goods there in order to reimburse him.[6]

This is a major characteristic, rightly pointed out by the French economists; but there is also another, equally important one, which is in fact simply *the other side of the same coin*:

> By making it possible to transfer funds without transporting coins, exchange by bills enabled intra-European merchandise trade to develop without liquidity constraints at a time when local merchants constantly complained about the shortage of metallic coins of good quality and their manipulation by the princes.[7]

Let it be clear, here, that 'without liquidity constraints' means that liquidity was not created *at will*, without limits, but only so as to suffice within the strict limits dictated by the needs of trade and of its effective expansion. Such a system creates liquidity, but without a liquidity constraint – without, that is, reversing the relations between real economy and the conditions to finance it. This is why the liquidity principle cannot be said to be more efficient than the *clearing* principle. Actually, one might go as far as to put it the other way round: the clearing principle works without the constraints of the liquidity principle, generating the *possibility* for growth without making it *necessary*. Furthermore, the two principles answer to diametrically opposed rationales, implying a totally different nature for money and for finance. Where the clearing principle holds, money is not a commodity but a measure, and cannot be a store of value. In the case of the Clearing Union we saw that Keynes had contemplated purging the currency of the characteristics of liquidity, store and commodity by applying costs for holding currency in the form of negative interest on credit. The idea behind this is clear enough; for this is a matter of distributing a loss among all the players in the game, so that it would not be perceived as loss but rather as a contribution, due from all, towards achieving equilibrium – or, in the case of finance, towards reaching its goal and end, namely the payment of debts.

In the case of Lyon, loss was distributed in a different but equally interesting way. Given that the *écu de marc* was pure money of account with no metal equivalent, its value in relation to other currencies could not be determined through the bargaining of the market forces: the only market taken into consideration here was the commodity market, and there was no room for a money market that served only to denominate and pay. Thus the exchange rate was fixed through the deliberation of a narrow circle of merchant–bankers whose task in the system was to supply money against bills (exchange *per arte*): every three months the merchant–bankers would decide upon a 'conto', or exchange tariff, in which the local money of account was evaluated in the terms of the money of the fair.

How, then, was it possible to produce the estimate, the list of exchange rates between local money of account and the fair's unit of account? The latter had the virtue of making all possible clearing between agents perfectly feasible, bringing to light the net position of each; but what were the terms of reference? Actually, the exchange rate for the money of account of each of the markets was determined in such a way as to reflect the *relative* abundance or scarcity of real money in the respective market, which derived in turn from the state of the market's balance of trade. In a market in surplus, real money tends to run short in relation to the use that needs to be made of it to pay for the goods sold there, and the exchange rate therefore goes up. This will have the effect of orienting the trade of the following quarter in the direction of equilibrium. For a market in deficit, the contrary is the case.

Unlike the systems we have seen so far, the Lyon exchange rates were neither fixed nor flexible: that is, they were neither publicly fixed by a state that publicly committed its credibility to maintaining them, nor privately negotiated on a market that fundamentally entailed no commitment. The rates were *adjustable*, with a view, not to equilibrium in the demand and supply of money, but to equilibrium on the commodity market. The quarterly settlement of accounts, matching all the creditors with all the debtors, was arrived at in such a way as to ease the convergence to equilibrium, and not to offer support to the indefinite and onerous sustainability of disequilibrium.

Such, then, was the public function of that private system – the international corporation of central merchant–bankers – on which they made systematic gain, in other words seignorage. In fact, the rates *from* Lyon were systematically higher than the rates *for* Lyon, the difference amounting to the sum of the seignorages applied by the states involved in the exchange operations. In this way the merchant–bankers' gain was nobody's loss. The system generated through the Lyon fairs amounted to a particular pattern of *loss distribution*. It was in fact precisely for this reason that the seignorage of the fairs was no distortion of, or exception to, the 'rules of the game', but a strict application of them. The merchant–bankers were able to conduct an international orchestra simply because the symphony of international trade opened with an explicit recognition of the *discretional power* entrusted to the conductor, who was *not an interested party*. The significance of the seignorage exercised by the 'central merchant–bankers' by fixing the *conto* was in diametrical contrast with the modern-day seignorage, exercised as this is through the adjustment of the rate of *discount* – made by the central bank of the country acting as fulcrum – to an international monetary system based on the identification of international with national currency. While the *conto* is fixed with the sole aim of achieving equilibrium among the participants in international trade as a whole, adjustment of the discount rate and, in general, the monetary policy of the hegemonic country has to (but at the same time is unable to) reconcile two different needs: the expansion of international trade and the equilibrium of its own external accounts.

An international monetary and credit system based on the principles of non-interference from the state and explicit subordination of finance to real trade: this is how we might describe the system that mediated volumes of international trade from 1533 to 1575, which amounted on average to four times the French GDP of the time.

So why did it have to end? It stopped working when a country

– France, as it happened – started tampering with it, intent on bending the credit circuit of the trade bills towards financing the crown's war debt. Apart from historians, few are acquainted with the story of the *grand parti de Lyon* – a loan made by the merchant–bankers to the king of France by way of sidetracking bills of exchange: it finished in widespread bankruptcy, with the first funding of public debt, going through an identification of the French unit of account with a quantity of metal, before the game came to its sorry end. Such was the monetary reform of 1577, which was eventually aborted.

While this prompted ruin for Lyon and serious difficulties for the financing of international trade, it also opened the way for the rise of another fair centre which, formally, applied the same exchange mechanisms as those used at Lyon. The system was known as the Bisenzone fairs. They were convened upon by the Genoese bankers in various places to begin with, then for a long period of time in Piacenza, and subsequently in Novi Ligure. Their sole aim was to finance the Spanish crown, and their history thus closely reflected the fortunes of Spanish power. Above all, however, having this particular goal to pursue while they retained the formal structure of the exchange fairs, they had to change the constitution of the *écu de marc*. No longer was it to be an international unit of account, but simply the denominator of a basket of effective currencies – a metal standard.

Henceforth bills of exchange were to be bent to the endeavour of instituting an international credit market based on a commodity currency with demand and supply based in its turn on interest – as yet not explicitly provided, but in practice calculable through the implicit mechanism of the exchange with reexchange (*ricorsa*), amounting to a systematically distorted use of the bill of exchange, no longer associated with the movement of goods, but with the need to continuously postpone the moment of payment.[8] As was noted by an observer of the time, Bernardo Davanzati:

> It is not people purchasing merchandise that go there [to Bisenzone], but only fifty or sixty exchangers with a quire of sheets, taking there the exchanges made in almost all Europe, and returning them with the due interest, not ruled but by the intention to operate in such a way that the game can go on [. . .]. Part are abuses, tricks *and not live debts or effective credits.*[9]

At Bisenzone, the fixing of the metal standard and the legitimization of interest on loans already become the pillars of a system that would be completed with the British reforms. In a matter of just a few years, a system that could not survive state interference evolved into a system that would have collapsed without constant state tending. At the same time, while the settlement of accounts had once kept the credit system healthy, it was soon to prove a deadly threat for a structure that could only survive by systematically postponing the moment of truth – a system holding in check its fundamental instability by constantly raising the stakes. We have finally reached the turning point in our backward journey through history.

PART III

Politics

1

Double or quits?

In concluding our anabasis towards the origins of the financial markets, we wrote that a real turning point had been reached. Now we have to ask how and in what sense the transition from the fairs of Lyons to those of Bisenzone *really* marked a watershed in financial history and, more generally speaking, in what sense all of the history re-examined can still prove relevant today, in the twenty-first century, for an understanding both of the ongoing crisis and of the institutional path that should be taken if we are to emerge from it adequately and with dignity.

The decision to start from the end in reconstructing the history of the financial system did not in fact result from a purely intellectual idiosyncrasy, but reflects the point of the book as a whole. The end of finance, in the sense of its purpose, can again become a serious subject of discussion only if we examine the threat of an end, understood as termination, which is inherent in every crisis. It is, however, precisely the fact that this crisis may reveal – not, of course, the chiliastic 'end of the world', but, in a very concrete form, the possibility that a way of conceiving and practicing finance has come to its end that makes the ability to conceive of an alternative to the present institutional framework truly essential. Given that this can coincide neither with some impossible 'abolition of finance' nor with the subordination of largely unidentified 'market forces' to an even less precisely identified public control (normally associated with 'statism'), the alternative cannot be attained solely through mechanical juxtapositions and reversals.

This is so not least because our backward reconstruction of western financial history has revealed nothing whatsoever in the way of an inevitable evolutionary process of a 'take it or leave it' character.

It is only for as long as progress continues to be the object of a *mythic construction* that 'leave it' will unequivocally mean a reactionary attitude of turning one's back on the future.

Very different horizons open up if we dispense, not with progress, but with its mythic and evolutionary construct. What manifests itself clearly in this case is that, despite the undeniable role of financial innovation, the present system and its innate propensity for crises are not at all the result of evolution and improvement, but have rather emerged through problematic junctures that have usually remained unresolved and hence critical. The only true progress from this viewpoint would be the decision to stop avoiding them.

When the problems are addressed, financial innovation ceases to look like the driving force of evolution and manifests itself as a surrogate for the failed institutional innovation that should have taken place. As regards the institutional structures of the financial market, the only decision taken with any real consistency has been the decision not to decide.

Our backward reconstruction has highlighted something that tends not to be made apparent in an evolutionary perspective and indeed to be dogmatically suppressed, namely the fact that innovation is not *in itself* a vehicle of improvement. Given the way in which the financial market has been established, its constant inclination is rather to resolve the structural imbalance out of which it was born and on which it feeds by means of a pure and simple strategy of raising the stakes. Jacques Rueff spoke, and certainly with little enthusiasm, of the perpetuation of the expedient with respect to the way in which attempts were made in his day to escape from the Triffin dilemma.[1]

The 'incremental evolution' that Eichengreen speaks about, and indeed not always in necessarily positive terms, is thus revealed as the constantly reiterated attempt to provide contingent responses to a structural instability that we have been able to trace back to the very nature of liquidity. The dilemma identified by Triffin in the Bretton Woods system – namely that it cannot be both stable and capable of fostering growth at the same time, which was linked in that case to the ambiguous position of the dollar with respect to the need for convertibility – is in actual fact the dilemma of all financial systems based on liquidity. Triffin's dilemma is a striking manifestation of the far more crucial *dilemma of liquidity*. The institutional construction of money as a commodity, and hence as a store of value, lies at the root of the structural instability of all the monetary and financial systems that people have endeavoured to construct on the basis of this dogma, from the classic gold standard to the post-Bretton Woods non-system.

The current evolutionary reading of our financial history makes it impossible to account for, or indeed even to recognize, the nature of the crises that have marked its course from the outset – including, *a fortiori*, the present crisis – and hence to take into sober consideration the possibility of an alternative form of finance. As stated above, this is not a matter of 'take it or leave it'. What we should really learn to leave behind us is rather the constitutive 'double or quits' approach, whose anything but clear structure has been shown to run all the way through the dilemma of liquidity.

The entire history of finance as financial market has thus appeared to be marked by a constitutive institutional deficit with a tendency to generate crises to which it invariably responds by raising the stakes in such a way as to increase the system's capacity for expansion, and in a certain sense its elastic resilience – but only at the cost of a radical exposure to increasingly violent crashes. The result is therefore the disappearance of any possibility that finance can count on a concept of equilibrium worthy of the name.

The history of modern finance has thus emerged as the history of liquidity *and its crisis*. At the institutional level, the history of liquidity manifests itself as a succession of liquidity crises, to which the constant response is to make the conditions of liquidation less rigid (for instance through a relaxation of the conditions of gold convertibility, where the initial gold dogma gave way to indefinite suspension). At the dogmatic level, the same history is instead presented, quite paradoxically, in the form of a gradual strengthening of the underlying dogma: the more commodity money works as a source of fragility for the system, the more this very representation is circulated as something self-evident and with no alternative.

The apparent absence of dogmatic alternatives can in turn account for the phenomena of the 'decision not to decide' and of the perpetuation of expedients. When the alternative is no longer even thinkable, 'decision' and 'reform' must assume the form of an increasingly less far-sighted, not to say blind, acquiescence to a demand for strengthening. When power becomes a complete synonym for truth, the watchwords of efficiency and, above all, *sustainability* become dogmatic and theoretical surrogates for the requisites of equilibrium and stability that have accompanied finance starting from the word itself.[2] Prevented from pursuing its end, namely closure, a finance identified with the financial markets endeavours and equips itself to live with no end, and indeed in no relationship with any end, to the point where its capacity for survival – in the form of a constant over-strengthening of its operative capacities and of an equally constant detachment from any constitutive relationship with the economy – comes to be mistaken for efficiency. As we have seen, this is a form of efficiency capable of supporting both production and destruction, indiscriminately; above all, it is totally compatible with the lack of distinction between peace and war, which has marked the history – with no qualifying adjectives – of the modern West with ever-increasing intensity.

The purpose of our investigation was, however, precisely to strip the supposed lack of alternatives of all its apparent cogency and to show it more concretely as the dogmatic effect of a repression. The alternative does not exist, first and foremost, because we are no longer capable of conceiving it. And we are no longer capable of conceiving it essentially because we no longer think about the base of the present financial system. Its foundation is assumed as a dogma, which reigns all the more undisputedly as there is less need even to mention it. This is why we had to work back along the trajectory, reaching the point at which the dogma can once again be seen *as such*. Asking *where the crisis originated* made it necessary to identify turning points at which what was institutionally involved was precisely a choice between principles, and in particular the choice between maintaining the principle of liquidity and resorting to the decidedly alternative principle of clearing, as in the case of Bretton Woods, or the choice, manifest at the beginning of our history, between maintaining the principle of clearing and abandoning it, tacitly and unavowedly, in favour of the principle of liquidity.

Various more or less convincing reasons can of course be put forward to justify the triumph of the principle of liquidity over clearing. If the aim is, however, not to justify but to explain, all those reasons are informed by the same logic that informs the principle of liquidity. Insofar as the *raison d'être* of liquidity and its strength in the short run lie precisely in postponing the moment of payment, and hence of decision, postponement has also been the element underpinning the way in which the structural problems of the modern finance have been 'tackled'. With a consistency that is implacable in its own way, these problems, and especially those of instability and crisis, have been resolved 'pragmatically' – but actually in total and dogmatic submission to power and its enhancement – through a growing institutionalization of the deferral of the 'moment of truth'. Failure to solve the problems has led to its opposite, namely the progressive entanglement of a Gordian knot whose ever-increasing intricacy has provided further grounds for continuing not to decide. As we wrote elsewhere, in relation (among other things) to the classic gold standard:

> Every time the modern monetary system has had to choose between paying a debt and postponing it, it has invariably chosen the latter. Suffice it to recall the way in which we arrived on the one hand at a gradual relaxation of the conditions of convertibility, from the gold standard to the gold exchange standard and then to the dollar standard, and on the other to the suspension of convertibility (and the resulting collapse of all three systems) first by Great Britain in 1914 and 1931 and then above all by the United States in 1971.[3]

The history we have recounted is the history of liquidity and of its underlying paradox, of which the Triffin dilemma is only a peculiar form, given that the dilemma is already to be found at the basis of the institution in which the modern financial system was officially born, namely the Bank of England: the systematic abandonment of the backing in gold for paper money is required by the system's need for expansion, but it constitutes at the same time a weakening of the requisite of stability, on which the same system rests.

Like every dilemma, Triffin's demands resolution while seeming to admit none at the same time. The tension inherent in the dilemma admits only expedients, albeit these are described as 'pragmatic solutions', in an attempt at ennoblement. Despite this appeal to common sense, however, these 'solutions' are nothing but purely performative acts – that is, acts retroactively judged to have been 'right' on the basis of their 'success', to the point where raising the stakes really appears to be the only possibility. An alternative does, however, become thinkable once again, precisely when this pragmatism is no longer regarded as sufficient, and in the name not of 'higher ideals' but of a *more concrete idea of praxis*. The solution to the Triffin dilemma, and to the institutional dilemma of liquidity in general, *admits alternatives* to simply raising the stakes. And it is when this possibility opens up that raising the stakes also begins to be seen for what it is: not a pragmatic solution to a problem, but simply a way of putting it off indefinitely.

The 'solution' to the dilemma of liquidity has consisted, all throughout its history, in systematically subordinating the requisite of stability to the requisite of growth or, to be still more precise, in subordinating the need that debts should be paid to the need for a credit susceptible of indefinite expansion. The decisions taken at the institutional junctures, which led from the gold standard to the gold exchange standard, from the gold exchange standard to Bretton Woods, and from Bretton Woods to the present non-system have meant greater instability of the new system with respect to what it replaced. Every system has made the payment of the debts, which was underpinning its existence, *more improbable* – even the Bretton Woods system, where this 'non-payability' did not manifest itself empirically through recurrent crises but in one fell swoop with the instantaneous and definitive suspension of convertibility.

The financial markets have become, and are destined to become, increasingly fragile: the price of saving finance has been to create a system that is more vulnerable and more dangerous than ever before.[4] And this is because the defence of a central nucleus of fragility has increasingly necessitated the deployment of highly peculiar tools of stabilization and reassurance, the reliability of which has been counted upon *despite* the fact that they involve no idea of stability in themselves, and therefore no limitation on growth. It is, however, precisely this that has been required of financial innovation, with always greater urgency and quite paradoxically: the provision of tools making it possible to discount and bypass any regulation that could cause anything to look in any way like a limit. Stabilization has not sought *stability*, but only the indefinite *sustainability* of imbalances in the name of growth.

In other words, the decision to free the financial markets progressively of every criterion of limitation *with a view to payment*, in other words to deprive money of its use as a measure, had to be accompanied by a form of financial innovation that has claimed, in increasingly dogmatic terms, to obviate the instability of the market *through the market itself* – a market placed, with always greater determination, in a condition of self-referential autonomy, one that is increasingly deregulated in the name of self-regulation.

The idea that the market could protect itself from the market through the market is clearly at the root of the exponential spread of derivatives. In 2004 Greenspan was still claiming that, thanks to derivatives, 'not only have individual financial institutions become less vulnerable to shocks from underlying risk factors, but also the financial system as a whole has become more resilient'.[5]

If the market is used as a bulwark against the instability that it itself structurally generates, its stabilization through innovation entails that the market can, and indeed must, always 'function'. It is, however, precisely this requisite of functioning that explains the increasing importance, in a financial market that wishes to be private and therefore deregulated, of the public dimension – in the form of the increasing importance attached to the role of the *lender of last resort*. The very market dogmatically asserted as self-regulating and self-reforming has entailed an increasingly 'strong' state as a structural condition for its existence, albeit in the form of a power – not of constriction, and still less of regulation and limitation, but quite literally of *seduction*.

Despite all claims to the contrary, the state and the market are inextricably linked, precisely in the birth of the financial market. Unlike every other market, which can ask the state to provide the normative framework for its participants to operate in, but can also, *for this very reason*, ask it to do nothing else, the financial market is the only one that cannot exist if the state does not continue to watch over it – and, what is more, in the ambiguous form of a controller that is also a debtor and a subsidizer dependent on those it subsidizes.

We have already discussed at some length the ambiguous role of the 'Greenspan put' as resolving the crises of the 1980s and 1990s and as paving the way for the present crisis. What history has enabled us to see more clearly is, however, the structural and preventive necessity of the lender of last resort, a necessity imposed as such at the very beginning of the construction of the financial market. In short, there is really no financial market without a lender of last resort, whose role cannot but increase in step with the instability of the system, given that this instability is *at the same time* the origin of growth and crisis, of boom and crunch.

History also enables us to see how the dual necessity of instability and stabilization eliminates *in principle* any possibility of a 'discourse of moderation', that is, any possibility of distinguishing between the rule and its violation in the form of excess. Where finance is organized into financial markets hinging on the lender of last resort, there is no possibility of distinguishing between normality and excess *other than a posteriori*: once the bubble has burst, when the excess of monetary liquidity has turned into what it already was, potentially and structurally, namely a lack of liquidity on the markets. It is, however, precisely in this situation of a lack of liquidity and drop in 'confidence' that the role of restoring liquidity, which is peculiar to the lender of last resort, appears inevitable to the point of being hailed as 'salvation'.

It should now be clearly seen in what sense the 'normality' that it is loudly called upon to restore can only coincide with a raising of the stakes and with further excess. If we may be allowed recourse to a parable, the lender of last resort tends to present himself like the father of the prodigal son, who accepts his son's repentance for extravagance and excess, welcomes him back into the ancestral home and reinstates him in the position he had irresponsibly abandoned. The reality is very different, however. The lender of last resort is rather a father who acts even more childishly than the son and confines himself to providing him with fresh funds, so that he can be just as prodigal (if not indeed more) having a greater sense of security, at least until his next 'repentance': a father who fails to act like a father and plays at being God and forgiving all the debts.

But what form can this 'playing at God' take? What we must see, dropping the metaphor, is that the lender of last resort can act as it does – and as it has been doing ever since the beginning of the current crisis – not because it is a more far-sighted creditor than the remorseful ones, whose lack of confidence threatens to perpetuate the crisis, but only because it is an *even more irresponsible* debtor than every other creditor and debtor ('irresponsible' being of course understood in a strictly logical and legal rather than moral sense). The lender of last resort is a debtor required to comply with no criterion of responsibility whatsoever, not even the one it can itself proclaim with sovereignty, simply because it confines itself to *lending a debt that it is not required to repay*. The lender of last resort is in reality a debtor, constructed so that it can never be called upon to pay up, and therefore able in principle to extend this singular property to *the financial market as a whole*.

While playing at being almighty, however, the lender of last resort is in actual fact forced to exercise this omnipotence *in just one direction*. If we look at what especially the American treasury and the Fed have done in practice since the liquidity crisis became clear and manifest, it is easy to see that their efforts have not been aimed at getting finance back on an even keel by changing its form and by introducing a principle different from liquidity, but simply at using the socialization of losses to increase the sustainability of a system based on the private appropriation of the income generated by liquidity – a system that the crisis reveals to be actually unsustainable.

Some will object that history is not a teacher of wisdom. This is certainly true if the expression is to be understood as meaning that history must provide obligatory lessons. At the same time, however, we may now have enough evidence to deduce that the way in which attempts are being made to find a way out of the present crisis actually *coincides* with entry into the next, an entry that looks as attractive as the crisis is distasteful, only because it takes the form of a boom. In this perspective, crunch and boom follow each other, having inverted roles with respect to the structure of what we call a financial bubble. The linchpin of this inversion is, once again, liquidity. Injected in huge amounts since the beginning of the crisis, money continues for the moment to stagnate and to create deflation. Given the way in which it is accumulating, however, the possibility of its inflationary return onto the markets – the financial markets in particular – at an unforeseeable but dogmatically certain point in the future is already becoming quite plausible.

Well, everything's all right then, isn't it? It is in this very cheerful light that the 'lesson of history' still tends to be read today. All crises come to an end sooner or later. If we survived the crisis of 1929, we will survive this one too, as long as we go on being optimistic and 'believing in the markets'.

The question arises, however, of why we never read the lesson of history in the other possible sense and see that all the booms come to an end sooner or later. In other words, what kind of suicidal optimism are we being led by? Perhaps the optimism derided by Giorgio Gaber, of the type that 'puts off suicide' by setting up groups of study and moral self-awareness, possibly even in the form of international summit conferences whose increasingly packed agendas now give birth only to magniloquent proclamations, and especially to arrangements for new and finally decisive meetings. Can the postponement of suicide through temporary measures and through raising the stakes really be enough?

The fact is that the 'strategy of postponement', to which the whole recent history bears monotonous witness, is, or will be, literally *self-reproducing*, at least until some alternative to this form of behaviour becomes conceivable.

It must, however, be stated clearly: no alternative will ever be conceivable until we make at least the effort to *conceive one in concrete terms*, to think out something rather than simply dreaming it up, making impassioned appeals for reforms and 'new rules' and basing everything on the 'will' and 'optimism' of those who proclaim – with a mixture of oversimplification and arrogance, not least from lofty public positions: 'Together we'll manage.'

And perhaps we will; *but to do what?*

If 'managing' were really just a matter of determination and optimism, the present system should be functioning perfectly and going through no crises at all. The condition was in any case clearly stated by John Law, at the very beginning of modern finance: 'the system is essentially sound [. . .]. All we need, to make it as stable as it is useful, is unreserved commitment.'[6] In short, we will be able to 'manage', but on condition that nobody ever opens her eyes and asks what we are doing. If 'managing' means this, then the 'trust', or rather faith, upon which the financial markets have always been based depends on nothing but the will to have it.[7] Such faith is, however, *totalitarian* in all respects, a faith that admits no doubt from anybody. It is a faith that requires everyone to relinquish their freedom in order to be able to take part in the production of the freedom of all – in the form of a democratization of finance, for example. A faith that admits no doubt is, however, a false faith. To say the same thing in 'positive' terms, it is a *nihilistic faith* corresponding to a very precise form of 'institutional nihilism', which the most clear-sighted jurists have been concerned about for quite some time.[8] The institutional nihilism underpinning the present financial system is not something to be defeated by will, not even (and perhaps especially not) when this will proclaims itself to be 'good'. Good for what and with respect to what? What common yardstick do we possess already, that makes it possible in the institutional field to distinguish between good will and bad will, innovators and speculators, finance at the service of the real economy and 'gangster' finance?

This is not a matter of taking it or leaving it. It is a matter of getting out of this apparent alternative, and of doing so by abandoning the logic of raising the stakes, the logic of 'double or quits'. This is only possible, however, if we abandon the realm of liquidity. And, once again, even though it imparts no obligatory lessons, history is the one that offers us some pointers here.

2

The way out of liquidity: The Gordian knot and utopia

Precisely because it is not a one-way process, the history of western finance is not only the history of liquidity and its ascent but also a history of forms, institutions, instruments and operative arrangements that elude the logic of liquidity – at least for as long as they can, as long as they succeed in maintaining their own institutional physiognomy.

Attentive readers will in fact not have failed to notice that credit institutions wholly unconnected with the principle of liquidity are by no means absent from our reconstruction. Moreover, forms of credit can still be found today that are based – or seek to base themselves – on the preservation rather than dissolution of the relationship between debtor and creditor. It may indeed be that the way out of the 'liquidity trap' – which hinges primarily on *seeing money as liquidity* – and into the perspective of reform and of an alternative approach can begin with a reappraisal of existing credit institutions.

It is basically only because bank credit was born in the form of the creation and preservation of the relationship between debtor and creditor – as the formula 'originate and hold' still recalls – that the process of securitization set in motion with subprime loans ('originate and distribute') can now be seen as an attempt, as explicit as it is clumsy, to dissolve the indissoluble – namely the risk inherent in the relationship between debtor and creditor.

This is not only a matter of pointing out that many more or less traditional financial instruments, from bills of exchange to mortgages, can be subordinated to the logic of liquidity only through degeneration from the principle that made them possible. The history of finance is one in which the principle of liquidity clashes not only with institutions and instruments that are incompatible with it, but also with an alternative principle, namely what we have called the 'principle of clearing'. We shall have to speak of this again. When all is said and done, what must be underscored is that this principle is to be found not only at the point where the history we retraced began, in the chapter dedicated to the Lyons fairs – and hence as a waning principle, on the point of being swept away by history. It is to be rediscovered in the British proposal at Bretton Woods, where it is asserted without any concessions to the nostalgia for a glorious past. As far as European history is concerned, it is to be found in the first place in the European Payments Union, operating effectively and as an alternative to the Bretton Woods system reshaped by the American amendments. If one looks with due caution and makes all the appropriate distinctions, one can also see it resurfacing, at least as an assertion of the need for an alternative principle, in the official Chinese stance of March 2009. This blunt statement appeared in an article signed by Zhou Xiaochuan, governor of the Chinese central bank:

> Back in the 1940s, Keynes had already proposed to introduce an international currency unit named 'Bancor', based on the value of 30 representative commodities. Unfortunately, the proposal was not accepted. The collapse of the Bretton Woods system, which was based on the White approach, indicates that the Keynesian approach may have been more farsighted.[1]

That this is a reference made in full knowledge of the facts, and connected precisely with the paradoxical structure of liquidity, is shown by the fact that, just a few lines above, Zhou had written as follows: 'The Triffin Dilemma, i.e., [the fact that] the issuing countries of reserve currencies cannot maintain the value of the reserve currencies while providing liquidity to the world, still exists.'[2]

The Triffin dilemma is the dilemma of liquidity. The fact that it has been resolved traditionally – as we must now put it – by raising the stakes and by subordinating stability to growth in no way means that alternatives do not exist and cannot be enunciated. If the principle of liquidity is neither historically nor logically the only possible principle on which to base the financial system and its connection with the monetary system and with the real economy, then the Triffin dilemma, with its incompatibility between stability and growth, is not something to be addressed by opting for one or the other of its horns.

This dilemma is in actual fact something that it is both possible and advisable to avoid by adopting a different approach from the pure and simple attempt to regulate what is by definition wholly resistant to regulation – namely liquidity and the financial markets. Precisely because it is based on jettisoning this attempt, the new approach must be authentically political and not simply technical, legal, regulatory and bureaucratic.

The approach becomes genuinely political in direct proportion to the extent to which it tackles the basic dogmatic issue. Though simple to frame, the question is one that it is wholly impossible to get round, as both our historical reconstruction and our phenomenological survey have clearly shown. *Is money a commodity or not?* Is money really money when it is a commodity or when it is not? The question is simple when its legitimacy and priority have been recognized, and the answer must also be simple: yes or no, *tertium non datur*. And the possibility of placing the political and economic issue of the architectural principle of finance on new and more solid foundations depends on the answer given.

Despite the constantly lurking temptation to claim that a problem has been solved simply because it has not been faced, the question has become increasingly unavoidable. The clear answer it has been awaiting for a long time, if not indeed from the very outset, has become still more urgent, ever since the practical and ideological collapse of the planned economy opened the way to a purely Darwinist ideology of market supremacy. It is precisely since the planned imposition of prices on production and distribution definitively proved to be an economic, political and ideological failure that the question of what a market economy is, of what it can and must be, has become still more delicate and crucial. Above all, it is an issue that depends to a great extent on the way in which the question of money is addressed and understood in all its real implications.

Asserting that money is not a commodity in no way means denying space for the exchange of goods, and hence for the markets. What it means is asking instead under what conditions markets can *really* perform the task of allocation assigned to them by economic theory.

Given that we cannot do either without money or without markets (as Keynes said in the 1920s, with reference to Mussolini, prices cannot be dosed with castor oil), the question is whether money markets are also necessary. If the markets are to make possible the signing of *fair* contracts, that is, contracts that it makes sense to comply with and to enforce, if they are really to express *equilibrium prices*, that is, prices that really bring producers and consumers together in accordance with a shared measure, is it necessary for this measure to be constructed in turn as an object of exchange or for it to be institutionally taken out of the market?

In order to answer, it should be specified that taking money out of the market *in no way means regulating the prices of goods*. It means creating the institutional conditions to regulate *the value of money*, its debt-paying power, and this solely with a view to making possible the payment of debts. The alternative presented by this crisis is not one between the market and planning, between liberalism and statism. This is simply the spectre raised by those who declare their readiness to change everything while actually seeking to change nothing at all. There is no better way to avoid facing the question of the future – and indeed of the present – than by conjuring up the ghosts of the past. And if these do return, they are never in the same clothing, but dressed up so as to look new.

The alternative that the question of money reveals, in all its relevance and crucial character, is between capitalism and the market economy, or rather between capitalism and the economy *tout court*. From the outset, we have given precise indications as to how this difference is to be understood: capitalism is a market system with one market too many, namely the money market, and hence structurally exposed to the risk that none of its markets may be a market in the true sense.

In this perspective, history provides indications that it could prove truly suicidal to ignore in the present situation. Taking money out of the market means adopting clearing as the architectural principle of a possible reformed financial system. It is true that the financial system as we know it was born precisely when the principle of clearing, and the particular configuration of the relationship between money and credit that it entails, were jettisoned in favour of the principle of liquidity. It is also true that, later on, that principle was to triumph precisely because of its greater power. The greater power of the principle of liquidity is, however, accompanied by the ever-increasing power of the crises it generates as an 'inevitable concomitant' of its normal functioning. If all this is true, then can we not perhaps see this crisis (whose possible duration and damage are things no one can claim, *in all honesty*, to know at the time of writing) as the right time to ask whether the state of extreme delicacy and complexity that characterizes now the relations between the components of the present system of markets and states (which constitutes the global economy) does not require an adequate and carefully considered return to the principle of clearing as the principle upon which to *rebuild finance*?

'It may be fine in theory but it doesn't work in practice,' some may well object. You can talk about reforms, and even about principles of reform, in theory; but practice is too complex to fit in with the simplicity of a principle.

We should, however, begin to recognize that the present complexity, reference to which is wholly legitimate, derives historically from the 'incremental evolution', which has proved in turn to be a result of the logic of raising the stakes and undermining the foundations, and which prompted us to describe the present-day financial structure as 'architecture with no architect'.[3]

The dominant system is not just 'complex'; it is not a 'dense network of institutions'. To be precise, it is an *institutional tangle*, made possible by the very fact that it has been left to its own devices. The demand for reform finds itself facing not a system of greater or lesser complexity, but one that *hides within itself the riddle of its own complication*. In this sense, finance as we know it is an authentic Gordian knot.

While nothing could be more disastrous today than to think of slicing through the Gordian knot with a blow from a sword, nothing is more urgent than the need to unravel it. If this cannot be achieved through determination and power, on the basis of an 'optimism' that is only an ill-concealed pessimism, then how can it be achieved?

Perhaps it can be achieved by aiming directly at the riddle at the very heart of the knot. The basic essence of all the reforms that it will make sense to implement in every specific field, in an effort to get out of this crisis in a way that does not prepare the terrain for another, possibly even more serious one, can be summed up as an action designed first and foremost to *strip money of its character as liquidity* wherever this is possible. But this means stripping money as we know it of its fundamental institutional character, namely the character of a commodity. Nothing less, but nothing more either.

Nothing more. Setting this objective in no way entails the need to abandon the terrain of the economy and politics, and especially the perspective of feasibility, for the 'glowing' but impracticable space of utopia. 'Utopia', which literally means 'no place', was the term used by Bernardo Davanzati for the Bisenzone fairs, based as they were on the delocation of finance and on the elimination of any distinction between money and credit. A way to avoid this placelessness may be found precisely in Keynes's Clearing Union project of reforming the finance through the explicit institution of a well-structured place of exchange and measure: 'not utopia, but *eu*topia', as he put it.[4]

At the same time, however, even if this is not a utopia in the sense of an unattainable objective, who is to say whether the proposal of a form of finance grounded in the removal of money from the class of commodities does not mask a nostalgic and regressive attitude, purely 'romantic' at best and effectively reactionary at worst? The fight against financial capital (the '*raffendes Kapital*' of Hitler's diatribes, with its ethnically unmistakable corollary of 'vampires' and 'leeches') was one of the war horses of the reactionary ideologies of the twentieth century. What kind of fundamentalism may be lurking behind the call for a non-capitalist reform of finance? Moreover, even if there is no fundamentalism involved, the risk could simply be of falling into a culpably naive anti-modernism – a systematic failure to appreciate the freeing of energies historically connected with the emergence of the financial markets. Without financial markets there would be no investments and therefore no development, no growth, no progress. Thus speaks the current gospel.

Are we perhaps calling for the abandonment of everything that the financial intelligence of the West has produced in the last few centuries and for a return to the fairs of Lyons? Are we perhaps thoughtlessly underestimating, or indeed reprehensibly keeping quiet about, the fact that, until three centuries ago, in other words before 'capitalism' and the industrial revolution, the 'economy' meant 'feudalism', that is hierarchy, immobilism and exploitation?

Of course not. We are not advocating a return to the past, for exactly the same reason why we cannot be content with an unconditional prolongation of our present into the future, and to the same degree. Both 'solutions' are inadequate because both underestimate the institutional and political (and basically economic) deficit historically marking the way in which the West began to move away definitively from a static and hierarchical society three centuries ago. What cannot be underestimated, except at the cost of a permanently increasing risk, is the fact that the undeniable liberation of energies and potential effectively brought about by 'capitalism' has been accompanied by forms of economic slavery and exploitation even less acceptable than those it had put an end to. Less acceptable because they are unavowable; unavowable because they are less and less visible; less and less visible because they are increasingly indistinguishable from the benefits that effectively accompany them, those benefits that prompted Keynes to write as follows: 'the *economic problem* may be solved, or be at least within sight of solution, within a hundred years. This means that the economic problem is not – if we look into the future – *the permanent problem of the human race*.'[5]

Keynes adds, however, that this state of freedom from the economic problem can only be attained if we learn once again to recognize the difference between what he calls 'absolute needs' and 'relative needs'. It is not only Keynes who speaks in these terms, but also the illustrious sociologist of globalization Zygmunt Bauman, who was recently prompted by the current crisis to point out that a model of life grounded on the possibility, seen as a right, to have on credit what you cannot have through work is anthropologically unsustainable. Before it can take a prescriptive character and become a 'discourse of moderation', however, the difference between absolute and relative needs can only be adequately learned if a relationship with measure has been instituted.

This is the point. When money is the kind of commodity that it costs nothing to produce and is therefore construed in such a way that there can always be more of it, the only limit and the only measure of its growth and 'sustainability' becomes, in a wholly intolerable way, the crisis itself. But why should free and progressive human beings fatalistically accept, as an 'inevitable concomitant' of their progress, the fact that the limit is imposed upon them by an element of chance for which they themselves provide fuel, ignoring its nature and its importance for the economy and continuing to labour under the illusion that an indefinitely produced commodity money can dissolve all risk and support all growth?

It is precisely when there is no measure for the economy – when the deeper sense of financial innovation takes precisely the form of making inoperative any form of preventive limitation, and in consequence the economy grows and develops as the very process of abolishing every measure and every limit; in short, when measure and rule *are blurred* – that crises become the inevitable concomitant of 'normality' and slavery the undesired but necessary concomitant of prosperity. Slavery arose historically as 'debt bondage', in particular bondage for debts that the victims were unable to pay. What form of slavery, even more subtle, is engendered when debts are incurred so as not to be paid? It is no coincidence that Alan Greenspan once let slip an extremely revealing remark, to the effect that, the more debts workers have, the less free they are to strike – in other words, the less they can hold their heads up and insist on respect for their dignity. The dignity of labour has been more and more surreptitiously replaced, even among workers, by the 'lordly attitude' of the *rentier*, a process aided and abetted by a form of finance that induces slaves to think that they can play at being masters, and makes debtors imagine that they can pass themselves off as creditors.

This absolute lack of any distinction between economic slavery and freedom is, however, precisely the situation in which what is referred to in this book as 'capitalism' and carefully distinguished from the market economy became fully operative after the fall of the Berlin Wall and at the end of the myth of the planned economy – that is, the myth of 'just prices' collectively administered by state bodies.

Pre-1989 capitalism was simply required to be 'better' than 'state socialism'. As long as it was economically juxtaposed to the Soviet type of planned economy, the only thing asked of it was that it be a more efficient system of production, even at the cost of some inequality – which could be compensated in turn through a redistribution based on welfare state policies. Much more has been demanded of it since the 1990s. It is now required to be *good*. Now that the competition for the most efficient way of organizing growth has been decided, the 'end of history', in economics, has taken the form of a dream of achieving not only production, but also the *redistribution* of wealth through the market.

On croit rêver. How is it possible on the one hand to assign this task to capitalism, and on the other to assert, blithely, that crises are a concomitant of the way it works? Even if the net result of the alternation between growth and crisis is, in the long run, positive in terms of the production of wealth, it can hardly be said that this is also true of the distribution of the income thus produced. Can we really claim, in all intellectual honesty, that the best way to distribute wealth in accordance with the basic principle 'to each his own' is a system in which every so often 'stuff happens' and 'tough luck for the losers', not to say worse?

It's like a dream. Or perhaps like something else. Certainly, this new capitalism has also been imposed by American unilateralism. As this is essentially a doctrine of war, it has also entailed a type of wartime finance in which, as the German general staff said during the Great War, *Geld spielt keine Rolle*: money is not an issue, you can always produce as much of it as you need, whenever you want. We must, however, also take into account the fact that, if you are to impose something, *you really have to believe in it.*

The fact that the ideological issue at stake in these last few years has been nothing less than *the love of capitalism* may make us smile, as may the opening of a long pamphlet that enjoyed great success – also with the left, if not indeed especially there:

> Capitalism, or more precisely, the free market system, is the most effective way to organize production and distribution that human beings have found. While free markets, particularly free financial markets, fatten peoples' wallets, they have made surprisingly little inroads into their hearts and minds. Financial markets are among the most highly

> criticized and least understood parts of the capitalist system. [. . .] Yet, as we argue, healthy and competitive financial markets are an extraordinarily effective tool in spreading opportunity and fighting poverty.[6]

It should not be forgotten, however, that this dogmatic move also made it possible to imagine the creation of a 'new world order', based on the full and unconditional compatibility of 'democracy' and 'the market' – a compatibility to be built primarily through the expansion of the global financial markets. Thus, supported operatively by an expansionary monetary policy, the globalized finance of the last twenty years also adopted the ideological form of a movement for the democratization of finance.

But then, once again, what does 'the democratization of finance' mean? In a nutshell, it means the creation of as much credit as possible, with no preventive limitation of financial leverage – only, this time, in the name not of profit and riches just for some, but of unconditional access for all to all the credit thus created. The channels of this access were precisely the financial markets, regulated by nothing but their ability to offer *more and more credit.* The underlying ideological hypothesis was in fact that access to credit made everyone freer, and free first of all from need, also known more bluntly as 'poverty'. Up until just a few months ago Francesco Giavazzi was still preaching that finance is made for the poor in his editorials.[7]

The concept was expressed still more clearly last year, on the site lavoce.info, in the following terms: the financial markets must be able to make it possible for credit to be granted *also to those who do not deserve it.*[8] This means, to those who cannot pay for it, those classified as subprime borrowers in traditional banking practice: debtors who offer insufficient guarantees of solvency; in other words, both the poor in the traditional sense and the 'innovators'.

There is no need to repeat here what we have already shown about the crucial nature of the relationship between debtor and creditor in the historical and phenomenological sections. It is, however, worth pointing out that financial capitalism was able to present itself, from this perspective, no longer as an extreme form of anti-social behaviour but, on the contrary, as *the most complete form of social market economy*, as a structure capable, in itself, both of lending to the 'poor' and of providing *all the guarantees* against the risks thus generated.

This unprecedented form of 'social security' took the form of the 'deregulation' and proliferation of derivatives, held in massive quantities also by pension funds and supported and practiced by the Fed under Alan Greenspan, who was certainly very consistent in seeking all this.

In this way 'the market', presented as the up-to-date synonym of capitalism without any distinction being made between them any longer, could be seen as the most efficient vehicle not only for the *production* of a surplus, in accordance with the traditional liberalist version, but also for its *social distribution*. The democratization of finance made it possible to 'think' that social policies such as public housing could be carried out, not after and alongside the market – by means of taxation and redistribution within the framework of welfare and income policies – but through the market and through financial innovation. This was the *utopia* underlying the system of unconditional liquidity, which was plunged into crisis with the collapse of subprime mortgages.

While the present crisis is of course helping to lift the first veil from this ideological representation, the definitive veil is evidently still in place. The liquidity crisis is not yet seen as the crisis *of* liquidity, as is shown by the fact that the attempts being made today are still to 'restart the machinery', in the hope that, if regulated a little more and a little better, it would be able to go on producing in the same way, but with fewer hitches. Never mind if this restarting involves a further relaxation of the bond between debtors and creditors, or even a more or less generalized moratorium on payments – that is, a shifting of the burden onto future generations. Even though some 'speculators' are justly punished – but at the same time held up barbarously to public scorn as the only ones responsible for a *systemic* crisis – the utopia of the abolition of debt and liability – along with the dignity involved in honouring one's debts – has not been abandoned yet. The question remains, however, of whether all this has a politically acceptable sense, or rather whether it is compatible with human dignity, which politics certainly does not create but which it is nevertheless called upon to protect against any (again, very human) tendency to forget about it in the name of more immediate advantages.

Well then, this is precisely what is at stake here. What we have to see in the crisis and what it shows us is the opportunity to institute a new relationship with money, one that may enable the market economy to display all its capacity for the free generation of wealth, but without freedom of economic action being mistaken for the right to avoid bearing a proportionate share of the risks; in other words, and in positive terms, without freedom of action being detached from responsibility and merit.

The 'principle of clearing' – and hence a form of finance based on money that is not a commodity and an unpayable debt, but a measure for the exchange of goods and for the payment of debts – has of course never yet truly formed the basis of an economy *geared to freedom*. It is, however, for this very reason that the reform of finance must also involve a rethinking of money. We are not in fact in a situation where waving a magic wand or brandishing a sword can instantly solve all problems and reverse the course of events.

If it is to become a politically practicable objective, the detachment of money from liquidity will involve learning to unravel – with delicacy, and hence calmly *but firmly* – the Gordian knot resulted from centuries of history, with their wealth of events as well as untaken decisions. In other words, it will involve learning to identify the institutional points upon which action can be taken, carefully estimating the form and timing of this action, and carefully weighing up the problems inherent in the transition from the principle of liquidity to the principle of clearing.

In this connection, it becomes crucial to develop the ability to focus on contingent events, along with a capacity for encompassing long-period aims, understood as the architectural principles that must be prior to contingency – given that any partial solution can only be a solution if it is coherently related to the whole of which it forms part.

In point of fact, the transition from one form of money to another also involves transition from a configuration of the relationship between money and credit based on their indistinguishability to one based on the possibility of distinguishing. This 'faculty of distinguishing' must, however, be learnt all over again in a certain sense.

History gives indications but issues no prescriptions. The reform of finance has to do not with excogitating remedies doomed to obsolescence a moment later, but with the construction from scratch of spheres in which it is possible to borrow with a view to payment and no longer possible to put off paying indefinitely, shifting all the burdens onto the fiction of a lender of last resort, which is such only because it is a debtor who never pays up.

On the basis of these monetary and financial principles, it is possible to begin looking for somewhere to start drafting 'new rules' and at the same time to judge the institutional tenor of the proposals and operations through which attempts have so far been made to find a way out of the crisis. This is what we shall do in the next three chapters.

3

Prevention or cure? The structural paradox of the anti-crisis policies

In the current debate, the political reactions to the crisis normally fall under two headings: stimulus and regulation. The countermeasures put into effect, or simply proposed, can in fact be traced back to two underlying approaches. On the one hand, we have an action designed to promote economic recovery so as to find a way out of the standstill at all costs, and as quickly as possible, on the assumption that any delay will entail still higher real costs and that all concern as regards financial sustainability must therefore be shelved for the moment. On the other hand, we have what is, as yet, mostly proposals for an action designed to regulate the financial system so as to avoid the repetition of similar episodes and to ensure that finance is actually placed at the service of the real economy.

As is more or less explicitly confessed, however, the major political predicament lies not so much in the difficulty of devising and implementing measures of regulation or stimulus, as in the apparent incompatibility of the two approaches. Prevention and cure are both equally necessary if one is to address the clearly manifested pathology that is undermining the economic and financial system at present – and not for the first time either. Nor do they have to be mutually exclusive in principle. In actual fact, however, most of the remedies designed to solve the current crisis threaten instead to accentuate the imbalances that generated it and could pave the way for a still more serious relapse. On the other hand, the measures aimed at attenuating the imbalances and excesses made possible by deregulation, and hence aimed ultimately at squaring the private, public and foreign accounts threaten to accentuate the present hardship and to endanger the recovery.

We shall endeavour in this chapter to outline the characteristic features of the two approaches, lay bare the roots of their incompatibility, and suggest a perspective within which their goals can prove compatible. As the key is provided by the whole of the examination carried out so far and recapitulated in the last two chapters, it can perfectly well be stated in advance here. What makes the two approaches incompatible is essentially their common feature of identifying money with liquidity. The advocates of both approaches share this dogmatic assumption at the theoretical and institutional level, and it is precisely this that prevents them from reaching agreement in the practical sphere. The dilemma of prevention and cure, stimulus and regulation, is nothing but the form in which the dilemma of liquidity reappears today, in a manner as urgent as it is contingent. Let us therefore examine the peculiar characteristics with which the recrudescence of the endemic conflict that has been undermining the financial system for centuries manifests itself today.

The primary objective of the first group of measures is to put a stop to the crisis. To this end, attempts are made to avoid any worsening of the contraction, to limit its effects on the real economy and to facilitate its resolution in the shortest time possible. In other words, the approach is to implement measures of crisis management – meaning management of the effects of the crisis – with a view to overcoming it. Provisions of this kind include bailouts, recapitalization, tax incentives, monetary expansion, devaluation and other more or less veiled forms of protectionism. The feature they all share is the intention of *restoring the liquidity of the financial markets*.

On the other hand, the aim of the second group of measures is primarily to prevent any repetition of such a crisis. Attention is accordingly focused on drawing up new rules for the sound functioning of the financial system, bringing the old rules up to date with the new developments constantly spawned by innovation, standardizing the existing rules and extending them to cover previously excluded areas, and setting up supervisory bodies endowed with broader powers to ensure their application. These are measures of crisis prevention, designed to prevent a crisis from taking place, and can be divided into subsets. The first comprises preventive measures aimed at reforming banking regulations (Basel II), in particular to correct and integrate mark-to-market accounting criteria; to increase reserve requirements, especially in phases of expansion; to define legally the role of rating agencies and to clarify their responsibilities; to revise the criteria of remuneration for executives. The purpose of the second subset is to extend regulation to instruments (derivatives), subjects (hedge funds) and areas (off-shore centres) previously subjected to no regulation at all, or to requirements of a very bland nature. The third subset contains provisions to foster the strengthening, coordination and possible integration, at international and intersectoral level, of the bodies of financial oversight. The intention underlying all these measures, albeit in different ways and to differing degrees, is to decrease the leverage and to *increase the liquidity requirements of financial intermediaries*.

As the measures involved are in any case political, they can only be introduced by national governments. International coordination is, however, crucial to the effectiveness of any action undertaken both to prevent further crises and to remedy the one still underway.

In the absence of international coordination, any expansionary manoeuvre will in fact have counterproductive side-effects. The country implementing it will either achieve the goal of boosting its internal economy, but at the expense of foreign competitors (for instance through devaluation, tax relief for domestic industry or duties on imports of foreign products) or favour foreign competitors involuntarily at its own expense (for example through policies that prove conducive to foreign investments or imports). At the same time, in the absence of international coordination, any regulation will prove to be completely inefficient as long as financial activities can be transferred to more favourable jurisdictions and countries introducing more restrictive measures are systematically penalized. There is indeed unanimous agreement on this point, at least at the verbal level: the response to a global crisis of the global markets must be globally coordinated.

The crucial importance of coordination explains the whole succession of international conferences held ever since the outbreak of the crisis. As they have no decision-making power but can only put forward guidelines, the proliferation of such meetings threatens to cause a glut of recommendations and proposals, whose effectiveness is inversely proportional to their repetition. As has been opportunely pointed out, the vacuousness of the declarations of intent formulated and reformulated at these gatherings can be measured by the number of assertions of such vagueness that no disagreement is humanly possible.[1] The veil of rhetoric serves only *to mask* differences in approach even with respect to shared objectives, *to avoid* having to discuss concrete measures that could reveal conflicting national interests, and *to duck* commitments at the international level that may prove unpopular at home.

International coordination has in fact only been achieved so far, and to a limited extent, in blocs of countries that adopted one of the basic approaches or the other. The USA and the UK have agreed on the need for immediate and massive intervention with expansionary monetary and fiscal policies, whereas the countries of continental Europe have insisted especially on the need for tighter regulation and have reached some (albeit vague) agreement on the main lines of action. This juxtaposition reflects the basic characteristics of the two areas involved and corresponds to the historical division of the industrial economies into Anglo-Saxon capitalism and Rhineland capitalism.

In the first, the financial system is traditionally market-based, in the sense that the credit required for production (and, to an increasing degree, also for commerce and consumption) is made available through the issuing of securities on the market; these include not only shares and bonds, but also commercial paper and ABS (asset-backed securities), most notably in the recent period. It is therefore comprehensible that in such a system the primary concern of the government and of the monetary authority in facing a crisis should be to get those markets working again, even at the cost of massive injections of liquidity; for they constitute a vital and indispensable source of supply for all economic activities.

The financial systems of continental Europe are instead traditionally bank-based. The credit required by firms (and, more recently, also by households) is supplied by the banks, mainly through participation in company capital or loans. In this case, the attention of politicians naturally focuses in the first place on strengthening the solidity and credibility of the banking system through regulation.

It should be noted that the supposed juxtaposition of liberalism and statism appears to be increasingly irrelevant in the definition of these alignments. State intervention and the functioning of the market are in fact both crucial and indispensable elements on both sides, regardless of the smokescreen raised by the ideological stances that still tend to be adopted around this polarization.

On the one hand, and even though they may not admit it explicitly, even the champions of the market as the most efficient mechanism for the allocation of savings and of 'market discipline' as the most effective form of regulation cannot dispense with the existence of a monetary authority, which undertakes authoritatively to provide all the liquidity that the market requires in order to function.[2] The point of reference is initially the central bank. As Alan Greenspan himself had to acknowledge, however, the central bank cannot work without the state. Nor is this the 'minimal state' of liberal ancestry, but rather a prodigal state *that also spends money it does not have*. He was forced to admit this at the end of the 1990s. Faced with the persistent budget surpluses of the Clinton administration and having called for their use to pay off the whole of the public debt, he realized with some consternation that, in the absence of state bonds, he would be without sufficiently secure assets to cover his emissions of liquidity.[3] In short, if it is true that there is no market without liquidity, it is also true that there is no liquidity without a central bank acting as a lender of last resort, no lender of last resort without an irredeemable consolidated debt, and no irredeemable debt without an immortal state.

On the other hand, even the most outspoken advocates of the need for regulation on both sides of the Alps, who are busy considering the prefects' intervention towards rationing the credit and declaring the end of Anglo-Saxon economism, take good care not to dispense with the market, or even with securitization alone.[4] No country appears to be willing to relinquish the benefits of participating in national or international financial markets as a debtor or as a creditor, not even China. State and market are seen less and less as a dichotomy and more and more as an inseparable dyad.

If these are not the poles of attraction, what, then, is the source of this apparently irrevocable juxtaposition in the strategies for resolving the crisis? Why are the two objectives of stimulus and regulation not seen as complementary, but rather as alternative – so much so that they can only be pursued in different places or at different periods? In short, why is it impossible for prevention and cure to take place at the same time?

The measures comprised under the heading of stimuli all involve increasing *the liquidity of the market* in one way or another: facilitating access to credit through emissions on the market, first on the part of banks and then, through the same, of firms and households; increasing the overall capacity for borrowing; paying off old debts with new debts, private debts with public debts. In this case, the liquidity that must never be found wanting is *on the liabilities side of the financial intermediaries' balance sheets* and consists of securities issued or loans contracted on markets whose liquidity is guaranteed by the state or by the central bank in the role of the lender of last resort.

Conversely, the provisions and proposals for regulation are aimed in one way or another at increasing *the liquidity of banks*. In this case, the liquidity that must never be found wanting is *on the assets side of the financial intermediaries' balance sheets* and consists of the reserves and deposits that should enable them to meet their commitments in due time. For this reason, regulatory measures are designed to tighten the constraints of obligatory reserves, to ensure that liquid assets are sufficient to cover short-term commitments, and in general to bring in line assets and liabilities in terms of their risk and maturity profiles.

The reason why the two approaches are structurally conflicting may appear clearer at this point. Both seek liquidity, but one seeks it on the markets and the other in the banks; one wants it in circulation and the other in reserve; one as a liability and the other as an asset. One wants more liquidity to be emitted by the central banks, the other less. The contrast between the two approaches is still more evident if each of them is taken all the way to its extreme, but now by no means unrealistic, consequences.

The stimulus strategy means in fact that every debtor in difficulty will be directly or indirectly financed by the lender of last resort, that every debt can therefore be paid off with another debt, and that ultimately no debt is paid. The underlying principle of all stimulation and indiscriminate expansion of the credit system is this: Thou shalt not pay. This is precisely the course of action taken by the bailout plans implemented especially in the USA and the UK for the recapitalization of banks and the purchasing of toxic debt.

Conversely, the regulatory crackdown that aims at strengthening the solidity of banks in such a way as to ensure their liquidity – conceived of in the sense of an ability to meet one's commitments when due, both in foreseeable and in *unforeseeable* circumstances – involves the provision of no credit at all.[5] This is indeed what is implied by the recent recommendations of international bodies designed to protect banks against the liquidity risk.[6] The underlying principle of all regulation and prudent supervision of the credit system is this: Thou shalt not lend. Each time the commandment is of course qualified, as required, within specific limits. Do not lend more than twelve times the amount of money you actually have (the principle of the 8 per cent prudential reserve). Do not lend for ten years money that you must repay in a month (the principle of maturity matching). The question of what margins remain in order to exercise the banking profession does, however, arise when the injunction becomes not to lend if you are not sure beyond any shadow of a doubt, reasonable or *unreasonable*, of being repaid. This is, however, precisely what the new guidelines, if taken literally, require of banks.

This dilemma was in any case pointed out in fairly similar terms by Jean Tirole with reference to the crises connected with international loans: 'Preventing crises is not a goal in itself; after all, prohibiting foreign borrowing would eliminate the threat of foreign debt crises altogether!' Moreover, 'creditors collectively would be better off if each (hypothetically) could commit to roll over any claims'.[7] In other words, the surest way of preventing crises is by never granting loans, and the most effective way of managing crises is by never demanding the payment of debts.

Seen from this viewpoint, in the light of the fundamental principles upon which they rest, the two objectives of prevention and cure obviously cannot do other than generate constant conflict. Even when, as is normally the case, we are not at either end of the scale, every step towards one of the two objectives means moving away from the other.

Is it possible, as Barack Obama suggested in a recent interview with the *Financial Times*,[8] for the two approaches to be regarded by the press (and, let us add, championed by politicians) not as irreconcilable alternatives (either/or) but as complementary solutions (both/and)? Most importantly, in what conditions would that be possible?

What might have appeared in the interview with Obama as no more than a remark made in order to soothe and reassure has instead proved to constitute the essential rationale of what the newspapers have blown up as the most important proposal for reform since the New Deal. While this is not the time or the place for a detailed analysis of the 'Obama plan', attention must be drawn to the following points. The text presented to Congress on 19 June 2009 refers to the breakdown of the traditional relationship between debtors and creditors brought about by securitization. We take note that the subject has been raised and we observe that, for Obama, repairing this relationship will involve safeguards for debtors *but also* for creditors, respect for Wall Street *but also* for 'Main Street'; in short, a balancing act with elements that will remain irreconcilable *as long as the principle of liquidity is in force*. In actual fact, while pointing out the need to restore the relationship between debtor and creditor severed by securitization, the document never asks whether this can really take place in a market, and above all whether the financial markets do not already, by definition, entail a relationship between state and market that can never be kept in balance except through the constant strengthening of both. Until the question of liquidity is seen as such, all that remains is the resolution, quixotic at best, to seek what Obama referred to in his presentation of the plan as a careful balance between free market and state intervention.

It may be worth stating this point still more bluntly. As long as the distinction remains blurred between market and state, that is, between the market and the rules for the market, the only market that really matters, also for states, is the market of rules, to be understood as a situation in which the movements of capital prompt a competition between financial systems that manifests itself, essentially and exclusively, in efforts to eliminate any possible limitation on those movements.[9]

Closer examination shows that the real problem is not the incompatibility between prevention and cure, but rather the fact that, due to the way in which they are pursued, both objectives involve the risk of undermining the fundamental structures of the fiduciary relationship between debtor and creditor, albeit in different ways. There are two inseparable prerequisites for this relation if it is to exist: it must be possible to make promises; and it must be possible to do so with credibility and reliability.

Instead of this, the regulation approach threatens to compromise the granting of credit in order to safeguard credibility, while the stimulus approach threatens to undermine the basis of credibility in order to ensure the granting of credit. If the financial relationship is one of opening with a view to closing, that is, one of granting credit with a view to the repayment of the debt, the greatest importance attaches to the junction of these two elements. It makes no sense to give priority alternatively to one or to the other. It is essential that both should exist and be in a well-structured relationship. If this is to be achieved, it will be necessary to jettison the logic that sets one up against the other.

If what we have described so far is a dilemma, we certainly cannot confine ourselves to pointing it out. What is necessary is rather to expose its paradoxical nature, and especially the underlying dogma upon which it rests – namely the dogma of liquidity, the view of money and credit as interchangeable. As long as money and credit are constantly interchangeable on a market or discountable in a bank, the closing of the relationship can have no appropriate connection with the opening, but must instead appear either as the moment whose indefinite and unconditional postponement is the cornerstone of the entire financial system, or as the moment whose simultaneous and equally unconditional arrival would bring the system crashing down. And, as long as finance is balanced between these two extremes, crisis can only be an inevitable concomitant of its functioning. What is at stake is therefore not a matter of managing the dilemma, but of finding a way out of the paradox.

Jettisoning the logic of liquidity would mean setting off seriously along a third path, which is not purely theoretical but has actually been proposed, albeit in a still vague and ambiguous form, by two emerging countries, namely Russia and China. We refer to the proposal mentioned above and given its most explicit and reasoned formulation in an article by the governor of the People's Bank of China. As noted, the declared intention of the proposal is to avoid the perpetuation

– albeit in different forms – of the same dilemma, namely the Triffin dilemma, which is essentially the dilemma of liquidity.

It is natural that the question should be raised first of all by China. The extraordinary volume of credit accumulated with respect to other countries over the last decade and the persistent balance of trade surplus make that country the most eligible to take over from the United States as the linchpin of the international financial system. This could mean the gradual replacement of the dollar with the yuan as a means of payment and reserve at the global level, which is indeed precisely the possibility foreshadowed to a certain degree by the loans that China has begun to grant other countries in the form of currency swaps. China has, however, let it be understood, through the statement of Governor Zhou Xiaochuan, that it has no desire whatsoever to assume a role that has already proved unsustainable and counterproductive in the long run and that would be so not only for China, as an emerging country and creditor, but also for the United States, as a hegemonic country and debtor, and ultimately for the financial stability of the global system as a whole. In the light of everything we have seen, why indeed should China have any interest in repeating, in the twenty-first century, the mistakes of England in the nineteenth and of America in the twentieth? A lust for power and hegemony? While the Italian saying that things always come in threes may be true, there may also be a limit to the short-sightedness of such aspirations.

In any case, apart from its generally favourable reception on the part of politicians and markets, the result of the G-20 meeting of March 2009 can be seen as a way of responding to this need. It was in fact decided then to boost international liquidity and credit, but by increasing the resources at the disposal of the International Monetary Fund rather than the international circulation of a national currency, and hence the international debt of one particular country. This is the solution suggested by Triffin to the dilemma that bears his name: the creation of international liquidity, denominated not in dollars but in Special Drawing Rights (SDRs).

This solution does not, however, offer a way out of the logic of liquidity. It simply transfers the source of liquidity from an unquestionably unsuitable national centre to one that is international, but in no way really supranational. Endowing the Fund with the function of a lender of last resort would ultimately mean focusing upon it and upon the division of its quotas and its governance the opposing interests of the major political and economic blocs. It would do no more than shift the dilemma from the USA to the IMF, which would be set up as a sort of international central bank, with the power and the task of issuing 'international currency' in the form of SDRs. The name of this 'currency' already suggests, however, that it would actually be a form of credit granting the holder the right to draw on the IMF's resources. The question would then arise of the assets that are supposed to guarantee the IMF's liabilities. Are these debts to be paid or not? In short, even if this were a way out of the Triffin dilemma, the dilemma of liquidity would still remain.

The Chinese proposal merits more serious and concrete consideration, and probably also on the part of China itself.[10] Nor are the official G-20 meetings necessarily the best place for this. It is indeed very probable that such a delicate question as the replacement of the dollar in its function as international currency can only be discussed in diplomatic settings, away from the media circus and its potentially destabilizing effects on the markets. Before the start of negotiations behind closed doors, however, public debate on the question and on its possible solutions at the institutional level would be most welcome. And it is here that all the parties are called upon to contribute in terms of their areas of competence, economists first of all.

For our part, we must observe, in relation to the path followed so far, that in all the debate on policies designed to tackle the crisis the truly crucial issue is the one about which least has been said, namely the reform of the international monetary system. In this connection, one potential new development is the explicit reference to Keynes's *bancor* by Zhou Xiaochuan. It really is a matter of 'going back to Bretton Woods', not in order to repeat the mistakes that were made on that occasion and that lie at the root of the present imbalances, but in order to seize the opportunity that was then lost.

It has been observed that Keynes's project is a blueprint ready for implementation. While a great deal has certainly changed since then, the problem is the same and, if possible, still more urgent: to create credit, but without leverage; to create money, but without liquidity. It is not therefore a matter of simply putting forward, once again, the structure of the Clearing Union just as Keynes designed it, but of rethinking its underlying principles in such a way as to delineate a framework within which the reforms proposed can also acquire meaning and prove compatible. So what are these principles? How are we to conceive them? What concrete indications can they provide for a reform of the present-day financial system that may offer a way out of the crisis (both the present crisis and the permanent possibility of crisis)? This is what we shall try to see in the next chapter.

4

Another finance

If the current crisis is regarded as a liquidity crisis, a simple increase in liquidity can also be regarded as a possible solution. And it might even work. By dint of refinancing banks and firms, it will also be possible to limit bankruptcies and get banking and production back on their feet. By dint of flooding the markets with public money to purchase shares that have plummeted, it will also be possible to raise their prices. By dint of increasing the amount of money, it will also be possible to induce those who have it to begin lending and spending it again. It will then also be possible for demand to pick up again in all its components: consumption, investment and exports. And the more convincing the public declarations of the authorities responsible for implementing these expansionary policies prove in foretelling their virtuous effects, the sooner these effects will be achieved.

Prices could of course also rise together with the demand. The risk of inflation could be particularly high at the beginning of recovery, when production could struggle to keep up with the increase in demand. The rise in prices could then heighten the tension in negotiations between the social partners over how the corresponding rise in income is to be divided between wages and profits. At the same time, this probable tension could also be alleviated if it proved possible – even more so than over the last thirty years – to channel the surplus liquidity into the financial markets and thus to ensure that it would be share prices that went up, rather than the prices of goods. In this way it would not be wages or profits to increase, as much as rents through capital gains on financial investments, always greater participation in shareholding, and the growth of funded pension systems. More than the income of one social class or another, the wealth of all would increase, 'democratically'. In this way, if everything 'goes right', the inexhaustible source of liquidity might render the dream of peace and prosperity possible once again.

Nevertheless, it would still be just that: a dream – the pipedream of finance with no end, fuelled by regained optimism and destined to last only until – at some unspecified and unforeseeable place and time – there will be, again, a call for debts to be paid and for money to purchase goods rather than securities. Once more, the rude awakening from this daydream will then necessarily take the frenzied shape of crisis in any of its possible forms, such as depression, hyperinflation or stagflation. And the new crisis will prove all the more traumatic – in direct proportion to the massive injections of liquidity used to doctor the previous recovery.

A liquidity crisis is like a withdrawal syndrome. You can alleviate it with methadone, but the attempt to cure drug addiction by administering such substances, even though in controlled conditions, involves the risk of inducing an even stronger state of addiction. In terms of the less extreme and more customary metaphor of depression, pharmacological treatment may be useful, but if you really want to be cured of cyclothymia and do not resign yourself to regarding the alternation of euphoria and depression – or 'manias and panics', to cite a classic of the history of crises[1] – as a physiological fact, you have to find a relationship with reality that does not take *the form of escape* in one way or another. In non-metaphorical terms, while it may prove indispensable to alleviate overdue debt temporarily by granting further credit, if you really want to get private and public finance back on an even keel, steps have to be taken from the very outset to ensure that all debts are payable when due and that payment is not deferred indefinitely. Only in this way is it possible for finance to regain contact with the reality of economic life.

If what we want is not just to solve a liquidity crisis, but rather to find a way out of the crisis of liquidity that has plagued the financial system from the very beginning of its capitalist configuration, we will have to abandon liquidity entirely as the architectural principle of the financial system and jettison the dogma of liquidity. But how? What does it mean to reform finance by relinquishing liquidity? As suggested back at the opening of this book, if we are to reform finance, we must first learn how to think about it. While it might even be true that there are no architects in this sphere, it is also true that, if there is to be financial architecture in the real sense, there has to be at least an *arché* or a recognized principle from which the construction and reconstruction of the financial system can draw their *technical* measures. And we have repeatedly said what this principle is: the end of finance, understood as its purpose, is to reach an end, understood as termination or closure, so as to make way for the production and distribution of goods. If this is to happen, we need money and credit in the true sense.

Both these ends of finance can be attained only when money and credit, each in its own way, are constructed so as to disappear at the right time and make way for goods, for their production and exchange. To this end, it is necessary on the one hand that credit should not be an indefinitely transferable commodity, but a relationship between a creditor and a debtor that is appropriate, in terms of legal structure and deadline, to the purpose for which the loan was granted; and, on the other hand, that money should not be a commodity susceptible of indefinite accumulation, but a means of payment and exchange within a clearly defined economic and political space. In short, it is necessary that debts should be paid and that money should be used to pay them. The answers given in the first chapters of the book to questions about the true nature of money and credit can now serve as indications of the criteria that any real monetary and credit system must be able to meet in order to be such. In other words, they can serve as nominal definitions of money and credit.

These definitions give rise to a series of distinctions, which, as preliminaries, are all the more necessary as the current language of the financial *doxa* is full of concepts that are commonly confused, or treated as synonyms when they should be kept distinct. These are distinctions to be re-established both at the conceptual and at the institutional level, as the incapacity to distinguish reflects not only a lack of thought, but also a lack of thought that has turned into a lack of institution.

The identification of money with liquidity is regarded as a matter of fact by the current *doxa*, but this does not mean that it must also be considered a fact of nature. This is not even the result of a purely intellectual operation of a subjective or collective kind, like a dangerous illusion to be avoided or a useful convention to be adopted. Money becomes liquidity rather on the strength of a *legal fiction*, an institutive act: money as liquidity is the putting into effect of a dogma. Stripping money of the property with which it has thus been endowed is therefore possible, but solely on condition that the operation is carried out at the same level: not through theoretical exercises or moral appeals, but through an institutive act, in accordance a science capable of drawing distinctions.

The first distinction to re-establish is precisely the one between *money* and *credit*. In current language and practice, the character of money no longer unambiguously identifies an object legally assigned the function of paying debts, but rather a 'quality' that belongs, to varying degrees, to every form of financial asset, to the point where it has become possible to use 'money' as an adjective and 'moneyness' as a synonym of liquidity.[2] If liquidity is a realm of indistinction between money and credit, this is therefore the first distinction to be reinstated in order to break free of the logic of liquidity.

Distinguishing between credit and money means in turn distinguishing between what serves to denominate debts and what serves to pay them, in other words between money as a *unit of account* and money as a *medium of exchange*.[3] Once again, these are entities that have been made identical and indistinguishable ever since money institutionally assumed the form of an object bearing upon itself a number expressing its value. Distinguishing between unit of account and means of exchange also means reopening the political space of the definition of their relationship – that is, beginning to think of monetary sovereignty *solely* as the prerogative of defining the value of money.

In turn, it is precisely this political definition that legally endorses the distinction between *money* and *commodity*: the fact that its value is neither irrevocably fixed nor left in the hands of the capricious calculations of the market, but made the object of political responsibility. As we have already written, this is not a question of assigning to politicians the power to set the price of goods, and thus raising the spectre of centralized planning, but rather one of entrusting the monetary authority with the task and the responsibility of setting just one price, namely the price of money, its debt-paying power. By doing precisely this, we would be in good company. Adam Smith explicitly recognized, as a public office, the function of the judge to reach settlement between debtor and creditor through the redefinition of the value of money with a view to the payment of debts.[4]

It is only if money is not a commodity that goods can truly be exchanged as such, and something like a market can therefore properly exist. The distinction between money and merchandise is therefore at the root of the distinction between *capitalism* and the *market economy*, as was outlined here from the opening pages on. The market, properly understood, is the place where it is possible to exchange goods freely, and nothing but goods. Capitalism is instead an economic system in which things that are not goods, and money in particular, are also traded on the market.

Moreover, recognizing the political dimension of the definition of the value of money means recognizing the need not only for politicians capable of performing this task, but also for a connection between every type of money and the economic and political space that it belongs to. In other words, it is a question of recognizing, once again, that money is always *the* money of a clearly defined community of exchanges – defined not necessarily in territorial terms, but also, or alternatively, in functional terms (say, with reference to the circulation of a particular type of goods). Hence the need to distinguish not only between *national money* and *international money*, but also between national and local money, and in general between different forms of money intended for different purposes and spheres of circulation.

If money is not a commodity, credit is not its temporary loan at a price. Credit is rather, and more originally, the deferral of payment or investment of capital in an enterprise with no possibility of establishing its profitability preventively, in terms of a set rate of interest. Credit is not a loan in return for some set interest and independent of its purpose, but rather a loan in which the mechanism and the timing of payment are closely connected with the purpose for which it is granted. Hence the need to distinguish between *commercial credit* and *investment credit* and between the corresponding legal forms.

The same considerations must hold *a fortiori* for international financial relations. If money is not a commodity that crosses every border, it makes no sense to think of savings as an amount of money previously set aside, which can legitimately go in search of the highest remuneration on the international financial markets, in this or that country. At the international level too, the only economic operations that really count in the end are the exchange of consumer and investment goods, and hence payments on *current account* and capital movements in the form of *direct investments*. Both require corresponding forms of credit.

If these distinctions make sense, then crucial importance attaches to the question of whether there are monetary and financial institutions capable of making them operative and freely acceptable. The reform of such institutions may take different periods of time. These can prove compatible, however, insofar as they rest on the same principles, so that the pursuit of one need not clash systematically with the reforms designed to put the others into operation.

The identification of institutional forms in line with the principles stated here can also take advantage of references to history, but not with a view to resuscitating, with no modifications, institutions that managed to work in times and conditions unlike those obtaining today. The problem is rather to find now a new answer to the question that lies at the heart of every true financial system: to make payments possible.

Let us therefore start from the principle that seems, more than any other, to belong to history and to moral precepts and religious beliefs that are, if not completely superseded, at least relegated to the dimension of private life, namely the prohibition of interest-bearing loans. Understood in the strict sense, as *interest*, and not in the broad sense of an *excessive* interest, usury is no longer banned, not even by the social doctrine of the church. While all of the three great monotheistic religions traditionally repudiated lending at interest, today only the most orthodox followers of one regard it as a sin.

What is known as 'Islamic finance' already shows, however, in the extraordinary variety of its instruments, that lending at *no interest* does not simply mean lending *disinterestedly*, that is, free of charge and out of pure solidarity, but rather that the creditor's 'interest' in lending can take forms other than that of a percentage on the amount lent – for instance a participation in the profits (or losses) of the investment financed. The fact that this form of loan is not only possible on a purely ideal and religious plane, but can also be desirable and appropriate in strictly economic terms is attested by its ever greater spread also among non-Muslims, as well as by the existence, in the advanced and most modern economies, of a typically European financial institution that is based on the same principle, at least in its pure form, namely venture capital.

Venture capital funds collect money from subscribers for long-term investment (an average span of three to five years) in the form of participation in the risk capital of innovative companies. Venture capital funds differ from private equity funds in that they provide not only capital and financial expertise but also specific industrial and managerial skills. For this reason too, venture capitalists do not receive a set return on their investments but participate in the firm's increase or decrease in value, sharing the risk with the entrepreneur for better or worse. The relationship thus created between creditor and debtor is as close as possible to the 'marriage' of savers and entrepreneurs called for by Keynes.

It may be objected that this very form of finance made a significant contribution to swelling the bubble of the new economy. The use of venture capital in that case was, however, greatly distorted by the possibility of listing the companies financed on the stock exchange *even before* they began to generate any profit. Flotation through initial public offering (IPO) dissolved the specificity of venture capital in the circuit of liquidity, thus making it possible to finance the most chimerical projects, as long as the market of new technologies was able to attract increasingly large flows of money. Where it takes the shape not of short-term financing with a view to flotation but of long-term financing with a view to return on real investment, however, venture capital does not suffer from financial cycles and, most importantly, does not fuel them, but instead remains anchored in and subordinated to the solidity and economic profitability of the new technologies it finances.

As the name suggests, venture capital is the form of credit specifically designed to finance economic activities whose results cannot be in any way calculated in advance. As we have pointed out with reference to Keynes, however, this is the characteristic peculiar to all investment, all entrepreneurial activity, all economic enterprise: relying on the force of soul, on 'animal spirits', to support and supplement pure calculation.[5]

Foregoing the rate of interest does not in fact mean foregoing economic calculation as a whole, but rather putting yourself in a position to calculate in the true sense, refraining from anticipating what cannot be anticipated, abandoning the bookkeeping artifice of calculating the present value of future cash flows, and shifting from the patrimonial logic of fair value accounting to an approach based on cost and revenue accounting. If money cannot be represented as capital that generates returns, still less can the firm. No matter what the theorists of shareholder value may claim, just as money is not to be seen as capital awaiting certain remuneration, the firm has no need whatsoever to be assessed on its ability to provide returns on the money invested. It is money rather that must be invested, in view of the firm's ability to pursue its aim.[6]

Also trade, as investment, can be financed without any need for interest-bearing loans. Here too, loans can take the form of a delay or a respite in payment, with no involvement whatsoever of money previously set aside. This form of lending does not even necessitate the existence of a *physical amount of money*. As we have seen with reference to the trade fairs of Lyons, the Clearing Union and the European Payments Union, all you need is a centralized system of bookkeeping to carry out the necessary compensations. In other words, it is sufficient to have a form of bank money used as a unit of account – money that can be created at a stroke of a pen whenever it is needed to carry out a transaction.

As we have seen, this kind of money is often accused of being inflationary. It would be very easy to object that *fiat* money, as we know it, is potentially far more inflationary, as it can also be created *ex nihilo* and *ad libitum* but, unlike the book money we have just described, it has no connection whatsoever with the actual exchange of goods. There is, however, an even more telling objection. Insofar as the faculty of creating money out of nothing in order to foster exchange also means the possibility of destroying the money that is in excess of requirements, clearing systems simultaneously avoid both the deflationary and the inflationary potential structurally inherent in the various phases of the *fiat* money system. What is possible with a pure unit of account is instead impossible with a reserve currency. We have already seen one way of carrying out this destruction in a precisely calibrated and measured way: it was at work in the Clearing Union, in the form of a charge on the balances of surplus countries.

In more general terms, the destruction of liquidity can take place through the imposition of a sort of 'circulation tax' – a rate of demurrage, as it is appropriately called – acting as a negative interest rate on money that is not used. The idea of *Schwundgeld*, money that depreciates (or, more literally, 'vanishes'), was formulated by the unorthodox economist Silvio Gesell and then taken up, analytically reformulated and warmly championed by Keynes in the *General Theory*.[7] This idea is not held only by 'monetary cranks', to use Keynes's own term. It also constitutes the foundation of the proposal put forward, albeit in a different form, by the far more orthodox American economist Irving Fisher.[8] Still more significantly, it is not only an idea, but also an institutional practice adopted in places and periods sometimes very distant from one another (and most of all from ours). Forms of depreciating currency have in fact been known in economic systems as disparate as those of Renaissance Europe, Mogul India and some rural areas of Austria and America struck by the Great Depression.[9] In all these cases, the imposition of a depreciation rate proved to be an effective measure to discourage hoarding and to foster the circulation of money, which thus maintained its liquidity, understood as the *ability to flow*, without being itself liquidity – that is, purchasing power susceptible of *indefinite* accumulation.

It is clear, however, that there is no possibility whatsoever of a depreciating currency being successfully used and achieving its purpose as long as it can be unrestrictedly exchanged for other currencies, not subject to demurrage. Placed in competition with accumulable money, depreciating money really would be bound to vanish, but immediately and definitively, as has actually happened each time when such a competition has come into effect in the course of history. No monetary rule, including the rule of demurrage, can survive in conditions of monetary exchangeability.[10] This is why a monetary rule can only be truly established if its jurisdiction is defined. And this is why the only political act that money requires is the definition of its sphere of validity. Money can only exist inside a clearly defined political space. Money is a tool of autonomy in the dual sense of demanding it and strengthening it.

The same principle also makes clear the advisability of drawing a distinction, institutionally, between national money and international money, and in general between internal money and external money, with a view not to the autarkic separation of economic spaces but to the possibility of making compatible, and indeed really *complementary*, the equilibrium of the domestic economy with the equilibrium of the balance of foreign trade. This was the declared intent of the proposals put forward not only by Keynes, but also by the liberal economist Einaudi,[11] and even by Ricardo.[12]

It is not necessary, however, that the sovereignty presiding over money should have the exclusive form of the nation–state. The theory of optimal currency areas has gained support over the last few decades and is in fact also the basis of the European Monetary Union. At the same time, there is no reason why an *optimal* currency area should not be *infra-national* rather than international in extension. Nor can it be ruled out that the appropriate criterion to define a monetary union be *functional* rather than simply territorial. There has been an enormous growth in the number and variety of experiments with local currencies over the last few decades. This has admittedly happened in most cases with no clear understanding of what issuing a currency really involves in political and economic terms,[13] and hence at the risk of repeating the shortcomings of the official monetary and financial system on the local scale – but with the aggravating circumstance of operating outside any framework of legality.[14] In this case too, however, we learn less from news reports than from history, and especially from comparative history, which is full of examples of currencies of a local, communitarian character, or variously circumscribed in their sphere of circulation and powers of payment.[15] In their great variety, these examples already give some indication of the feasibility and advantages of such forms of monetary organization. It would be a good idea to foster their spread, not through imposition by the central authorities but rather by leaving it to the initiative of the exchange communities, on the basis of a principle of *monetary subsidiarity*, whereby the task of the central authority would be primarily that of establishing a normative framework for the definition of the principles with which a currency must comply in order to be defined as such.

In any case, for as long as an accumulable currency exists in the world and is exchangeable with the others, it will continue to be accumulated as a store of value, in preference to any other form of money *and to goods*. For this reason, despite the possibilities of adjustment at the local and national level, the problem of reforming the monetary and financial system must necessarily be addressed also at the global level. And all the distinctions we have drawn so far must apply also at this level in the definition of international money and credit, if money is to be spent and debts are to be paid.

In the first place, a clearing system for international trade based on the model of the Clearing Union and European Payments Union is necessary, but also, and above all, feasible, even in the short term. This means taking seriously the proposal and the considerations put forward by the Chinese central bank. We need a medium of exchange serving exclusively for the payment of international trade, and solely for circulation. In order to avoid its being hoarded by some countries and then loaned to others at interest, it must be subjected to a rate of depreciation. We would thus have an international currency that is truly international and truly currency, in other words money capable of performing its function in virtue of its speed of circulation and not of its quantity. Liquidity, in the sense of the actual amount of money, would prove wholly irrelevant.

In the second place, international investments must take the form of direct rather than portfolio investments.[16] This does not mean prohibiting the latter. As noted above, the existence of a clearing system tends by its very way of operating to render the movements of capital in this form useless and uneconomical. At the same time, this does not mean preventing transnational relationships of credit and debt from being established, but indeed ensuring that such relationships are stable and lasting: that they have a long-term rather than a short-term perspective. The transfer would not be exclusively one of money, but also, and always, one of knowledge and skills. While portfolio investments tend to accentuate financial imbalances and complicity between debtors who do not pay and creditors who 'get rich' by not demanding payment, direct investments involve a real relationship of joint responsibility between creditor and debtor, oriented towards the maturation of the investment and the payment of the debt. It would therefore be desirable for most international financial relationships to take this form. In this case, liquidity – understood as the constant and generalized transferability of securities on global financial markets – would prove completely irrelevant.

Finally, with a view to reducing still further the advantage of money over goods as a way of storing wealth, it would be a good idea, as a precautionary step, to remove the primary obstacle to the accumulation of commodities, namely the huge costs of storage and deterioration to which the owner is liable and the uncertainty with regard to future selling prices. Attempts have been made, with little success, to assign this function to the market, especially through forward transactions. The results are visible to all in the ever greater swings in commodity prices of raw materials, which in no way correspond to the meeting of demand and supply, but rather reflect the difficulty of attaining it. Nevertheless, attempts are still being made today to present the market as a solution with no alternatives. In actual fact, the solution has existed for a long time, and takes the form, not of abolishing the market, but of supplementing it with public storage programmes for raw materials and foodstuffs.[17] The adoption of similar systems of buffer stocks at the international level could help significantly to stabilize the prices of primary goods, to the benefit of producers and consumers alike, absorbing the surplus in periods of abundance and offering supply in periods of scarcity. A return to the traditional principles of food administration would make it possible for primary goods to regain their character as reserves, to be built up and distributed promptly and fairly when needed. In this way goods, rather than money, could perhaps once again be seen as wealth par excellence. Liquidity, understood as the character of money as a store of value, would prove wholly irrelevant.

Here, in a nutshell, are the principles and tools for a real reform of the financial system. It is not at all a question of abolishing finance but, much more concretely, of transition from finance based on the market to finance for the market.

While this could unquestionably take a long time, it would be as well to make a start for that very reason. And if we are to make a good start, we have to begin from the first principles. This does not mean issuing prescriptions, establishing hierarchies or, still less, substituting skills, but rather drawing upon the skills already in existence, so as to make the whole still more concrete. Until the economists who have long ceased to find support for their work in the prevailing financial dogma decide to assess the soundness of the principles and guidelines succinctly outlined here, the same principles can serve as tools to examine what has been done and proposed and what has not been done. This is what we shall do in the next chapter.

5

The (rare) 'green shoots' of a possible reform

The idea of reforming the financial system could appear unrealistic if it involved turning upside down a system consolidated for centuries, fully capable of performing its function, open to no substantial criticism, and above all with no alternatives. This is, however, not the way things stand in any sense.

First and foremost, this is not a matter of turning anything upside down but of learning how to jettison, not a system, so much as faith in its supposedly automatic mechanisms. Second, the crisis itself has not only brought to light the flaws in the financial system, but also opened up the possibility of redesigning it. And if this situation has seen a great many proposals put forward for the sole purpose of 'plugging the leaks' at all costs, suggestions have also emerged that are wholly consistent with the possibility of implementing the reforms outlined in the previous chapter.

We shall therefore examine the primary measures adopted and suggested and assess them on the basis of their ability to serve the ends of finance and to bring out the need for payment, considering first the expansionary manoeuvres of a fiscal and monetary character, then the proposals for regulation, and finally the efforts for coordination at the international level.

There can be no doubt that the expansionary manoeuvres, the legacy of a form of crisis management that began with the New Deal, are precisely the ones designed to plug the leaks, and that they therefore entail a price that is not taken sufficiently into consideration. At most, it is suggested that, when the patient is seriously ill, it is not the time to worry about the side effects of the drugs administered. The authoritative scholars who have put forward this view in authoritative fora have completely failed, however, to ask themselves whether this metaphor is applicable to drugs that are themselves the cause of the illness.[1]

In a period of recession, when the tax yield cannot be expected to rise, every increase in public spending will eventually mean an increase in the public debt. Bailing-out firms, recapitalizing banks, tax relief for consumers, investments in infrastructures, and in general all the programmes of fiscal stimuli implemented by governments can alleviate private indebtedness only at the cost of aggravating public indebtedness. In short, they boil down to the substitution of private debt that has become irredeemable, through public debt constructed so as to be irredeemable. Even if they do fulfil the most optimistic expectations and succeed in halting the collapse of the productive and financial system by boosting internal demand, they also create two further problems without solving the basic one, at the root of the crisis, which consists precisely in the previous accumulation of unpayable debt.

The first problem is that, with massive public intervention in the financial sector through bailouts and nationalization, partial or total, the regulating authority becomes even more deeply involved and at risk of structurally losing its already historically feeble capacity for impartial regulation. Fears in this sense were expressed in a recent speech by Christopher Cox, president of the Securities and Exchange Commission (SEC): 'Conflating the roles of market regulator and market actor would ultimately threaten the integrity of the regulatory system, and is certain to produce dangerous unintended consequences.'[2] These fears were well grounded, given that $6,400 billion of federal resources had already been allocated at the time of the statement to help banks and firms in trouble. Intervention on such a scale inevitably generates a structural conflict of interest, which remains such despite the good intentions and the good faith of the parties concerned. The legitimate demands for control of the new public shareholder, to protect the taxpayer inevitably, come into collision with the equally legitimate demands for autonomy of the old private shareholders, to safeguard not only their private interests but also the particular public interest that consists in freedom of competition and initiative. This conflict has already emerged, for example, with respect to executives' earnings, the conditions offered to customers and strategic alliances.

The very fact of placing public intervention side by side with private initiative makes it increasingly difficult to manage the relationship between state and market necessitated by the very structure of the financial markets. By improperly taking on the role of actor on the market, the state compromises its ability to perform its function and prerogative of regulating the market, which is also indispensable for the market's traders. If the regulator is to be truly such, it must be *super partes*, just as the market, if it is to be truly such, cannot claim the right to lay down the rules for its own functioning. The programmes of fiscal stimuli put into effect by governments to address the present crisis simply put the regulator and the regulated on even more of an equal footing. As we have seen, the endemic conflict is then resolved through the compromise of temporal alternation, whereby the state assumes the role of the particular actor that is *occasionally* called upon to foot the bill, so that all the others can start earning for themselves again once the storm has passed.

This compromise involves a very concrete price, namely the growth of the public debt. Here we have the second problem aggravated, if not indeed created, by the programmes of fiscal stimuli. We have become accustomed to the idea that the problem is the 'sustainability' of the public debt, in other words the possibility of always finding new purchasers for the government bonds – issued to replace those that reach maturity and to cover the new deficits – without having to offer prohibitively high rates of interest. The most indebted countries are in fact already paying the price of their creditors' misgivings in terms of higher rates on long-term securities, high costs of insurance against default, and devaluation of the exchange rate. This is what has happened to the United Kingdom, so much as to suggest the possibility of a downgrading of government bonds on the part of Standard & Poor's, and the same is also beginning to happen to the United States. It should be recalled, however, that the interest paid on the public debt, be it high or low, constitutes a cost for the taxpayers as a whole, which should be recompensed with an equally general benefit and a set term of closure.

Given the scale of the losses in the financial sector and the risk of further and still more widespread losses throughout the economic and social system, governments have been able to argue that it is in the general interest to intervene, and therefore also to finance the intervention. At the same time, in order to obtain the funds at reasonable costs (that is, in an attempt to prevent their own bonds from being the financial assets struck by the next crisis), they have immediately presented repayment plans. It is, however, legitimate to suspect that the projections upon which these plans are drawn have far more to do with the governments' hopes than with reasonable and generally acceptable expectations. What need would there be for state intervention, if the investments in question were really profitable? Would there not be a rush of private investors in that case? It is legitimate to suspect that the state has to intervene precisely because it can allow itself not to pay up in circumstances in which the payment of the debt is anything but guaranteed. The growth of the public debt simply defers the moment, and indeed the very possibility, of the payment of debts.

The central banks have stood alongside and supported the governments in this. Fiscal expansion has been accompanied by an unprecedented monetary expansion as regards the scale and the variety of the provisions adopted. In the first place, all of the major central banks have made utmost use of the traditional tool of monetary policy. The discount rates applied by the Bank of England and by the European Central Bank (ECB) are at their historical minimum, and the Fed fund's target rate is close to zero. The central banks have not, however, confined themselves to making their loans less onerous. They have also increased the categories of potential beneficiaries, broadened the range of assets accepted as collateral to include those of the 'toxic' variety, and extended the maturities. Finally, in an attempt to reduce the long-term interest rates (and also to provide tacit support for the growing public debt), many central banks have allocated huge amounts for the purchase of government bonds.

The most aggressive policy has been put into effect by the Fed, whose total assets and liabilities doubled between March 2008 and March 2009, going from $1,000 billion to $2,000 billion (Figure III 5.1), as a result of the measures adopted.

Examination of the composition of the Fed's assets shows that the expansionary manoeuvre consisted largely in increasing the forms of security accepted on its loans. On 25 November 2008, for example, the Fed announced the start of a programme for the purchasing of GSE (Government-Sponsored Enterprises) bonds and of MBS (Mortgage-Backed Securities) guaranteed by the GSE for a total of $600 billion, plus a credit line of $200 billion, to be lent against ABS (Asset-Backed Securities) covered by consumer loans or loans to small businesses.[3] In March 2009, in collaboration with the Treasury, the Fed launched a new plan called, the TALF (Term Asset-Backed Securities Loan Facility), described in the press release of 25 November 2008 as 'a facility that will help market participants meet the credit needs of households and small businesses by supporting the issuance of asset-backed securities (ABS) collateralized by student loans, auto loans, credit card loans, and loans guaranteed by the Small Business Administration (SBA)'. The American central

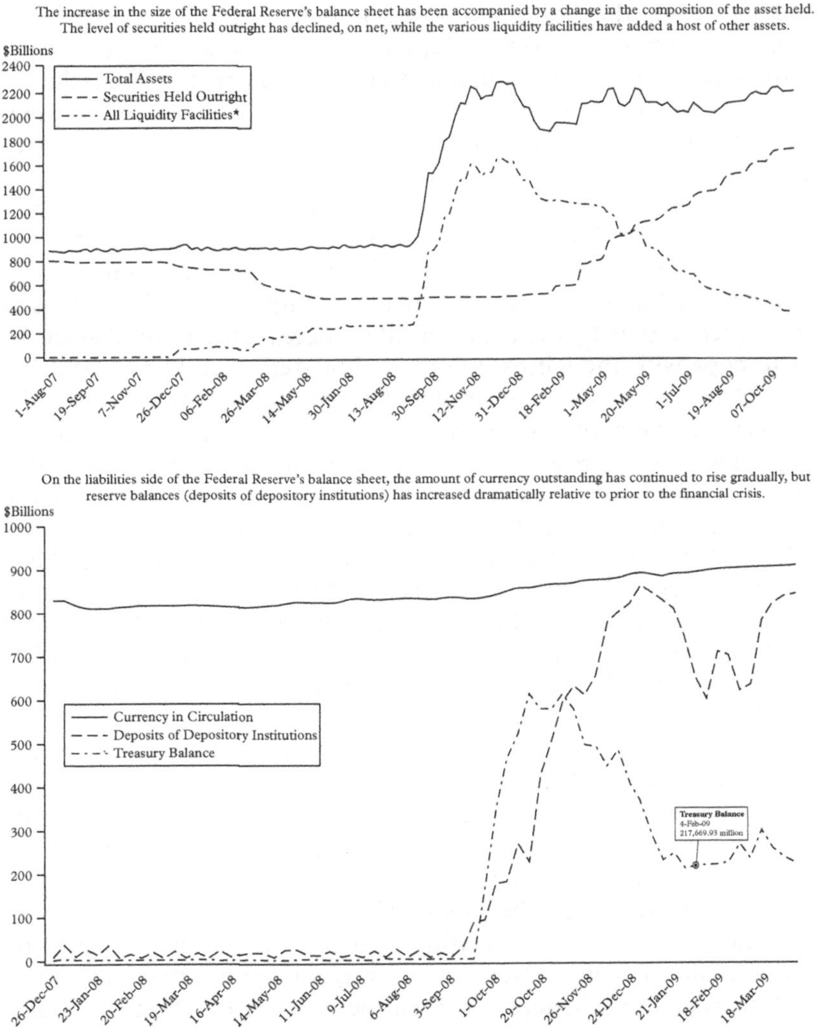

Figure III 5.1 Composition of Fed assets and liabilities

Source: Board of Governors of the Federal Reserve System, Credit and Liquidity Programs and the Balance Sheet. Available at http://www. federalreserve. gov/ monetarypolicy/bst_recenttrends. htm

bank's injections of liquidity are therefore substantially covered by junk bonds.

In this way, by acting as a depository for toxic bonds until things pick up again, the Fed has *already* assumed in all respects the role of the 'bad bank' that some still persist in regarding as a remedy yet to come. The attempt to restore liquidity to the markets by purchasing junk bonds constitutes an updated and even more drastic version of the Greenspan put. Even if it does work, there is no reason to think that this 'Bernanke put' can be anything but a raising of the stakes for the next crisis.

The situation is no more encouraging if we examine the structure of the liabilities. The monetary expansion in the United States has taken the form of an increase, not in the number of banknotes in circulation, but in the reserves held by banks at the Fed. This is motivated in turn by the banks' need to increase their liquid assets so as to cope with the increase in their short-term liabilities – or debts payable on demand – constituted by deposits. In other words, the increase in the supply of money has served entirely the purpose of coping with an increase in the demand for money as a store of value (for precautionary or speculative purposes), and not with an increase in the demand for money as a medium of exchange (for the purpose of transactions). The liquidity injected by the central banks has been almost entirely absorbed by hoarding. The more money the banks receive, the less willing they are to lend it, in case they do not get it back. As Michael Darda, head economist of MKM Partners LLC in Greenwich, Connecticut, commented: 'It's like spitting in the wind.'[4]

The result is that the total reserves held at the Fed are above the obligatory level to the tune of $600 billion. This means that about half of the $1,300 billion supposedly pumped into the economy by the Fed in the space of a year[5] has come back to it in the form of deposits *without ever getting into circulation*.

Which brings us to the point. The fact of thinking in terms of quantity, and hence of equating monetary policy with regulating the amount of money issued, in no way guarantees that the money will circulate, and hence that it will perform its function as money. No monetary policy can even think of achieving its aim until money ceases to be liquidity. The amount of money issued could suddenly prove excessive and result in inflation.[6]

This is indeed the objection, understated in its form, but precisely aimed and devastating in its substance, raised by Albert J. Hettinger Jr, one of the directors of the National Bureau of Economic Research (NBER), against the now fashionable view put forward by Milton Friedman and Anna Schwartz as regards the possibility of avoiding crises like the crash of 1929 simply by injecting 'high-powered money':

> With possibly unjustifiable oversimplification in description on my part, the basic weapon in the authors' arsenal may be termed their concept of high-powered money. Their treatment of its role is consistent and brilliantly analytical in depth. One point only disturbs me. There is no question as to the mathematical demonstration. If high-powered money could be increased by the Federal Reserve without that very move setting other forces in motion, unforeseeable both as to source and intensity, I would have no reservations. I lack competence to pass judgment. This is not a controlled experiment, with high-powered money increased and all other factors remaining constant.[7]

In other words, it may well be a nice idea but we have no grounds whatsoever for expecting it to be applicable – for expecting that the money made available by the central bank will actually be used and therefore will actually be money. Once again, one wonders on which side the utopia lies.

In point of fact, the Fed's mounting debt, like the Treasury's, can only continue as long as the readiness of the banking system and private investors to hold its liabilities (money and deposits) grows at the same rate. Bernanke has tried to argue that these liabilities have increased in order to meet an increased demand for liquidity, that is, for safe forms of saving, and that they can therefore be reabsorbed just as soon as this demand drops again.[8] In saying this, however, the governor seems to ignore the fact that the money he creates can alternatively be used (spent and lent) or not used (kept as a reserve) *while the holders are under no obligation to account for their decisions to him.* Today, in an attempt to increase the money in circulation, Bernanke thus issues money that does not in fact circulate and expects that tomorrow, when nobody will any longer ask for money in order not to use it, the money will be returned to him without anybody feeling tempted to spend it or lend it. This is so hard to believe that it is reasonable to suspect he does not believe it himself.

Proof of the soundness of this hypothesis is provided by the fact that, with a view to reabsorbing in due course the enormous amount of liquidity created in order to cope with the crisis, the Fed is considering the possibility of bonds for sale on the market so as to take money out of circulation. The idea is doubly perverse, however, both as regards the Fed's private budget and in view of its public role. In the first case, it would mean relinquishing its main source of revenues. If seignorage consists in the faculty of incurring debt at no cost, why in the world should the Fed give up this prerogative in order to incur debt at a cost? The only plausible reason would be an improvement in its capacity to perform its institutional functions, insofar as issuing bonds in exchange for money would enable the Fed to reduce liquidity and hence the risk of inflation. But why do so by *paying* those who *agree to stop* holding money in exchange for safe assets? Would it not be a more immediate and direct solution to achieve this by *penalizing* those who *hold* money by imposing a cost on money that is not spent, in other words by means of a rate of demurrage?

This hypothesis opens up a crucial horizon as regards the reform called for here. The power to create liquidity out of nothing, which central banks have possessed for centuries now, must be accompanied and balanced by the symmetrical power to destroy the liquidity thus created. The encouraging sign is that the need to make possible the adoption of negative rates of interest, and hence of costs on the holding of money unspent, is starting to be discussed in positive terms even in the more conservative circles, from a paper by Marvin Goodfriend of the Federal Reserve Bank of Richmond to a recent article by Brendan Brown in the *Financial Times*.[9] Another way to pursue the same goal with the present tools of monetary policy consists in the explicit setting of a *minimum* rate of inflation by the central bank, as suggested by Mishkin and Leunig in the *Financial Times* and by Mankiw in the *New York Times*.[10] It is indeed for this very purpose that the Fed recently inaugurated a policy of transparency as regards its target of planned inflation, which is indicated explicitly as not only a maximum but *also a minimum* objective: 'Also, increased clarity about the FOMC's (Federal Open Market Committee) views regarding longer-term inflation should help to better stabilize the public's inflation expectations, thus contributing to keeping actual inflation from rising too high or falling too low.'[11]

Planned inflation could have the effect of a negative rate of interest, and a credibly announced inflation target could prove easier to attain. Asking precisely this of the central banks while their institutional function remains the defence of the purchasing power of money would, however, mean expecting them to declare in a credible way that they are not credible. In its present configuration, unlike in the situation called for by Einaudi in his 'apology for imaginary money', monetary policy cannot set the value of money.[12] Even if a carrying cost of money is accepted as a necessary objective, seeking to achieve it in this form will mean remaining confined to the sphere of the 'unscientific expedients' to combat the tendency of money to accumulate, which was described by Keynes in 1923 as a makeshift not free of unknowns and undesired effects, in other words as a pure and simple surrogate for a monetary reform grounded on scientific considerations.[13]

After eighty-five years, some hyperinflation and a great many crises, the time has thus perhaps come to raise the question of *monetary reform* explicitly. All of the policies adopted by the monetary authorities can essentially be traced back to two objectives: to keep the value of money under control and to ensure that the money issued is actually used – spent or lent. Even though the recent innovations may appear daring and unprecedented, the tools for this purpose at the disposal of the central banks only succeed in achieving one of the two objectives, and to a very incomplete and uncertain degree, often at each other's expense. All that is needed is perhaps just to be more precise rather than daring, and explicitly to equip the central banks with tools more appropriate for the task in hand, namely the power to set the value of the medium of exchange, in terms of a unit of account distinct from it, and the power to promote its effective circulation through a rate of demurrage. In other words, it would be enough to assign the monetary authority the sole task of providing a measure or rule for truly free exchanges.

This is instead the only rule missing in the list drawn up by those – above all, in continental Europe – who have seized the opportunity of the crisis to call for a tightening and extension of regulation in order to avoid the explosion of financial assets wholly unconnected with the real economy. While they can be strengthened and expanded, the tools of regulation are bound to remain insufficient for this purpose until the dogma of liquidity is called into question and the institutions in which it is embodied are modified accordingly.

Consider, for example, the attempt to redefine the criteria of remuneration in the sector of finance with a view to reducing the incentive to focus attention on short-period objectives and to assume systemic risks (that is, risks that materialize in the long run, in our sense). Can we really ask traders to pursue long-period objectives, in other words to 'look to the future', when the financial market is organized in such a way that this would always endanger their 'present' competitiveness and hence ultimately their survival as traders? Should we not try instead to change the very form of competition, its institutional framework, in such a way that the short period be structurally subordinate to the long, and behaviour be suitable for the individual trader only if it does not clash with the general interest? To a certain degree, this can already be done at the level of corporate strategies for the remuneration of employees, which could give more importance to the risk manager than to the asset manager, unlike what has been the case so far.[14] Since businesses also have to balance their books, however, such a change in relative importance is really possible only to the extent that the bookkeeping criteria allow suitable weight to be given to the two functions.

Fair value has come to predominate over the last twenty years as the primary principle of bookkeeping. Its spread has been supported in particular by the FASB (Financial Accounting Standards Board) on the grounds that it is the only principle capable of taking into account the 'facts' reflected in market prices. According to its advocates, the approach does not cause losses but simply confines itself to registering them. We should therefore be consistent and admit that there is no crisis from this standpoint, in the sense that there is no possibility of distinguishing a situation of balance from one of imbalance, given that even the most dramatic collapses in share prices would simply register a new balance.

Few have shown willingness to put their trust consistently in this formulation, however, when the losses have come to be such as to jeopardize an entire financial system. Thus it is that the American Bankers' Association (ABA) recently asked the SEC to limit the application of the principle of fair value to banks.[15] Moreover, when there is no longer a market and hence not even a price for assets, as has happened in some cases, the principle proves wholly inapplicable. The Geithner plan has become indispensable in order to restore liquidity to the markets and hence their ability to formulate evaluations, that is, to form prices. It is, however, precisely this intervention – justified by the failure of the market or the assumption that the market was mispricing certain assets – that undermines any claim that the market is the one and only oracle of 'true value'.

The assertion of the principle of fair value was the result of economic science shirking the task of formulating a theory of value, in other words the task of defining a 'fair price' that may differ from the market price. The abandonment of that principle, which is now advocated by many, essentially means reopening a question that has played a crucial role in the history of economics, namely that of the relationship between value and prices. While making no claim to have come up with a solution, we do know that this is a question that economics must necessarily address both at the theoretical and at the institutional level.[16]

At the institutional level, claiming that the market price is the only true measure of the value of a financial asset means postulating that there is a market for every financial asset and that every credit relationship therefore takes the form of a standardized negotiable security. This is precisely the direction taken by most of the financial innovations of the past few decades. The spread of securitization, the proliferation of derivatives and the growth of hedge funds have all helped to create liquidity and thus to ensure that there is always a price for every financial asset.

As long as liquidity remains the principle and purpose of every financial asset, all attempts to regulate these instruments are of course bound to end in a *temporary* suspension of deregulation. As we have repeatedly observed, however, there is no need for the relationship between creditor and debtor to take the form of a negotiable security. Alternative forms exist that are perfectly in line with the various functions of financing the economy, permitting its growth without imposing it as a prerequisite for stability. Support for our view comes from proposals to promote forms of commercial respite in order to finance exchanges and forms of participation in profits, so as to finance investments while preserving the distinction between the two. In this spirit, Nigel Lawson, the former chancellor of the exchequer, recently proposed the reintroduction of the Glass-Steagall Act, passed in 1933 and repealed in 1999, which provided for the separation of commercial banks from investment banks. Others have called for the promotion of venture capital, also through the use of public funds, thus following the Chinese model of policy banks.[17]

A further signal of the need to distinguish between value and price and of the impossibility of making the market solely responsible for the determination of all value is already given in the present configuration of financial relationships by *the very existence* of rating agencies. The function of these agencies is supposed to be precisely that of evaluating creditworthiness. The crisis has now shown, however, that the agencies' ratings are not necessarily more accurate and reliable than the market prices. Moreover, as many have (subsequently) pointed out, the agencies operate in a situation of structural conflict of interests, since they are paid by those who issue the securities (the debtors), they base their assessments exclusively on information supplied by the debtors, and they often act as advisers to the debtors on the best ways to obtain a good rating.[18]

At the same time, we cannot expect this conflict to be resolved, as some claim, by making it obligatory for the agencies to be entered in a public registry, on condition that they prove able to meet certain requisites. It is in fact basically impossible for rating, in its present form, to be anything but a *surrogate* for an independent third party in relations between debtors and creditors. On the one hand, rating is indispensable as long as the debtor/creditor relationship takes the form of a negotiable security. On the other, it can never be truly impartial as long as the rating agencies continue to be what they are:

not only arbiters, but also actors in the market. Institutional endorsement of the public role of rating agencies would change nothing at all with respect to the reality of this situation. Nor can we look for a solution in the greater competition between agencies, by instituting a 'rating market', since this would make it necessary, by the same logic, to admit rating agencies for the market of rating agencies, and so on ad infinitum.

In any case, until it is clear what setting a rule for finance actually means, the role of the public regulators will also be subject to the same risk of infinite regress. First came calls for the reform and centralization of oversight at the national level. Then it was suggested that regulation should be extended to every sector, instrument and market. Given the global scale of the financial markets, it was finally suggested that coordination should be instituted between national bodies, or even that an international supervisory body should be created. Now, however, in order to avoid having to stop at this level and thus finally being obliged to set rules for finance, this is no longer conceived as a permanent institution with its own statute, but as a continuous process of reforming the rules.[19] There is no end to the regress, and so, just as rating is a surrogate for judgement, regulation becomes a surrogate for rules.[20]

The same fate appears to have befallen the International Monetary Fund. The G-20 meeting decided on an increase in endowments and on the issuing of special drawing rights in April 2009. Discussion is now under way of a revision of quotas, and there have been calls for further strengthening its lending powers through expansion of the New Arrangements to Borrow and through an increase in bilateral support.[21] At the same time, an increase in the size of the Fund will necessarily mean an increase in the problems connected with its institutional deficit. As we have seen, the IMF was conceived in 1944, as a body to safeguard a 'regime of stable exchange rates'. For the last thirty years, however, it has performed the far more ambiguous task of preserving a 'stable regime of exchange rates', thus leaving the system of the international trade with no yardstick.

The need to redefine the regime of exchange rates has received little attention as yet. It is, however, a matter of crucial importance, especially at a purely factual level. Exchange rates have undergone massive fluctuations since the outbreak of the crisis, thus helping to accentuate the speculative movements of capital. The resulting increase in international uncertainty has contributed in turn to a drastic reduction of the volume of international lending and to a decrease also in direct investments, which are structurally more exposed to exchange rate risk. Nevertheless, there has been no improvement as regards imbalances in the balance of payment, which could lead to further large-scale adjustments of the exchange rates between major currencies, especially between the dollar and the yuan. Even if these imbalances do not give rise to a devaluation of the dollar, as it would seem logical to expect in view of the 'basics', they will remain as factors of 'basic uncertainty'. What reliability can an exchange rate have that only remains stable because – and for as long as – the party that could sell a currency refrains from doing so?

While there would thus be very cogent reasons for a reform of the exchange rate system, these are nothing but contingent manifestations of the underlying problem of international liquidity. Every currency is international liquidity as long as it can be traded against other currencies like a commodity, at the price determined on the international markets. If international money is to stop being liquidity, it will be necessary to stop *that price* from being determined by the market – necessary, in other words, to institute a regime of adjustable pegs, where the exchange rates are adjusted through political decisions, possibly agreed upon at the international level on the basis of previously established rules.

The main objection to such a regime has traditionally been, and still is, the scarecrow of competitive devaluations. If every country were free to set its own exchange rate, there would be the risk of arbitrary reductions in order to increase the competitiveness of exports at the expense of international competitors. Closer examination reveals this to be a hypocritical objection that overlooks the fact that such a strategy is quite feasible also in a regime of flexible exchange rates, and has in fact been adopted by China for some years now.

We should really ask ourselves what importance we can attach, with respect to all this, to the risk that a country *with a deficit* embarks unilaterally on a competitive devaluation, as envisaged by the Keynes plan for Bretton Woods. Where the prerogative to decide exists, there is of course always the possibility that the decision will be wrong. There is also, however, always the possibility of detecting and punishing mistakes. In other words, it will be a *responsible* decision if taken within a closely organized institutional framework. This does not mean that it cannot be wrong, but simply that you pay for your mistakes.

The primary risk today is that of emerging from the crisis through an effort of will and a projection of desire. There is a whole ritual made up of policymakers' announcements, public opinion polls and media campaigns aimed at instilling new confidence in entrepreneurs and consumers. It may have some effect. With the beginning of spring and President Obama's observing 'green shoots' in the US economy, the improvement in market sentiment, as registered by the rise of share indexes, has been accompanied by an improvement in the mood of traders as measured by the indicators of optimism and confidence.

Far from being anything to be taken as a concrete signal and as a solid fact, all this could simply mean that the market itself, in its capacity for self-regulation, is the object of an act of faith and an ideology – especially the financial market. Some still cling stubbornly to this ideology despite the financial market's clear manifestation of its incapacity for self-regulation with the crisis. The view of the crisis as the result of the failure of self-regulation is indeed put forward not only by adversaries of deregulation – historical or newly converted – but also by a man who has always been a resolute and openly declared champion of the market's – especially the financial market's – ability to regulate itself, and who continued to be so even when he assumed the role of regulator of that very market and held it for twenty years. In the hearing on 'the financial crisis and the role of federal regulators' held by the Congress Committee on Oversight on 23 October 2008, Alan Greenspan, governor of the Fed from 1987 to 2006, explicitly recognized that the view informing his every action, namely the assumption that the markets were more efficient than any regulation, was actually an ideology, and a false and harmful one at that.[22] While in his performative perspective Greenspan regards this as false insofar as it is harmful, it is actually still more false when it does not seem to be harmful but presents itself in the guise of a benefactor, as it has been able to do for centuries now.

Does this crisis therefore mark, opportunely, 'the end of laissez-faire'? We must answer 'yes', but with the immediate provision that the laissez-faire that must come to an end is only of the variety regarding money and investments, which is indeed what Keynes meant when he wrote the essay bearing that title. If money is not a commodity, it makes no sense to leave the fixation of its price to a market.

The price of money takes three forms. It can be defined with respect to the entire set of goods produced and exchanged inside its space of circulation; with respect to other forms of money circulating in other spaces; and with respect to another moment in time. The internal value of money is expressed by its purchasing power; the external value, by its exchange rate; and the intertemporal value, by the rate of interest.

All three of these values should be taken out of the market's hands. While this may look like an extreme assertion, closer examination shows that it is exactly what every central bank tries to do, but *without possessing the tools required for the purpose.* The central bank is forced to act on all three fronts with the single tool of the discount rate, in an attempt to control – or at least influence – the trends of prices, the structure of the interest rates and, if necessary, also the exchange rate with other countries.

The power to regulate the value of money in all three of its forms should be explicitly assigned to the monetary authority, possibly organized into three distinct bodies. Taking the purchasing power of money out of the market's hands means distinguishing between unit of account and medium of exchange. Taking the exchange rate out of the market's hands means instituting a system of adjustable exchange rates. Taking the interest rate out of the market's hands means instituting demurrage on currency, clearing for commercial credit, and participation in profits, but also in risks, for investment credit. These distinctions would finally provide the monetary authority with different tools to pursue different objectives. It would thus be equipped with adequate *tools* to define and pursue its objectives; with the *discretionary powers* needed to modify these objectives when necessary; and with *responsibility* for their correct definition and their effective attainment.

The end of the money market would not be the end of the market. On the contrary, it is only by putting an end to the market of money and credit that we can finally start to have markets in which everything that is truly an economic good and hence also a commodity can be bought and sold for what it is. The end of the financial market could be the beginning of every other market. The end of capitalism could be the beginning of a true economy.

So why not try?

6
If not now, when?

A backward leap of over two centuries will help us to arrive directly at the heart of these final reflections. The year was 1795 and Europe was faced with a choice. A war had just begun in which a new political form, namely France's republicanism, was threatened by the determination of traditional states to impose a restoration, and therefore it took action to defend its political conquests. But the way in which it did so affords a glimpse into the possibility that a war begun with a view to establishing peace for all nations and the right of a people to self-determination might instead take the conflict to a more dangerous and uncontrollable level. The very difference between war and peace was in doubt. For precisely this reason, however, the state of crisis called for a reflection on peace that would be truly capable of addressing the situation. This was the context in which Kant wrote his essay on perpetual peace.

The important thing was in fact not to leave peace to the good intentions of any one party, or indeed of all, but to anchor it in a political configuration capable of making it, to begin with, clearly distinguishable from a simple truce. The distinction between peace and a truce is one that 'will appear merely academic and pedantic', Kant says, if 'the glory of the state is placed in its continual aggrandizement by whatever means'.[1] If it is not, he adds, then this distinction alone will make it possible to construct an order capable of *guaranteeing* the *possibility* of peace, not indeed 'with sufficient certainty for us to *predict* the future in any theoretical sense, but adequately from a practical point of view, making it our duty to *work toward* this end, which is not just a chimerical one'.[2]

Practical certainty is sufficient for Kant precisely because peace is not, and will never be, the automatic product of a scientific calculation that takes mankind as it is in its natural state, that is, a state of war, and expects to lead it to a state of peace on that basis. There is no 'science of peace' because peace is in no way simply 'natural' but rather, Kant says, a space that must be *established.*[3] The space of peace is not technical, but political, and does not arise by itself through evolution or partial adjustments but must be expressly established, so as to be adequate to what it must ensure.

Why this long preamble? Not only because the question of war and peace and of their lack of distinction in modern finance has appeared repeatedly as a crucial theme of our reflections, but also (and quite simply) because in economics *making peace* means *paying up*. In the same way, when 'the glory of economies' is placed so as to be exclusively in the pursuit of unconditional growth, the systematic postponement of payments is nothing but a truce.

Therefore Kant's problem concerning peace arises also for finance and payment. Now as it did then. So much so that, in order to be wholly consistent, our position should be stated as follows: finance, understood as the settlement of accounts in due form, can never be the automatic product of a scientific calculation, because payment is not simply 'natural', but must be *established*. The space of payment is not technical, but political, and does not arise by itself, through evolution or partial adjustments, but must be expressly established so as to be adequate to what it must ensure.

We do not simply wish to suggest a parallel, but rather to recall a fact that has been repeatedly highlighted here, *namely that the possibility of peace is also historically bound up with the possibility of payment.* This is why our concern about the risk of this financial crisis being 'solved' through a truce in the form of a raising of the stakes is not only economic in character, but also indissolubly political. The persistence of global financial imbalances *structurally* vitiates the possibility of global, political and economic peace.

Let us now return to Kant. As is known, he argues that what can guarantee the pursuit and attainment of perpetual peace is not an absolute superstate, a super*power*, but a federation of republics that are truly *independent*, from their own power in the first place. And so, for Kant, also independent from the particular form of finance that is based on the *money of power*.

To proceed in an orderly fashion, the preparation of the space of perpetual peace entails in the first place the assertion, made in accordance with a certain number of articles, of principles that are shared and such as not to fuel a tendency to war, which Kant rightly identifies in the very principle of power: the principle whereby the increase in power pursued by each party is the sole prerequisite of the 'balance' between all of them, so that war becomes the paradoxical prerequisite of 'peace'.

From the standpoint of power, war not only becomes increasingly manageable in technical terms, but also tends to establish itself as the most immediate instrument in handling the relations between states. Standing armies predominate among the tools serving this purpose. Imprinted as it is by the logic of power, the standing army can mean only one thing for Kant: an arms race, a race by all and sundry to overcome one another.

This build-up of military power has a necessary corollary for Kant: standing armies also make a finance of war a permanent necessity. It is therefore hardly surprising that the article 'Standing Armies (*miles perpetuus*) Shall in Time Be Totally Abolished' is immediately followed by the article 'National Debts Shall Not Be Contracted with a View to the External Friction of States'.[4] Kant's discussion of peace explicitly intersects with the question of finance at this point.

It is therefore well worth reading extensively the arguments put forward by Kant. If the public debt serves for the 'establishment of stores against unfruitful years' – that is, for financing buffer stocks – and in general for the purposes of the domestic economy, this instrument is 'above suspicion':

> But as an opposing machine in the antagonism of powers, a credit system which grows beyond sight and which is yet a safe debt for the present requirements – because all the creditors do not require payment at one Time – constitutes a dangerous money power. This ingenious invention of a commercial people [England] in this century is dangerous because it is a war treasure which exceeds the treasures of all other states; it cannot be exhausted except by default of taxes (which is inevitable), though it can be long delayed by the stimulus to trade which occurs through the reaction of credit on industry and commerce. This facility in making war, together with the inclination to do so on the part of rulers – an inclination which seems inborn in human nature – is thus a great hindrance to perpetual peace. Therefore, to forbid this credit system must be a preliminary article of perpetual peace all the more because it must eventually entangle many innocent states in the inevitable bankruptcy and openly harm them.[5]

Kant regards finance based on the perpetual postponement of payment as one of the primary obstacles to perpetual peace. As long as 'endless finance' makes possible, at no cost, the indefinite postponement of peace and payment and their replacement by more or less lasting truces, war becomes, to all appearances, the pragmatically least expensive alternative. This impression obtains to such an extent as to suggest that there are no alternatives and that 'peace' is nothing but a chimera good for 'philosophers'; but then the reckoning comes all at once, in the form of a political and financial crisis that no one can escape.

In 1795 Kant put his finger on something that could only appear obvious to a mind as acute as his. Two centuries later, we can count not only on his indications, but also on the fact that what is to be seen has become still more obvious after a few wars and a few crises.

Some might of course object that things have become more complicated in the meantime and that the risk of a global crisis is precisely what will rule out the possibility of a war between debtors and creditors that is no longer to anyone's 'advantage'. Was it not indeed Kant who wrote in the same essay that it will be commerce to avoid war?

> The spirit of commerce, which is incompatible with war, sooner or later gains the upper hand in every state. As the power of money is perhaps the most dependable of all the means included under the state power, states see themselves forced, without any moral urge, to promote honourable peace and by mediation to prevent war wherever it threatens to break out. They do so exactly as if they stood in perpetual alliances.[6]

The very financial power that Kant indicated as the cause of the certain ruin of the relations between states and as 'the most dependable weapon'[7] is now invoked as a tool to pacify them. Is Kant contradicting himself? Or is he simply getting carried away and making sweeping statements before coming to terms with the practical realities, as often happens with philosophers? Neither one nor the other, unfortunately. After discovering something essential, Kant sets about covering it up again. The tool of this operation is dialectics, *speculation*. Peace is guaranteed by its opposite. War divides human beings so deeply that commerce alone can reunite them. The globalization of peace comes about through the globalization of commerce. We seem to be hearing familiar arguments, even if those who put them forward would hardly admit the idea of globalized finance having a philosophical origin.

Through this cover-up, Kant helps to blur the distinctions he himself made so acutely clear. So much so that the blur is all we are left with today. If we have tried to show anything at all in our story, it is in fact precisely the gradual blurring of the possibility to distinguish between wartime economy and peacetime economy, and at a still deeper level between war and peace. This blurring, which seeks to present itself dialectically as the 'cunning of reason', may be able to defer a war for much longer than would be possible if it were necessary to make clear-cut choices. Perhaps. Deferring war is not, however, to eliminate its possibility. It is not even working to establish a state of international economic relations that can be recognized as authentically *pacific*. Moreover, the 'permanent alliances' – such as the one that some might conjecture between China and the USA, which would be based precisely on their mutual interest in not paying the debts accumulated and not demanding payment for them – could prove to be not so permanent. In point of fact, after the arms race that characterized the Cold War and its peculiar 'balance of terror', the race for power could today involve the accumulation of imbalanced positions as regards both credit and debt. The present crisis could then be seen as the crisis of the third postwar period, and its solution as the perfect surrogate for a world political order based no longer on military terror but on 'economic seduction'.

This crisis clearly shows that the geopolitical relations upon which the world's equilibrium has been based so far – globally precarious and locally conflict-generating though it is – will no longer be the same. It is equally true, however, that the hegemonic claim the West has always asserted with respect to globalization might not lose its apparent legitimacy so easily. In other words, the crisis may not become the catalyst of a clash of civilizations. It may be possible to find a way out with a *stabilizing compromise* that will definitively consign every effort to conceive an authentic reform to the category of pipedreams of noble spirits.

In reality, the claim to *know* that war has become 'useless' and therefore 'highly improbable' is far more of a pipedream than the attempt to shed light on the conditions in which an economy is really and only an economy and not a (cold) continuation of (cold) war by other means. While waiting to see how things will go, we can learn something important from the crisis straight away, namely that finance as we know it prevents us from distinguishing what we need to be able to distinguish, and, by contrast, that finance grounded on different principles is not only possible but also desirable.

With the proviso put forward by Kant,[8] what strikes us as most important to consider is not his dialectical acrobatics but the method he illustrates immediately after stating the preliminary principles for the attainment of perpetual peace.

Kant distinguishes between principles 'of that strict kind which hold regardless of circumstances'[9] and principles which, 'while not exceptions from the rule of law, nevertheless are subjectively broader [. . .] in respect to their observation, containing permission to delay their execution'.[10] The distinction is between what he calls leges strictae ('strict laws') and leges latae ('permissive laws'). The latter include the possibility 'to delay their execution without, however, losing sight of the end. This permission does not authorize [. . .] delaying until doomsday (or, as Augustus used to say, *ad calendas Graecas*)' but only 'a delay to prevent precipitation which might injure the goal striven for'.[11]

This is an indication that holds also for the reform of the financial system. And it is a precious distinction for us too, precisely because, if this crisis in no way *obliges* us to change course, neither does it prove that there can be no concrete alternatives. *If correctly considered, it allows us rather to measure more precisely what the failure to change might cost.*

The possibility thus remains of simply taking consistent stock of what has become clear in the present crisis (but has actually been so for much longer) without therefore adopting rigid positions. Accepting the principle that the only fitting way to enter into the debt/credit relationship is to assume the risk it involves is the work of a moment. The construction of institutions to put this principle into effect will instead take time, and indeed different periods of time. And we must know how to take all the time needed for construction. But the time needed and no more: the periods of time for each of the principles on the basis of which finance can regain both its end as purpose and its end as conclusion may differ among themselves, but they are not infinite.

The institution of a clearing system for international commerce on the basis of the principles stated by Keynes at Bretton Woods could take a few months to draft and a few weeks to implement. This is indeed what happened for the European Payments Union, which had a gestation period of just nine months and, once in place, as Robert Triffin observed, 'drastically shifted overnight the whole structure of intra-European settlements'. Our thinking on this is the same as Buiter's claim that 'unbundling currency and numéraire is something that can be done over the weekend'.[12]

If no time were lost, international trade, which has dropped by 30 per cent with this crisis, could already be carried out in accordance with the new rule within six months. Absorption of the global imbalances accumulated so far would instead take far more time and, above all, a further degree of political negotiation; but it could perhaps be made more practicable by the simple fact that the new system would make it possible to avoid their constant aggravation.

In the same way, the adoption of this system would perhaps be facilitated by parallel agreements for the stabilization of commodity prices through buffer stocks. Keynes tried, with convincing arguments, to show the marked synergy existing between the attempt to strip money of the property of liquidity through clearing and the attempt to give liquidity to primary goods, foodstuffs and raw materials through buffer stocks, and hence to make attractive the holding of wealth in the form of commodities. Precisely because the holding of wealth is no bad thing at all in itself, it would be as well for the ways in which this holding takes shape to be such as not to contradict a *real* concept of wealth.

Circuits of local currency – designed not to replace but to complement the national currency, for example through the assurance of full convertibility guaranteed by funds set aside in the official currency equal to the amount of local currency issued, and hence with 100 per cent backing – could be made possible in a reasonably short space of time by a framework law laying down the terms of the subsidiarity they involve and introducing clarity in a sphere simply left to spontaneous initiative so far. At that point, the effective birth and bottom-up spreading of systems of complementary local currency would be grounded solely on the associative capacity and needs of local communities.[13] It is to be assumed that neither will be found wanting. In the same way, it is first of all at this level that effective trials could be carried out on the introduction of *carrying costs* for money.

The path for a reform of the national credit systems is something indicated not only by us, but also by many bankers and scholars of banking: a move in the direction enabling banks to act as true intermediaries between the readiness to lend by savers and the need to borrow of businesses and families rather than selling financial products and fuelling a potentially infinite lever. In this perspective, the principle of profitability must simply be subordinated to the principle of specialization and of correspondence between the intermediary's structures of assets and of liabilities, reducing to the minimum the recourse to wholesale funding for banks.

Finally, all these changes would clearly entail a rethinking of accounting regulations, that is, of the way in which all economic actors are called upon to account for their actions. Mark-to-market accounting has long been the object of criticism, to which a deaf ear has been turned regardless of the critic's authority. It is now the crisis itself that reveals the destabilizing potential of this conception of accounting and makes the previously ignored criticisms perhaps still more authoritative.

Just as it took time to demolish every traditional barrier to the 'bookkeeping innovation', but just a second to decide to proceed in that direction, a second would also be enough to reverse course. The 'rewriting of the rules', so often called for, could take place not through authoritative prescriptions designed to predetermine what economic agents *do*, but much more liberally, through the requirement of transparency in what they *say*, in other words through their balance sheets. Here too, it will be as well to take all the time one needs. It would be as well, in other words, for those concerned with economics – and not just with supplying an ideological justification for deregulation – to lend their expertise so as to make this approach feasible.

This crisis has made it possible to tell the truth about the Emperor's new clothes, and not necessarily with naïveté, smugness or ideological rancour. The way in which the crisis broke out and the way in which it has developed show that the dogmatic assumptions that finance has explicitly chosen as its cornerstones for the last thirty years are wholly untenable, and have been so for a lot longer.

The Emperor is naked. We can only agree. We must, however, immediately add that the crisis shows that the Emperor's nakedness is also the nakedness of his subjects, led by their ruler to believe that they can be rulers too, if they really want. Only one condition: *nakedness is never to be mentioned* – and any innocent child so obstinate as to expose the conspiracy of silence by pointing out the non-existence of the finery flaunted by Emperor and subjects is to be 'silenced'. There are many ways to impose censorship and to shut people up. The most modern and effective one, precisely because it is the most completely nihilistic, does not involve eliminating the voice of dissent, but drowning it in the sea of 'opinions'.

The most depressing thing about the present day is precisely this: the tacit accord – made all the stronger by the absence of any need for explicit agreement – not to recognize the crisis for what it is. The hope that sustains this understanding, and leaves even the most apparently irreconcilable views to subside in an unexpressed plebiscite, is that everything can remain as it is and that the sea will be calm again once the storm has passed. What is hoped for is the long run of the living dead.

This observation brings us, however, to the crux. It has been pointed out by many, more or less timidly and pertinently, that, insofar as it is the crisis of a system, this economic crisis is also a crisis of the economics that made the construction of the system possible.

An ancient maxim telling theologians to say nothing of matters beyond their ken (*silete theologi in munere alieno*) has been updated in Italy for application to economists, who have been asked to keep quiet.[14] In certain respects, however, this is precisely what they have done, in every sense. The economists who monopolized the dogmatic theoretization of financial capitalism in recent years have certainly not provided satisfactory explanations of the crisis; but neither have they admitted their inability to do so, and still less their earlier mistake of failing to recognize the extremely dangerous nature of market-based finance. Moreover, this silence has yet to be broken by voices that, in addition to presenting themselves as alternatives, are also convincing. And this is not the worst. After proclaiming the collapse of faith in the free market in definitive accents, the *Financial Times* announced the opening of a forum devoted to developing 'new ideas' to indicate what can and must take the place of the now abandoned faith. Those invited to speak were, however, precisely the best known champions of that superseded ideology. It is a bit like proclaiming the collapse of communism and asking Stalin to guide the transition to market economy. Given the course of events in East Europe, we are indeed not so far away from reality.

And so, not only do those who are part of the problem fail to point out the Emperor's nakedness, but their own nakedness also tends to escape notice. If everyone is naked, no one is naked. Everyone pretends that everything is fine, in the hope that, once the storm has passed, they can go back to producing theories, dogmas and models just like before. Or rather, needless to say, even better than before. Just as people pretended after the First World War that the *belle époque* was not the cause of the war, but an ideal state that we should endeavour to regain, the hope that has been cherished ever since the beginning is that, once the crisis has loosened its grip, it will be possible, and above all right, to go back to work as though nothing has happened.

If the economic and financial crisis is also the crisis of a way of thinking about the economy and finance, then *thinking is the only way out*. And thinking means, in the first place, pointing in the direction of what shows: indicating – without measuring what is said solely in relation to the more or less probable resistance that may be put up by vested interests, which have been allowed to prosper in the shade of a dogmatic construction of finance that was economic only in appearance. Gauging an idea of reform by these criteria would in fact be like gauging a doctor's indications solely on their ability to please the patient.

Even before this, however, thinking means speaking in such a way that others will begin to think on the basis of their own knowledge and skills.

Keynes said, in the 1930s, that his goal was to 'put economic considerations into a back seat [. . .]. For the next twenty-five years in my belief, economists, at present the most incompetent, will be nevertheless the more important group of scientists in the world. And it is to be hoped – if they are successful – that after they will never be important again.' If we were to take this seriously, we should say that the economists of recent years have not been capable of doing their job correctly. This means, however, that we need a new generation of economists. What we have written here is intended as a contribution to regenerating our relationship with the economic sphere and its expertise.

Notes

Part I Phenomenology

Introduction

1 'Keynes and the Crisis', Centre for Economic Policy Research (CEPR), May 2008, Policy Insight No 23.
2 From an oral interview; see below, Part I, Ch. 5, p. 49.
3 This quotation is given more amply, together with the full reference, in Part I, Ch. 6; see p. 59.

Chapter 1 Do we know what the financial markets are?

1 See for example the list put forward by M. Vitale in 'Sbagliare non era obbligatorio', *Il Sole 24Ore*, 24 May 2009. See also I. Maes, 'Alexandre Lamfalussy: An Early Cassandra on Financial Fragility', paper delivered at the STOREP 2009 conference, Florence, 5 June 2009.
2 This is literally the closing observation of an article by Alberto Alesina in *Il Sole 24Ore*, 20 May 2009. The argument had already been put forward in A. Alesina and F. Giavazzi, *La crisi. Può la politica salvare il mondo?* Milan: Il Saggiatore, 2008.
3 B. Eichengreen, *Financial Crises and What to Do about Them*. Oxford: Oxford University Press, 2002, p. 4.
4 See in this connection J.-C. Michéa, *L'Empire du moindre mal. Essai sur la civilisation libérale*. Paris: Flammarion, 2007.
5 As regards the risk of a possible drift of democracy into authoritarian and managerial attitudes, we attach great importance to the observations developed by Alain Supiot in recent years. See in particular his 'L'Europe gagnée par "l'économie communiste de marché"', in *Revue du MAUSS permanente*, 30 January 2008, available at http://www.journaldumauss.net/spip.php?article283 last accessed 3 May 2011. See also C.

Lasch, *The Revolt of the Elites and the Betrayal of Democracy*. New York: W.W. Norton & Co, 1995.

6 R. Rajan and L. Zingales, *Saving Capitalism from the Capitalists: Unleashing the Power of Financial Markets to Create Wealth and Spread Opportunity*. New York: Crown Business, 2003, p. 1. It should be noted in passing that the application of Schumpeter's concept of creative destruction to the financial markets is rash to say at least. Schumpeter regarded the capital markets as part of Walrasian circular flow, which is constantly repeated in identical form. It is bank credit that, by creating money beyond the measure given by the amount of assets present, enables the entrepreneur to interrupt that potentially ossifying repetition so as to introduce innovation and shift the system from 'statics' to 'dynamics'. We thank Yuri Biondi for bringing this point to our attention.

7 Eichengreen, *Financial Crises*, p. 2.

8 Ibid.

9 Ibid.

10 In the same sense, Marx wrote as follows in an early work: 'Because in the acute and precise formulae to which they [economists] reduce political economy, the basic formula, if they wished to express that movement abstractly, would have to be: In political economy, law is determined by its opposite, absence of law. The true law of political economy is chance, from whose movement we, the scientific men, isolate certain factors arbitrarily in the form of laws.' K. Marx, Auszüge aus Mills Eléments d'économie politique [1844], published in K. Marx and F. Engels, *Gesamtausgabe*, Part I, vol. 3. Berlin: Marx-Engels-Verlag, 1932. (The title refers to Mill's work in the French translation simply because Marx, for whatever reason, read a translation of Mill's book, by J. T. Parisot, Paris, 1823.)

11 Eichengreen, *Financial Crises*, p. 3.

12 Ibid. The author uses the same expression, in a sense that is certainly not positive, also in *Globalizing Capital. A History of the International Monetary System*. Princeton: Princeton University Press, 1998, p. 63.

13 P. Slater and W. G. Bennis, 'Democracy Is Inevitable', *Harvard Business Review* (September/October 1990), p. 171.

14 See Rajan and Zingales, *Saving Capitalism*, p. 3, and the comment in note 6 above.

15 Eichengreen, *Financial Crises*, p. 4.

16 Ibid., p. 4.

Chapter 2 At the root of the possibility of crisis: Liquidity and risk

1 Financial Services Authority (FSA), available at *Financial Risk Outlook*, 2007, http://www.fsa. gov.uk/pubs/plan/financial_risk_outlook_2007. pdf, last accessed 4 May 2011.

2 See also A. Greenspan, 'We will never have a perfect model of risk', *Financial Times*, 16 March 2008, available at http://www.ft.com/cms/s/0/edbdbcf6-f360-11dc-b6bc-0000779fd2ac.html#axzz1LN4GJGv0 (last accessed 4 May 2011).
3 J. M. Keynes, 'The General Theory of Employment', *The Quarterly Journal of Economics*, 52.2 (February 1937), pp. 209–23; reprinted in *The Collected Writings of John Maynard Keynes*, 1971–89. London and Cambridge: Macmillan and Cambridge University Press, vol. 14 (1973), pp. 109–23, at p. 116.
4 J. M. Keynes, *The General Theory of Employment, Interest and Money* [1936], in *Collected Writings*, vol. 7 (1973), p. 155.
5 L. Fantacci, 'J. M. Keynes: Escaping the Liquidity Trap', Bocconi University, ISE Working Paper 2/2005, p. 2.
6 The proper use of money will be addressed more broadly in Chapter 4. See also M. Amato, *L'enigma della moneta*. Milan: Et al., 2010.
7 Keynes, *General Theory*, pp. 154–5.
8 Compare the interview with Chuck Prince, 'Investment Banking Revenues', *Financial Times*, 10 July 2007: 'When the music stops, in terms of liquidity, things will be complicated. But as long as the music is playing, you've got to get up and dance. We're still dancing.' In the game of liquidity, dancing means buying and sitting down means selling. When the time to sit suddenly comes, there are not enough chairs for everyone. This metaphor of musical chairs was also used by Keynes to describe how the financial markets work in chapter 12 of his *General Theory*.
9 Keynes, *General Theory*, p. 155.
10 What does 'acting normally' mean? Simplifying slightly (but without departing too much from reality), we could say that it means forecasting and managing risk through systematic and conventional use of the normal distribution as a representation of the future movements of the market and of its standard deviation as a measure of the risk implied by such movements. Even though it is empirically known that extreme events are far more frequent than is envisaged by the normality hypothesis, technological innovation has so far led, above all, to the proliferation of forecasting models based on that hypothesis.
11 In financial terms, this means selling just before a radical change in direction takes place on the markets.
12 Keynes, *General Theory*, p. 155.
13 In this connection see M. Basili and C. Zappia, 'Keynes's "Non-Numerical" Probabilities and Non-Additive Measures', *Journal of Economic Psychology*, 30.3 (2009), pp. 419–30.

Chapter 3 What is credit?

1 See for example C. M. Reinhart and K. S. Rogoff, 'The Aftermath of Financial Crises', paper delivered at the conference of the American

Economic Association *International Aspects of Financial Market Imperfections*, San Francisco, 3 January 2009, available at http://ws1.ad. economics.harvard.edu/faculty/rogoff/files/Aftermath.pdf (accessed 4 May 2011); now published in C. M. Reinhart and K. S. Rogoff, *This Time Is Different. Eight Centuries of Financial Folly*. Princeton: Princeton University Press, 2009, pp. 223–39.

2 'Preventing crises is not a goal in itself; after all, prohibiting foreign borrowing would eliminate the threat of foreign debt crises altogether!' J. Tirole, *Financial Crises, Liquidity, and the International Monetary System*. Princeton: Princeton University Press, 2002, p. 44.

3 See M. Amato, *Le radici di una fede. Per una storia del rapporto fra moneta e credito in Occidente*. Milan: Bruno Mondadori, 2008, esp. pp. 16–24.

4 According to information received from Marco Vitale, this was claimed for example by the *Harvard Business School Bulletin* in October 1997: 'In fact, using Merton's formula [to calculate the price of derivatives], it becomes possible to construct a portfolio that is virtually risk-free.'

5 Compare F. Vella, 'Dalla parte del popolo dei subprime', in L. Pellizzon (ed.), *Il mondo sull'orlo di una crisi di nervi: origine, sviluppi, responsabilità della crisi che ha sconvolto l'economia globale*. Roma: Castelvecchi, 2009, p. 197; also available at http://www.lavoce.info/articoli/pagina2877-351.html (accessed 4 May 2011).

6 Cf. p. 71 below.

7 This has been the primary argument in favour of the liberalization of the credit market ever since Jeremy Bentham's *In Defence of Usury* (1787).

8 The conditions capable of making this potential convergence concrete will be illustrated at a later stage (Part II, Chapters 5 and 6) through references to the European Union of Payments and to Keynes's plans for an International Clearing Union.

Chapter 4 What is money?

1 For the question of the concept of 'the long term' (or long period) in the recent economic literature, see E. Sanfilippo, *Short Period and Long Period in Macroeconomics: An Awkward Distinction*. Working Paper no. 95, series published by the Department of Economics, University of Rome III, 2008.

2 See M. Amato, *Le radici di una fede. Per una storia del rapporto fra moneta e credito in Occidente*. Milan: Bruno Mondadori, 2008, pp. 8–16, and L. Fantacci, *Storia di un'istituzione mancata*. Venice: Marsilio, 2005, pp. 262–72.

3 J. M. Keynes, *A Tract on Monetary Reform* [1923], in *The Collected Writings of John Maynard Keynes*, 1971–89. London and Cambridge: Macmillan and Cambridge University Press, vol. 4, p. 124; our italics.

4 J. M. Keynes, *A Treatise on Money*, vol. 1: *The Pure Theory of Money* [1930], in *Collected Writings*, vol. 5, pp. 3–4.

5 The need to distinguish between market economy and capitalism will be the subject of broader discussion in Part III, Chapter 6.

Chapter 5 Finance starting from the end

1 The details of all this constitute the subject matter of Part II.
2 J. M. Keynes, *A Tract on Monetary Reform* [1923], in *The Collected Writings of John Maynard Keynes*, 1971–89. London and Cambridge: Macmillan and Cambridge University Press, vol. 4, p. 124.
3 J. M. Keynes, *A Treatise on Money*, vol. 1: *The Pure Theory of Money* [1930], in *The Collected Writings of John Maynard Keynes*, 1971–89. London and Cambridge: Macmillan and Cambridge University Press, vol. 5, p. 4.
4 Cf. B. Eichengreen, *Financial Crises and What to Do about Them*. Oxford: Oxford University Press, 2002, p. 4: 'writing and enforcing contracts that anticipate the relevant contingencies is particularly difficult'.
5 As we have written elsewhere, it is worth recalling that, 'if wealth is held in the form of an object of use, a drop in its market price does not entail the loss of the thing itself. This is not true of shares. A share that has no market value is wastepaper' (M. Amato and L. Fantacci, 'La sbornia finanziaria è finita', *Libertaria* 3–4 (2008), pp. 4–9, at p. 6).
6 Cf. E. Helleiner, *States and the Reemergence of Global Finance: From Bretton Woods to the 1990s*. Ithaca, NY: Cornell University Press, 1994.
7 A. Smith, *An Inquiry into the Nature and Causes of the Wealth of Nations* [1776], London: Methuen & Co., 1904, book II, chapter 2, §100; also available at: http://www.econlib.org/library/Smith/smWN7.html (last accessed 5 May 2011).
8 This question is raised, albeit in slightly different terms, by A. Gigliobianco, 'Abolire il capitalismo. Economia politica e lessicografia', in G. Dosi and M. C. Marcuzzo (eds), *L'economia e la politica. Scritti in onore di Michele Salvati*. Bologna: Il Mulino, 2007, pp. 34–46.
9 O. Pianigiani, *Vocabolario etimologico della lingua italiana*. Genova: Melita, 1890, s.v. 'finanza'; also available at http://www.etimo.it (last accessed 5 May 2011).
10 J. M. Keynes, 'Proposals for an International Clearing Union' (second draft, 18 November 1941), in *Collected Writings*, vol. 25, p. 47.

Chapter 6 Capitalism and debt: a matter of life and death

1 J. M. Keynes, *A Tract on Monetary Reform*, in *The Collected Writings of John Maynard Keynes*, 1971–89. London and Cambridge: Macmillan and Cambridge University Press, vol. 4, p. 65.
2 Ibid.; italics in original.
3 From considerations regarding the dignity of labour, for example. In this connection, see the above-cited work by Alain Supiot, 'L'Europe

gagnée par "l'économie communiste de marché"', in *Revue du MAUSS permanente*, 30 January 2008, available at http://www.journaldumauss.net/spip.php?article283 (accessed 5 May 2011).

4 As Jean Cocteau said, '*Les miroirs feraient bien de réfléchir un peu avant de renvoyer les images*' ('Mirrors would do well to reflect a little before presenting their images') – and so perhaps would speculators.

5 'From time to time' is the expression used by Keynes in ch. 4 of the *Treatise on Money* to indicate the timing of state intervention on money. See his *Collected Writings*, vol. 5, p. 59.

6 J. M. Keynes, *The General Theory of Employment, Interest and Money*, in *Collected Writings*, vol. 7, p. 162. For a contrary view, see the purely irrationalistic interpretation of animal spirits given by G. A. Akerlof and R. J. Shiller, *Animal Spirits. How Human Psychology Drives the Economy, and Why It Matters for Global Capitalism*. Princeton: Princeton University Press, 2009. It is interesting to note that the two authors acknowledge (pp. 3–4) that the expression cannot mean 'irrationality' in good English. It is, however, also remarkable that they should accept the erroneous interpretation established in current academic discourse, which sees animal spirits as some sort of 'a restless and inconsistent element' by which 'sometimes we are paralyzed', and above all that they should attribute it to Keynes.

7 Keynes, *General Theory*, p. 148. See also, in the same chapter, the description of the formation of expectations on the financial markets as expectations not about the event, but about the average state of expectations, through the celebrated metaphor of the beauty contest.

8 Keynes, *General Theory*, p. 152.

9 Ibid., pp. 151–2. This is not only easy to show, but it is actually demonstrated by Keynes in ch. 4 of his *Treatise on Probability* (*Collected Writings*, vol. 8).

10 Keynes, *General Theory*, p. 153.

11 M. Bloch, *Esquisse d'une histoire monétaire de l'Europe*. Paris: Colin, 1954, p. 77.

12 See M. Amato, *Le radici di una fede. Per una storia del rapporto fra moneta e credito in Occidente*. Milan: Bruno Mondadori, 2008, p. 26.

13 R. Rajan and L. Zingales, *Saving Capitalism from the Capitalists: Unleashing the Power of Financial Markets to Create Wealth and Spread Opportunity*. New York: Crown Business, 2003, p. 1.

14 The discount rate is the rate at which credit maturing in the future is transformed into money by the central bank.

15 In the financial sense, *realizability* unequivocally means *monetizability*.

16 Rajan and Zingales, *Saving Capitalism*, p. 1.

17 Ibid.

Part II History

Chapter 1 From credit risk to liquidity risk (2008)

1 IMF, *Global Financial Stability Report*, April 2009.
2 Obviously, there is a personal property guarantee for *asset-backed securities*. However, it is one thing for an asset taken as guarantee to be fungible, and so reasonably saleable, and quite another thing for it to be real estate, for which *continuous revaluation is assumed.*
3 R. J. Shiller, *The Subprime Solution*. Princeton and Oxford: Princeton University Press, 2008, p. 25.
4 'Global Banking: Paradigm Shift – Managing Transition', speech delivered by Malcolm D. Knight, General Manager of the BRI at the Federation of Indian Chambers of Commerce and Industry (FICCI) – Indian Banks' Association (IBA) Conference, Mumbai, 12 September 2007. Actually it was also possible to criticize the new model and to signal the risk that it might get out of hand. See for example R. Rajan, 'Has Financial Development Made the World Riskier?', NBER Working Paper no. W11728, November 2005.
5 The figure should in fact be adjusted to take into account the many who lost their homes through the crisis. The figures will be provided in the next chapter; suffice it here to note that the balance is negative.
6 Shiller, *The Subprime Solution*, p. 25.
7 For the first two years.
8 This, we believe, is a good empirical illustration of the proposition we had occasion to refer to somewhat frequently in the first part, to the effect that regulation is deregulation.
9 See on this point the observations in P. Mottura, 'Crisi bancarie: un problema di governance?', "Bancaria", 12 (2008), pp. 15–28.

Chapter 2 The globalization of capital (1973)

1 J. L. Borges, 'The Zahir', in *The Aleph and Other Stories*. London: Penguin, 2004, pp. 79–88, at p. 80.
2 Thus it is defined for example by Mottura and Forestieri: 'Liquidity is directly associated with two factors: the intensiveness of trading and the negotiability of the instruments' (P. Mottura and G. Forestieri, *Il sistema finanziario*. Milan: Egea, 2005, p. 172).
3 The difficulty in distinguishing between 'predatory lending' and 'subprime lending' had been pointed out as early as the year 2000, in the context of a hearing of the US Congress; see US Congress, *Predatory Lending Practices: Hearing Before the Committee on Banking and Financial Services, U.S. House of Representatives, One Hundred Sixth Congress, second Session, May 24, 2000*. Washington DC, 2000. See also US Department of Housing and Urban Development and US Department of Treasury, *Curbing Predatory Home Mortgage Lending*. 1 June 2000,

available at http://www.huduser.org/portal/publications/hsgfin/curbing.html (accessed 14 May 2011).

4 For a chronology, see for example P. Isard, *Globalization and the International Financial System: What's Wrong and What Can Be Done*. Cambridge and New York: Cambridge University Press, 2005, pp. 131–52.

5 UNCTAD, *Comprehensive Study of the Interrelationship between Foreign Direct Investment (FDI) and Foreign Portfolio Investment (FPI)*. Mimeo UNCTAD/GDS/DFSB/5, 1999, pp. 24–9.

6 Here we can see that the problem lies not so much in the particular instrument used (in this case, shares rather than bonds or derivatives) as in the liquidity that washes away all distinctions, since they are all convertible into money through the financial markets where they can be bought and sold.

7 See for example Charles Kindleberger, *Manias, Panics, and Crashes. A History of Financial Crises*. New York: John Wiley & Sons, 1996, p. 7.

8 Center for Responsible Lending, 'Subprime Lending: A Net Drain on Homeownership', in *Centre for Responsible Lending, Issue Paper*, 14 (27 March 2007), available at www.responsiblelending.org (last accessed 4 May 2011).

9 B. Eichengreen, 'Capital Account Liberalization: What Do Cross-Country Studies Tell Us?', *The World Bank Economic Review*, 15.3 (2001), pp. 341–65.

10 For a parallel between portfolio investments and IPOs, see R. Martell and R. M. Stulz, 'Equity Market Liberalizations as Country IPOs', *American Economic Review*, 93.2 (May 2003), pp. 97–101.

11 For a recent review, see M. A. Kose, E. Prasad, K. Rogoff, and S. Wei, 'Financial Globalization: A Reappraisal', IMF Working Paper, WP/06/189 (2006), especially pp. 23–31.

12 W. B. Wriston, 'Technology and Sovereignty', *Foreign Affairs*, 67 (1988), p. 71; for the reference to Eichengreen, see above, pp. 10–11.

13 J. Bhagwati, 'The Capital Myth: The Difference between Trade in Widgets and Dollars'. *Foreign Affairs*, Vol. 77, No. 3, May/June 1998, pp. 7–12, at p. 12.

14 See above, p. 9.

15 E. Helleiner, *States and the Reemergence of Global Finance: From Bretton Woods to the 1990s*. Ithaca, NY: Cornell University Press, 1994, pp. 8–14.

16 Ibid., p. 18.

17 '"Greenspan put" may be encouraging complacency', *Financial Times*, 8 December 2000. The Fed funds rate is the rate of interest at which banks lend each other federal funds.

18 Interview with Peter Bernstein, 'View From the Top', *FT.com*, 10 February 2008.

19 The expediency of accompanying the refinancing of the banks with a renegotiation of the terms of mortgage loans was appropriately

underlined by Zingales when he proposed a 'Plan B', 11 October 2008, 'Plan B', http://www.voxeu.com/index.php?q=node/2390 11 (accessed 4 May 2011).

20 See on this point the editorial in the *New York Times* of 22 September 2007, which was highly critical of the position taken by Bernanke and Paulson and was significantly entitled 'When Markets Are Too Big to Fail'.

21 Federal Reserve Bank of New York, *Forms of Federal Reserve Lending* (April 2009), available at http://www.newyorkfed.org/markets/Forms_of_Fed_Lending.pdf (accessed 4 May 2011).

22 A. Greenspan, 'Fostering Financial Innovation: The Role of Government', in J. A. Dorn (ed.), *The Future of Money in the Information Age*. Washington, DC: Cato Institute, 1997, pp. 45–50, at p. 49, also available online at: http://www.cato.org/pubs/books/money/money6.html (accessed 7 May 2011).

23 The doubts are waxing ever more insistent. See 'Beijing Is Caught in "Trap" over Dollar', in *Financial Times*, 25 May 2009. The Chinese authorities themselves have on a number of occasions expressed concern – also officially – over the fact that they continue to accumulate reserves in dollars, as happened for example on the occasion of the visit by Treasury Secretary Geithner in May 2009.

24 Acquisitions of long-term US securities by official investors increased from $173 billion between October 2006 and September 2007 to $230 billion over the following twelve months, only to fall back to a net sale of $44 billion in the six months from October 2008 to March 2009 (Department of the Treasury, *Treasury International Capital Data*, published on 15 May 2009 in http://www.treasury.gov/tlc; accessed 4 May 2011).

25 N. Chowdhury, 'China Takes a Small Step Away from the Dollar', *Time*, 6 April 2009.

Chapter 3 '*Fiat* dollar'. And the world saw that it was good (1971)

1 R. Nixon, 'Address to the Nation Outlining a New Economic Policy: The Challenge of Peace' (15 August 1971), in *Public Paper of the Presidents of the United States, Richard Nixon*. Washington, DC: U.S. Government Printing Office, 1972, p. 886.

2 Federal Reserve Act, Section 16: 'Note Issue', 1. Issuance of Federal Reserve Notes; Nature of Obligation; Where Redeemable (12 USC 411).

3 The expediency of restoring dollar–gold convertibility has found isolated advocates over the years, being granted space in the press only in the wake of the crisis. See for example R. Duncan, 'Bring Back the Link between Gold and the Dollar', *Financial Times*, 23 November 2008.

4 PL 90-269; see G. G. Munn, F. L. García, and C. J. Woelfel (eds), *The St James Encyclopedia of Banking and Finance*, 9th edn. Chicago: St James Press, 1991.

5 PL 95-147 (31 USC 5118), comma b.

6 A. Greenspan, 'Fostering Financial Innovation: The Role of Government', in J. A. Dorn (ed.), *The Future of Money in the Information Age*. Washington, DC: Cato Institute, 1997, pp. 45–50, at p. 49; also available online at: http://www.cato.org/pubs/books/money/money6.html (accessed 7 May 2011).

7 As stated in Article 1 of the first version of the Federal Reserve Act, law of 23 December 1913, ch. 6, 38 Stat. 251.

8 Federal Reserve press release of 20 October 1987, quoted in M. Carlson, *A Brief History of the 1987 Stock Market Crash with a Discussion of the Federal Reserve Response*. Washington, DC: Finance and Economics Discussion Series, Divisions of Research & Statistics and Monetary Affairs, Federal Reserve Board, 2007, available at http://www.federalreserve.gov/Pubs/feds/2007/200713/200713pap.pdf (accessed 4 May 2011).

9 Although the possibility cannot be ruled out that this limitation, adopted by the European Central Bank for example, can apply precisely because the Fed does not respect it, taking it upon itself to do the 'dirty work' of supplying liquidity to the whole world – as we will see.

10 Nixon, 'Address to the Nation', p. 886.

11 J. S. Nye, *Bound to Lead. The Changing Nature of American Power*. New York: Basic Books, 1990, pp. 31–2.

12 G. Gaber, 'Far finta di essere sani', *Far finta di essere sani*, Milano: Carosello, 1973.

13 Quoted in H. James, *International Monetary Co-Operation since Bretton Woods*. Washington, DC and New York: International Monetary Fund and Oxford University Press, 1996, p. 210.

14 Nixon, 'Address to the Nation', p. 889.

15 P. Isard, *Globalization and the International Financial System: What's Wrong and What Can Be Done*. Cambridge and New York: Cambridge University Press, 2005, p. 29.

16 *Nixon Tapes*, Conversation n. 69b, 16 August 1971 (10.10–11.27), Cabinet Room, available at www.nixontapes.org (accessed 4 May 2011).

17 Quoted in B. Eichengreen, *Globalizing Capital. A History of the International Monetary System*, Princeton: Princeton University Press, 1996, p. 133.

18 Or, in the terms of Article 4, Section 5, 'fundamental disequilibrium'.

19 Greenspan, 'Fostering Financial Innovation', p. 49.

20 *Articles of Agreement of the International Monetary Fund*. Washington, DC: IMF, 1993, art. IV.

21 P. Kenen, 'Refocusing the Fund: A Review of James M. Boughton's Silent Revolution: The International Monetary Fund 1979–1989', *IMF Staff Papers*, 50, 2003, p. 296.

22 *Articles of Agreement of the International Monetary Fund*. Washington, DC: IMF, 1993, art. XXX (f).

Chapter 4 The Eurodollar chimera (1958)

1 R. Triffin, *Gold and the Dollar Crisis. The Future of Convertibility*. Yale University Press, New Haven 1960, graph 2.
2 S. Battilossi, 'The Eurodollar Market and Structural Innovation in Western Banking, 1960–1985', in D. Ross and M. Pohle Fraser (eds), *Investment and Savings: Historical Perspectives*. Aldershot and London: Ashgate 2009, vol. 1 (in press). See also P. Einzig, *The Euro–Dollar System. Practice and Theory of International Interest Rates*, 5th edn. London: MacMillan, 1973, p. 30.
3 E. J. Frydl, 'The Eurodollar Conundrum', *Federal Reserve Bank of New York Quarterly Review*, 1982 (spring), p. 12.
4 On average, from 66 to 103 basis points, according to the calculations of Battilossi, 'Eurodollar Market', table 4.
5 Einzig, *Euro–Dollar System*, p. 65.
6 R. Mundell, 'The Monetary Dynamics of International Adjustment under Fixed and Flexible Exchange Rates', *Quarterly Journal of Economics*, 74 (1960), pp. 227–57.
7 E. Helleiner, *States and the Reemergence of Global Finance: From Bretton Woods* to the 1990s. Ithaca, NY: Cornell University Press, 1994, p. 84.
8 Einzig, *Euro–Dollar System*, p. 52.
9 The need to 'draw a line' between money and credit, regardless of precisely where that line is drawn, has been pointed out in practically the same terms by economists who are normally at loggerheads on the conception of money – such as M. Friedman ('The Euro–Dollar Market', *Federal Reserve Bank of St Louis*, July 1971, p. 17) and Keynes (*The General Theory of Employment, Interest and Money* [1936], in *The Collected Writings of John Maynard Keynes*, 1971–89. London and Cambridge: Macmillan and Cambridge University Press, vol. 7 (1973), ch. 13, note 1).
10 Einzig, *Euro–Dollar System*, pp. 63–74 and 111: 'Because it provides additional facilities for speculation and for disturbing arbitrage, the Euro–dollar system has created new problems relating to international liquidity. Above all, the possibility that some international crisis is liable to bring about a sharp contraction in the volume of Euro–dollars and in the volume of credit based on them must be borne in mind'.
11 Einzig, *Euro–Dollar System*, p. 113.
12 J. Niehans and J. Hewson, 'The Eurodollar Market and Monetary Theory', *Journal of Money, Credit and Banking*, 8.1 (1976), p. 12.
13 Ibid., p. 15.
14 Battilossi, 'Eurodollar Market'.
15 Battilossi, 'Eurodollar Market'.

Chapter 5 The European Payments Union (1950)

1 Between October 2007 and September 2008, the net purchase of US government securities by foreign agents, public and private, exceeded 760 billion dollars. To put this in perspective, in the same year net purchase abroad of stocks and shares of private American companies came short of 18 billion dollars (Table 1 in Bureau of Economic Analysis, 'US International Transactions Accounts Data', *US International Transactions*, 17 December 2008 version, available at www.bea.gov; accessed 4 May 2011).

2 After a fall in the early months of the crisis, the effective exchange rate of the dollar started rising again in April 2009, showing appreciation by some percentage points over the levels of June 2007 (Bank for International Settlements, *Effective Exchange Rates Indices*, available at http://www.bis.org/statistics/eer/index.htm, last update 15 April 2011, accessed 4 May 2011).

3 To use the graphic figure of speech that Jacques Rueff coined in 1971 in order to stigmatize the paradoxical approach taken to the issue even then (*Le Péché monétaire de l'Occident*. Paris: Plon, 1971, p. 177; English trans. *The Monetary Sin of the West*. London: Macmillan, 1972, p. 131).

4 See B. Eichengreen, *Reconstructing Europe's Trade and Payments. The European Payments Union*. Manchester: Manchester University Press, 1993, pp. 10–11.

5 J. J. Kaplan and G. Schleiminger, *The European Payments Union. Financial Diplomacy in the 1950s*. Oxford: Clarendon Press, 1989, p. 14.

6 B. Eichengreen, *The European Economy since 1945: Coordinated Capitalism and beyond*. Princeton: Princeton University Press, 2008, p. 73.

7 R. Triffin, *Europe and the Money Muddle. From Bilateralism to Near-Convertibility, 1947–1956*. New Haven, CT: Yale University Press, 1957, pp. 143ff.

8 Kaplan and Schleiminger, *European Payments Union*, pp. 16–17.

9 Ibid., p. 18.

10 Leaving aside significant ulterior motivations regarding the US political interest in strengthening western Europe and its stance against the USSR.

11 Triffin, *Europe and the Money Muddle*, p. 161; our italics.

12 Ibid., p. 204.

13 Of the 46.4 billion dollars of surplus and deficit registered among the countries belonging to the European Payments Union, about half were settled on a multilateral basis, a quarter on intertemporal basis, and less than a quarter in dollars or gold (see Kaplan and Schleiminger, *European Payments Union*, Table 10).

14 Eichengreen, *Reconstructing Europe's Trade and Payments*, pp. 30–2.

15 Ibid., ch. 6.

16 Rueff, *Péché monétaire de l'Occident*, p. 24; English trans. *Monetary Sin*, p. 23.

17 Ibid., pp. 24–5 (English trans. p. 24). The spirit here is clearly very close to that of Keynes's appeal not to expect to ease the post-war hardships of Europe's countries with 'red cross philanthropic plans' (see below, p. 123).
18 Triffin, *Europe and the Money Muddle*, p. 199.

Chapter 6 Bretton Woods: the plan that might have made it (1944)

1 'Articles of Agreement of the International Monetary Fund, December 27, 1945', in A. J. Peaslee, *International Governmental Organizations. Constitutional Documents*. The Hague: M. Nijhoff, 1956, pp. 259–87, at p. 259.
2 Bureau of Economic Analysis, *US International Transactions Accounts Data*, published on 15 December 2008. The figure refers to 2007. It is a figure 17 times greater *in real terms*, given that 4 billion dollars of 1944 correspond to 48.46 billion dollars of 2009 (US Department of Labor. Bureau of Labor Statistics, CPI *Inflation Calculator*, available at http://stats.bls.gov/data/inflation_calculator.htm, accessed 4 May 2011).
3 J. M. Keynes, *Activities 1940–1944. Shaping the Postwar World. The Clearing Union*, in *Collected Writings*, vol. 25, pp. 276–7. (Quoted above, Part 1, Chapter 5, footnote 9.)
4 Net of endowment of any foregoing assets, and in particular gold reserves – an issue we will return to later on.
5 J. M. Keynes, 'The Bank Rate', *The Nation and Athenaeum*, 7 March 1925, reprinted in *The Collected Writings of John Maynard Keynes*, 1971–89. London and Cambridge: Macmillan and Cambridge University Press, vol. 19, pp. 336–7.
6 J. M. Keynes, 'Proposals for an International Clearing Union', 15 December 1941, in *Collected Writings*, vol. 25, p. 74.
7 See the complete quotation above, p. 38.
8 Etymologically, 'clearing' derives from the same Indo-European root as the Latin *kalendae*, which evokes the idea of a term. In late Imperial Latin the *calendarium* was the financier's due register (see M. Amato, *L'enigma della moneta*. Milan: Et al., 2010, p. 91).
9 J. M. Keynes, 'The Objective of International Price Stability', *Economic Journal*, June–September 1943, reprinted in *Collected Writings*, vol. 25, p. 31; our italics.
10 D. H. Robertson, 'The Post-War Monetary Plans', *Economic Journal*, December 1943, p. 359; quoted in F. Cesarano, *Monetary Theory and Bretton Woods. The Construction of an International Monetary Order*. Cambridge: Cambridge University Press, 2006, p. 150.
11 'Characteristic of money that each man is at the mercy of his neighbours' (Cambridge, King's College Modern Archives, *Keynes Papers*, TM/2/286-308).
12 An initial attempt to do so is in L. Fantacci, 'J. M. Keynes: Escaping the Liquidity Trap', Bocconi University, ISE Working Paper 2/2005.

Chapter 7 Bretton Woods: the system that found implementation (1944)

1 A question Keynes himself effectively raised in 'Notes on the Memorandum for Post-War Currency Arrangements' and in the cover letter with which he sent the notes to Richard Hopkins and Sir Frederick Phillips on 3 August 1942 (reprinted in *The Collected Writings of John Maynard Keynes*, 1971–89. London and Cambridge: Macmillan and Cambridge University Press, vol. 26, pp. 158–67).
2 See for example B. Eichengreen, *Globalizing Capital. A History of the International Monetary System*. Princeton: Princeton University Press, 1998, p. 94.
3 Against the 26 billion dollars proposed by Keynes, compare Eichengreen, *Globalizing Capital*, p. 97.
4 H. D. White, 'Preliminary Draft Proposal for a United Nations Stabilization Fund and a Bank for Reconstruction and Development of the United and Associated Nations', April 1942, Part III, quoted in J. K. Horsefield (ed.), *The International Monetary Fund, 1945–1965. Twenty Years of International Monetary Cooperation*, Vol. 3: *Documents*, Washington, DC: International Monetary Fund, 1969, p. 79.
5 White, 'Preliminary Draft', pp. 81–2.
6 As pointed out by M. de Cecco, 'Origins of the Post-War Payments System', *Cambridge Journal of Economics*, 3 (1979), pp. 49–61.
7 Quoted in de Cecco, 'Origins', p. 50; our italics.
8 'The Monetary Conference', *New York Times*, 1 July 1944; our italics.
9 J. M. Keynes, *Activities 1941–1946. Shaping the Post-War World: Bretton Woods and Reparations*, in *Collected Writings*, vol. 26, p. 96.
10 Ibid., p. 149.

Chapter 8 The standard crisis (1929)

1 J. M. Keynes, *The Economic Consequences of the Peace* [1919], in *The Collected Writings of John Maynard Keynes*, 1971–89. London and Cambridge: Macmillan and Cambridge University Press, vol. 2, pp. 133–4.
2 Ibid., pp. 194–5.
3 On this issue, see G. Alvi, *Il secolo americano*. Milan: Adelphi, 1996.
4 Keynes, *Economic Consequences of the Peace*, pp. 177–8.
5 Ibid., p. 189.
6 J. M. Keynes, *Notes on the Monetary Reform of Solon* [1920], in *Collected Writings*, vol. 28, p. 226.
7 J. M. Keynes, *A Tract on Monetary Reform* [1923], in *Collected Writings*, vol. 4, p. 36.
8 For comparison of this system with the system envisaged by Keynes, see L. Fantacci, 'Complementary Currencies: A Prospect on Money from a Retrospect on Premodern Practices', *Financial History Review*, 12.1 (2005), pp. 43–61.

9 The first economist to highlight this feature was Rueff, *Le Péché monétaire de l'Occident*. Paris: Plon, 1971 (English trans. *The Monetary Sin of the West*. London: Macmillan, 1972).

10 See, for a broad outline, the paper by R. Artoni and C. Devillanova, 'Dal 1929 al 2008', *Short Note*, N. 5 (2008) (Econpubblica, Università Bocconi, Milano).

11 B. Eichengreen, *Golden Fetters: The Gold Standard and the Great Depression, 1919–1939*. Oxford: Oxford University Press, 1992, p. 13.

12 See the opening considerations in Part I, Chapter 2.

13 Rueff, *Le Péché*, p. 18 (English trans. *The Monetary Sin*, p. 19). The same idea is repeated at p. 31 (English trans. p. 28): 'it was the collapse of the house of cards built on the gold-exchange standard in Europe that turned the recession of 1929 into a Great Depression'.

14 See Eichengreen, *Golden Fetters*, Table 7.1, pp. 188–9.

15 J. M. Keynes, 'Economic Prospects 1932', in *Collected Writings*, vol. 21, pp. 39–40.

Chapter 9 Orchestra rehearsal. The international gold standard and the dissolution of gold (1871)

1 'It is commonly said that the pre-1914 Gold Standard was really a Sterling Standard' (M. de Cecco, 'From Monopoly to Oligopoly: Lessons from the pre-1914 Experience', in E. Helleiner and J. Kirshner (eds), *The Future of the Dollar*. Ithaca, NY: Cornell University Press, 2009, p. 130.

2 B. Eichengreen, *Globalizing Capital: A History of the International Monetary System*. Princeton: Princeton University Press, 1998, p. 32; our italics. M. Amato (*Le radici di una fede. Per una storia del rapporto fra moneta e credito in Occidente*. Milan: Bruno Mondadori, 2008, pp. 235–56) offers an interpretation of the positions taken by Kindleberger and Eichengreen on a scale that goes beyond our scope here.

3 Cf. J. M. Keynes, 'The Economic Consequences of Mr Churchill' [1925], *Essays in Persuasion*, in *The Collected Writings of John Maynard Keynes*, 1971–89. London and Cambridge: Macmillan and Cambridge University Press, vol. 9, p. 220.

4 See above, Part I, Ch. 6.

5 De Cecco, 'From Monopoly to Oligopoly', p. 136.

6 Ibid., p. 120.

7 Ibid. The same observation on the shifting of liquidity from credit to liability in the modern banking institutions underlies the entire critical reconstruction undertaken by P. Mottura, 'Crisi bancarie: un problema di governance?', *Bancaria*, 12 (2008), pp. 15–28.

8 De Cecco, 'From Monopoly to Oligopoly', p. 126.

9 Ibid., p. 124.

10 Ibid., p. 127; our italics.

11 Among the various chance factors, there was also the discovery of South African gold, which led to the doubling of the world's gold stock in the space of just a few years but afforded the gold standard no escape from the vicious circle in which it was embroiled.
12 De Cecco, 'From Monopoly to Oligopoly', p. 133; our italics.
13 L. Einaudi, *Preparazione morale e preparazione finanziaria*. Milan: Ravà, 1915.
14 Quoted by G. Carli in the preface to C. M. Cipolla, *Le avventure della lira*. Bologna: Il Mulino, 1975.

Chapter 10 Money before and after the gold standard (1717)

1 See Part I, Ch. 2, p. 47.
2 However, seignorage did not necessarily yield a gain in every case; in the case of low intrinsic value silver coin, it could in fact entail a loss. See M. Amato, *Le radici di una fede. Per una storia del rapporto fra moneta e credito in Occidente*. Milan: Bruno Mondadori, 2008, p. 69.
3 For a detailed analysis of the conditions under which the possessors of metal experienced no loss, not even from the point of view of their economic balance sheets, see L. Fantacci, 'The Dual Currency System of Renaissance Europe', *Financial History Review*, 15.1 (2008), pp. 55–72.
4 I. Fisher, 'A Compensated Dollar', *The Quarterly Journal of Economics*, 27.2 (1913), pp. 213–35.
5 We have examined them in depth elsewhere: Amato, *Le radici di una fede*, pp. 39–86; Fantacci, *La moneta. Storia di un'istituzione mancata, Venice: Marsilio, 2005*, pp. 25–111.
6 L. Einaudi, 'Teoria della moneta immaginaria da Carlo Magno alla Rivoluzione francese', *Rivista di storia economica*, 1.1 (1936), pp. 1–35; English trans. 'The Theory of Imaginary Money from Charlemagne to the French Revolution', in L. Einaudi, R. Faucci, and R. Marchionatti (eds.), *Luigi Einaudi. Selected economic essays*, London: Palgrave Macmillan, pp. 153–181.
7 See R. Triffin, 'The Myth and Realities of the So-Called Gold Standard', in B. Eichengreen and M. Flandreau (eds), *The Gold Standard in Theory and History*. London: Routledge, 1997, pp. 152–3.

Chapter 11 Money for nothing: The invention of central banking (1694)

1 Such is the unconditional line of argument followed by T. J. Sargent and F. R. Velde, *The Big Problem of Small Change*. Princeton: Princeton University Press, 2002.
2 This is how, without stretching the point too far, we may interpret the parallel drawn by de Cecco between oligopolistic competition in the late nineteenth century and the present situation, above all subsequent to the crisis of 2007; see M. de Cecco, 'From Monopoly to Oligopoly: Lessons

from the pre-1914 Experience', in E. Helleiner and J. Kirshner (eds), *The Future of the Dollar*. Ithaca, NY: Cornell University Press, 2009.

3 See N. Ferguson, *The Cash Nexus: Economics and Politics from the Age of Warfare through the Age of Welfare, 1700–2000*. London: Allen Lane, 2001.

4 See on this point M. Amato, *Le radici di una fede. Per una storia del rapporto fra moneta e credito in Occidente*. Milan: Bruno Mondadori, 2008, pp. 127–58.

5 The phrase 'financial revolution' was coined by P. G. M. Dickson, *The Financial Revolution in England*. London: Macmillan, 1967. Among those insisting on the need to link this financial revolution with the British monetary reforms, we find – apart from Amato, *Le radici di una fede*, pp. 191–4 – also L. Desmedt, 'Les Fondements monétaires de la révolution financière anglaise: Le tournant de 1696', in B. Théret (ed.), *La Monnaie dévoilée par ses crises*. Paris: Editions de l'EHESS, 2007, pp. 311–338, and G. Ingham, *The Nature of Money*. Cambridge: Polity, 2004, p. 129.

6 J. K. Horsefield, *British Monetary Experiments: 1650–1710*. London: LSE Press, 1960, p. 128. Horsefield knew what he was talking about, for he was also one of the official historians of the Bretton Woods system.

7 H. V. Bowen, 'The Bank of England During the Long Eighteenth Century, 1694–1820', in R. Roberts and D. Kynaston (eds), *The Bank of England. Money, Power and Influence 1694–1994*. Oxford: Clarendon Press, 1995, pp. 5–6; our italics.

8 Quoted by H. V. Bowen, 'The Bank of England', p. 3.

9 J. Broughton, *Remarks upon the Bank of England, with Regard More Especially to Our Trade and Government*, 1705, quoted in Bowen, 'The Bank of England', p. 12; our italics.

10 With this observation we depart radically from the fairly widespread commonplace that sees the seignorage of the central bank as an expropriation at the expense of the 'people'. The problem is not seignorage itself, but the way it works.

11 De Cecco, 'From Monopoly to Oligopoly', p. 134, italics added.

12 Decree of the Central Executive Committee, 3 February 1918, Article 1, in M. McCauley (ed.), *The Russian Revolution and the Soviet State 1917–1921*. London and Basingstoke: Macmillan, 1975, p. 235.

13 As has recently been demonstrated anew by S. McMeekin in dealing with the financial mobilization of the Bolshevik regime: see his *History's Greatest Heist: The Looting of Russia by the Bolsheviks*. New Haven and London: Yale University Press, 2009.

14 The 'efficient breach of contract' doctrine was formulated in the context of economic analysis of the law (law and economics), and in particular by R. Posner; see for example his recent article 'Let Us Never Blame a Contract Breaker', *Michigan Law Review*, 107.8 (2009), pp. 1349–63. To simplify without oversimplifying, the gist of the doctrine is this:

whenever the economic advantage I have in not keeping my word, given in a contract, exceeds the penalty I would have to pay for failing to respect my promises, I have the 'right' not to keep it.

15 M. Heidegger, *Die Geschichte des Seyns* [1938–40], in *Gesamtausgabe*, III. *Abteilung, Unveröffentlichte Abhandlungen, Vorträge, Gedachtes*, vol. 69. Frankfurt am Main: Vittorio Klostermann, 1998, p. 208.

16 Ibid.

17 On this particular point, see L. Fantacci, *La moneta. Storia di un'instituzione mancata*. Venice: Marsilio, 2005, pp. 180–91.

Chapter 12 The International Currency of the Trade Fairs (1579)

1 Beginning with the version formulated by B. Hildebrand, 'Naturalwirthschaft, Geldwirthschaft und Kreditwirthschaft', in *Jahrbücherfür Nationalökonomie und Statistik*, 2 (1864), pp. 1–24.

2 M. T. Boyer-Xambeau, G. Deleplace, and L. Gillard, *Private Money and Public Currencies: The 16th Century Challenge*. Armonk and London: M. E. Sharpe, 1994, p. 207.

3 Boyer-Xambeau et al., *Private Money*, p. 30.

4 See C. Marsilio, *Dove il denaro fa denaro. Gli operatori finanziari genovesi nelle fiere di cambio del XVII secolo*. Novi Ligure: Città del silenzio, 2008, pp. 47–8.

5 It is worth noting that the tariff was not an obligatory list tariff but a benchmark, which also allowed for off-the-list transactions on various markets.

6 Boyer-Xambeau et al., *Private Money*, p. 26.

7 Ibid., pp. 129–130; slightly modified translation.

8 It is the same practice that was adopted by English and Scottish banks in the eighteenth century and that was fiercely criticized by Adam Smith as the 'pernicious tendency of drawing and redrawing': *Inquiry into the Nature and Causes of the Wealth of Nations* [1776]. New York: Modern Library, 1994, p. 337.

9 B. Davanzati, 'Notizia de' cambj' [1582], in P. Custodi (ed.), *Scrittori classici italiani di economia politica, parte antica*, vol. 2. Milan: Stamperia e Fonderia di G. G. Destefanis, 1804, pp. 61–9; our italics. On the Bisenzone fairs as a degeneration of the exchange fairs and as a first example of a financial market, see, apart from Boyer-Xambeau et al. above, L. Fantacci, *La moneta. Storia di un'istituzione mancata*. Venice: Marsilio, 2005, pp. 197–205, and M. Amato, *Le radici di una fede. Per una storia del rapporto fra moneta e credito in Occidente*. Milan: Bruno Mondadori, 2008, pp. 87–124.

Part III Politics

Chapter 1 Double or quits?

1 Cf. Rueff, *Le Péché monétaire de l'Occident*. Paris: Plon, 1971, p. 7 (English trans. *The Monetary Sin of the West*. London: Macmillan, 1972, p. 11): 'The art of monetary expedients has been refined to such a point over the last ten years that no one can predict what artificial devices can be generated by the fertile minds of experts. One thing is certain, however: while additional innovations may stave off the gradual deterioration of the system for a while, they cannot change the outcome.'

2 See for example the obsessive recurrence of the terms 'sustainability' and 'sustainable' in the final document of the G-20 meeting of 3 April 2009.

3 M. Amato, *Le radici di una fede. Per una storia del rapporto fra moneta e credito in Occidente*. Milan: Bruno Mondadori, 2008, pp. 253–4.

4 'Three trillion dollars later. . .', *Economist*, Leaders, 16 May 2009.

5 A. Greenspan, 'Remarks at the American Bankers Association Annual Convention', New York, 5 October 2004, available at http://www.federalreserve.gov/boarddocs/speeches/2004/20041005/default.htm (accessed 10 May 2011).

6 J. Law, *Œuvres complètes*. Paris: Librairie du Recueil Sirey, 1934, vol. 2, p. 110.

7 See Amato, *Le radici di una fede*, p. 244.

8 See N. Irti, *Nichilismo giuridico*. Rome–Bari: Laterza, 2004.

Chapter 2 The way out of liquidity: the Gordian knot and utopia

1 Z. Xiaochuan, 'Reform the International Monetary System', Speech by the Governor of the People's Bank of China, 23 March 2009, available at http://www.bis.org/review/r090402c.pdf (accessed 11 May 2011).

2 Ibid.

3 See Part 1, Ch 1, p. 10.

4 Cambridge, King's College Modern Archives, Keynes Papers, 24/W/6/1/252–9: 'The International Clearing Union'.

5 J. M. Keynes, 'Economic Possibilities for our Grandchildren', *Essays in Persuasion*, in *The Collected Writings of John Maynard Keynes*, vol. 9, pp. 321–32, at p. 326 (emphasis in the original).

6 R. Rajan and L. Zingales, *Saving Capitalism from the Capitalists: Unleashing the Power of Financial Markets to Create Wealth and Spread Opportunity*. New York: Crown Business, 2003, p. 1.

7 'The financial markets are first of all an opportunity for the poor' (F. Giavazzi, 'Il mercato e la finanza', *Corriere della Sera*, 20 September 2008).

8 F. Vella, 'Dalla parte del popolo dei subprime', in L. Pellizzon (ed.), *Il mondo sull'orlo di una crisi di nervi: origine, sviluppi, responsabilità della crisi che ha sconvolto l'economia globale*. Roma: Castelvecchi, 2009, p. 197;

also available at http://www.lavoce.info/articoli/pagina2877-351.html (accessed 4 May 2011).

Chapter 3 Prevention or cure? The structural paradox of the anti-crisis policies

1 C. Giles, 'Grammar Fails to Make Up for Lack of Gravitas', *Financial Times*, 16 March 2009: 'The first test that any statement purporting to be weighty should pass is the "no test". The test assesses whether any reasonable person could disagree with any part of the statement.'

2 The speed with which some supporters of the market have applauded the massive intervention of the central banks is therefore hardly surprising, even though it may give rise to legitimate doubts.

3 A. Greenspan, *The Age Of Turbulence*. London: Allen Lane, 2007, pp. 212–14.

4 See for example the statement made by President Sarkozy at the joint press conference with Angela Merkel on the eve of the G-20, 1 April 2009: 'We are not against the principle of securitization [. . .]: what we want is traceability.' Retrievable at: http://www.ambafrance-uk.org/London-G20-summit (accessed 11 May 2011).

5 At least for as long as regulation takes the form of purely quantitative balance-sheet requirements that link the volume of liabilities to the volume of assets – rather than the form of qualitative requirements that link the form of funding to the form of lending. In the next chapter we shall return to this possibility, as it is put into effect, for example, by separating commercial banks and investment banks.

6 See for example Basel Committee on Banking Supervision, *Principles for Sound Liquidity Risk Management and Supervision*. Basel: Bank for International Settlements, June 2008, where 'funding liquidity risk' is defined as 'the risk that the firm will not be able to meet efficiently *both expected and unexpected* current and future cash flow and collateral needs without affecting either daily operations or the financial condition of the firm' (p. 1; our italics).

7 J. Tirole, *Financial Crises, Liquidity, and the International Monetary System*. Princeton: Princeton University Press, 2002, pp. 27 and 44.

8 Interview, 27 March 2009, available at http://www.ft.com/cms/s/0/5ee69cb2-1c8d-11de-977c-00144feabdc0.html#axzz1M2EujDpU (accessed 11 May 2011).

9 To the best of our knowledge, Alain Supiot is one of the few to have focused seriously on the unsustainable and senseless character of the phenomenon currently known as the 'market of rules'. See in particular his 'Le Droit du travail bradé sur le marché des normes', *Droit social*, 12 (2005), pp. 1087–96.

10 And to a greater extent than the press has done, e.g. in Fred Bergsten, 'Beijing's currency idea needs to be taken seriously', *Financial Times*, 9

April 2009. Bergsten's proposal substantially envisages the conversion into Special Drawing Rights, through the IMF, of the $5,000 bn held as a reserve by all of the world's monetary authorities. Implementation of this proposal would not solve the problem of liquidity, and not even the problem of the dollar. The new 'international currency' would be nothing but a new coat of paint over the old one, and the IMF would end up being a sort of 'bad bank' for the '(increasingly) toxic debt' held by the central banks in the form of reserves in dollars.

Chapter 4 Another finance

1 C. P. Kindleberger and R. Aliber, *Manias, Panics, and Crashes: A History of Financial Crises*. Basingstoke: Palgrave Macmillan, 2005, which describes crises as 'hardy perennials'.

2 See F. A. von Hayek, *Denationalisation of Money: The Argument Refined (An Analysis of the Theory and Practice of Concurrent Currencies)*, 3rd edn. London: The Institute of Economic Affairs, 1990, p. 56: 'it would be more helpful for the explanation of monetary phenomena if "money" were an adjective describing a property which different things could possess to varying *degrees*'.

3 The economic advisability of this distinction was underscored not only by Einaudi but also more recently by W. Buiter, 'Negative Interest Rates: When Are They Coming to a Central Bank Near You?', available at http://blogs.ft.com/maverecon/2009/05/negative-interest-rates-when-are-they-coming-to-a-central-bank-near-you/ (accessed on 11 May 2011).

4 See above, p. 48.

5 The connection between the unexpected and surprising character of innovation and the nature of the credit assigned the task of financing it was recently pointed out – surprisingly enough – by an economist awarded the Nobel Prize precisely for the models with which he tried to present the innovation of a crucial factor of economic growth: R. Solow, 'Stories about Economics and Technology', opening address at the ESHET Conference, University of Macedonia, Salonika, 2009.

6 See in this connection the work of Yuri Biondi, especially *Azienda, moneta e contabilità nella nascente economia aziendale*. Padua: Cedam, 2002.

7 J. M. Keynes, *The General Theory of Employment, Interest and Money* [1936], in *The Collected Writings of John Maynard Keynes*, 1971–89. London and Cambridge: Macmillan and Cambridge University Press, vol. 7 (1973), pp. 234 and 355–8.

8 I. Fisher: *Stamp Scrip*. New York: Adelphi Company, 1933; *Mastering the Crisis*. London: Allen & Unwin, 1934.

9 See, respectively, L. Fantacci, 'The Dual Currency System of Renaissance Europe', *Financial History Review*, 15.1 (2008), pp. 55–72; I. Habib, 'Monetary System and Prices', in T. Raychaudhuri and I. Habib,

Cambridge Economic History of India. Cambridge: Cambridge University Press, 1982, vol. 1, p. 361; W. Broer, *Schwundgeld*. Innsbruck-Vienna-Bolzano: Studien Verlag, 2007; B. Champ, 'Stamp Scrip: Money People Paid to Use', *Economic Commentary*, Federal Reserve Bank of Cleveland, April 2008, available at http://www.clevelandfed.org/Research/commentary/2008/0408.cfm (accessed 11 May 2011).

10 This is nothing but a corollary of the general principle that no rule survives in the market of rules.

11 The reference is not only to Luigi Einaudi's 'Teoria della moneta immaginaria nel tempo da Carlomagno alla Rivoluzione francese', *Rivista di Storia Economica*, 1 (1936), pp. 229–65 (English trans.'The Theory of Imaginary Money from Charlemagne to the French Revolution', in L. Einaudi, R. Faucci, and R. Marchionatti (eds.), *Luigi Einaudi. Selected economic essays*. London: Palgrave Macmillan, pp. 153–181), but also to his 'The Medieval Practice of Managed Currency', in Arthur D. Gayer (ed.), *The Lessons of Monetary Experience*. London: Allen & Unwin, 1937, pp. 259–68.

12 As recently pointed out by G. Deleplace, 'Ricardo and Keynes on the Gold Standard: Foes or Bedfellows?', ESHET Conference, University of Macedonia, Salonika, 2009.

13 Cf. M. Amato, 'Qu'est-ce que la monnaie? Réflexions sur l'enjeu de l'institution monétaire', in J. Blanc (ed.), *Exclusion et liens financiers. Monnaies sociales*. Paris: Economica, 2006, pp. 43–57; G. Rösl, 'Regionalwährungen in Deutschland. Lokale Konkurrenz für den Euro?', in *Deutsche Bundesbank*, Diskussionspapier, Frankfurt, 43 (2006), available at http://www.bundesbank.de/download/volkswirtschaft/dkp/2006/200643dkp.pdf (accessed 11 May 2011).

14 See on this point M. Amato and L. Fantacci, 'Monete complementari per i distretti di economia solidale', in *Distretti di economia solidale in Lombardia. Rapporti delle attività di ricerca e di sperimentazione, iniziativa comunitaria EQUAL 'NuoviStiliDiVita'*, 2004–7.

15 See in this connection the monographic issue of *Financial History Review*, 15 January 2008.

16 See J. Bhagwati, 'The Capital Myth: The Difference between Trade in Widgets and Dollars', *Foreign Affairs*, 77.3 (May/June), 1998, pp. 7–12.

17 In addition to the proposals put forward in this sense by Keynes in connection with the Clearing Union project, attention should be drawn to the plans drawn up in the 1950s, for the Food and Agriculture Organization (FAO), by R. F. Kahn (see L. Fantacci, M. C. Marcuzzo, A. Rosselli, and E. Sanfilippo, 'Speculation and Buffer Stocks: The Legacy of Keynes and Kahn', in *Gli economisti post-keynesiani di Cambridge e l'Italia*. Proceedings of the conference held at the Accademia dei Lincei, 11–12 March 2009), and in the 1960s, on behalf of the UNCTAD, by A.G. Hart, N. Kaldor, and J. Tinbergen ('The Case for an International Commodity Reserve Currency', in N. Kaldor, *Essays on Economic Policy*.

London: Duckworth, 1964, vol. 2, pp. 131ff). See also L. St Clare Grondona, *Economic Stability Is Attainable*. London: Hutchinson, 1975. The latter proposal is explicitly advocated by R. Harrod and N. Kaldor in their forewords to the book.

Chapter 5 The (rare) 'green shoots' of a possible reform

1 It has been aptly observed that, unlike new drugs, financial innovations are not subjected to severe testing designed to assess their effects on health as far as possible before they are offered to the public. See R. Boyer, 'History Repeating for Economists. An Anticipated Financial Crisis', *Prisme*, 13 (2008), available at http://www.centrecournot.org/?wpfb_dl=13 (accessed 11 May 2011). This strikes us as a good argument both for considering the introduction of preventive control of this type and for discontinuing the use of ill-advised metaphors. See D. Besomi, 'Crises as a Disease of the Body Politick. A Metaphor in the History of Nineteenth Century Economics', paper delivered at the STOREP Conference, Florence, 5 June 2009.

2 C. Cox, 'Address to Joint Meeting of the Exchequer Club and Women in Housing and Finance', Mayflower Hotel, Washington, DC, 4 December 2008, available at http://www.sec.gov/news/speech/2008/spch120408cc.htm (accessed 11 May 2011).

3 Board of Governors of the Federal Reserve System, press releases of 25 November 2008, available at http://www.federalreserve.gov/newsevents/press/monetary/2008monetary.htm (accessed 11 May 2011). The credit line is guaranteed by $20 billion allocated by the Treasury. See US Department of the Treasury, Secretary Paulson Remarks on Consumer ABS Lending Facility, HP-1293, 25 November 2008, available at http://www.treasury.gov/press-center/press-releases/Pages/hp1293.aspx (accessed 11 May 2011).

4 C. Torres and S. Lanman, 'Fed Risks "Spitting in the Wind" with New $800 Billion Pledge', *Bloomberg*, 26 November 2008, available at http://www.bloomberg.com/apps/news?pid=newsarchive&sid=ag3TJyGD73qk (accessed 11 May 2011).

5 From November 2007 to November 2008; see Fed, 'Factors Affecting Reserve Balances of Depository Institutions', 20 November 2008, available at http://federalreserve.gov/releases/h41/Current/h41.pdf (accessed 11 May 2011).

6 J. P. Hussman, 'The Fed Can Provide Liquidity, but Not Solvency', *Hussman Funds*, Weekly Market Comment, 17 March 2008, available at http://www.hussmanfunds.com/wmc/wmc080317.htm (accessed 11 May 2011).

7 A. J. Hettinger Jr, 'Director's Comment', in M. Friedman and A. J. Schwartz, *The Great Contraction. 1929–1933*. Princeton: Princeton University Press, 1963, pp. 127–8.

8 B. Bernanke, 'Federal Reserve Policies to Ease Credit and Their Implications for the Fed's Balance Sheet', Speech delivered at the National Press Club Luncheon, National Press Club, Washington, 18 February 2009, available at http://www.federalreserve.gov/newsevents/speech/bernanke20090218a.htm (accessed 11 May 2011).

9 M. Goodfriend, 'Overcoming the Zero Bound on Interest Rate Policy', *Federal Reserve Bank of Richmond*, WP 00-03, August 2000, available at http://www.richmondfed.org/publications/research/working_papers/2000/pdf/wp00-3.pdf (accessed 11 May 2011); B. Brown, 'The Case for Negative Interest Rates Now, *Financial Times*, 20 November 2008, available at: http://blogs.ft.com/economistsforum/2008/11/the-case-for-negative-interest-rates-now/ (accessed 11 May 2011).

10 F. Mishkin, 'In Praise of an Explicit Number for Inflation', *Financial Times*, 11 January 2009 available at: http://www.ft.com/cms/s/0/9fafc180-e013-11dd-9ee9-000077b07658.html#axzz1M5EAgCYL (accessed 11 May 2011); T. Leunig, 'Co-Ordinated Inflation Could Bail Us All Out', *Financial Times*, 16 February 2009; G. Mankiw, 'It May Be Time for the Fed to Go Negative', *New York Times*, 19 April 2009.

11 Bernanke, 'Federal Reserve Policies'; our italics.

12 L. Einaudi, 'Teoria della moneta immaginaria nel tempo da Carlomagno alla Rivoluzione francese', *Rivista di Storia Economica*, 1 (1936), pp. 229–65; English trans.'The Theory of Imaginary Money from Charlemagne to the French Revolution', in L. Einaudi, R. Faucci, and R. Marchionatti (eds.), *Luigi Einaudi. Selected economic essays*, London: Palgrave Macmillan, pp. 153–181.

13 J. M. Keynes, *A Tract on Monetary Reform* [1923], in *Collected Writings*, vol. 4, p. 9.

14 See A. Sironi, 'La crisi finanziaria internazionale un anno dopo: Quali lezioni per le banche e le autorità di vigilanza?', *Economia e management*, 5 (2008), pp. 3–11.

15 Letter of the American Bankers' Association to the Securities and Exchange Commission (SEC), 13 November 2008, available at http://www.aba.com/Industry+Issues/recentcommentletters.htm (accessed 11 May 2011).

16 Among those who have long taken seriously the need to address this question, particular attention should be drawn to Yuri Biondi (see, for example, Y. Biondi and X. Ragot, 'Les dangers de la "juste valeur": une analyse économique', N. Véron collection coordinator, AFG and FFSA, Paris, 15 December 2004; Y. Biondi, X. Ragot, and V. Bignon, 'An Economic Analysis of Fair Value: The Evolution of Accounting Principles in European Legislation', with a comment by R. Barker (Cambridge University, IASB Scientific Committee) and a reply by the authors, in *Prisme*, 4 (2004)).

17 A. Lee, 'Innovation: Learning from China's Banking System', *Business Week*, 16 March 2009.

18 E. Helleiner and S. Pagliari, 'The G20 Leaders' Summit and the Regulation of Global Finance: What Was Accomplished?', *Web exclusive CIGI Policy Brief*, 11 (1 December 2008), p. 6.
19 B. Eichengreen, 'Not a New Bretton Woods but a New Bretton Woods Process', in B. Eichengreen and R. Baldwin (eds), *What G20 Leaders Must Do to Stabilise Our Economy and Fix the Financial System*. London: CEPR, 2008, pp. 25–28.
20 See A. Supiot, *Homo juridicus. Saggio sulla funzione antropologica del Diritto*. Milan: Bruno Mondadori, 2006.
21 F. Bergsten, 'Needed: A Global Response to the Global Economic and Financial Crisis', *Peterson Institute for International Economics Monitor*, 18 March 2009.
22 'The Financial Crisis and the Role of Federal Regulators', Hearing Before the Committee on Oversight and Government Reform of the House of Representatives, Washington: U.S. Government Printing Office, 2010, p. 46, available at http://house.resource.org/110/org.c-span.281958-1.pdf (accessed 11 May 2011).

Chapter 6 If not now, when?

1 I. Kant, *Perpetual Peace: a Philosophical Sketch* [1795], available at http://www.mtholyoke.edu/acad/intrel/kant/kant1.htm (accessed 11 May 2011).
2 Ibid.
3 Ibid.
4 Ibid.
5 Ibid.
6 Ibid.
7 Ibid.
8 'But one condition the author of this essay wishes to lay down. The practical politician assumes the attitude of looking down with great self-satisfaction on the political theorist as a pedant whose empty ideas in no way threaten the security of the state, inasmuch as the state must proceed on empirical principles; so the theorist is allowed to play his game without interference from the worldly-wise statesman. Such being his attitude, the practical politician – and this is the condition I make – should at least act consistently in the case of a conflict and not suspect some danger to the state in the political theorist's opinions which are ventured and publicly expressed without any ulterior purpose.' Kant, *Perpetual Peace*.
9 Ibid.
10 Ibid.
11 Ibid.
12 W. Buiter, 'Negative Interest Rates: When Are They Coming to a Central Bank Near You?', available at http://blogs.ft.com/maverecon/2009/

05/negative-interest-rates-when-are-they-coming-to-a-central-bank-near-you/ (accessed on 11 May 2011).

13 M. Amato and L. Fantacci, 'Monete complementari per i distretti di economia solidale', in *Distretti di economia solidale in Lombardia. Rapporti delle attività di ricerca e di sperimentazione, iniziativa comunitaria EQUAL 'NuoviStiliDiVita'*, 2004–7.

14 For a comment on Giulio Tremonti's views, see M. Amato, 'È l'ora di ripensare la moneta', *Via Sarfatti 25*, 6 March 2009, available at http://www.viasarfatti25.unibocconi.it/notizia.php?idArt=4313 (accessed 11 May 2011).

Index